Patrick Duncan, who contributed to and edited this book, and Leslie Franks, who also contributed some of the puzzles, are two of Britain's leading crossword compilers. Their puzzles have appeared in many of Britain's leading magazines.

By the same author

Crossword Compendium 1

Crossword Compendium 2

Edited by Patrick Duncan

This edition published 1994 by
Diamond Books
77–85 Fulham Palace Road,
Hammersmith, London W6 8JB

First published by Panther Books 1984

These puzzles were previously published in three volumes
under the titles:
Fourth Granada Book of Crosswords
Fifth Granada Book of Crosswords
Sixth Granada Book of Crosswords

The Author asserts the moral right to be identified as the
author of this work

Set in Times

Printed in Great Britain

Introduction

As in the first Crossword Compendium, this collection of cross-words contains 300 puzzles catering for all moods and abilities. Whether you're a beginner, an average solver or a Senior Wrangler of the crossword world there should be plenty here to keep you entertained, challenged and mentally stretched.

Section One (Nos. 1 to 81) contains the easier puzzles. Those new to cryptics should limber up on these. More experienced solvers may want to time themselves.

Section Two puzzles (Nos. 82 to 210) are designed to entertain the average regular solver, while Section Three puzzles (Nos. 211 to 300) by Leslie Franks are calculated to make even experienced solvers chew their pencils.

Enjoy them all; if you get stuck, all the solutions are at the back of the book.

Patrick Duncan

1

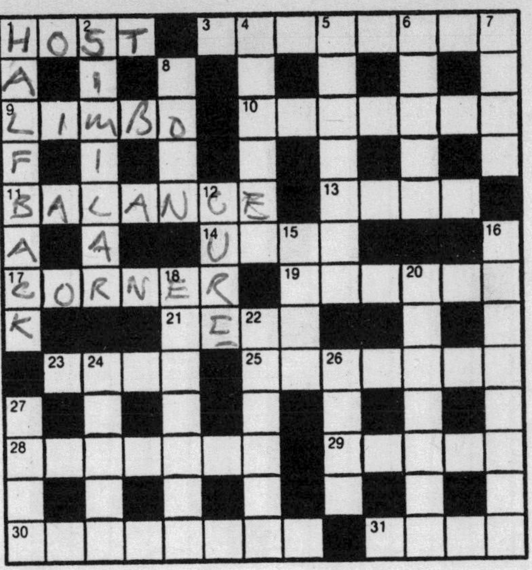

ACROSS

1 A lot of people find him entertaining (4)
3 Get it all together (8)
9 West African dance for forgotten people? (5)
10 The joy you can get from pure art! (7)
11 Money in the bank to keep you from falling? (7)
13 Shorten sail when there's possible danger at sea (4)
14 Make a loose arrangement to take off (4)
17 Things might improve when we turn it (6)
19 Country song about a sailor (6)
21 Take it out of someone else's book for example (4)
23 Carl leaves town for somewhere over the water (4)
25 Funny you should confuse Reg with Stan! (7)
28 One of the twelve has got a job in beer (7)
29 Bird with uplift? (5)
30 There's laughter when a man or a girl swallows it (8)
31 Fruity cover for a huntsman (4)

DOWN

1 Not entirely restored to the team? (4-4)
2 It shows what one can do with a needle (7)
4 Show a film or maybe hide it? (6)
5 Top person giving the rep more trouble (7)
6 Uncouth character with inner depression (5)
7 Girl with a Pole on the level (4)
8 Giving light enough to do a second job? (4)
12 It makes for better feeling (4)
15 Five hundred a foot—that's crazy! (4)
16 Something to eat and we will say goodbye (8)
18 He has to make a political choice (7)
20 Slavery in 007's time? (7)
22 Cap set to give a particular look (6)
24 Earth thrown up to cause damage (5)
26 Sway to the music? (4)
27 Place where you might clean up? (4)

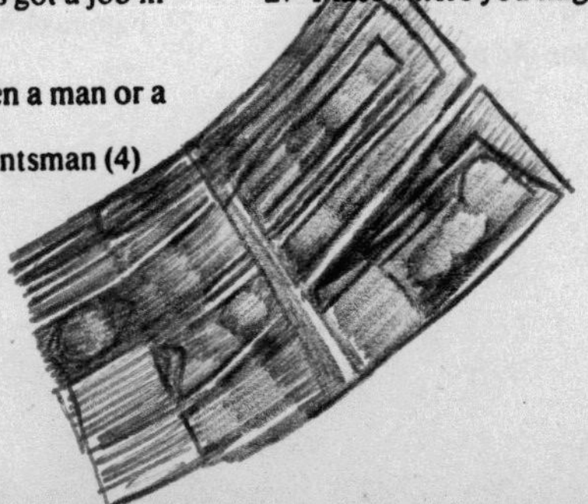

2

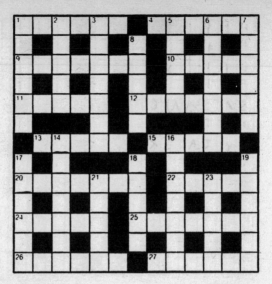

ACROSS

1 Demented Abyssinian prince in India! (6)
4 A taxi coming back to take us—you can count on it! (6)
9 Sink the ship that might carry coal (7)
10 What fun it is to go on one! (5)
11 Measure of drink big enough to see? (5)
12 Get the young bird to move and have a throw (7)
13 It's read to see how much you have to pay (5)
15 Pile-up in the snow (5)
20 Find a substitute for the car Peel crashed (7)
22 There's something crooked about this sort of work! (5)
24 Do without some of the plum duff or golden syrup (5)
25 The point of separating pounds from pence (7)
26 It enables you to dig in a very small way (6)
27 What a nut the old man turned out to be! (6)

DOWN

1 Mother's bed might bring you luck (6)
2 You can't be certain when you're in it (5)
3 Something to read? Here's just the thing! (7)
5 Foundation provided when one is in voice (5)
6 Personal transport makes little difference in the city (7)
7 It might follow Bob down the mountain (6)
8 Sound like a disagreeable horse? (5)
14 Pat and Rose tumbling in the grass (7)
16 Cad, liar? Maybe he's a politician! (7)
17 Something to be gained when the expert is in good health (6)
18 The sort of money you have in hand? (5)
19 It comes down in a winking (6)
21 Sailor taking a poem home (5)
23 Famous lover of the city circle (5)

ACROSS

1 It helps one to come clean (4)
6 It's inclined to be a swindle (4)
9 There's probably something in it (9)
10 Always and at any time (4)
12 Quite an amount in one lump (4)
14 For sending a stiff message? (8)
15 Bird hiding in the hibiscus (4)
16 Not much good at making a pudding? (4)
18 One of those things that happen (8)
20 Nobody we know (8)
21 It sounds the proper ceremonial (4)
22 Dispatched from the nest (4)
24 Putting coats on may be work for them (8)
28 Something growing in a shoe? (4)
29 It might just occur to you (4)
30 The haughtiness you get from Grace and Nora (9)
31 Looking out for danger (4)
32 It sounds a negative tie-up (4)

DOWN

1 Take one to get ahead (4)
2 Conquerors of kings (4)
3 Wine left for sailors (4)
4 Moving as quietly as a thief (8)
5 You may be frightened to get it up (4)
6 Just so you won't forget to give Dr Ermine a turn! (8)
7 Oil man in a different bar (4)
8 Get by with Father on the ship (4)
11 He didn't have to be pressed (9)
13 You can make a name for yourself with this (9)
17 Praise for getting rid of that bulge? (8)
19 Ivan and Carl involved in revelry (8)
22 Agitation in the kitchen? (4)
23 Not far from being a fine artist (4)
24 Where typists are in the swim? (4)
25 Credit for a mark of approval? (4)
26 Paradise for nudists (4)
27 A taste for seamanship? (4)

4

ACROSS

1 Eric Steel's turn in town (9)
8 Naive return to a French resort (5)
9 He's got a lot to learn (7)
10 Give the girl a small operation for a lump (6)
11 It helps to make employment pleasant (7)
13 You've reason to apply it (5)
15 Penetrated by lack of interest? (5)
16 Not the way to meet people (5)
18 Reclining figure under the rails (7)
21 Goes around out of this world? (6)
22 The higher the better (7)
23 Flower girl given a black eye (5)
24 They may be open to a top person here (9)

DOWN

2 Inspiring fear in the cheeriest circumstances (5)
3 Men at the top (6)
4 Let an animal guide you! (5)
5 Not new in the tyre world (7)
6 Not the place for the big build-up (7)
7 He'll soon see what's wrong (9)
11 It has production in its keeping (9)
12 Finds work a paying proposition (5)
14 Just what you'd expect to see in that dump! (7)
15 Assistance to make the wheels go round (7)
17 Toast proposed by the Medical Officer? (6)
19 See the employment of a parasite (5)
20 More than you bargained for! (5)

5

ACROSS

1 No danger of lack of function in this system (4,4)
5 It may be good to express satisfaction (4)
9 Come up for a pay increase (5)
10 Let raid go wrong when pulled behind (7)
11 There's no going to extremes here (6)
12 Sound means of keeping in touch (5)
14 In all I might upset the girl (6)
16 Might show you which way the wind is blowing (6)
19 Take it easy after six when you come to call (5)
21 Something heavy about the wig (6)
24 There's something to be learnt from him (7)
25 It's all in your head (5)
26 It might give you the wind-up (4)
27 It helps you to discover what might otherwise go unnoticed (8)

DOWN

1 Panic adjustment to the wing camber? (4)
2 Letter giving you a start (7)
3 Important factor in your advance (5)
4 Would he be healthier in the workshop? (6)
6 Given extra ventilation by the enemy? (5)
7 Very good weather conditions in those big spaces? (4-4)
8 A few scouts on duty? (6)
13 Rising store? (8)
15 Dramatising the fact that the appointment's only temporary? (6)
17 Outlet for giving fatigue? (7)
18 Take action when straightforward steering isn't advisable (6)
20 Quite a performance to stop overnight? (5)
22 Dispute as to what to send out? (5)
23 It's not clear what's intended here (4)

6

ACROSS

1 Use verbal wit to make a thrust in India (6)
4 For weighing the fish you've caught? (6)
8 Leave high and dry on the beach (6)
10 Where one might get to grips with a racket (6)
11 They have their ups and downs at the seaside (5)
12 Request to be sure there's something to enjoy (4)
14 Scene of high living? (5)
15 The higher the faster (5)
17 The hard stuff at Gibraltar (4)
19 Their identification is certain (4)
20 Knock up a total of twenty (5)
21 Taking part in public orgies, the dog! (5)
23 Quiet time with maybe a storm to follow (4)
26 Sounds in a beastly temper (5)
28 You can't see where it is when it is (6)
29 Don't go on in the old-fashioned way (6)
30 On a horse in old Yorkshire? (6)
31 Written in confinement (6)

DOWN

1 Hand over the wine to assist the traveller (8)
2 Hurry up and have a bit of sense, sister! (5)
3 Sally's the one to throw things at! (4)
5 Get along without effort at the seaside (5)
6 Finding accommodation at the gatehouse? (7)
7 Took off in the garden perhaps (4)
9 Entertaining change of route? (9)
10 Top man meeting the directors connected with bedding (9)
13 Request to start a skilled trade (3)
16 Sold a tie somehow by oneself (8)
18 Made a bit obscure by bad weather? (7)
19 Shelter put up for a slippery creature (3)
22 Where it's just a matter of putting the ball in (5)
24 Organisation for joining (5)
25 Burn to be of service in the home (4)
27 It's too dry among these reed-beds (4)

ACROSS

1 Vegetables reached by long drives? (6)
4 Disney getting on in Surrey? (6)
7 Just a part of the final product (9)
9 Quite a blessing Bolton has no centre! (4)
10 Just the stuff for the lubrication addict? (4)
11 They may carry water to the fire (5)
13 Wearing fewer clothes in class (6)
14 He becomes saucy after giving Ruth a start (6)
15 Questioned about obtaining petrol? (6)
17 Lady in explosive surroundings as the occupier (6)
19 Taken in hand for removing a tyre (5)
20 Impossible humbug! (4)
22 Mark of a seaside borough (4)
23 Promise to protect the purchaser (9)
24 It's painful for a short time (6)
25 Lacking some sound qualities? (6)

DOWN

1 Sounds a chancy way to have fun (6)
2 Note a rise in education (4)
3 Take a drink with a peer's son even if only soda (6)
4 No. 1 performer in competitive sport (6)
5 Come down on the estate (4)
6 We in our little home are most up-to-date! (6)
7 The sort of interest you might take in the canteen? (9)
8 It allows for very little variation (9)
11 You might find people quite accommodating here (5)
12 Very good description of the better sort of petrol (5)
15 Quite a lot of pay! (6)
16 Stage reached at a university (6)
17 Court activity for people with rackets (6)
18 Hatter's turn to suggest future trouble (6)
21 Go around in a music-hall act? (4)
22 Apply the closure to prevent leaks (4)

8

ACROSS

1 Attack for not working? (6)
4 Sequence of command? (5)
7 Go down briefly for a swim (3)
8 Come together unexpectedly (7)
9 Indicate the position (5)
10 Close to disaster with 11 (4)
11 Bad shot, girl! (4)
12 Jack sounds grateful (3)
14 Boots the old bombers (11)
18 Be quick to pull the cord (3)
20 In truth, Vera has found the place! (4)
21 Face giving you the figure (4)
23 Cross island (5)
24 Nothing to eat – that'll cause big talk! (7)
25 Quite a commotion among leading citizens (3)
26 Burn to produce a note (5)
27 An unlicensed dog off course (6)

DOWN

1 Not the first to give assistance (6)
2 See real change in liberation (7)
3 Keep on needling in a big way (4)
4 Some sort of number over the way? (8)
5 Not a go-ahead movement (5)
6 After this you're back where you started (6)
7 No tag inside to show what it's called (11)
13 Bleak cod manoeuvre to prevent supplies getting through (8)
15 Number one gets the rise wrong causing more row (7)
16 Cards to play when not suited (6)
17 All you need and more! (6)
19 Current low-flying hazard (5)
22 Not a brilliant result but it gets you by (4)

ACROSS

1 Fearsome female from a progressive school (6)
4 Makes sure the squares are perfect? (6)
8 Mark me returning first and last (6)
10 The traffic flows all round it (6)
11 Give an indication of direction (5)
12 The unsociable motor-cycle? (4)
14 Fills a gap in the road network (5)
15 Revolutionary aid to progress (5)
17 A beastly place for a port (4)
19 Contributes one more to the stock of tools? (4)
20 No setback if you've got the money (5)
21 I moan when she comes back (5)
23 Use a stick to get production started (4)
26 Not a southerner at the races (5)
28 Rest and do some more modelling (6)
29 It's quite usual to give a girl fifty (6)
30 Go-ahead vegetables? (6)
31 Things ought to be much better after this (6)

DOWN

1 Foreigners can be encountered here (8)
2 He's not on the Government's side (5)
3 It might be taken to make a little progress (4)
5 Made to get there in a hurry (5)
6 Given a lift by admirers (7)
7 Swagger to be expected from the team? (4)
9 Adapt the miners' ode to bring it up to date (9)
10 Economic trend in the tyre trade? (9)
13 Do it up in a confession (3)
16 Sure to make a comeback after a swing (8)
18 It used to be enough to give an instance (7)
19 Poisonous creature encountered in Las Palmas (3)
22 Mother and child in the building trade (5)
24 Romantic figure adding nothing to capital (5)
25 Surely not a slow type of motor racing! (4)
27 Just a big book as far as I'm concerned (4)

10

ACROSS

1 Force to become a soldier (7)
5 Complains at what the sleepers have to carry (5)
8 Figure there's enough for a row (5)
9 Game possibly presented as an act (7)
10 Top speed for the law-abiding (5)
12 There's space for a big fight here (5)
14 Thank the piggery for what's enjoyable to eat (5)
16 Half a dozen depart for a Spanish port (4)
17 Something growing in a boat, maybe (4)
19 Gets along without revolution (5)
21 Girl coming back for a possession (5)
23 He's no friend of ours (5)
26 You'd do better to let the little devil move around (7)
27 Try not to be a contact man (5)
28 She may be encountered by accident (5)
29 The man who advances a shilling doesn't grow fat (7)

DOWN

1 Turn of the tide (4)
2 Activity in the corner? (7)
3 Needed for repair, perhaps, having emerged looking healthy (6)
4 Steal from the police station! (4)
5 For those in a hurry to take off (6)
6 Send out the matter in dispute (5)
7 He may have a job keeping afloat (8)
11 Possibly containing the spirit of motoring (4)
13 The sort of spirit we find uplifting (8)
15 It has its ups and downs at the seaside (4)
18 Make a new shape (7)
19 Caressing movement of the piston? (6)
20 Bless you for that small explosion! (6)
22 Very good as an extra actor (5) quality (5)
24 Walk up and see the animals! (4)
25 Clothes to be changed to get ahead faster (4)

ACROSS

1 It's a matter of who you are (8)
5 Some of the teachers cause discomfort (4)
9 Freewheel at the seaside? (5)
10 Intending to have some significance (7)
11 A message to the train driver (6)
13 It's progress when you get this (5)
15 It's most satisfactory to have a halo! (4)
17 Kindly get out of Ealing! (6)
19 Fresh burden for the great scientist (6)
21 Tyrannical old fiddler (4)
23 Continue when ready for an attack (5)
25 The thing that makes us protest (6)
28 Tile man's changes causing some ill-feeling (7)
29 Greek character at the river mouth (5)
30 One may be needed to do a job (4)
31 Not enough violence for a serious match? (8)

DOWN

1 It causes a lot of irritation (4)
2 The joy of seeing one of the family lose his head (7)
3 The big fellow has it in brown (5)
4 Fall for a sort of drier (6)
6 Capital atmosphere in business (5)
7 Attractive enough to be planning marriage? (8)
8 A taste for what our friend had for dinner (6)
12 Can do! (4)
14 Not knowing how to break the NATO ring (8)
16 He thinks he's better than some of us (4)
18 It may give singers a certain standing (6)
20 Given some amusing touches (7)
22 Right animal for a bad person (6)
24 A lot of shooting might be a friendly gesture (5)
26 Consider how sober the fellow is! (5)
27 Her follower is a little sheepish (4)

12

ACROSS

1 Does he represent the nation in a beastly way? (4,4)
5 Current requirement for reduced illumination (4)
9 I make a distribution that can't be faulted (5)
10 It's amazing to have the car turn back with a mile! (7)
11 Have a couple after taking me back for a cuddle (7)
14 Corrupt archdeacon accepting a pound (5)
15 Something should be done, it's felt (4)
17 Totter in a snaky fashion? (5)
19 This might be the point if you're trying to find gold (5)
21 Group a little creature hasn't got in (4)
24 It makes a very smart coat (5)
25 The real difference is in the material (7)
27 Goes into action as an all-rounder? (7)
28 She's in a fine state of apprehension! (5)
30 Not much to pay, though it involves a number of notes (4)
31 The stuff there's no getting away from (8)

DOWN

1 Not the man to stay outside the Woodworkers' Union? (6)
2 He has nothing inside for gardening (3)
3 Answers a light wood requirement (5)
4 Useless material that might be given to Jack (6)
6 Giving protection from a Scot in some nonsense (9)
7 She might be all set to do a turn (6)
8 With his skill he's able to go places (6)
12 Game for some show jumping? (9)
13 It should put an end to the trouble (4)
16 It's been gone through by a man inside (4)
18 Grounds for breaking up a tea-set (6)
20 Has fun and games (6)
22 Not prepared to admit (6)
23 Making a mark on the cricket field (6)
26 She seems to have a wrong number (5)
29 Go downhill in sporting fashion (3)

ACROSS

1 He knows he's got a lot to learn (7)
5 Scottish cattle man (5)
8 It's left over from the old days (5)
9 It gives one a certain standing (7)
10 It might be smart to put it on (5)
12 In some headgear he looks vulgar (5)
14 Unpleasantly fat quantity (5)
16 Make progress with a little bread? (4)
17 Goddess of two little islands (4)
19 Given sound reception (5)
21 Let the motor depart by ship (5)
23 Blue dog county (5)
26 Gear for it may be in the bag (7)
27 Frolic I can't get sorted out (5)
28 Try to produce a piece of writing (5)
29 Gasp at the girl being a beast! (7)

DOWN

1 Enabling an ace to make the top (4)
2 For the traveller who has everything? (7)
3 Achieving a tie-up in footwear (6)
4 Tyres keep them off the ground (4)
5 High living may have its place in them (5)
6 Get along without power (5)
7 It just shows where you might be going (8)
11 Something shady in a city back-street (4)
13 Giving more than the usual support for the pedal-pusher (8)
15 Island vessel under way (4)
18 Make longer use of the elastic? (7)
19 Bully for you if you want to start playing it! (6)
20 Keep back Ted and Ian when they're upset (6)
22 It would be a mistake to go off them (5)
24 Put an end to that carry-on! (4)
25 Mark of nothing less than a film award (4)

14

ACROSS

1 Might be needed to make up for lost time (12)
8 One of the usual lines of communication? (7)
9 Possibly provided by agitated aides (5)
10 Part of the journey accomplished on foot? (3)
11 Splendid weather for taking money (4)
12 Cause delay in a front seat? (5)
15 Sufficient to make one return with a cry of disgust (6)
16 Letting higher authority know there's been an explosion? (6)
19 Used to convey a message by radio-telephony (5)
21 He sounds a colourful character (4)
22 One feels elevated walking on it (3)
25 Hang on to Heather after a century (5)
26 Suitable sort of action when a meeting is not desired (7)
27 In which one might take a turn outside (8,4)

DOWN

1 Marble in London (4)
2 Prepare for examination under pressure? (4)
3 Coming down from upstairs maybe (7)
4 Got out the festive barrel (6)
5 Grasps what's on the branches (5)
6 You might get the message from him (8)
7 Keep apart one thus delayed (7)
13 Starting some tennis during your engagement? (7)
14 Given this you know where you are (8)
17 There'll always be one in song (7)
18 The art of doing a turn that could mean trouble (6)
20 Great bird for a spread (5)
23 Pet fog dispersal system? (4)
24 Look up and down (4)

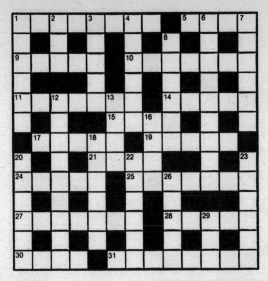

15

ACROSS

1 They're probably after the heavy lorries (8)
5 Cat taking a little time off to be an employer (4)
9 Take pains to be well turned out? (5)
10 The worrying kind, like Nellie (7)
11 Not to be spared for the best that money can buy (7)
14 He helps to seat somebody stand.ng (5)
15 Impulse to get out of our genteel suburb (4)
17 Put your foot down to exert it in a car (5)
19 A bit of a row with Mother might cause one to sniff (5)
21 Exports are sent over them (4)
24 A fight in the neighbourhood (5)
25 They let you down lightly when the going's rough (7)
27 He can provide colourful cover (7)
28 A walk back to see a strange animal (5)
30 The spirit of motoring may be found here (4)
31 Sporting partner? (8)

DOWN

1 Tried the set-up on Mr Heath (6)
2 His Highness could start a garage business (3)
3 Scene of many a holiday take-off (5)
4 Vehicle not yet needing a tow (6)
6 He's expected to play the game (9)
7 Last place to spend a holiday if all else fails? (6)
8 He can give directions as we go along (6)
12 In favour of progress to a higher position (9)
13 There'll be no mistake if you make it (4)
16 Surprise air intake (4)
18 It may provide grounds for producing rubber (6)
20 Driver's animal kept underfoot? (6)
22 Among the stars of fast rally driving (6)
23 Made to get away from an unpleasant situation (6)
26 Get together for a testing trip (5)
29 Name a dame who can do without me! (3)

16

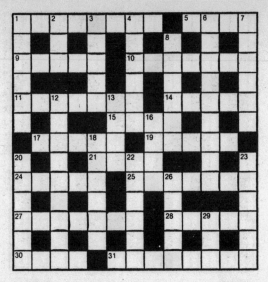

ACROSS

1 Maybe a flap will keep the dirt off (8)
5 Chooses a different post (4)
9 Fear you may have five hundred to plough through (5)
10 We and France have it between us (7)
11 The horseman might put his foot in it (7)
14 Trying to keep the wedding guests quiet? (5)
15 Smart enough to do without water? (4)
17 Still remaining singularly eligible? (5)
19 Land of the plane crash (5)
21 Feeling it might be easy? (4)
24 A few quick shots for breaking out (5)
25 It may be handed to you with telling effect (7)
27 Going the other way in a shop? (7)
28 Get together in Monte Carlo (5)
30 Making a little progress, one may take it (4)
31 It's used to prepare a football for kicks (8)

DOWN

1 Not too revealing fashion on the street (6)
2 Give his to the devil! (3)
3 Where everything's on top of you (5)
4 It could be quite instructive in the kitchen (6)
6 It's made to take a bashing (9)
7 It's sure to come when you're on the staff (6)
8 It should be returned by the officer it's given to (6)
12 Often subject to inflation (5,4)
13 Prepare for take-off (4)
16 Change a ten to put something in the kitty (4)
18 Eastern country where rubber is produced (6)
20 Ancestor of the computer? (6)
22 Bob's double (6)
23 Not the type to give up and go (6)
26 March past (5)
29 The man who had everything? (3)

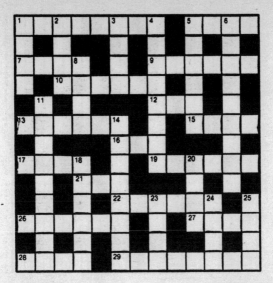

ACROSS

1 It's strongly in favour of hair (8)
5 Outstanding man at the top (4)
7 Fly this way with endless art (4)
9 John Buchan's hero has a girl inside (6)
10 Move in for the kill (6)
12 Try to establish deep understanding (3)
13 To take the gun away might be mad, sir! (6)
15 Invalid having no effect (4)
16 Taking part in the balloon race without exception (3)
17 Food for an old service consumer (4)
19 This is too much! (6)
21 Came down when caught in the beam? (3)
22 Recompensed agent with assistance (6)
26 Just one of those things (6)
27 Turn up with a couple of pounds to get something moving (4)
28 Speed tangle (4)
29 Cook eggs in an emergency (8)

DOWN

1 It might be doubled in attack (4)
2 Cut down what's come up (4)
3 Be worthy of some special learning (4)
4 He's clued about the timetable (8)
5 Gracious fellow mixing a drink (6)
6 Ali is best to make a steady arrangement (9)
8 One's turn comes round in it (4)
11 Order which way to go? (9)
14 Something soft covering the hair (8)
18 Hurried retreat in the air (6)
20 Cut out at speed (4)
23 Not much good being like Clare? (4)
24 Nothing to be said for our beastly friends? (4)
25 Not happy at having to squander money? (4)

18

ACROSS

1 It might provide background for an artist (6)
4 Get a spread out of it (6)
8 Sung by people of standing (6)
10 It might go to your head (6)
11 Message that might tie things up? (5)
12 A lot of people giving a party? (4)
14 Decoration that can't rub off (5)
15 It's certainly not the popular feeling (5)
17 Double over in the air (4)
19 Vegetable head (4)
20 Not the ones we have here (5)
21 Capture a girl with a ring (5)
23 No denying it when one is faithful (4)
26 Switch lamps during the song (5)
28 Fool turning round with an exclamation in the bathroom (6)
29 Goes openly on foot (6)
30 Carrier for a ball game (6)
31 My dole harmoniously arranged (6)

DOWN

1 Opening for a fuel supplier (4-4)
2 Observes where a stone has been turned (5)
3 He's smart enough to cut a lecturer short (4)
5 He has a right to be a foreigner (5)
6 Plunder from the drug era? (7)
7 Go to it for the big build-up! (4)
9 Just the man for your protection (9)
10 Line men's shoes? (9)
13 Where there's room for a novel (3)
16 What was spread out below the airport? (8)
18 They've got a lot to say for themselves (7)
19 Somewhat improved, you can wager! (3)
22 Out of this world, there's no limit to it! (5)
24 Enabling you to hear what the waves are saying (5)
25 Striking form of social organisation? (4)
27 Compel to be constructive (4)

ACROSS

1 They may come to hand in the cockpit (8)
5 Old aircraft lacking fire (4)
7 Plenty of possible buys at the auction (4)
9 Split for a share-out (6)
10 One act of confusion in the fuel rating (6)
12 Brightly enabling the position to be fixed (3)
13 In a fever of excitement (6)
15 Equipment that may have to be changed (4)
16 The fighter from Australia (3)
17 The man who starts a lawsuit makes it plain (4)
19 It's just looking for trouble (6)
21 Brief activity involving half the soldiers (3)
22 Sounded like some sort of bird (6)
26 She might be all set to come round (6)
27 It all comes out in the wash (4)
28 Cut the people on board (4)
29 Making a light contribution to aircraft construction (8)

DOWN

1 Cry of a visitor (4)
2 Body found in London at one o'clock (4)
3 That's the wrong goal, girl! (4)
4 Lose height without taking the plunge (8)
5 Economy in rescue work? (6)
6 It should tell you something (9)
8 He probably gets off free (4)
11 It's all round the airfield! (9)
14 Part of the engine almost arrived with the handle (8)
18 Grasp the idea of pursuit? (6)
20 That was the time! (4)
23 Failed to contact in poor visibility (4)
24 Only half the change from a dime (4)
25 Light on one side (4)

20

ACROSS

1 Theatre performances (10)
7 Eager to knock David's head off (4)
8 Message about great elm being chopped up (8)
10 Provoked by injections? (7)
12 Cattle man? (5)
14 Get land in a muddle (7)
17 Needing nursing (3)
18 You could go round the bend in one (3)
19 It might cover surgical work (7)
22 More like one of a cast of thousands (5)
23 Trying to find a drawing? (7)
26 Instruction given on the railway? (8)
28 Angry about feeling discomfort? (4)
29 Do they show what food has been spilt on the bed? (4,6)

DOWN

1 We don't want him in the ward! (3-7)
2 Something slippery in the elastic bandage (3)
3 Time to be majestic (6)
4 Terrible fellow! (4)
5 Supporter of a cyclist (6)
6 Book in one long sentence (4)
9 Insufficient to make me rage around (6)
11 Sends out with a bang (10)
13 Movement of the swallow (4)
15 Ben sat around when not here (6)
16 It might be thrown into bed (4)
20 Given key protection (6)
21 Taking part in a quarrel is her enjoyment (6)
24 Space to tie up the other way (4)
25 Abrasive courage? (4)
27 Dropped in for a cool drink (3)

ACROSS

1 One sort or another might keep you going (10)
8 It's quite a different thing at this time (5)
9 Flying isn't easy in such conditions (7)
10 He might have been the last of those conscripted (3)
11 It may permit only a one-way passage (5)
12 Where the drama is taking place (5)
13 The side of privilege (5)
15 Keeps to one plane amid all the manoeuvres (4)
16 It could be a worry when it goes to the top (4)
18 Sail from an Italian port (5)
20 You can see she's got something when she makes a comeback! (5)
22 Describing a boom in air travel (5)
23 Light going round the bend? (3)
24 Encroach by giving too much of a run-around? (7)
25 Chance of a toss-up? (5)
26 It might give you some idea of what lies ahead (3,7)

DOWN

2 The sort of service conscription didn't give (7)
3 Club that might land you in a hole (6)
4 You'll have people after you if you're in it! (4)
5 Put up money and lose your shirt? (6)
6 Hospital tender (5)
7 Allusions to one's working record (10)
8 It's just a matter of knowing where you're going (10)
14 If discharged, there'll probably be a report (3)
17 Cutlery provided where you eat (7)
18 Make rapid progress as a rider (6)
19 Try to attain a higher level (6)
21 Let it off to avoid an explosion (5)
23 It's in rather a flap seeing it's in church (4)

22

ACROSS

1 Bad-tempered blow on the side? (9)
8 Game for a trip on your own? (4)
9 He may be taken for a ride (9)
11 Slight depression caused by a smile perhaps (6)
13 Not too talkative in the helicopter service (5)
15 Indicating the derivation of the wrong form (4)
16 Small proportion mostly under canvas (5)
17 Gives examples of the towns I leave (5)
18 Drink business doubled with a letter (5)
19 A girl from one of the tele-communication channels (4)
20 A little man in a representative capacity (5)
22 Cancels the action (6)
25 Allusion to some point on the map (9)
26 Needled by an adaptation of the news (4)
27 Levels of excellence at which flags are displayed (9)

DOWN

2 See what's in the book (4)
3 Method for carrying out a function (6)
4 They conribute to a bird's upkeep (5)
5 Eden adapted according to requirement (4)
6 It's just a part of the assembly (9)
7 Foremost point of contact with the runway (9)
10 Fissures visible at the first change (5)
12 Not in line to arrive on schedule (3,6)
13 Try for a landing (5-4)
14 More than you bargained for (5)
17 Satisfy a consuming interest? (5)
19 Girl flier with a letter (6)
21 Safe to show this light (5)
23 The passenger has his place here (4)
24 Keeping cool when endangered by outside condition? (4)

ACROSS

1 Such spirit the flier needs! (8)
8 Away and have a seizure if you've got all the equipment (6)
9 It tells us what to expect (8)
10 Get off at a lamp-post (6)
12 An occasion for politics? (5)
14 Cash for the runner-up? (6)
16 Professional one in a lodging (4)
18 Give some indication of approval (4)
19 Half a minute back by road transport when rain threatens (6)
20 Panic directions about transport (5)
23 Scene of a lot of shooting (6)
26 Trouble in UN case possibly (8)
27 Not much cover where an atom bomb exploded! (6)
28 Class division (8)

DOWN

2 Instrument for a girl (5)
3 A chap with representative functions (5)
4 One-horse race in the Middle East? (4)
5 Furniture missing when important people appear (7)
6 Lines of authority (7)
7 Lovely girl on the menu! (4)
11 One may not be conscious of being in it (6)
12 They need instruction in our eyes (6)
13 Comedown from 19 possibly (4)
14 Not in the Concorde class (8)
15 Somewhat authoritarian lady (4)
17 Scorn for what might be said badly in a row (7)
21 Sound of something dropped in error (5)
22 One in a hurry to get there first (5)
24 Make a neat adjustment (4)
25 Incline to have a go with the lance (4)

24

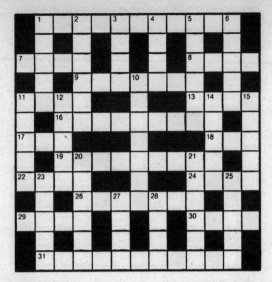

ACROSS

1 They make a telling contribution to safe flight (11)
7 Is this a record? (4)
8 Flier noted for direct navigation (4)
9 Flow with more than usual force (7)
11 Naval cipher ship providing Government communications (4)
13 Raises a query when jobs aren't begun (4)
16 The delight of getting shifted? (9)
17 Indicating the route taken is a bit of a deviation (3)
18 An unnamed person is just a number (3)
19 It might provide the answer to current demands (9)
22 He'll probably get a mention at Christmas (4)
24 It might be sinister in heraldry (4)
26 The heart of the matter (7)
29 In the course of a long trek I eventually find a foreign city (4)
30 Chaplains responsible for engine movements? (4)
31 In which you might get a grounding in flight procedure? (4,7)

DOWN

1 Used to talk like a native (5)
2 Brief moment on the hill in one area (6)
3 Brought up by the last man (4)
4 Just one item in a calculation of distance (4)
5 Drink to get out of a trance (6)
6 Dismay occasioned by current contact (5)
10 Not the first to go into action (7)
11 Offer direction in a safe place (5)
12 Entertainment for an overnight stop (5)
14 What's coming to you in the future may be in it (5)
15 It may present a knotty problem of calculation (5)
20 Associated with one in an airliner (6)
21 Shakespearian dream king (6)
23 College window? (5)
25 Said to indicate a permanent refusal (5)
27 A purchaser might put money in it (4)
28 She certainly isn't a well-known artist! (4)

25

ACROSS

1 Queer togs give that fantastic look (9)
6 The rest is familiar from Spike Milligan's comeback (3)
8 Land us with a letter in a song (7)
9 Used for making a cut on the propeller? (5)
10 Diamonds perhaps giving cover (4)
11 You might expect to have a hot time in them (7)
13 One for one was the Biblical exchange rate (3)
14 There hasn't been much of a build-up in this district (5)
15 Go after it in the freight hold (3)
16 Foul arm movement that might solve the problem (7)
18 To be worn in an exposed position? (4)
20 Blew up when given the wrong grade (5)
21 Damaged with some fuss in a storm (7)
22 Not the right thing to do in the strawberry season (3)
23 Len's prone to upset Service folk (9)

DOWN

1 Zeppelin was one who had a note on fliers (4)
2 Not easy to see how to adapt B course (7)
3 Flier discovered in rather regrettable circumstances (5)
4 Exercising fractional authority in the stores? (13)
5 Tangle me up to do some cooking (7)
6 In which a soldier looks browned off (5)
7 Request certain to give gratification (8)
12 By means of compulsion of necessity (8)
14 Circle overhead to collect stragglers? (5,2)
15 Officer inclined to get stuck into a killer (7)
17 He may be said to have got the message (5)
18 Carried to make the vehicle move (5)
19 Bad enough to cause whistling (4)

26

ACROSS

1 Make a hit in command (6)
4 No inclination to put a girl among learners (5)
7 Keeping cool won't avert this danger (3)
8 Sortie by the padre? (7)
9 Burning to commit an offence (5)
10 Flag girl (4)
11 Hurries back in a tizzy (4)
12 Weight put up at high speed (3)
14 Promotion from sergeant not justified? (11)
18 A right briefly to display skill (3)
20 Ceremony taking place in the Criterion Restaurant (4)
21 See the point (4)
23 Uniform item cut in a different way (5)
24 Do something in the theatre (7)
25 Not quite royal relations (3)
26 Calls for some personal adornment (5)
27 Smoothed out the hard way (6)

DOWN

1 Top choice for an international meeting (6)
2 He's carelessly said to be in a hurry (7)
3 Get together with needles (4)
4 Under instruction to get a pound by working (8)
5 Something for the caller to pay (5)
6 Getting straight inside material (6)
7 I spin around and get food – great idea! (11)
13 Drinking-place and torture instruments in private accommodation (8)
15 Provide the key to what used to be obvious (7)
16 Superior person of degree (6)
17 Be there some time and start dancing (6)
19 Saw a number added (5)
22 Change direction ever confusingly (4)

ACROSS

5 Shakespeare river (4)
7 They might cause a drop in flying (3-7)
8 Eager to express sorrow? (4)
9 Aircraft for taking your baggage East (4)
12 Gives out at different times (5)
13 Sounds like a horse when she gets fuddled with gin (6)
14 Point of subtle detail (6)
16 It might slip past the aircraft (6)
18 Three points of support (6)
19 Go in as a competitor (5)
20 Otherwise I leave a girl (4)
23 You might find this record over (4)
24 Enabling the engines to provide stable flight? (10)
25 Capital solo crack-up (4)

DOWN

1 Inclination to change direction (4)
2 Worry about some kind of work (4)
3 It might be their turn to get tight (6)
4 Put your name down again as you go out (6)
5 Puts the question invitingly (4)
6 Work in the theatre? (10)
10 They're on the cards for some people (10)
11 American flyer (5)
15 Not a paying proposition, it's said (5)
17 Goes by road spending very little time on the hills (6)
18 Used to hold a gun in the old bomber (6)
19 It provides a sound return (4)
21 Rule on some point where tennis is played (4)
22 He's entitled to make a girl lose her head (4)

28

ACROSS

1 Remove the possibility of an explosion (6)
4 Time said to be consumed (5)
7 Girl encountered in a cross-Channel flight (3)
8 Organise a fight to give more authority? (7)
9 The man who is one presumably won't be back (5)
10 Chance of coming unstuck, one takes it (4)
11 County in which one has landed? (4)
12 Drink in a big way! (3)
14 More dignified than simple jobs? (11)
18 Impersonal person (3)
20 Unwarily one might fall into it (4)
21 Certainly not getting the wind up (4)
23 Take off—or it might be for landing (5)
24 Involved in a rite that requires no great effort (7)
25 Briefly given business status in America (3)
26 The talk of ancient Rome (5)
27 Classified as unsuitable for general consumption (6)

DOWN

1 Start to become rather distant? (6)
2 Something from the wreck that hasn't sunk (7)
3 It might cause obstruction if you get the drift (4)
4 It's up to him to provide the power you need (8)
5 Decent chaps in a small way (5)
6 Sailor encountering a Scot on the airfield (6)
7 Concerned with the flow of air from my one car aid (11)
13 Domestic revolution in the air? (4,4)
15 It might give one a certain pull on the farm (7)
16 Some sort of fin on the top (6)
17 Striking quality of a devilish performance (6)
19 For instance, a brief return might get you the bird (5)
22 This is the place! (4)

ACROSS

1 Great book of the big race? (7)
5 Advance in formation (5)
8 Service doctor taking tea when coffee is wanted (5)
9 Scotsman shortly to get the wind up (7)
10 Quite an amount when you add it up (3)
11 City vehicle taking one in at the roundabout (5)
12 Animals you can't quite weigh up (5)
13 The kid's natural protector (5)
14 Standing in the station? (4)
15 Be a sport in the theatre? (4)
17 Girl's hair needing key treatment? (5)
19 Compel to use troops (5)
21 Mean to be drunk (5)
23 There'll be time for it in the afternoon (3)
24 Wish Ali could be made intelligible to Africans (7)
25 It's understood I'm in diplomacy (5)
26 Tart answer? (5)
27 The case of the covered-in engine (7)

DOWN

1 Funny business taking some of the mickey (5)
2 A lot gets knocked down at one (7)
3 Time for a rendering of 'Water Boy'? (6)
4 Letter about lines of some sort (13)
5 Solomon's birthday (6)
6 Origins of growth (5)
7 Virtue of a certain sweetness about a good man (7)
14 Not accepting reconditioned seal fur (7)
16 Record one unfinished call as making sense (7)
17 Ex-Servicemen in this are many (6)
18 Not moving to interfere with reception (6)
20 Land where it's right to provide a different meal (5)
22 A name for nobility (5)

30

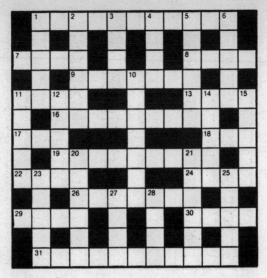

ACROSS

1 It provides a mixture to keep the engine going (11)
7 There's sure to be a big disturbance when it's dropped (4)
8 Exhibit a mad enthusiasm (4)
9 Paper you might find absorbing (7)
11 Make a mark to ensure there's no escape (4)
13 American lake back in the Ould Country (4)
16 They may be found in a mess (9)
17 Fighter doing a bit of a line (3)
18 Garland to be sure when you've time to spare (3)
19 High-level indication of which way to go? (9)
22 Not now indicating the North (4)
24 Make some impression as an artist (4)
26 He may be called on when things are getting too heated (7)
29 Two similar pieces of mink for one girl (4)
30 She may be pipped after lunch (4)
31 Mac to perish in a mix-up concerned with the air (11)

DOWN

1 Near enough to see a hundred suffer defeat (5)
2 Possibly a building after the raid (6)
3 Cancel a performance before take-off? (4)
4 The big blow-out doesn't start this way (4)
5 There could be fire coming out of it (6)
6 Singer's old man (5)
10 It might help to make the canteen situation a bit sticky (7)
11 Light pole? (5)
12 Turn this way to avoid bashing on (5)
14 Having found a tenant for a small piece of land? (5)
15 He'd get involved with it for her (5)
20 Not too strong in company (6)
21 It looks expensive on the surface (6)
23 Laugh if you get a letter in Israel (5)
25 Funny how the company begins to take the mickey! (5)
27 Rags about making a cage? (4)
28 Legend of the lisping lady? (4)

ACROSS

1 Is it clogs involved in supply and transport? (9)
6 Time to be sure of a rub-out (3)
7 Letters in Germany (3)
9 Souvenir from the derelict mansion (5)
10 Put your foot down on the tyre (5)
11 Bury the painter when his father's gone (5)
12 Caught after putting the chopper back—that's right! (5)
13 It's held to indicate high rank (5)
15 Choose to put someone in the office (5)
17 Small picture as part of a series (5)
21 Used a cat to demonstrate room space? (5)
23 Operate the emergency pilot's exit (5)
24 Take the lady on as a flier (5)
25 They have a big part in reporting progress (5)
26 What dental service personnel learn on parade? (5)
27 Not very clever with the lighting (3)
28 Fool to cut the relationship short (3)
29 People at work (9)

DOWN

1 Regret spending a morning in a period of abstinence (6)
2 The path up here might be deceptive (6)
3 Middle East bigwig with a fruity wife (6)
4 Urge to be mutinous (6)
5 Pay up and sink down (6)
6 Confirmed as being part of the authorised strength (11)
8 Gets artists reclassified as war planners (11)
14 Unnamed person giving a number (3)
16 Close to base? (3)
18 Just a little one that might be netted (6)
19 Offer to be gentle (6)
20 Sheep in more trouble (6)
21 Subjected to unauthorised removal procedure (6)
22 Some of you learn to be different, it may be fancied (6)

32

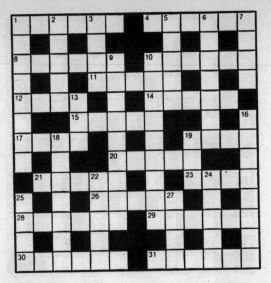

ACROSS

1 Bather disturbed by a girl (6)
4 Talk of a possible Common Market customer (6)
8 Where the beast might cross the river (6)
10 No disruption in this football team? (6)
11 Taken to be sure the job's done properly (5)
12 Slip of the tongue (4)
14 Nothing in the department for the distribution centre (5)
15 Serves a turn in the workshop (5)
17 Just like the model (4)
19 Something to drink as it's half-time (4)
20 All-round path or only part of it? (5)
21 Chap with a bit of a name for miraculous food (5)
23 Provide direction if the animal won't start (4)
26 Wear away a poem after some hesitation (5)
28 Caught a race in want (6)
29 Has someone been pulling at him? (6)
30 The power to push ahead (6)
31 Going in a bit for a break (6)

DOWN

1 Possible tie-up at low level (8)
2 Fast turn to the right to prevent sinking (5)
3 It might require pluck to play it (4)
5 Plunge in without washing (5)
6 Ian's not disturbed by such states (7)
7 Don't let anyone see the leather! (4)
9 The aim of many pub players (9)
10 Menial person beneath the driver? (9)
13 Work at a job that's simply finished (3)
16 Cause dismay by removing hair? (8)
18 Man of growing importance in rubber production (7)
19 Put away inside (3)
22 Requires dense redistribution (5)
24 Leg joint (5)
25 Tie up at some speed? (4)
27 With this there should be no difficulty (4)

ACROSS

1 Height of Mahommed's readiness to move (8)
5 Information about a fool and his fix (4)
7 Cut at some speed (4)
9 The usual open space (6)
10 Understand there's a fall (6)
12 Smith might work it in Hastings (3)
13 One for a quick discharge (6)
15 One doesn't work to get it (4)
16 She comes before the big day (3)
17 King Frederick's inner man (4)
19 Time for a song from Porgy and Bess (6)
21 Food for a bad actor (3)
22 Reception of the gullible? (6)
26 One might be given time for a stay here (6)
27 The noble fellow's nearly in New York! (4)
28 Advantage provided by a knife (4)
29 Too languid to have any inclination? (8)

DOWN

1 Jeer when it's not the real thing (4)
2 One bit of service (4)
3 Put a bar up for the foreigner (4)
4 Subtle distinctions of approved neckwear (8)
5 Ask to add men in new formation (6)
6 Revolutionary means of getting things going (9)
8 Influence of the tractor? (4)
11 Accommodated in divisions (9)
14 This is the end! (8)
18 Said to be pursued – but never caught? (6)
20 The opportunist is on it (4)
23 Throw to a vessel (4)
24 You'll have no trouble with this (4)
25 With the addition of a cross (4)

34

ACROSS

1 Advance this way (7)
5 The man with skill in the middle (5)
8 Left on the other side (5)
9 Is he in charge of a keep-fit exercise? (7)
10 She appears before the big day (3)
11 Union stick returned in style (5)
12 Much may turn on this (5)
13 Good word for a final departure (5)
14 They follow the car in glass vessels (4)
15 Make a loose arrangement (4)
17 Power possibility? (5)
19 It has the makings of an unworldly tower (5)
21 Our foreign friend (5)
23 Island personality (3)
24 Where the drama of war takes place? (7)
25 Understood to be at present inside (5)
26 Permission to take time off (5)
27 Revolutionary flying machine (7)

DOWN

1 Tree on the road before all the others (5)
2 How rules are applied when one is shaken? (7)
3 Following like a bird (6)
4 Breaking off the battle or the marriage? (13)
5 The climber's achievement (6)
6 Tremulous growth (5)
7 Explosive device to give poor Ted a break (7)
14 Aircraft city (7)
16 Ian's turned up and Robin's not quite finished in Africa (7)
17 Girl in the shrubbery (6)
18 It carries the means of making progress (6)
20 Twirl a rope for our entertainment (5)
22 Animal in the pound (5)

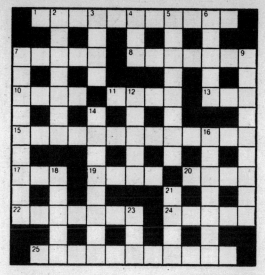

ACROSS

1 Upkeep of a ceremonial cap (11)
7 Some breakfast that might be saved (5)
8 Strife when you take the string off? (7)
10 Birds given a certain amount back on a note (4)
11 Made for each other (4)
13 There'll be time for that after lunch (3)
15 It just shows what the serviceman has to look after (3,10)
17 Put in when the row starts (3)
19 It gives me a turn to see it in the list (4)
20 A bit of a stinker provides the drink (4)
22 They help to distinguish items in the book (7)
24 Box-kite? Well, some old aircraft (5)
25 They may be the means of getting things done (11)

DOWN

2 Story of where the money's gone? (7)
3 Days of wonder (4)
4 Chum taking a day off at last (3)
5 Take away some kind of summary (8)
6 Hit 150 before being dismissed (5)
7 Detailed analysis of what's gone wrong? (9)
9 Suitable trousers for running away? (9)
12 Quite enough to confuse me, pal! (5)
14 Something that happens to make an impression at last (8)
16 It's happening in a flash at this moment! (7)
18 Not the type to slope away (5)
21 Among the discomforts of the Normandy beaches (4)
23 Worth very little if it's less than sound (3)

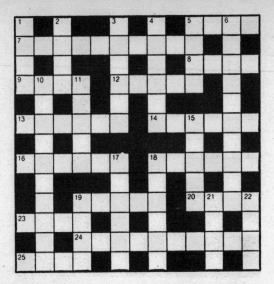

ACROSS

5 No longer with us, being unpunctual? (4)
7 Movement in the air causing a commotion (10)
8 Dial one might be ashamed to lose? (4)
9 Scheme to show the arrangements (4)
12 Move quickly for the kill? (5)
13 A Norfolk feature overseas (6)
14 Magician in a former line of business (6)
16 Amuse by sending elsewhere (6)
18 Radio interference getting you nowhere? (6)
19 The way the needle points (5)
20 It might help to lend one (4)
23 He might have a man sat on by the Turks (4)
24 House title altered as an aid to identification (10)
25 Advantage of being an outsider? (4)

DOWN

1 Don't go on piling up trophies (4)
2 The extent of what you see from the basement window (4)
3 A hundred and fifty the wrong dose – shut up! (6)
4 At one's best, one can tell (6)
5 The Socialist side (4)
6 Man with the workshop know-how (10)
10 Prepared to take easily to revolution? (10)
11 A hanging matter can make one so different! (5)
15 Get to the point where you can see a bit of river (5)
17 Shiver of excitement (6)
18 One might be sent here as a matter of course (6)
19 No sense putting this part in front (4)
21 Bet there's room in the mess (4)
22 Action document (4)

ACROSS

5 Present an American Serviceman on a great day in 1945 (4)
7 It provides a chance to look into things (10)
8 Laos in ruins as well (4)
9 Violent character of East End embrace (4)
12 Not moving one with a rent adjustment (5)
13 Estimate of value of money in cloth (6)
14 Take lunch in after a quarrel (6)
16 Unit in current supply (6)
18 Outlaw group that has it (6)
19 There's no reasoning with one (5)
20 Songs of the hen? (4)
23 Seen in Sicily before turning back (4)
24 Real outing diverted as a rule (10)
25 Let out at no expense (4)

DOWN

1 Inclination to put down certain items? (4)
2 Bible man in the Saudi Arabian capital (4)
3 Not yet confirmed in the theatre? (6)
4 Show the quickest way to go (6)
5 Insignificant little flier (4)
6 It's a help in landing, as far as one can see (10)
10 He's most superior at school (10)
11 Show how to go and get lampooned, it's said (5)
15 No more after this one! (5)
17 Hire to get into a fight (6)
18 Few took part in that of Britain (6)
19 Uncovered an animal, did you say? (4)
21 Old enemies at the centre of revolution (4)
22 Bag this as a defence aid! (4)

ACROSS

1 Yearning to get away from the meridian? (9)
6 Cry of wonder at a hundred spectacles (3)
7 Damage the other arm (3)
9 Hang on like a peach (5)
10 Mad elephant you can't trust (5)
11 Dame Edith as a girl meeting Poles (5)
12 It might be brought up to scratch (5)
13 Land of the leg, it appears (5)
15 Capital also including Kentucky extremists (5)
17 I do it the mad way! (5)
21 He puts an additional note and that's plenty (5)
23 Probably kicking too! (5)
24 Make an adjustment in the special terms offered (5)
25 Try to become one of the high-ups (5)
26 I'm in the majority, being slightly wet (5)
27 And so on in wretched succession (3)
28 It takes time to achieve it (3)
29 Dealing with applied science in making a nice latch adaptation (9)

DOWN

1 American serviceman in wrong goal providing cover (6)
2 The pleasant quality of precision? (6)
3 Frozen hanger (6)
4 Old city chap in a hurry (6)
5 Go aboard and see me turn over and imitate a dog (6)
6 A document to establish fact (11)
8 Having the duty of making an answer (11)
14 Astrological man (3)
16 A person who is singularly anonymous (3)
18 It can't be changed if undamaged (6)
19 Standing at the airport (6)
20 You can see what's in it (6)
21 Exciting new arrangement of the ICC (6)
22 Creature that might be crackers (6)

ACROSS

1 Uncommon Act II that tells us something (13)
8 Instruments of wood? (5)
9 We are living in the Queen's (5)
10 It's fearfully rousing! (5)
11 Ring the chaps for indication of what's coming (4)
12 Anything taken out of the slaughter (5)
14 Really grim – that's the way to get the bird! (5)
17 Come in like a pigeon (4)
18 Accurately adjusted to the facts (4)
20 Ray's radioactive! (5)
23 Like a silent Serviceman (5)
25 So elevated at the beginning of dinner (4)
26 Non-exclusive bay (5)
28 Give up the product (5)
29 Order our country to sea wrongly (5)
30 No use to HM Forces (13)

DOWN

1 Deal with the problem of covering the bishop? (4)
2 At least put a skirt on the old lady! (7)
3 Clumsily unlash Germany's old soldiers (6)
4 Deception or reception? (6)
5 Give a chap a breather – he may be in flight (6)
6 Seeing it's not this on the cake (5)
7 A number of links in times past (8)
13 It's said to indicate approved reception (5,3)
15 Part of the late afternoon intake (3)
16 Drink making one feel queer? (3)
19 Tart lot of theatrical talk (7)
20 Silent flier (6)
21 Law I am breaking in Africa (6)
22 Shrewd expression of disapproval in a rough sea (6)
24 Opinions of men of vision? (5)
27 This is the place (4)

40

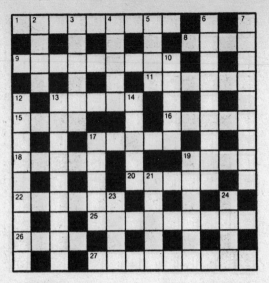

ACROSS

1 Permission to go—by taking a jump? (9)
8 Said not to be found in bad visibility (4)
9 It shows how acid or tin can change (9)
11 Land at last near the centre for a meal (6)
13 Had an old-fashioned time with a girl? (5)
15 It's even when a craft is steady (4)
16 He will be given a ring as a greeting (5)
17 He's in court briefly exposing the front (5)
18 Limit of a stretch of river (5)
19 Bring up to be one of the followers? (4)
20 Let an animal give directions (5)
22 Sharp craft? (6)
25 Ability to strike with fatal effect (4-5)
26 Land part of an heiress's inheritance (4)
27 Such navigation as the old Chinese might have used? (9)

DOWN

2 The chain connection? (4)
3 Only a beast would turn Alma in! (6)
4 Knowing there's fighting to the East (5)
5 Note half a dollar rise for a piece of earth (4)
6 One of the air crew is trying to communicate (9)
7 It's right on the ship (9)
10 Proper privilege (5)
12 It's expected to explode in the air (3-6)
13 Something new on going away (9)
14 Put something on, perhaps a uniform (5)
17 Most important for the cook to include one (5)
19 Deliver the facts with a bang? (6)
21 It's where we hope to get (5)
23 Better pay on promotion? (4)
24 She's just one girl among several (4)

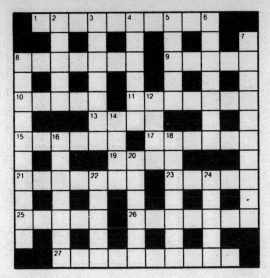

41

ACROSS

1 It might provide cover when you're swinging (4,6)
8 The number that might turn it green (7)
9 Ingredient of Shakespearian comedy (5)
10 Dieting Jack (5)
11 We're in such a state when we get married! (7)
13 Otherwise I leave a girl (4)
15 A different result is needed to demonstrate brilliance (6)
17 They may be employed for giving out soup (6)
19 Monstrous loch (4)
21 Their outpourings can be quite refreshing (7)
23 Broken rut and then a rough bit in Cornwall (5)
25 Having an obligation to indicate nothing (5)
26 This gal gets off somehow! (7)
27 Gangsters muscling in on the sports equipment market? (10)

DOWN

2 On target by a different route (5)
3 Not one to give up without a struggle (7)
4 They're despatched with a bow (6)
5 Get your hands on some dough (5)
6 Mixing a drink during work causes some upset (7)
7 Obviously not running footwear (5-5)
8 Separation on an island? (10)
12 They may be caught at length (4)
14 Borrowed time? (4)
16 Cause great surprise at different times? (7)
18 Just a step and you're in the saddle! (7)
20 Grounds for using one sort of car (6)
22 You can see it will easily give you a nip (5)
24 For keeping people quiet at the wedding? (5)

42

ACROSS

1 Helpful in forming a band? (12)
8 Left ale around to convey a message (7)
9 Nonsense brought back to the doctor to get things going (5)
10 Are coming back for a time (3)
11 Dog dispersing fog somehow (4)
12 Many find it irritating to come down in the sea (5)
15 Matters carrying little weight with the general staff (6)
16 Just look at that airfield! (6)
19 Saw a number put on (5)
21 Noble listener as a student (4)
22 Outcome of drilling at sea (3)
25 Happen to suffer a business reverse with some low creature (5)
26 They show the same pressure all along the line (7)
27 Being tired of the hard stuff the cause of a crack-up? (5,7)

DOWN

1 Doing nothing to let the engine turn (4)
2 Don't go when support is needed (4)
3 Doing a manoeuvre like the Stones? (7)
4 High-level traveller in remote crash (6)
5 Agree about Mother being a wanderer (5)
6 Get off the ground to gain it (8)
7 Make sport of a cherry (7)
13 Position somewhere along the line (7)
14 High point reached by fifty in a vessel (8)
17 Its travel figures go up and come down (7)
18 Much thanks for someone to take over! (6)
20 Lady of the manor (5)
23 Report on a hair-style (4)
24 Ground in water (4)

ACROSS

1 Ribbon right in the ship (8)
5 Put money by to rescue (4)
7 Pull backward (4)
9 Vibrates like a bulkhead in short dislocation (6)
10 Aircraft from the North and South states (6)
12 Container from an unknown Continental port (3)
13 Set of clothing for the unit (6)
15 The way the guard might protect (4)
16 I did this in the Middle East! (3)
17 They may be mastered by degrees (4)
19 Some petrol that might be nearly all gone (6)
21 He's finished off a Russian! (3)
22 It's the way things work when my sets are broken (6)
26 Fighter in a small way (6)
27 People in a hurry? (4)
28 Better cancel the race and have a drink! (6)
29 Assembled to get other arrangements made (8)

DOWN

1 Pride of the team? (4)
2 Way out of a Broadway show (4)
3 No permissiveness here in Ireland? (4)
4 Got train going around (8)
5 The jumping season? (6)
6 It gives one the shakes (9)
8 Shorten the way if it's for a homeless child (8)
11 Make the revolution easier (9)
14 Send St Martin round (8)
18 Easy catch for a model (6)
20 Stagger up and look lascivious (4)
23 Very lilttle to pay for entertainment (4)
24 Make a mess of the spuds (4)
25 Clothes to change in the car (4)

44

ACROSS

1 Capital as seen about that time (6)
4 Don't go away when you get punishment (5)
7 Sharp reduction (3)
8 Gunnery or balloon flying (7)
9 Ready for action if the beer is right (5)
10 Destroy with light lines, we hear (4)
11 Establishment run by people of breeding (4)
12 Shelter from the battle early on (3)
14 Not caring what's changed after gaining entry (11)
18 Carry on needling (3)
20 Head supporter (4)
21 Not in time to avoid a fatality? (4)
23 Due .o the circle displayed on one side (5)
24 Road not damaged in a storm (7)
25 Colour he wraps round you at last (3)
26 River right in the camp (5)
27 Brief international law preserved (6)

DOWN

1 Prince one might keep watch on (6)
2 The edge of the world, as far as one can see (7)
3 Such a miss is almost disastrous (4)
4 Regular staff display (8)
5 Perfect when I hand out cards (5)
6 Youngster providing equipment number (6)
7 Documentary proof of the fact (11)
13 Time for a new date (8)
15 Falls between Canada and USA (7)
16 One with another (6)
17 Give the facts about wine (6)
19 Sound of the complaining drinker? (5)
22 Hard stuff in the bag perhaps when one's on course (4)

ACROSS

1 Its lines go up and down the globe (9)
6 Eggs the dean to get out of the girls' school (3)
7 Healthy enough to have a seizure (3)
9 Minimum quantity that might turn stale (5)
10 Can be bribed to take the back road after five (5)
11 Nothing but bees buzzing around could be so fat (5)
12 One transaction that couldn't be better (5)
13 Big part of a regular German force (5)
15 Put off making a little gentleman cleaner (5)
17 Sound of a departure from the bow (5)
21 You 'finish in debt at first appearance (5)
23 As far as you can shoot in the mountains (5)
24 It carries little weight as a feline (5)
25 He takes things philosophically (5)
26 Still kicking, man! (5)
27 Big hit number (3)
28 State shortly to be in poor condition (3)
29 Ice regent doing an active turn (9)

DOWN

1 One inclining to be more slim (6)
2 Miss Dean, fellow dreamer (6)
3 Picture of how the game is reformed (6)
4 Such a great number kept in the dark? (6)
5 One might have cause to create one (6)
6 More to be expected from Russian engines? (11)
8 The oil trace not established by research (11)
14 Means of delivering explosive (3)
16 The day before the lady appears (3)
18 Extra accommodation for a girl on the river (6)
19 Means of reducing friction for a great start with no difficulty (6)
20 We come to this at last (6)
21 Leave unexpectedly in the Sahara? (6)
22 Working like a living computer? (6)

46

ACROSS

1 Line of thought of radio distinction? (10)
8 Act it out in an upper room (5)
9 Plant information on poor Tina (7)
10 Dropped in for a cool drink (3)
11 Sharing a piece of meat? (5)
12 Spreading of a thickness (5)
13 It could be spread with limbs stretched outwards (5)
15 Took off in the hangar? (4)
16 Drink left on board (4)
18 Pigeon poet? (5)
20 Code of communication (5)
22 Measure of spirits by eye? (5)
23 Go in with some striking intentions (3)
24 Run late diversion without commitment (7)
25 Sing as you fish (5)
26 No longer in service after firing (10)

DOWN

2 Quite a step when one's in the saddle (7)
3 Rouse to give a thrilling performance (6)
4 Slight advantage for the outsider (4)
5 The sort of man who has a blonde preference? (6)
6 Dangerous when unkempt? (5)
7 Not of decisive importance so one's not complaining (10)
8 Jam Ted's nut so that it needs putting right (10)
14 Yorkshiremen swear by it! (3)
17 Result of leaving the door open? (7)
18 Romantic suit? (6)
19 Right animal for a decadent person (6)
21 Ammunition circle? (5)
23 It's just meaningless talk (4)

ACROSS

1 You're probably getting somewhere if you're in it (7)
5 Just a little bit of a fight (5)
8 Water under the bridge (5)
9 Providing a gas outlet could make one weary (7)
10 Do the human thing (3)
11 Show pain when you gain a couple of notes (5)
12 Small flier Ed having trouble with a Mig (5)
13 He's to turn over the ones over there (5)
14 Sounded as cocky as sailors (4)
15 Keep it up to maintain spirits (4)
17 Keep striking for money (5)
19 The lad with the lass (5)
21 Young flier throwing the towel in (5)
23 Mr Gladstone's boy (3)
24 He wilts perhaps but can take a blow (7)
25 They may be open to receive visitors (5)
26 Sounding a bit thin (5)
27 Keep back for later use (7)

DOWN

1 Worth the trouble for quick propulsion (5)
2 It's what one expects with a go-ahead commander (7)
3 Setter about to show the way (6)
4 Describing the reaction of the hydrogen bomb (13)
5 Plan to use a little science when he is ahead of me (6)
6 Golfer's slice? (5)
7 Sort of bombing that shows the attacker's design? (7)
14 Nothing to do with the dispute with Iceland! (4,3)
16 The case of the hidden gun (7)
17 How one looks sitting in an advantageous position? (6)
18 Tricks for avoiding a contact man? (6)
20 There's something to be said for using it (5)
22 Try to find out if it's what you like (5)

48

ACROSS

1 Surgery on a friend in relation to Service activity (13)
8 Look for a delay (5)
9 Eccentric character of a piece of machinery (5)
10 Circulation pump (5)
11 There'll be a row if we get into it (4)
12 A clean-up before sinking? (5)
14 It moves for very little time at a height (5)
17 One of those things in the newspaper (4)
18 Not agitated when there isn't a blow (4)
20 Throw back an attacker (5)
23 Animal in the pound (5)
25 Not the exclusive part of Copenhagen (4)
26 Able to get on as a churchman (5)
28 Anything that might come out of the slaughter (5)
29 Cover with a curtain (5)
30 Keeping people amused, that's it! (13)

DOWN

1 There's something to be said for such an examination (4)
2 Look at what was once a source of fuel (7)
3 Song of national standing (6)
4 Not damaged in diplomacy (6)
5 Possibly trance-inducing drink (6)
6 Everybody turns up before Mother becomes a beast (5)
7 A hook may be thrown out in port (8)
13 Skipper taking a long time navigating by landmarks on a map (8)
15 Have an obligation to get out of the control tower (3)
16 A person who is not named (3)
19 Declare one's years to be far from exceptional (7)
20 A clergyman to put us right? (6)
21 Father takes a fellow up a waterway (6)
22 Capital beginner getting on with a chap (6)
24 During which one has a dark experience (5)
27 Not the way one wants to go (4)

ACROSS

1 Coming in like a pigeon? (6)
4 Marvellous what comes out of one's purse! (5)
7 One politician can be a devil! (3)
8 Out of this world character (7)
9 Throw out in an emergency (5)
10 Make an impression by finishing a drawing (4)
11 Courage needed to display some integrity (4)
12 Cut the German off in the light (3)
14 Good enough to use in the Forces (11)
18 Funny fellow moving the dog-end (3)
20 One side needing help in the attack (4)
21 Highlight provided by a top performer (4)
23 Brown to get moving in a dance (5)
24 Not making a fighting commitment (7)
25 Fool of a girl losing her head! (3)
26 Quite a pile-up in the stores (5)
27 Expense of free-range egg production? (6)

DOWN

1 Get in the way of the basket (6)
2 It's wonderful to be able to pull a car up in the distance! (7)
3 You're quite right to hit it on the head! (4)
4 Let scrap take on a ghostly appearance (7)
5 Keep pushing for papers (5)
6 Having some value as a sailor (6)
7 Not complete breaches of the rules? (11)
13 Put too much on board (8)
15 Subsequently given a pound at the side (7)
16 Move quickly on and off (6)
17 Vulgarly held to give personal protection (6)
19 Sail from an Italian port (5)
22 Double piece of luck finding her! (4)

50

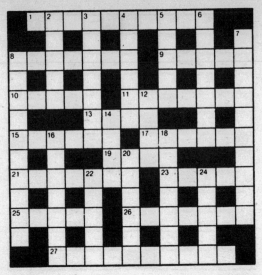

ACROSS

1 Where rallying can be rather a gamble? (5,5)
8 Recreation that might be catching (7)
9 Get along without power (5)
10 Prepared to go quietly? (5)
11 Break her shin with some sort of wine (7)
13 Ultimately lack success as a player (4)
15 He wants to get there quickly (6)
17 Behind you when all at sea (6)
19 Among the tastier types of tipple (4)
21 Just a moment, this one's happening now! (7)
23 They sound the last things you might find amusing (5)
25 Fear being beheaded by mistake (5)
26 Handled in a hospitable way? (7)
27 Where the city is not united (10)

DOWN

2 Bird finding employment inside (5)
3 Let wild Ted do a turn! (7)
4 Invest one grand in vehicles later reduced to ashes (6)
5 Like some thoroughly dishonest creature? (5)
6 Force eleven holocaust at the opening (7)
7 Given the power to dispense with brute force (10)
8 Standing in the kitchen maybe (5,5)
12 Raising the temperature in the theatre (4)
14 In North Africa where nothing moved (4)
16 Banning the guitar might be the cure! (7)
18 Easy catches for portrait painters? (7)
20 In time for a ninefold saving (6)
22 On the domestic front (5)
24 The French and the English doing a workshop turn (5)

ACROSS

1 I film ace's crash – or something very like it! (9)
6 Push back to cause damage (3)
7 Everything obtainable for a couple of pounds (3)
9 If you know them you won't get in a tangle (5)
10 He plans to make a hit with me in flight (5)
11 Disposed of internally (5)
12 Happen to take place (5)
13 Troubled by a superior group (5)
15 Trunk with tangled roots (5)
17 Call up all right with a girl around (5)
21 Polite learner among musicians (5)
23 Get up a North Yorkshire waterway (5)
24 Berry senior (5)
25 The beast Lily might take to (5)
26 Scope for the morning part (5)
27 Refreshing outpouring (3)
28 Not a priestly song? (3)
29 Female fliers in a very small way (9)

DOWN

1 Spectacular all-rounders (6)
2 Asinine incentive (6)
3 Striking effect of a collision (6)
4 Put inside when the rent is sorted out (6)
5 Time for an egg (6)
6 It may provide a figure for the distance (11)
8 Air city (11)
14 RAF man of the lesser kind (3)
16 It lessens the friction when things get moving (3)
18 Suffering from the loader's error (6)
19 Go wrong and there'll be a mission for you (6)
20 Uproar at the centre when there's some bubbly (6)
21 Worse alternative (6)
22 Heavenly of them to back plays! (6)

ACROSS

1 The way to keep going (8,5)
8 Part of the line-up on the personal front, maybe. (5)
9 Follow America in conveying water through Portugal (5)
10 Try to make a catch on the corner (5)
11 Read the gossip before the lad comes back (4)
12 It keeps going round (5)
14 The German can get by here in England (5)
17 Friend in the fight (4)
18 Information about preserving old aircraft canvas (4)
20 Line up to take cover (5)
23 Try for quality (5)
25 Animal getting cross at the top (4)
26 Concerning one's birth in South Africa (5)
28 Entertainment work needing time (5)
29 An improvement once more! (5)
30 Suitability for flying around with ears on, sir (13)

DOWN

1 Depressed area where there might be oil (4)
2 Aid Carl to become an old-time extremist (7)
3 Away from the shore (6)
4 It might provide fighter cover (6)
5 A break for Terry where the blood flows (6)
6 Number doing some sort of reel (5)
7 One who took off for the wide open spaces? (8)
13 It might be described as a projectile being affected by gravity (8)
15 You might lend one to the speaker (3)
16 Transport payment going up (3)
19 Function like communications personnel (7)
20 It goes around providing some current needs (6)
21 Amount of space in a former shelter (6)
22 Sausage girl with her French friend (6)
24 Point of attack (5)
27 It's our responsibility (4)

ACROSS

1 The old man's game to provide proof of identity (8)
8 Anxious about redeploying the RAF when help is needed (6)
9 Pancake when there's a panic getting a lift (8)
10 Duty-free? (6)
12 The old one's seen a lot of service (5)
14 Damages goods taken for loot (6)
16 Getting lighter in old age (4)
18 Make a call in the Shetlands (4)
19 A load off your mind when someone else takes over! (6)
20 Turn it to increase the pressure (5)
23 Distributes soup in fifty different deals (6)
26 No runway for fliers here (8)
27 Expert not turning at once (6)
28 Terriers in action? (3-5)

DOWN

2 Concede the lot with a pained cry (5)
3 Brown as pie, maybe (5)
4 Sort of message passed by word of mouth (4)
5 Mimics a pilot? (5,3)
6 In short, have some cheese before you take off (7)
7 Get along with difficulty without a stiffener? (4)
11 Turn to wall for a light (6)
12 Railwaymen may get the message (6)
13 We're reformed in jug (4)
14 Falls over the brick carrier, being careless (8)
15 Mystic taken over by the supervisor (4)
17 Gen Lily processed, for crying out loud! (7)
21 Island where the corn is tropical (5)
22 Ground for a change of heart (5)
24 Offhand about ventilation? (4)
25 Sell when the game's up (4)

ACROSS

1 Liking to end at the cricket ground (8)
8 Breezy chap in blue? (6)
9 Morecambe taken in by a chap from the States (8)
10 Provide off-course entertainment? (6)
12 Song about waving palms (5)
14 Observe a cutter that has its ups and downs (6)
16 Is this what dishes the Irish? (4)
18 Green linen? (4)
19 Protection is held to be possible here (6)
20 Magistrates in the workshop? (5)
23 He takes a healthy interest in people (6)
26 Attack by outsiders (8)
27 Oil mixed in French wine – it's a fiddle! (6)
28 One of the criminal crowd (8)

DOWN

2 Gets rid of water from shoes? (5)
3 How life in the country can be described (5)
4 It's a sin not to have the top rank! (4)
5 Where our country seems to be finished (5,3)
6 Unimportant half-dozen in test (7)
7 Made for each other (4)
11 Dig this for temporary protection (6)
12 Went along with the examiners' approval (6)
13 Fliers superior to royalty (4)
14 Giving guidance when it's green for a change (8)
15 Sound the alarm when there's fighting to the north (4)
17 No. 1 jet personality (7)
21 Moves slightly to avoid difficulties? (5)
22 Near the end (5)
24 Leave out nothing when a man is put up (4)
25 River to gain a victory on (4)

ACROSS

5 Family growth? (4)
7 The sameness of the Services? (10)
8 Unwind to gain release from it (4)
9 Out of the Worthington cask, certainly not stout (4)
12 Take steps to enjoy yourself (5)
13 Sitting thus, well placed to be put in the picture (6)
14 Give an account of the bang (6)
16 Means of catching the girl down below (6)
18 Personnel find the top performer a threat (6)
19 Possibly aided the revolution (5)
20 She may have a pad on the water (4)
23 Just the bird for a final song (4)
24 He regulates the comings and goings (10)
25 Liberated from the need to pay? (4)

DOWN

1 Wear it just in case? (4)
2 New Zealander getting a bit wild after losing some kit (4)
3 Robinson's man for twenty-four hours (6)
4 First to arrive at a contested conclusion (6)
5 City feeling the effects of inflation (4)
6 Cite cellar as being in a shocking state (10)
10 Answer to a nagging question of engine strength? (10)
11 Score a mark (5)
15 Committee for assembling instruments? (5)
17 Advanced again so you can relax (6)
18 Up-to-date fashion—ahead of the Navy (6)
19 On a never-to-be-repeated occasion? (4)
21 No use letting the engine run so slowly (4)
22 Measure of enclosed space? (4)

56

ACROSS

1 Slightly wet to reduce enthusiasm? (4)
3 Having no cover on top (4)
6 Offer to take the lot (3)
9 Find just a little bit (5)
10 Can leer in a less obscene way (7)
11 Keep away from the man who moved the railway wagons (7)
12 North African out in the country? (4)
14 It might make the revolution easier (6)
16 He provides our provisions (6)
19 The end of an animal (4)
21 The gain might be different when warmth is provided (7)
24 Go ahead and make a loan (7)
25 A bird for picking up? (5)
27 Give the old man fifty, friend! (3)
28 What a way to mash teas! (4)
29 Here's one way out (4)

DOWN

1 The girl has a point! (3)
2 Find the length of the dance (7)
4 Shopping is an undercover activity here (6)
5 He has some vision in mind (7)
6 Game to take a dust receptacle and depart (5)
7 Scandal in need of a clean-up (4)
8 Defeat in striking fashion (4)
11 Indication to put your name down (4)
13 Boast about card-playing? (4)
15 You can't hear anything in it (7)
17 Conditions for distributing mail, etc (7)
18 They go round when things are moving (6)
20 It comes under the hammer (5)
22 Support for giving the bishop a superior job? (4)
23 Artist meeting politician to expose a racket (4)
26 Function as a consumer (3)

ACROSS

1 Like air in a turbine (10)
8 Way of escape, possibly (5)
9 Bitterness makes a worker brave (7)
10 It's as low as one can personally get (3)
11 This trouble about the big end might be something to see! (5)
12 Device for giving a century of repose (5)
13 It gives us a rise in bread (5)
15 Someone dead in the group? (4)
16 If returning do use the fog disperser (4)
18 A knotty problem reckoning it? (5)
20 That's as far as you can go (5)
22 The girl from South America (5)
23 The man with the bag? (3)
24 Something of a strain in stone breaking (7)
25 A girl has it in her to show friendship (5)
26 Proper aspect of a square corner (5,5)

DOWN

2 Forced to distribute big dole (7)
3 One's well placed sitting thus (6)
4 Outside advantage? (4)
5 Take your choice among the best (6)
6 Plant man removed for a sailor (5)
7 Not going anywhere if there's a nasty riot around (10)
8 As far as one can see (10)
14 Wonder what's in the bottom drawer (3)
17 One starts to make a name with it (7)
18 Something the fixer might pull? (6)
19 Keep putting the wrong date in (6)
21 Not so important when one's young (5)
23 Tie up in the wood (4)

58

ACROSS

1 Enabled to climb to a higher level (8)
8 Unit from which one has emerged in good health (6)
9 A shout is no good and so is a knock-out here (4,4)
10 As high as you can get in negotiations (6)
12 Bad-tempered, probably having a trying time? (5)
14 Force to go ahead (6)
16 Agreement to return to see an island (4)
18 Hidden growth (4)
19 Local personage who might prove suitable (6)
20 Long-distance viewer finishing within range (5)
23 Pace extended in Russia (6)
26 He hasn't been here long (8)
27 Manoeuvre to gain advantage (6)
28 He knows how the machinery works (8)

DOWN

2 It's water under the bridge at Avignon (5)
3 Strength of a possibility? (5)
4 Instrument for raising plunder (4)
5 Animal form of drudge (4-4)
6 Have difficulty getting the talk started (7)
7 Start mine again, girl! (4)
11 Swimmer one might turn over (6)
12 Has met trouble in the river (6)
13 Revealing entertainment (4)
14 Card-player's virtue (8)
15 Crazy means of shifting wagons (4)
17 This way for river haulage (7)
21 Hit on the head for Her Majesty (5)
22 A bit you might say (5)
24 This side for sportsmen (4)
25 Tom's head with false hair added—catch on? (4)

ACROSS

1 Getting through in a rather dreary way (6)
4 Something of a fixture in commerce? (6)
8 A bit of a lark to mark a foreign sailor (6)
10 Means of getting ahead in the car trade (6)
11 Payments fixed for tuition periods? (5)
12 One may be afraid to get it up (4)
14 Put your foot on it for self-propulsion (5)
15 Neither side has the advantage here (5)
17 The story of nylon, maybe (4)
19 Look at the use of the horn (4)
20 The man the salesman's looking for (5)
21 Condition of the country? (5)
23 Finished in a superior position (4)
26 Feeling for a dramatic backward look? (5)
28 Quite a disturbance when people miss their sleep? (6)
29 Hidden trouble at one end of Leicester (6)
30 Stocking trouble helping you to rise (6)
31 Good quality wood on the surface (6)

DOWN

1 Get away with nothing finally in Zimbabwe (8)
2 Concerning the evil of varnish (5)
3 Smart enough to do without water (4)
5 Feeling the strain of numbers one way (5)
6 Talk about four being in the Army perhaps (7)
7 You get this way when you've paid off old scores (4)
9 Lying and finally quite crooked (9)
10 They're paid to be the people they are (9)
13 Private place at the end of the garden (3)
16 She might find you someone to talk to (8)
18 No longer among the 10 Down (7)
19 Is he paid for a supporting argument? (3)
22 It's a matter of what you fancy (5)
24 Not favouring this writing with an ad (5)
25 Good quality of a front-mounted engine? (4)
27 The only Frenchman in the entire neighbourhood, probably (4)

60

ACROSS

1 Mere tars can be employed making a pennon (8)
5 Take a beastly direction (4)
7 The work of stirring the soup (4)
9 Fair futility (6)
10 Drumming display? (6)
12 Position that can be deceptive (3)
13 Cry out in bad weather (6)
15 Get the message (4)
16 Employment in a good cause (3)
17 A girl who won't shoot well? (4)
19 Material help given back (6)
21 Go out after a rise (3)
22 See met. arrangements get proper respect (6)
26 He operates a cut-out procedure (6)
27 People in a hurry? (4)
28 Make a hit with a surprise item (4)
29 Mad pilot going around with a mission (8)

DOWN

1 Let's have no more carry-on! (4)
2 Old party in retreat (4)
3 Political extremist's obscure end (4)
4 Does it go around getting fired? (8)
5 Non-permissive standard? (6)
6 A gun you don't have to fire? (9)
8 Story of a fuel rise (4)
11 All you need to do the job (9)
14 Burdened with all that old furniture? (8)
18 Time for a ticket (6)
20 It never rolls when going out to sea (4)
23 Fall for an outing (4)
24 Injure at Maidenhead by intent (4)
25 The young man's way (4)

ACROSS

1 Time to start a new day (8)
5 One likely to go down in the fall (4)
9 Refuse to stir a stew (5)
10 Lacking an object of zero significance (7)
11 Cave man after a bit of grub (6)
12 Handle as a great pleasure (5)
14 It might be sought by refugees abroad (6)
16 Flower at some point behind (6)
19 Expensive sort of dive (5)
21 Go right in and take it! (6)
24 Go too far too fast? (7)
25 Old aircraft in a box (5)
26 Carry your bag, lady? (4)
27 RAF in relation to Britain (8)

DOWN

1 Cut down in a short time at two points (4)
2 Does try somehow to cause havoc (7)
3 Unable to move one over rent reform (5)
4 Bird meets boy in North London (6)
6 He's living among foreigners (5)
7 It's fierce where it's thickest (8)
8 One who is very good at taking the American position (6)
13 Father's game to provide identification (8)
15 He might give out when appealed to (6)
17 There was always one for wartime singers (7)
18 To live on others can be quite absorbing (6)
20 Standing up before the court (5)
22 Dutch talker (5)
23 The man most likely to succeed (4)

62

ACROSS

1 Plan to put American servicemen back into the study (6)
4 Come near to a shutdown? (5)
7 Somewhat notorious port (3)
8 He's nice in a devious sort of way, being foreign (7)
9 Plunder with a gun? (5)
10 Be miserable when a poem doesn't look right (4)
11 Not quite so near the ground when unaccompanied (4)
12 Fix up a source of oil? (3)
14 Do the honours with today's weapons (7,4)
18 Make it a highball (3)
20 Keen to see the old king lose his head (4)
21 It's trailing at the rear of the wing (4)
23 A sentry has to stand on it (5)
24 Go back when it's your round again? (7)
25 One to another in agreement (3)
26 Old-style royal house (5)
27 Reliable but corroded at the short end (6)

DOWN

1 Get away from temporary quarters? (6)
2 Chap in charge of the getaway? (7)
3 In the angle now seen between the hills (4)
4 A couple of stripes as some sort of punishment? (8)
5 Bargain suggestion (5)
6 Come out east and get together (6)
7 Have a look round the erection Ron rebuilt (11)
13 Man's man, for instance? (8)
15 Send Sam round? That's insanity! (7)
16 Fancy a getaway? (6)
17 He guards the way in to the south (6)
19 Make a mark that's new? (5)
22 Give a top performance in the Twinkles (4)

63

ACROSS

1 Wipe out the old boy if he can read! (10)
8 It might hold up current supplies (5)
9 Arrive holding the favourite and try to win (7)
10 Oh, that's what the Scots say! (3)
11 It's good when one's in favour (5)
12 Send a message to do air manoeuvres (5)
13 Follow points with a girl (5)
15 Bob's sister? (4)
16 No gunners for her! (4)
18 Just a bit of a fight (5)
20 There may be an attack round here (5)
22 One's presence is not required for this defence (5)
23 In the fire it means trouble! (3)
24 Refuse to go down (7)
25 Castle fliers? (5)
26 Having no views about how to press on? (10)

DOWN

2 Operations start when it goes up (7)
3 Don't worry about changes in one rig (6)
4 Make an impression as a craftsman (4)
5 Think well of me getting involved with a raid (6)
6 Make a change for me to get into the final! (5)
7 They give one quite a turn in flying! (10)
8 Grandpapa mixed up with nothing but psychological warfare (10)
14 You're senior to me, I say (3)
17 Threatening us after a brief time in spectacles (7)
18 Line under the kite (6)
19 Move to see what's happening in the area (6)
21 Happen to bring up the business with the dog (5)
23 A bad time coming, it's felt (4)

64

ACROSS

1 Way of working though in the Mediterranean briefly (6)
4 Get nowhere by flying? (5)
7 Many leave home at Plymouth (3)
8 Wave a card to indicate a plane (7)
9 Clergyman losing his head when there's firing (5)
10 The way to become an outsider (4)
11 Deposited back in the face (4)
12 Link some of the parties (3)
14 After exposure perhaps a negative achievement (11)
18 Come up for it after a dive (3)
20 Carry drink one way (3)
21 Land in an eastern Mediterranean port (4)
23 Room to display some curious lattice-work (5)
24 Not so erratic having signed on? (7)
25 Fool in a vessel (3)
26 Something to pay when the lagoon is enclosed? (5)
27 Notes an achievement in not winning (6)

DOWN

1 Old artist as teacher? (6)
2 It delivers power in brute revolution (7)
3 Said to be some sort of exam (4)
4 It casts a glow over the way forward (8)
5 Call half a dozen to take it easy (5)
6 Graded in rows? (6)
7 The crops lie damaged by aircraft (11)
13 Going up and down damaging an evil cart (8)
15 Body under an airship (7)
16 Tin covering a girl in the country (6)
17 Not for broadcasting (6)
19 The proportion now in operation (5)
22 Big fellow in no great hurry (4)

ACROSS

1 Likely to come a cropper even when lying down? (8-5)
8 Angry about a medal? (5)
9 Impatient to spend time among the Queen's letters (5)
10 Berry senior? (5)
11 Fight and return blows (4)
12 Get hold of the trick (5)
14 The Middle East might provide a subject (5)
17 Character with a message? (4)
18 Scheme to find one out of the ordinary (4)
20 Expert no good at making a point (5)
23 Somewhere to sleep in Number Thirteen (5)
25 For an old musician it's the absolute end! (4)
26 Girl getting home without me in a state (5)
28 One of those high-altitude nurses? (5)
29 It's not what one ought to do (5)
30 A nice spare pad makes a difference in the vanishing act (13)

DOWN

1 Support given at the end of a route march (4)
2 Does it fly in with cutting effect? (7)
3 Go absent in difficult country (6)
4 Pointer to the currently significant figure (6)
5 Go through and get a bit about right (6)
6 Has an obligation to get out of rough terrain (5)
7 It helps one to get a message (8)
13 The case for sheathing the sword (8)
15 You'll find the lady at the other end (3)
16 Chap given gold for cattle food (3)
19 Land disappointingly? (3,4)
20 Man to provide stimulation, let's say (6)
21 Nothing might be made clear by a know-all (6)
22 Look as if the note is not so high (6)
24 Storms when the gears go wrong (5)
27 Eye with amorous intent (4)

66

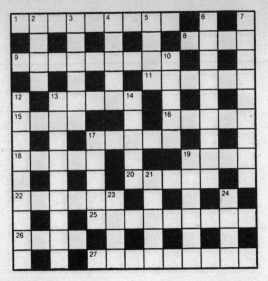

ACROSS

1 Maintenance by a clergyman? (9)
8 One of the feline nine (4)
9 Study the track where the passengers gather (9)
11 Move fast into line with nothing on? (6)
13 Leaves off after getting level (5)
15 Ammunition that takes some beating? (4)
16 Having been sent down inside (5)
17 Displeasure shown when the range is wrong (5)
18 She's always in excellent shape! (5)
19 Night-light (4)
20 Instruct the following (5)
22 Sweet shuffling of feet (6)
25 Freedoms far from the equator? (9)
26 Wind up a dance (4)
27 They are matters of concern (9)

DOWN

2 Where a boy might get collared (4)
3 There's nothing in it (6)
4 Find out the number (5)
5 Monstrous loch (4)
6 The way to give an order? (9)
7 Possibly dead by this calculation? (9)
10 There's a difference in the upper air (5)
12 Being under a vet for a change can be exciting! (9)
13 Having passed the necessary exams? Not absolutely (9)
14 This is something to see! (5)
17 One of those heavenly nurses (5)
19 Not enough time to get big? (6)
21 Turn her in as a flower (5)
23 Work for what you're paid (4)
24 The rhythm of police work (4)

ACROSS

1 Letting down the paratroops (8)
5 Control agitation (4)
9 Instructor of trade union eminence (5)
10 Appropriate foreigner on the way (7)
11 Just a bit of code left (6)
12 Fighting here might be a near thing (5)
14 Strike the girl this way (6)
16 Sixty miles in step (6)
19 Many are spoken in a lesson (5)
21 Strike at a point (6)
24 Forced out of some dip (7)
25 No timid Redskin (5)
26 Current movement in Egypt (4)
27 Pennon looking right in a vessel (8)

DOWN

1 Something to do on tour? (4)
2 Letters to be sent a long way from headquarters? (7)
3 Divides into components? (5)
4 Complain of a horse in the river (6)
6 Go away for a break (5)
7 Ready to turn paper a dangerous colour (8)
8 Part of a great facility for lubrication (6)
13 The best defender? (8)
15 Join up in silent disarray (6)
17 Get back by some extraordinary miracle (7)
18 Outlaw not allowed a hearing with it (6)
20 Sick man getting up to throw back invaders (5)
22 Figures a belt may be misplaced (5)
23 Drink better without being teetotal (4)

68

ACROSS

1 Let the next man know our secret (8)
8 Classical flier who ditched with wing trouble (6)
9 Not afraid to set the lass free to roam (8)
10 Move to show vigilance (6)
12 Very much inclined to dive or climb? (5)
14 Material of some significance (6)
16 Restrain a dog that starts biting (4)
18 Flood precautions expert (4)
19 Push the boat out (6)
20 Locating device going either way (5)
23 Military display of personal ornamentation? (6)
26 Belligerent old fellow supporting the cavalryman (3-5)
27 Part of the meal to follow? (6)
28 Batter at the bits that give protection (8)

DOWN

2 Warning to be watchful (5)
3 Material provided by some of the lesser German writers (5)
4 Quite prepared to receive outsiders (4)
5 Message to be sent with speed (8)
6 Unable even to drop five knives and forks? (7)
7 Fighting to take little Judy to a party (4)
11 In such excitement one might have a close shave (6)
12 There's no telling if we can keep it (6)
13 His lordship has got into real trouble! (4)
14 Human resources that give a fellow strength? (8)
15 One might go places without moving (4)
17 Guns stored for current use? (7)
21 It smells like the start of a romantic story! (5)
22 Something one has when a girl turns up (5)
24 Half the letters could go like a bomb! (4)
25 One likely to get a beating (4)

ACROSS

1 Up front for a protected person (7)
5 Funny enough for kids to read (5)
8 Churchgoers this way! (5)
9 Scene of a stoppage on the line? (7)
10 No sense in giving partial protection (3)
11 They enable progress to be made without revolution (5)
12 It's obvious no deciphering is needed (5)
13 The man who reformed Irene (5)
14 It's formed from grains, some thousands (4)
15 Smart animal! (4)
17 Inhibit the growth of aerobatics? (5)
19 Knowing there's a struggle on the way (5)
21 Where a brain will get you? (5)
23 Advance to get transport back (3)
24 Finished the tunnelling? (7)
25 In the popular German size (5)
26 There's likely to be shooting here (5)
27 Touched down in the wet (7)

DOWN

1 Panic movements (5)
2 He might involve us in Iran's trouble (7)
3 Not in favour of a poetic effort (6)
4 Made out to be illustrious (13)
5 Opportunity for a gamble (6)
6 State of the old lady in the East (5)
7 Car lent for going around in the middle of town (7)
14 Make a break from the arts (7)
16 Find not to be of this world? (7)
17 Safe to observe a dog inside (6)
18 Battle presented in a form you can swallow (6)
20 Airfield's domestic front? (5)
22 Fear the old Army man has taken in the engineers (5)

70

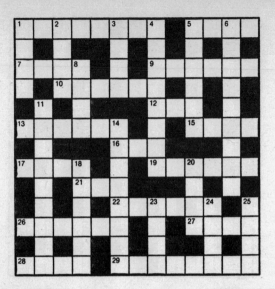

ACROSS

1 Is he given stripes as some sort of punishment? (8)
5 Try to find and interview at the King's Head (4)
7 Fishmonger's cake? (4)
9 Rather more unfeeling song? (6)
10 Fight back at the attacker (6)
12 He's not on our side (3)
13 Firm request to end mad manoeuvre (6)
15 Scold for speed? (4)
16 Shelter brought back for a swimmer (3)
17 There could be an opening for you here (4)
19 Scene of a bridge downfall (6)
21 He has a part in 'Pygmalion' (3)
22 Hot stuff, that redhead! (6)
26 Fix a good man in a morass (6)
27 Visibility is much reduced in it (4)
28 It keeps the car off the road (4)
29 Given a limited amount of dire NATO trouble (8)

DOWN

1 Thrown into a mould? (4)
2 See what a Red revolution signifies (4)
3 Capital lover losing nothing (4)
4 Stumble ashore? That's a long way ahead! (8)
5 Someone to add up in time (6)
6 Carrying out of an order to kill? (9)
8 A second letter from the Greeks (4)
11 Not the first to offer some sort of schooling (9)
14 He provides the shape of things to come (8)
18 Noise to frighten? (6)
20 Want Eden to be reconstructed (4)
23 Fresh start for Tommy as a small creature (4)
24 Not fair if it's falling (4)
25 Get along without further effort (4)

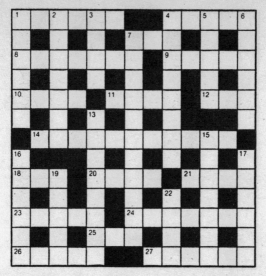

ACROSS

1 Reprimand for taking off into space (6)
4 Something to stand on to give protection (5)
7 In the throes of producing eggs (3)
8 Come down on Shrove Tuesday? (7)
9 Comes close to making contact (5)
10 It's hard to suggest a golf club (4)
11 Space to start a real attack (4)
12 Spoil some of the Samaritan's help (3)
14 There's likely to be a gun in it (11)
18 Game to get your head down? (3)
20 Terrible potential enemy (4)
21 She takes me back before meeting her mother (4)
23 Domestic cover (5)
24 Keeping in contact with a French affair (7)
25 Signal to hit a billiard ball (3)
26 Follow directions, girl! (5)
27 He may have to operate a cut-out (6)

DOWN

1 Go off to get something put right? (6)
2 Study the piece of paper and obey (7)
3 Brief appraisal of what you know (4)
4 Man required in a French trouble-spot (8)
5 Do something sound when danger threatens (5)
6 Run away and get rested maybe (6)
7 In a condition to be taken back (11)
13 We'll have friends fighting with us in this (8)
15 It could seem sin to tamper with fate (7)
16 Food for new recruits? (6)
17 Flag for the censor? (6)
19 Capital place to see 4 Down (5)
22 Lovers might find a way here (4)

72

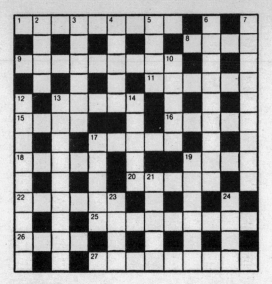

ACROSS

1 Think what might happen if a steel cup broke (9)
8 First man to give a girl a thousand (4)
9 He's not pulling his weight in the crew (9)
11 Remote manoeuvre in the air (6)
13 You can hear it's in good shape (5)
15 Space to tie up on the way back (4)
16 Release the old girl who's lost her head (5)
17 Show you're proud to give support! (5)
18 Top lady (5)
19 He's a bit of a maverick! (4)
20 One isn't paid to work as one (5)
22 Not liable for duty (6)
25 Small revolver (9)
26 Confine a hundred at a time (4)
27 Heavily attacked for being drunk (9)

DOWN

2 As high as one can get by climbing (4)
3 It's the usual thing (6)
4 Material indication of a route north (5)
5 The letter is for those people (4)
6 Excitement coming first (9)
7 Getting out at a time of crisis? (9)
10 Repel the brute in another way (5)
12 How often the vibrations are numbered! (9)
13 The royal gold? (9)
14 Game to put up a good fiddle (5)
17 Breaks for the pictures (5)
19 Develop out of a small revolver (6)
21 Foremost city, so it's said (5)
23 That's the end of the dog! (4)
24 Somewhat nasty excrescence impairing vision (4)

ACROSS

1 Not giving approval at the decisive moment? (8)
8 Offload production? (6)
9 Made kerb crooked as one got aboard (8)
10 Mission to dispose of Dr Arne (6)
12 Do it down before blast-off (5)
14 Move unsteadily before the fall (6)
16 Great story in little pictures (4)
18 Communicate with the fighting area (4)
19 It has the capacity to make further movement possible (6)
20 It warns of possible attackers going backwards and forwards (5)
23 Old aircraft that have been packed up? (6)
26 Explosive speech after escaping with some quick shooting (8)
27 It eases the tension for a sentry (6)
28 Militant in conflict (8)

DOWN

2 Capital ring for a lover! (5)
3 Impart skill at the station maybe (5)
4 A piece of it presents no difficulty (4)
5 It had a following among early navigators (8)
6 This ought to get things going (7)
7 Stream of hot water? (4)
11 Warning from a Red (6)
12 Hundred and fifty to the man who can produce a rev! (6)
13 It counts as one (4)
14 Imitates what a pilot does? (5,3)
15 Some power in dive providing cover (4)
17 Officer putting the lid on poor Tina (7)
21 Over eighteen in the majority (5)
22 Brief reply on an aircraft (5)
24 Wind up with a dance (4)
25 Beast cutting part of the journey short (4)

74

ACROSS

1 Taking steps to get ahead (8)
5 Information making one look a fool? (4)
7 Ecstatically dispatched? (4)
9 Result of firing with elevated barrel (6)
10 Plot danger removed (6)
12 Just like him to hang about! (3)
13 Where fuel is kept for one making a getaway? (6)
15 Carry drink on the way (4)
16 It's private for an investigator (3)
17 Panic cover (4)
19 Personal adornment by a drummer? (6)
21 Fighter in the locality (3)
22 Are you good enough to pass it? (6)
26 Wild South African victory time (6)
27 Eager to be able to make cuts? (4)
28 Colourful university athlete (4)
29 Send tin trams round another way (8)

DOWN

1 Catering chaos (4)
2 Call all round (4)
3 Given very cool treatment (4)
4 It's thrown down as a challenge (8)
5 Abscond in the wilderness (6)
6 Advance by means of publicity stunts (9)
8 It helped to make warfare more fluid (4)
11 Alexander's made one want to go to war (5,4)
14 Tim Green's new fighting formation (8)
18 There are grounds for such a display (6)
20 Walk right into Tel el Kebir very shortly (4)
23 Story of an eastern chief's turn-up (4)
24 Vision of losing five hundred – a lot of paper! (4)
25 Put the needle in in a big way (4)

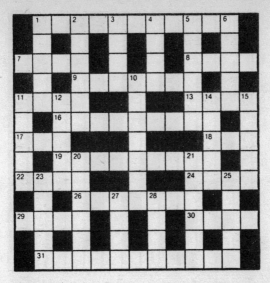

ACROSS

1 Contriving to employ skill in the workshop (11)
7 Cause great surprise with a strike (4)
8 Cut to achieve a balance (4)
9 Is he crazy for something to put his head in? (3-4)
11 Somewhere low as a starting-place (4)
13 Complains about the horses? (4)
16 Views we may have of the future (9)
17 Fliers are in their element here (3)
18 Breaking it might warm up the party (3)
19 Given a job that might cause the depot pain (9)
22 Flier at the end of the line (4)
24 Time for all-round experience (4)
26 Let go and see real involvement! (7)
29 Not the girl to make a hit (4)
30 Musically it's the absolute end! (4)
31 You might get the message from it (11)

DOWN

1 There's more to come from the next ration pack (5)
2 One might have a shot at doing his job (6)
3 The little creature might get on as a scientist (4)
4 There's a point at which it's all up with her (4)
5 Meaning to be under canvas (6)
6 Taking leave of one in a medal (5)
10 Unable to escape like a barrage balloon (7)
11 Dash for some harmless ammunition (5)
12 Traps arranged to catch fish (5)
14 Different ideas expressed privately (5)
15 Be emphatic in taking the oath (5)
20 Where one may aspire to be different (6)
21 Opening for one of small vision? (6)
23 I do get mixed up with it, being a fool! (5)
25 Make a change in the international terminal (5)
27 There's nothing to be gained by it (4)
28 Not in favour of giving one to the worker (4)

76

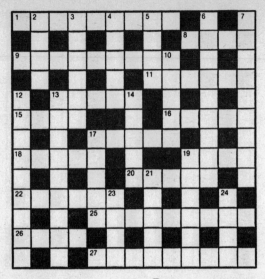

ACROSS

1 Swing coils around after a time (9)
8 They're made for each other (4)
9 Effected a touching meeting (9)
11 Guess it's heavenly! (6)
13 It's right at the corner of the square (5)
15. Take a new line through North Africa (4)
16 It might be left behind in vapour (5)
17 It's not smart to be ill (5)
18 Order that may be cited (5)
19 Go to it on the up train (4)
20 High point for one exerting pull? (5)
22 Reputation for not paying cash? (6)
25 It lets one down lightly (9)
26 It takes one to sea without moving (4)
27 A bomb to discourage paying the landlord (9)

DOWN

2 Expose to entertainment? (4)
3 Chant in a fashionable voice (6)
4 He's not far from the pub (5)
5 Done up with restraint (4)
6 He thinks he knows the line to take (9)
7 Ground for thinking the Atlantic fliers are on a northern route (9)
10 Not the sort of weather that provides pure snow? (5)
12 Move in to start a fight (9)
13 It just shows how far we've climbed! (9)
14 It happened in the seventies (5)
17 Comic take-off? (5)
19 The end of it is the edge of madness (6)
21 Speak with zero rapidity (5)
23 Record a red civil service tie-up? (4)
24 Strike as very surprising (4)

ACROSS

1 Going around giving information? (8)
8 Pleased to knock a beer back with a chap (6)
9 Building at journey's end (8)
10 Having a lazy time running the engines (6)
12 Say what the condition is (5)
14 Society girl gaining height in the red (6)
16 Wind up with a dance (4)
18 High time? (4)
19 There may be grounds for supposing you've drunk it (6)
20 One way to step out of this world (5)
23 Country in NATO manoeuvres (6)
26 Piston enclosure (8)
27 Line of smart trousering (6)
28 Playing for time before the dive? (8)

DOWN

2 How some gases make one feel? (5)
3 Business encountered in the air (5)
4 Come down to earth (4)
5 Rebel Ali can be depended on (8)
6 Fighting starts when it goes up (7)
7 No time to be generous? (4)
11 Look like a fine stroke (5)
12 Check security at the cinema? (6)
13 He starts coughing after a beer (4)
14 They're meant to keep the enemy out (8)
15 It may show you your duty (4)
17 Soldier in a pub – that makes sense! (7)
21 Committee redesigning plane (5)
22 Do it up to make a tidy profit (5)
24 Land after mass killing (4)
25 In one's ear it's dismissive (4)

78

ACROSS

1 He's got it coming to him (8)
5 Demonstration of method when given direction (4)
7 Just one of those things (4)
9 Drink carrier (6)
10 Gain reduced terms out of season (6)
12 It might colour one's prose (3)
13 They're not quick to carry accommodation with them (6)
15 Disposes of the rations (4)
16 Leaves in the late afternoon (3)
17 Flighty female? (4)
19 Its bridge is its downfall (6)
21 Drill outfit (3)
22 Adjusted to give different speeds (6)
26 Knotted art tie being what you're wearing (6)
27 One might go through it at the opening (4)
28 The creature sticks in one's throat (4)
29 Lack of supplies for a brief period (8)

DOWN

1 Fall below a cloud (4)
2 Sounded cocky as sailors? (4)
3 Put in possession of some underwear (4)
4 It may be taken as revenge (8)
5 How to make a hit without doing anything (6)
6 It's carried out with entertainment turning on it (9)
8 She has half a mind to be repetitive (4)
11 Do it in car crash – this shows the place (9)
14 Surprises by going into stepped formation (8)
18 Forgetting what has to be said about losing water (6)
20 Want change from Eden (4)
23 Voice that might get her joined up completely (4)
24 It's a stick-up, lady! (4)
25 At liberty to dispense with payment (4)

ACROSS

1 Barter or cut device for providing the mixture (11)
7 Lines of assistance to map-readers (4)
8 Improvise a sexy piece? (4)
9 Make mad notes on where the shooting is (7)
11 Question an attitude? (4)
13 Standing in line? (4)
16 Ill-tempered blow making progress tricky? (9)
17 States some of the ingredients of a sausage (3)
18 Point of punctuality (3)
19 Going far before hitting the target? (4-5)
22 Buzzer on the right if you want a drink (4)
24 Mary's turn to see some service (4)
26 It's put to work with deep effect (7)
29 Go back and start really being fearsome (4)
30 Observe the money! (4)
31 One doesn't need help to get going (4-7)

DOWN

1 Quite a load needed to make the vehicle move (5)
2 It's moved to give a new direction (6)
3 The one to provide employment (4)
4 Get this in revenge (4)
5 Express thanks for victory to the Navy in a pub (6)
6 Old-time city gent (5)
10 Positively told the fool to rewrite rude letters! (7)
11 Going down like lead (5)
12 Climb on a fish (5)
14 Dread disturbing a dangerous creature (5)
15 She takes the gamblers' money (5)
20 Suffering or is it just business? (6)
21 Paper turned up to catch stone (6)
23 Moves to the borders (5)
25 Engine giving very little time at height (5)
27 Painful rise of a god (4)
28 A joke turning up when one's past it (4)

80

ACROSS

1 It gives you the shakes (9)
6 There's water in some of these air inlets (3)
7 Application for employment (3)
9 Eat too much cheddar? (5)
10 Not standing up for truth (5)
11 Get along like a motor-boat in the drink (5)
12 Swallow a spirit (5)
13 This or that alternative (5)
15 Shoot in a spray (5)
17 Moves slowly like an outsider? (5)
21 Isn't he devilish brown from South Africa? (5)
23 Fear to make an alteration in cap (5)
24 Voice worth a few quid, we hear (5)
25 Laugh at it before one identifies the country (5)
26 Cold Comfort House? (5)
27 Spring in Belgium (3)
28 Talk about fuel! (3)
29 Alan truly reformed, as you'd expect (9)

DOWN

1 Disappear with the vehicle before his turn (6)
2 Not one of the choosy types (6)
3 Fearful of a loud attack (6)
4 The best arrangements the ladies can make (6)
5 One of the less feeling songs? (6)
6 Use those lit badly to show shadows (11)
8 Exciting times when things come out (11)
14 She comes before the big day (3)
16 One's just like another (3)
18 Shoot the person who might be a killer (6)
19 Make a dash for it! (6)
20 He drops a line to one in the swim (6)
21 In which one learns to play cards? (6)
22 Model of the sort that holds a leaf? (6)

ACROSS

1 Get the message that wasn't clear (6)
4 Message at some length (5)
7 East of England it's North (3)
8 Break up crate you can take (7)
9 Prone to deceit (5)
10 Too close for comfort, Miss! (4)
11 Gilbert's partner's terrible end (4)
12 Go down in the middle (3)
14 Give and take at the crossroads (11)
18 Damage with reverse thrust (3)
20 I didn't make a stand in the country (4)
21 Old man with two personal assistants (4)
23 Come down far from heavily (5)
24 Volume of timber just for the record (3-4)
25 Agree to see one to another (3)
26 A source of intelligence in front (5)
27 Fear of going wrong at some junction (6)

DOWN

1 Very good at avoiding exposure (6)
2 He could take charge of a ship or a company (7)
3 It might be beaten in a tattoo (4)
4 Clear and muddled dates (8)
5 Betty's head and mouth appearing on the screen (5)
6 Hire to put the gear in (6)
7 Fit for use by H.M. Forces (11)
13 Departed from the diet Dave might have been given (8)
15 Alluring look of Olga fuddled with rum (7)
16 She identifies me inter alia (6)
17 Vessel of some spirit (6)
19 The wild one's not one of the herd (5)
22 It gives you the shivers! (4)

82

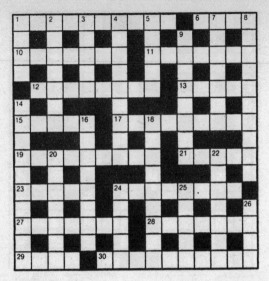

ACROSS

1 It gives the old regime quite a turn! (10)
6 So cool when the dice are thrown (4)
10 Just the person to represent the shop (7)
11 Suggests the little devil's untruthful (7)
12 Oblique ditty about idle reform (8)
13 Where there's shooting in the mountains (5)
15 Sound means of getting something done? (5)
17 Is it coal's troubles that make him a politician? (9)
19 Characteristic carry-on to show one's not dead yet (4-5)
21 It's more than all right for the upper classes! (5)
23 Make slow progress in the pool? (5)
24 We're both at sea, chum! (8)
27 Concentrated in a few on the Stock Exchange (7)
28 Ground for hesitation in railway travel (7)
29 His Lordship's nearly in New York (4)
30 Your young friend might have a dramatic success (10)

DOWN

1 Become dull by inaction? (4)
2 Compete with a bit of the RAF for television (7)
3 Go and get permission (5)
4 It's led you astray in a boring manner (9)
5 Due to receive some money (5)
7 The Chinese have started opposing Italian tipple (7)
8 They don't agree with the establishment (10)
9 They simply despised culture (8)
14 Socialist organisation for passing the hat round? (10)
16 Aspiring flier at home with Heather (8)
18 Study the transformation of my rich set (9)
20 Praise for being less exciting (7)
22 Hidden danger of a mining decline? (7)
24 It's very hard for David to be a politician (5)
25 It might bring us a message from Cheam or Sevenoaks (5)
26 Writer inclined to drift? (4)

ACROSS

1 Move to achieve a higher level (6)
9 It doesn't cost much to make the cinema cool for a change (10)
10 Shelter requiring some attention (4)
11 Consent to get into correspondence (5)
12 Lay stress on pronounced individuality (6)
14 The menace of the mad hatter! (6)
15 Actor responsible for the trouble in Spain (8)
17 Gathering after gathering (7,8)
20 Marks for being bad or saintly (8)
22 Take for granted if the sea's rough there's money in it (6)
24 The attraction of a second hearing? (6)
26 Having completed a take-off (5)
27 The last judgment of the day (4)
28 This is something like! (10)
29 Hit with lightning impact? (6)

DOWN

2 Dear sugar-beat? (10)
3 Place in the country left by the deceased? (6)
4 Rusted it, getting mixed up in the debris (8)
5 One's crazy for this brief occasion! (6,2,7)
6 Seek food on behalf of the old folk? (6)
7 Not much land for a Crusader port (4)
8 Eccentric pal with time to provide a typewriter part (6)
13 No tropical corn on this island! (5)
16 Cause of a fearful awakening? (5-5)
18 Shivering after five – that's not very precise! (5)
19 Becomes lazy and eases off? (8)
20 Stiffener in your food? (6)
21 Entice to show charm (6)
23 Bend over a snake in lower spirits (6)
25 Try to get water out of a shoe? (4)

84

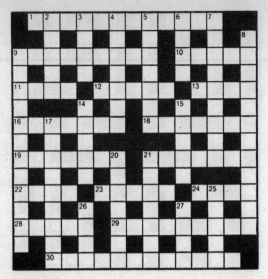

ACROSS

1 Another place to which you can't get elected (5,2,5)
9 Lost again in a muddle of old yearnings (9)
10 Note a new distribution of coke for a cold-blooded creature (5)
11 It's not cricket examining one's means (4)
12 If making a comeback at last it's the devil! (5)
13 Feeling heated when the warmongers get started (4)
16 The pubs can start selling beer at this time (7)
18 People see red when one appears (7)
19 She doesn't seem herself when working (7)
21 Lily might turn to give a man a nod (7)
22 One country's rebels query another country (4)
23 She devotes very little time to a change of air (5)
24 Very bad at indicating status (4)
28 Do your best to be very good before Lent (5)
29 It shows how much you fork out for one thing after another (5,4)
30 Poll's female admirers having anger at heart (12)

DOWN

2 Pull-up for caravans (5)
3 He sounded certain of being a writer (4)
4 Continuing to carry on before departing (7)
5 One's initially identified while driving (7)
6 New gear arousing fierce disapproval (4)
7 Can't raise the difference, being so narrow (9)
8 Vulgar buying and selling at a European gathering? (6,6)
9 The sort of industry we can all own (12)
14 Materialist revision of Lenin (5)
15 Apart from a speech to the audience (5)
17 Delights in finding opportunities to get inside (9)
20 One causing a hold-up in a bottleneck (7)
21 Good for an early greeting (7)
25 Surviving boxer to end the war in Europe (5)
26 It shows what the pitch is in Uncle Fred's case (4)
27 Make striking use of a police patrol? (4)

ACROSS

1 Means of travel in mind? (5,2,7)
10 Pale as one might be after a fire? (5)
11 Impressed by something dreadful (3-6)
12 Characteristics of a crazy artist (6)
13 Taking ten years to be so rotten? (8)
15 It's often referred to as one's plainest feature (4)
16 You know you'll succeed if you've got it (10)
20 Friendly association in a man's joint (10)
21 Drink offering some lasting benefit (4)
23 Corresponding in a family connection (8)
26 Dignified movement of a steed (6)
28 Cornering at 45 degrees all round (9)
29 Anything taken in by the King of Spain's daughter (5)
30 One hadn't expected this to cause ill-feeling (8,6)

DOWN

2 Work before play (9)
3 Where hungry travellers stopped and what they did for the native (6)
4 Ring a friend able to provide a stone (4)
5 The subject of myself? (5)
6 Dust a row that's turned away from the centre (8)
7 Estimate a measurement (5)
8 Be so bold as to accept the freedom offered? (4,3,7)
9 In a great hurry to express rage? (4,3,7)
14 Ornament raised by a person at the top? (4)
17 Reasonable number of stalls assembled (4)
18 Losing cat somehow reminding one of the good old days (9)
19 Not the person in the big house (8)
22 Salesman a good chap to offer a meal (6)
24 Not now alert for change (5)
25 Goddess with a heavenly body? (5)
27 Request of uncertain gratification (4)

86

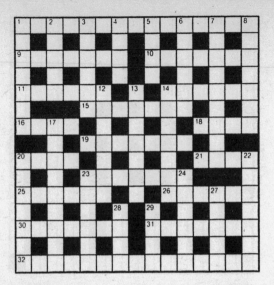

ACROSS

1 Pledge local government to become a world body (8,7)
9 Foreigner in a tail-spin reaching John in Scotland (7)
10 Don't allow for profit when you negotiate (7)
11 First get a man around to hear what we say (6)
14 Pass the other way, please (6)
15 It's competition that puts people in it (7)
16 It may be the custom to demand you pay it (4)
18 Contrives to get a man off for a long time (4)
19 Finally touch a girl for a cup (7)
20 Refusal to get on this time (4)
21 It might grow out of Brother Bernard's ear (4)
23 Flower crowd coming back to encompass defeat (7)
25 No joy when my rise is renegotiated! (6)
26 Remember to bring back someone who's been elected (6)
30 Difficult to kill and not easy to change (3-4)
31 Having more than enough to put Noel in trouble (7)
32 Discovered flagrantly employing Communists in the factory? (6,3-6)

DOWN

1 By no means everyone can do such work (7)
2 In which one learns to appreciate quality? (5)
3 One doesn't linger after a strike (6)
4 Vessel for thinkers? (4)
5 Island youngster getting a good mark (4)
6 Rough run-around at the end of the month (6)
7 Drink and eat with a girl endlessly (9)
8 Stay to adjust Len's rig (7)
12 Happening daily after work (7)
13 Pals he's misdirected must be unlucky (7)
14 Steelwork is a put-up job to him (7)
17 Claimant at last getting the social contract man to provide the bride's outfit (9)
20 I'm no cad to go around without settling! (7)
22 Out of date story turning up in retirement (7)
23 Any living person can draw this (6)
24 Fearsome female taking the short sea route to America (6)
27 Where being a top person gets you (5)
28 The traveller from Berlin to Poland will probably get over it (4)
29 Material taken from the log (4)

ACROSS

1 One tries to win support for the cause (10)
6 Hard-hitting association? (4)
10 Cite Hal as being good and honourable (7)
11 There's nothing new you can tell him! (4-3)
12 Give thanks for the right sweet course (4)
13 You might be prepared to pay this (5,5)
16 Continue for a further period to give a Frenchman direction (5)
17 Supporter breaking trust (5)
18 An attempt to indicate the past (3)
19 Expected to arrive before the two of us have finished our song (3)
20 It's common talk that one might use abuse (5)
21 Take it easy after six and be sociable (5)
22 Security provided by cousins? (10)
24 By no means the best on top! (4)
27 Hit at the crooked with brilliance (7)
29 Not quite certain to satisfy the examiners? Do better than that! (7)
30 Depression caused by a strike maybe (4)
31 They aren't working to achieve progress (10)

DOWN

1 He's in court briefly to represent the front (5)
2 A top Indian lady might hear a name badly (9)
3 Among the peculiar characters holding up the bridge (4)
4 One isn't free to work as a sea-cook apparently (6-5)
5 Charitable moose? (3)
7 Acquire knowledge of mixing ale with the Navy (5)
8 William the Licentious being the kids' father? (5-4)
9 Like those early years when we went dancing as a body? (9)
14 They certainly don't give one a brighter outlook (4,7)
15 Company car? (3-6)
16 I did cruel turns and was mocked (9)
18 Have dealings with a colleague (9)
23 One of St Clement's rhymers, near enough (5)
25 A people's leader has some trouble going south (5)
26 It's hard to be a duke like Wellington! (4)
28 Sympathetic accompaniment (3)

88

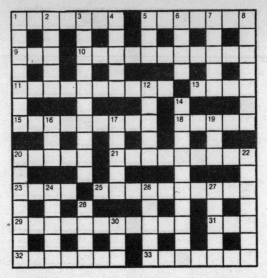

ACROSS

1 Talk with a radio amateur in Kent (7)
5 Doesn't agree with our aims? (7)
9 Some measure of good fellowship (3)
10 Making a mean fur cut in some other way (11)
11 Small faults show up when it's close (10)
13 That old car could make you a pile! (4)
15 The joy of getting somewhere (9)
18 He helps to make the wheels go round (5)
20 Keep the Communist quiet when there's a scrap (5)
21 They're finally reached in oil transport (9)
23 Achieve some turnover at the bakery (4)
25 Take a rest and a drink to withstand sea attack (10)
29 Experts needed to get advice from workers (11)
31 Big chief? With me it's a game! (3)
32 Tank use makes so great a difference (7)
33 Interview hotel lad when there's a leak (7)

DOWN

1 Bit of cheap obscurity for the man in the lab (7)
2 Mountains of maps? (5)
3 County of Hull (10)
4 Painter chap—and French! (5)
5 Take this and start flying (3)
6 He can give you a lift (4)
7 Rather uncouth before visiting the refinery (5)
8 Under the rail or in the night train (7)
12 Alter route away from the centre (5)
14 Hard stuff to get rid of? (5,5)
16 Music one can take in? (3)
17 Swimmer in a fur coat (5)
19 The grassland of Little America (3)
20 Smartens up some timbers? (7)
22 Come up from under as an expert wave-rider (7)
24 Nothing to put up before an attempt at language (5)
26 You might meet her during a champagne supper (5)
27 It goes to the countess' head (5)
28 Youngster with a letter for the country (4)
30 It provides some colour on the personal front (3)

ACROSS

1 James and Vanessa start to make some coffee (4)
3 There's trouble for you if you're in it (4)
6 To hear her you might think it was Christmas (5)
10 Where one can learn to make a pudding? (7)
11 Confection from the underground? (7)
12 Make a sea-rib stew (6)
13 Given portion of some assistance (7)
16 Not much left after cutting into slices (10)
17 Do very little inside getting paid less (4)
19 Every single fruit softly removed (4)
21 Such an attractive way to talk of getting married? (10)
24 A tingle of trouble when the jelly's made (7)
25 Quite old enough to have rum stirred with the tea (6)
29 Flavour of home about an article (7)
30 Old birds getting into hot water (7)
31 Has fun getting up early (5)
32 One character out of seven is on the level (4)
33 Take off the cover for a huntsman (4)

DOWN

1 Ladder man (5)
2 Hamlet to compete with rising bitterness inside (7)
4 Somewhere warm in Lady Godiva's place (4)
5 Made from an animal shot for dinner? (6,4)
6 They're fools to suggest chops (6)
7 Suitable sort of sugar for a genteel tea-table? (7)
8 Food that won't retain its juice, they say (4)
9 The doctor has the manner for it (7)
14 Faring badly with glass in the pastry (10)
15 Beauties in company (4)
16 Complain at what the joint might offer (4)
18 Food factor mentioned by letter (7)
20 One might improve the look of the place (4)
22 It provides many openings in the cheese trade (7)
23 They give support when food is consumed (6)
26 One responsible for a hold-up at the studio (5)
27 In good shape to provide some breakfast maybe (4)
28 No ordinary seaman is so clever! (4)

90

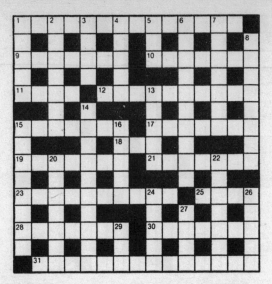

ACROSS

1 In the neat style of West Country activity (7,7)
9 Tugs may help to do so for late recovery (7)
10 Forced a change of air before reaching the Canaries (7)
11 That precious girl lost her head for a title! (4)
12 Warmly recommended for fuel economy (10)
15 We've got something to sell here! (7)
17 Provide a more expansive view (7)
18 Referring to what we have in the course of construction (3)
19 Colourful indication of wet weather ahead of the ship (7)
21 They give assistance for a very short time (7)
23 For skimming the surface of sea transport business? (10)
25 Deep sources of what might be burned (4)
28 It's said they don't care (7)
30 Just a matter of taste (7)
31 Comfort coming from a warm heart? (7,7)

DOWN

1 Lighter form of shove (5)
2 You can deduce a blazing refusal! (7)
3 Instrument for turning up the plunder (4)
4 The talk of ancient Rome (5)
5 Something up your sleeve (3)
6 Moving by water without using ships (10)
7 He's a well-known actor while I am in a musical (7)
8 They put their coats on even in the tropics (8)
13 Equipment is no good without them (5)
14 It may be used when there's inflation at sea (6,4)
15 Paying proposition giving power (8)
16 Enabling one to take a lofty view (5)
20 Able to sing an accompaniment to delivery (7)
22 Ian does a turn and Robin is cut short in Africa (7)
24 Just a fraction of Beethoven's output? (5)
26 A way of shouldering irresponsibility? (5)
27 Story of lost city wisdom (4)
29 One of the elements of Chinese activities (3)

ACROSS

1 American political figure? (9)
6 Where the people are likely to be cross? (5)
9 Conspirator at Fighter Command HQ (7)
10 Jack doing a star turn for some rough characters (7)
11 It's hardly enough to make an employee a consumer (10,4)
14 Victory girl on the move in Russia (5)
15 It gives the hat wearer an edge (4)
16 She's back from a meeting in Hammersmith (4)
18 No illusion about Lear's reform (4)
19 Top people's class establishment (4)
20 In such a state that no-one's boss (5)
22 American Communist likely to lay an egg? (5,6,3)
25 He doesn't believe in Cuba's leader (7)
27 Garment for a philosopher? (7)
28 Composer of regal variations (5)
29 Ethelred's turn to be protected (9)

DOWN

1 Pass around like fools (4)
2 Drink from morning on until a fuss is made (11)
3 Always going on about ten being outside (8)
4 If she's black she'll have the police running her (5)
5 I turn it on somehow to avoid starvation (9)
6 One of those to whom unlikely stories are told? (6)
7 Incline not to finish in the grass (3)
8 Held responsible for questionable practices? (10)
12 It keeps a patrol going when the Army isn't popular (8,3)
13 Speak highly of Paris or Eve will be upset (10)
15 Spa sailors make immersion a pleasure (4,5)
17 Top person above all others giving support (4-4)
21 Someone with a following (6)
23 Passage in a Scottish town (5)
24 Loud left-wing person (4)
26 Dress for the smaller figure (3)

92

ACROSS

1 Industry for those who can make it (12)
8 Just a little bit of a cat! (4)
9 They get things done in the theatre (10)
11 Did Eve's turn have to be contrived? (7)
12 Vessel that will never keep afloat (8)
14 Sailors disturb the saint who doesn't drink (8)
16 Where a youngster might be collared (4)
17 Sounds a summons to reward heroic actions (5)
19 In sometimes symbolic disorder (5)
21 Advance backwards in Sicily (4)
22 He gives a picture of what might be (8)
25 It need not be sent by water (8)
27 Suitable vessel for a Cook's tour? (7)
29 You can't just pour it away (5,5)
30 Obstinate creature going on foot maybe (4)
31 Got worse diet to reader in trouble (12)

DOWN

1 Make it one or another (6)
2 Possible pointer to how things are going (6)
3 Are they learning to travel by rail? (8)
4 Get together in one (5)
5 Incline to put a number on Don's head (4)
6 Russian turning up at the opening to conduct (8)
7 Get ores mined in an up-to-date way (9)
10 It makes it if it's reasonable (5)
13 Footballers in the park? (7)
15 It seems important for a short time (9)
18 Looked ferocious when beaten first ball (8)
19 Work force reduced by the Sex Discrimination Act? (8)
20 They support the devout at times (5)
23 Meal prepared in suitable vesels (3,3)
24 Be there to see a race finish (6)
26 Laugh at it before I get into a state (5)
28 Had a flowery get-up? (4)

93

ACROSS

1 Our feathered friend in the office? (9-4)
8 No good describing Ivan! (8)
9 Hot music? (6)
10 Inexperienced creature taking everything in (6)
11 They may be paid to a praiseworthy character (8)
14 You might have it in mind (4)
16 Put on record (10)
18 Surely his business isn't expanding (10)
19 Throw to the ship (4)
21 Troops of monstrous women? (8)
24 The sort of oil that upsets actors (6)
26 He's hooked on the stuff (6)
28 You may be the first to be given it (8)
29 It's his job to improve your outlook (6,7)

DOWN

1 Attendant providing food on a road shortly (7)
2 She can give us a song (5)
3 Hard work lubricating the joint? (5-6)
4 A chap to represent us (5)
5 Talk constantly of putting the salary up (3)
6 I claim to be cautious but I'm not! (9)
7 Take steps to enjoy yourself (5)
12 Trust in vice reform from which much may be learned (11)
13 They're not taken by the impartial (5)
14 Bring on in the dog (5)
15 It's very wearing to train it wrongly (9)
17 Pull up in the channel (3)
20 The one who sees what he's looking for? (7)
22 Provide funds for a final cry of pain (5)
23 It gives us something to talk about (5)
25 Tempting female giving a warning (5)
27 One thing and another (3)

94

ACROSS

1 Having a tune to provide the right atmosphere? (3-11)
10 Walked with Father just a short month back (5)
11 Man with evidence of debt being cunning in a nasty way (9)
12 Stop struggling if you've put a lattice up badly (10)
13 After this it may be time for a break (4)
15 Try to include rumpled lace that's sweet and sticky (7)
17 Sink a coal vessel? (7)
19 Got up weary after finishing that (7)
21 Hurried to find a bag and plunder (7)
22 What you might get in one vengeful movement (4)
24 Shield in one's arms (10)
27 Think of the future when you see what's in front of you (4,5)
28 Nothing fancy without colour (5)
29 Fencing for the Queen at Ascot? (5,9)

DOWN

2 Beginning to get tip in nice muddle (9)
3 Younger son in training (5)
4 We haven't seen this before (7)
5 Moves to action in Channel Islands set-up (7)
6 It's hard to get the lines out (4)
7 She appears to take part in one's tantrums (5)
8 Time for revenge when the bill is added up? (3,2,9)
9 He shouldn't be cramped on his way to the moon (5,9)
14 Go around giving entertainment (4)
16 A character one might take in hand (4)
18 Business quite good at a commercial gathering? (5,4)
20 Make out there's a record Ernie can't complete (7)
21 Circle in a sort of dance (7)
23 Blackwood may be troubled by one (5)
25 Deals successfully with ecclesiastical coverings (5)
26 Unbelievably high? (4)

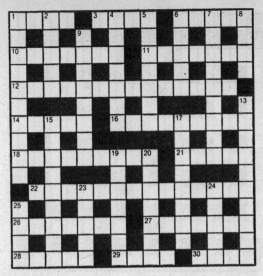

ACROSS

1 Floater right at the back of the ship (4)
3 He has land in the North (4)
6 Gets ready to go (5)
10 Comfort in the cabinet? (7)
11 Democratically ordered to the same degree (7)
12 Invitation to go on studying after the revolution (6,4,4)
14 Leading with an intellect (5)
16 German grub Mother brought back inside her (9)
18 It's difficult to find a way out of it (9)
21 A second letter has reduced effect when you call for favour (5)
22 It puts some warmth into one's lying (3-5,6)
26 He gives the bookkeeper a hearing, of course (7)
27 Her gift is sent round as goods (7)
28 Demonstration time? (5)
29 She may have a pad over the water (4)
30 Bring about sweetness at the tea-table (4)

DOWN

1 Place erect so as to hold things (10)
2 Uncomfortable seat for the uncommitted (5)
4 The beast isn't said to be honest (7)
5 It might be proved to bring about the destruction of Rome (7)
6 Underworld character raising the record for turning out (5)
7 Fellow worker having an association with an officer (9)
8 You could die crossing it (4)
9 Think of Eric mixing with Dons! (8)
13 He's looking for a place that might be mine (10)
15 Add some needling to a plain tale? (9)
17 Not having taken a snap (8)
19 No flat here, note (7)
20 Mixing half with rum will do you no good (7)
23 One whose craft is magic (5)
24 Mean to get drunk? (5)
25 Keep this to avoid panic (4)

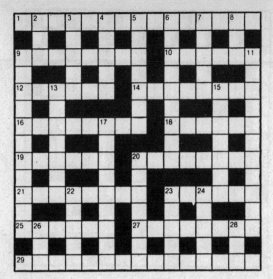

ACROSS

1 Gift of a bottle to enhance seasonable merriment? (9,6)
9 Felt dead possibly for lack of air (8)
10 It makes a nice change for inmates (6)
12 In which fish learn to swim? (6)
14 Non-violent tome read with difficulty (8)
16 Manner so strange for a fellow from reindeer land! (8)
18 No doubt he meets a lot of cool customers (6)
19 Santa Claus' home is traditionally within this circle (6)
20 Payment to keep a servant (8)
21 Turn red again when presented with a flower (8)
23 Picture in pieces (6)
25 Strange person to find in his wife's kimono (6)
27 He gives the police some telling assistance (8)
29 He does a turn on the pantomime stage (4,11)

DOWN

2 The man who's taken nothing in at Plymouth (3)
3 Build-up in very cold conditions (5)
4 Give the child a pound and that's all! (5)
5 Tummy upset bad sign (7)
6 Bank on a winter fall (4-5)
7 Send on a last underground journey (5)
8 No room here at the beginning of Christmas (3)
9 Sort out new England ties (11)
11 Not an experienced provision merchant if he sells vegetables? (11)
13 You can drive it for a time (4-3)
15 Gas gives Mother a turn and makes Naomi squiffy (7)
17 Protector in a fall (9)
20 One has no illusions about a set of items (7)
22 No alcohol it it? That's soft! (5)
23 Civilian cover for a soldier (5)
24 Little Holly? (5)
26 Somewhat riskier way to come down the mountain (3)
28 I myself for instance provide the ring (3)

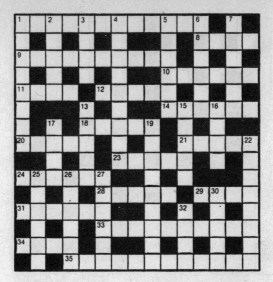

ACROSS

1 Use of hoses to avoid over-heating (5-7)
8 Party defeat? (4)
9 Talk you'd expect about North Sea resources? (7,3)
10 On the way to getting a rise (6)
11 Make progress in a pedestrian way (4)
12 Place of birth? (5)
14 Angry talk when one is in business (6)
18 Producer in creative role (5)
20 Give the doctor a lesser degree of excitement (5)
21 Going straight down to take soundings (5)
23 He won't do as he's told in the square below (5)
24 Gets along without engines (6)
28 Stay and be defiled (5)
29 Competent to be a seaman (4)
31 Medical man in a row suitable for the board (6)
33 Taxes a peer so as to cause annoyance (10)
34 Only half of these might be available (4)
35 Vulgar place to sell exports? (6,6)

DOWN

1 Sailors get a blow this side (8)
2 Add nearly everything to see what it comes to (5)
3 Not often gunners and sappers get together (4)
4 Vehicle unlikely to run out of fuel (3,6)
5 Injure with words (6)
6 Is he getting bigger in market gardening? (6)
7 Sounded pleased to be running smoothly (6)
13 Clever enough to feel pain? (5)
15 Suggest I am shortly to work steadily (5)
16 Lily offers us a drink (4)
17 Be grateful to the team providing transport (4)
19 Bob's taken on as a World War I general (9)
22 Best name perhaps for a depressed area (8)
25 Artist having a bad ride as an attacker (6)
26 Material available if crab is chopped up (6)
27 One thing after another in the river? (6)
30 Profitable state not approved by the union? (5)
32 A girl to rave about (4)

98

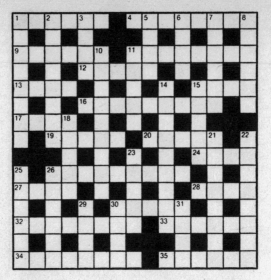

ACROSS

1 Take what you're given (6)
4 Provider of traditional protection for the Tories (8)
9 Two cats probably taking a beating (3-3)
11 Suggestive of love when Mr Action is around! (8)
12 Fanatical artist getting an offer (5)
13 Approval not granted in this corner (4)
15 Eager to make some cuts (4)
16 One is greatly in demand when people are enslaved (9)
17 Look out for your head! (4)
19 He's deeply involved in his work (5)
20 Smoke coming back from a tragic battlefield (5)
24 Half a meal and nothing more for an old fiddler (4)
26 Like brothers with a bird inside (9)
27 He's on our side at the end, naturally (4)
28 Great achievement of the Chinese (4)
30 Lamps arranged for singing in church (5)
32 Among politicians he is the one to formulate general principles (8)
33 Shout with pain if afraid (6)
34 Always something happening at such a time! (8)
35 Fear of Thomas starting to make a mistake (6)

DOWN

1 Out on May revolution to achieve self-government (8)
2 Quite a mixture in the Embassy grounds (8)
3 Not very good at making money? (4)
5 Robin giving protection in wet weather (4)
6 Catch a bit on the way up (4)
7 Strike first when you see an evil oppressor (6)
8 Take back what you said about humbug (6)
10 The Communist one made it easy to see revolution would follow (9)
11 Paul Robeson's old man? (5)
14 How well Marx wrote? (9)
15 After the knock-out was quick to produce Mohammed's book (5)
18 Artist up in do-it-yourself recordings (5)
21 If you've lost the last part you can get one from the shopkeeper (8)
22 The person who makes one a leader (8)
23 Railway fool among the high-ups (5)
25 New place in the North-east (6)
26 Cheat a sheepish character out of a coat (6)
29 The courage that's part of a person's integrity (4)
30 Land of pure chaos (4)
31 Nothing more than a pool (4)

ACROSS

1 Parrot a line that might be taken to be working-class (11)
9 He's learned to live with a reputation for absent-mindedness (9)
10 This way to the old slave states in America (5)
11 Steals from some unpleasant characters (6)
13 Authorise a penalty (8)
15 Groan horribly when there's nothing but obscurity from the farm business expert (10)
16 Put your foot in it and no mistake! (4)
18 Shakespeare said to be not allowed in! (4)
20 You'll have made an effort to achieve this (10)
23 Its residents are always in the swim (8)
24 Do some dredging in the river enclosure (6)
26 Some sort of reaction from the mountain line (5)
27 Keep asking for one politician or put on an air (9)
29 What we should all have in common, man! (11)

DOWN

1 One of the first of the Army diggers? (7)
2 Song in the modern manner (3)
3 Direction to knock a pound off the lowest amount (4)
4 Service chief initially suggesting the morning (3,7)
5 Small member of religious group? (6)
6 Feed in hours of trouble (7)
7 Particular outpost of the political police (7,6)
8 Proposed underground link with the French people (7,6)
12 Ireland's floating currency? (4)
14 Lacking the skill one's paid to employ (10)
17 Something up at Mother Brown's (4)
19 Growing talk among the stage crowd (7)
21 Defend with an argument from money (7)
22 Dictator who came from the foreign money circle (6)
25 Make a point of providing incentive (4)
28 Almost a street disturbance in South America (3)

100

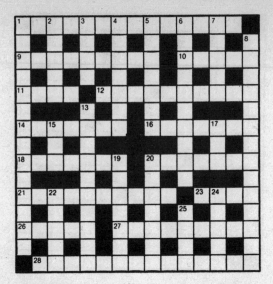

ACROSS

1 Not much of a change for a transport worker (7,7)
9 Given a raw deal when profit possibilities are realised (9)
10 Get along swimmingly as a toady (5)
11 Do business in the wood (4)
12 Red marines forming groups of those left over (10)
14 Not flat as you'd expect (7)
16 The sorrows of Ireland are associated with her (7)
18 Make a hostile demonstration to accommodate soldiers (7)
20 Tube traveller to induce that sinking feeling (7)
21 Machine of the kind given to a scribe (10)
23 Move with difficulty showing flexibility (4)
26 Former law to be precise (5)
27 He's on his way (9)
28 Fellow fighters on the left? (8-2-4)

DOWN

1 Some people want jam on it! (5,3,6)
2 Brown as pie might be (5)
3 Mighty small for a cat! (4)
4 Osbert or Edith might expand around it (7)
5 Late in life getting a round of applause for being an expert (3,4)
6 Nice in a dry way likely to cause a flare-up (10)
7 Knowing state without getting led astray (5)
8 Just what you need when you get a break in France? (7,2,5)
13 Time off with a drink on the beach perhaps (10)
15 Blackjack? (3)
17 Expected to arrive before the song is finished (3)
19 Kept on putting the needle in (7)
20 They provide low-level digital cover (7)
22 Philosopher of the Republic (5)
24 Possibly riled at not being one of the workers (5)
25 Exploited labourer quietly giving one a turn (4)

ACROSS

1 Cover an instrument to make peace (4,3,7)
9 Is it Clara who's mocking? (9)
10 It's Tom's turn to give us a few words (5)
11 Fearing far different help might be provided (6)
14 Proposal to get things going? (6)
15 Plan ice broken by bird! (7)
16 Dress for dismissal? (4)
18 Establishment of some cultivation (4)
19 They're not the ones to let go (7)
20 Shaped for final approval (4)
21 The churchman has a name for Nellie (4)
22 Talk with a radio amateur in town (7)
24 Fit one with stern twist (6)
25 Food provided if flap is moved (6)
29 A county council artist in West Africa (5)
30 Bird turning a lot in might achieve a better performance (9)
31 She looks lovely in repose! (8,6)

DOWN

1 On which it's a pleasure to work as usual (7,7)
2 Up or down it keeps going round (5)
3 Advice about a vessel for the vegetable (6)
4 Everyone in the teacher's class (4)
5 Capacity to be better than ordinary (4)
6 Vulgar as the wealth of Australia? (6)
7 Take out to excite art agitation (9)
8 No difficulty turning it to love in the spring (5,4,5)
12 The sweet joy of being Turkish! (7)
13 We disagree when in it (7)
14 For catching trespassers or getting a husband? (7)
17 Like serious music or a Greek goddess's looks (9)
22 Mark of a certain lack of smoothness (6)
23 Motorway anger – it's all an illusion! (6)
26 Goodbye to Frenchmen! (5)
27 A fairy is among the most superior beings (4)
28 Called to provide a step for the climber (4)

102

ACROSS

1 Hanging about at home in the country for bread? (7,4)
7 Sound affectionate with Bill? (3)
9 If you have to eat your hat, sir, what about this? (4-3)
10 Nourishment supplied already salted? (7)
11 She looks relatively pleasant when about to start eating (5)
12 These ones are great performers! (4)
13 Treat cakes as Alfred did (4)
15 Soup container needing time (6)
17 More crumbly when cut? (7)
19 One of the five could finish off the princes' fruit (7)
21 Offer to make the meat easier to eat (6)
23 A portion of cannelloni for the lady! (4)
24 Fill teacups for the French (4)
25 Boy starting learning to hand out the soup (5)
28 Warning of turning into hog (7)
29 Some idea of how to mark fish (7)
30 Go in quickly for some fondue? (3)
31 Different traces of sweetness (6,5)

DOWN

1 Birds from the post office in containers (6)
2 Some sort of pastry eaten in a restaurant or tea-shop (5)
3 To go with the pork? Nonsense! (5,5)
4 Tale Eve told so as to raise the level (7)
5 Natives perhaps providing a starter (7)
6 Not quite the side of the tart (4)
7 Murphy enabling you to have a ball? (9)
8 Fixed-charge meal, as is usual (8)
14 Breakfast offering of snowy grain? (10)
16 Causing tears at the start of a meal? (5,4)
18 Snubbed by being given the soft drink treatment? (8)
20 Tries to cadge some cakes? (7)
21 A bit of butter giving Erin trouble in making a casserole (7)
22 He's not the choosy type (6)
26 In action after getting up (5)
27 Last letter briefly incorporated in metal (4)

ACROSS

1 Going to the roots of political change (7)
4 One of Beryl's kind whirling in a mad reel (7)
8 Record the old folk we have as being put off (11)
11 Tandem girl endlessly providing a platform (4)
12 It's made to take a beating (4)
13 Difficult question for a model? (5)
14 There may be a slim chance of losing it (6)
16 Inventor backing no team (6)
18 Obeying the rules for using language (11)
21 Not long the fashion in Bermuda? (6)
23 Gin drinks to support injured members? (5)
24 No, this furniture item is not unimportant! (5)
25 Fat end of a duck (4)
27 Move to spread sweetness at teatime (4)
28 Some gibberish about paying for yourself twice over? (6,5)
29 They provide chances to get in among the competitors (7)
30 Go in and be offensive after shaking the tin (7)

DOWN

1 Feeling poorly after a road accident? (3-4)
2 The girl who can get round a pupil (4)
3 Answer a proposal engagingly (6)
5 In the home a great deal but not enough (6)
6 Its vibrations can sound musical (4)
7 Sparkling shape? (7)
8 One might leave here to get into the swim (6-5)
9 There's no saying how nasty this is! (11)
10 Enough material to provide full coverage (5-6)
15 One may be encouraged to take it (5)
17 Like Claud doing a grand turn (5)
19 Put aside one that's delayed so much (7)
20 Dear, it's different from riding side-saddle! (7)
22 Not easily moved by the horses (6)
23 One of many that might add to a dancer's glitter (6)
26 It's shown to one about to be dismissed (4)
27 Red let off when injury is shown (4)

104

ACROSS

1 The polite professional? (5,8)
8 Start with actors digging coal? (8)
9 Take the measure of this next entertainment (6)
10 They could be the start of something sickening (5)
12 He's on the fiddle! (9)
17 Coming up with small bursts (8)
18 A pattern of what's intended (6)
19 Little Diana having nothing on in the cold – that's foolishness! (6)
21 Keep up the argument (8)
22 Learned to repair Holly's car (9)
26 Start south and turn west to feed the Irish? (5)
30 Look at some of the boats in the summer-house (6)
31 Where there's a tie-up for the port workers' team? (8)
32 They have the makings of man's future car (13)

DOWN

1 Police on the way into the wood (5)
2 One gets up after five and starts making poison (5)
3 The one in front is in it (4)
4 Significance of sound and fury (7)
5 It's perfect when I handle distribution! (5)
6 Sent into the interior (5)
7 They help one to climb the ladder (5)
10 Little creature upset over receptacles for trash (7)
11 Rather abrasive nonsense? (7)
13 It's the cooler for the man who drinks! (3)
14 Go thou and do likewise! (7)
15 Their occupation makes them what they are (7)
16 Sort of sum to be made from disposing of refuse? (4)
18 Let fall a little (4)
20 Pass as an officer (3)
21 Having an air of having scattered old mice (7)
23 Something enchanting about all those goldfinches! (5)
24 Where a canoe is likely to capsize (5)
25 A stuck-up fool keeping his distance (5)
27 Try to discover what it's like to eat (5)
28 Makes pedestrian progress in the water (5)
29 Linen in the crude state (4)

ACROSS

1 Man with sound and solid reason for thinking progress has been made (9)
6 A vessel or where you might see one (5)
9 Musical occasion for mockery? (7)
10 Everything in entertainment that lacks profundity (7)
11 Buildings will go up here when the group is brought back (5)
13 He minds other people's business (5)
14 Water-line unfinished (3)
15 Pub anger when there's obstruction (7)
16 It has superior standing aboard (7)
18 Train to be quick? (7)
21 Reversing the vehicle inside the distance – it's uncanny! (7)
23 Chap to provide the equipment? (3)
24 Find the answer to love's strangeness (5)
25 Speaks unkindly of the pictures (5)
27 Circle the wing to get a view (7)
28 It used to be enough to provide a specimen (7)
30 Well-known to have refused a man (5)
31 He has to weigh things up as to merit perhaps (9)

DOWN

1 Ratings of the king in another world (5)
2 Vessel with cargo unloaded? (7)
3 Start skidding downhill (3)
4 Work to provide entertainment with half the team (7)
5 It couldn't be simpler! (7)
6 Big talk of seeing a snake on the way (5)
7 Polish coal has a place here (7)
8 But this is traditionally *not* the place to bring it! (9)
12 The sort of club that provides for overheads? (5)
15 Emergency analysis? (9)
17 Not the whole provision of replacements? (5)
19 Man making trouble as a loyal citizen (7)
20 There's nothing to be said for it (7)
21 Most likely to inherit the earth? (7)
22 The topical twist that might be mine (4-3)
24 Looked under cover (5)
26 Beast to do the navigating? (5)
29 Take this for a possible hit (3)

106

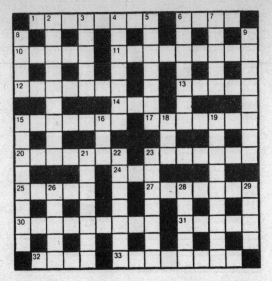

ACROSS

1 They go into liquidation without sinking (8)
6 Revolutionary basis for carrying a load (4)
10 Not fresh at half-time before the stop (5)
11 The business of providing temporary equipment (5,4)
12 Make up your mind to find the answer again (7)
13 Glide quietly in a niggardly way (5)
14 Note what's in these empties (3)
15 Tickets for the water boys (7)
17 One doesn't remember when one has it (7)
20 Music time and before (7)
23 Goods might go into it at the depository (7)
24 It might bear a welcome message (3)
25 The best note takes a lot of paper (5)
27 Great old steamship (7)
30 Futile hope in the main? (4-5)
31 Find out how the Navy goes to grass (5)
32 Smart enough to start the chat after a beer (4)
33 Unruffled character of foreign highnesses (8)

DOWN

2 Get-together of the musically employed (5,4)
3 One to copy for the studio shooting (5)
4 Train to put into words? (7)
5 Bird on the water in port (7)
6 Reforming this worker could be a strain (7)
7 With a bit of luck Gigi will lose her head for that foreigner! (5)
8 Do it up to make trouble! (4)
9 Agency typist not in time to display the required shape (8)
15 Picture the waves and the headland (8)
16 Head fastener? (3)
18 Encountered in our home territory (3)
19 Bit one might need after a break (5,4)
21 Disagree with a maid turning over a hundred without settling (7)
22 Put me up to bear down on a great lady (7)
23 Cook's vessel? (7)
26 Force to become an outsider (5)
28 It's not quite goodbye for the sage (5)
29 Just like Leo to take that many! (4)

ACROSS

1 Somehow pursuing what's trendy? (5,1,7)
8 Just how good the weather can be? (4)
9 Cause bafflement at Boston? (5)
10 It's nothing for tennis-players to express affection (4)
11 Feeling good after conquering Everest maybe? (2,3,2,3,5)
15 Put in a passion by a strange grandee (7)
17 Line Sam put round as a basis for development (7)
19 Vehicle pulling right back in front of a player (7)
21 Involve a German boy protecting his small brother (7)
24 Pub intake for a person of cultivation? (10,5)
29 Old enough to have got by without a man (4)
30 What the French take without asking? (5)
31 One vehicle for a terrible personality (4)
32 Strange stock in this old Dickensian establishment (9,4)

DOWN

1 Eastern religious leader at home once more (5)
2 Move the roots to find the trunk (5)
3 Put back the mineral after a lie-down (7)
4 Wrong girl around last month (6)
5 Best sort of purse for me (7)
6 In a very cold climate it can be accommodating (5)
7 Something fresh from a writer (5)
11 Easiest dance to learn? (7)
12 Damaged with some fuss in a storm (7)
13 Not at one's best after being in a street accident? (3,4)
14 All hide when a Philistine lady goes wild! (7)
16 Pull up to make a channel (3)
18 Crowd in the forum obviously out of hand (3)
20 Get a Shakespearian to come up with a greeting (7)
22 Complete control exercised by a teacher? (7)
23 Am I to follow a girl for something to eat? (6)
25 It makes sense to record one before starting to cook (5)
26 Down there in Australia (5)
27 Turn that's hair-raising for a familiar Dickensian (5)
28 Eat like a top boxer (5)

108

ACROSS

1 How the midwife might expect to be paid? (4,2,8)
9 A little cake before the ball is plenty (9)
10 Island starting to get chilly when the month isn't ended (5)
11 Take away the child and get some sleep (6)
14 They've given a refusal to have actress Diana around (6)
15 New gun role for someone hanging around (7)
16 Steal from the devil? (4)
18 Running hot water? (4)
19 Post causing a stoppage on the railway (7)
20 Fish one might overcook? (4)
21 Average lack of generosity? (4)
22 Hurried to show timeless courage and some bitterness (7)
24 Use my pole when it's broken (6)
25 Mix-up when led astray by the dirt (6)
29 Letter from Greece for the old lady after the American soldiers are back (5)
30 More than enough to give Len uplift maybe (9)
31 It enables one to take the long view (10,4)

DOWN

1 They're so different! (5,3,6)
2 Quite good at making a noise (5)
3 Suffering the destruction of the old era (6)
4 Hitting something might give this impression (4)
5 Right to be out of line (4)
6 Get caught shortly after six or he's won! (6)
7 Have offspring to make copies? (9)
8 Points of discomfort in dressmaking perhaps? (4,3,7)
12 Picture one of the harbour lights (7)
13 Come thus to grief because of the failure of a fix (7)
14 Month with no drink to achieve proper behaviour (7)
17 Pop might make this outpouring possible (9)
22 Go around getting a bit rough with the gallery (6)
23 Just like him to be out of town! (6)
26 Half-dead enemy of a writer (5)
27 Some of the pictures give a great story (4)
28 Look up and down (4)

ACROSS

1 Food peer in the joint? (5,2,4)
9 Remove a point to give freedom (5)
10 They're expected to cause quite a stir (9)
12 A Labour peer could be a good climber (8)
13 Rock fairy coming to the point (7)
14 It could be the basis for a lesson (7)
15 No particular commander? (7)
17 Prince of Russian opera (4)
18 Supporter of wind power (4)
20 Bit of a swindle when you've paid for a cooked meal? (3,4)
22 Put in a position to do without wages (7)
23 Polish the image of a fateful crossing (7)
25 One who exercises will power (8)
27 Diets once divided into portions (9)
28 Subject article meant to leave the worker out (5)
29 Is it such hard work supporting it? (6,5)

DOWN

2 Try to get a catch by degrees? (5)
3 Not a member of the establishment (8)
4 Result of progress by an emergent nation? (7)
5 There's no liberty behind them—except for publicans? (4)
6 Hot place for keeping tea in front (7)
7 Help a mere twister? Not for long! (9)
8 Tendency not to be on the level (11)
11 Put everything into a demonstration of Shakespearian justice (7)
13 Copperhead country? (6,5)
15 Make foolish progress in militarism (5-4)
16 Concealment for a Socialist in sore trouble (7)
18 Boatman I get involved with in Canada (8)
19 Arranging a meal after providing transport is sweet (7)
21 Thomas for one just doesn't believe it! (7)
24 Finished with Tom initially as we can see (5)
26 City famous for union breaking (4)

110

ACROSS

1 It shows how many can get along politically (13)
8 Point we take to study abroad (6)
9 Formerly an underground worker now having a testing time (8)
12 Circle imagined as bordering the hot part (6)
15 Cite difference in a New York matter of adjustment (6)
18 Note the account given by unions in the plant (6)
19 Man in a rape trial could be a political figure (15)
20 A necklace could be the death of you! (6)
22 Man or woman, I am the first! (6)
24 It's the end of the world when there's soil shortage! (6)
27 Mockery takes a cruel turn about Amin (8)
29 Person with a following (6)
30 Morale of an army corps breaking new ground? (7,6)

DOWN

1 Wave a wand to produce light (4)
2 The sort of man who deals with both sides (6)
3 Old enough to be naughty? (6)
4 Harmed by being put on so often (3,5,3,4)
5 Talk among some OPEC members (6)
6 I take a bit of a risk showing the flag (4)
7 Greatest of many Ebbw Vale heroes, some would say (3)
10 Logical argument as one is knocked about in the boxing arena (9)
11 He looks like a superior policeman (9)
13 RAF ace in crash – it must be the wine! (6)
14 They may take a man to the top (6)
16 Incentive to let private transport disintegrate (6)
17 Worked hard to reform the idle (6)
21 Don't accept any old rubbish! (6)
22 Man with a broken hip on edge (6)
23 Salesman having the manner to put things right (6)
25 Among the competitors for enduring fame as a national leader (4)
26 Abandoned by Socialists? (4)
28 One politician can be a devil! (3)

ACROSS

1 Expert on Channel one on output (10)
6 It tells when duty comes around (4)
9 Telling us what foreigners are saying in films (10)
10 Make a move to act as an agitator (4)
12 Children in dispute (5)
14 Quiet Communist cited as revolutionary as was foreseen (9)
15 Accommodation for Tom's rogue agitator (5-4)
18 Take steps to follow the band (5)
19 Something for teacher or a drink with Jack (5)
20 As far as you can go in political advocacy? (9)
22 Practise too much when it's evident bad weather is coming (9)
24 Musical journal? (5)
25 Don't go when support is needed (4)
26 Mike the wag could come round to supply the deficiency (4-6)
28 Grand chap at the top in Luxemburg (4)
29 He might attract a landowner's exclusive attention (10)

DOWN

1 Getting by without distinction (7)
2 The world of Sailor Bill (3)
3 The thing to do at a get-together (5)
4 Call for help on tee when in trouble (9)
5 Part of a government announcement carrying little weight (5)
7 Prominent among those who didn't get in (11)
8 A way to get across shortly? (7)
11 Cheat a bit in giving out notes (6)
13 His skill at work reaches a very high point (11)
16 Score a packet (6)
17 They produce a striking effect at sea (9)
19 Excited at getting employment in road-breaking (7)
21 You might get on terms if the big fellow reforms (7)
23 Song Robin (5)
24 It's often grand when it's not comic (5)
27 Just a lot of talk in the main? (3)

112

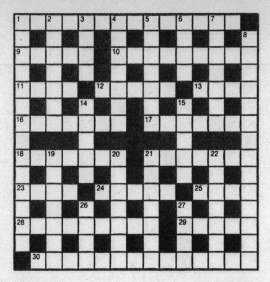

ACROSS

1 Refuse to stand in Gibbon's way? (7,3,4)
9 Musical orphan (5)
10 Not many ups and downs where he lives (9)
11 Horse race cancelled in North Africa? (4)
12 Do it fast for the early intake (5)
13 Wise man taking a day off on his own (4)
16 Aspired to break out of such gloom (7)
17 Not favouring the Moslem chief this month (7)
18 Make the most of this achievement (7)
21 Gravity takes a back seat when you complain (7)
23 Plan to limit consumption (4)
24 Try to catch a friendly dwarf? (5)
25 A bender for one of the members (4)
28 Looking top-left at the map (5-4)
29 D-Day beach city (5)
30 Condition of an adulterous part of America? (5,2,7)

DOWN

1 All those years together—and now a sparkling ceremony! (7,7)
2 Try to get votes in camp at Spithead (7)
3 Holly's one who takes to Roman law (4)
4 Ruler of a penguin colony? (7)
5 Falls and gets up again to become an artist (7)
6 The type you see at a christening? (4)
7 Make fun of a luminary with nothing on (7)
8 Some time this week maybe? (3,2,5,4)
14 On which the non-drinker hopes to make progress? (5)
15 Victory over the shivers? Not sure (5)
19 Seaside nonsense—that's all there is to him! (7)
20 Blast that crazy pet-door! (7)
21 Material for a festive outpouring (7)
22 Talk between India and Bangladesh maybe (7)
26 A question of substance (4)
27 Hang around at the bakery? (4)

ACROSS

1 Baking progress at a dance? (8)
5 Taking the biscuit perhaps for holding drink (6)
9 Timely virtue of fruit or cheese (8)
11 He has his nose in the chicken (6)
12 Quiver of emotion (5)
13 Ring the archdeacon for something hot (4)
16 He's not too daft to dish up some gooseberries (4)
17 What's the stone in aid of? Identifying cheese, it's said (9)
18 Of no importance if it's small (4)
20 Old person giving an entertainment (5)
21 A snug arrangement for a Scotsman (5)
22 The chap gets publicity as a top person (4)
24 Have a ball preparing meat or potato (9)
27 Turn up with Mother being a beast (4)
28 Story of a man's return from the Pole (4)
29 It's uncanny how a Scot can get round Joe! (5)
32 Dislodge and finally consume (6)
33 Its outpourings can't be identified (8)
34 Foreign victim of some jerk? (6)
35 Pelted with missiles to improve the flavour? (8)

DOWN

1 Incentive to get a donkey going? (6)
2 Breakfast for the sleeper? (6)
3, 4 Inclination to drink when the choice is offered? (4,4)
6 A counter put up for the foreigner (4)
7 Take the rise with the loss in preparing food (8)
8 Come down with the noble fellow who runs the pub (8)
10 Move to get a day's work done (5)
11 Be quiet or call the Queen for a dish (9)
14 A refusal is crazy when one has no fixed abode! (5)
15 Fat Irishman offering a spread (6-3)
18 Sandwich, chum? (5)
19 Cut a girl before you start an oriental dish (4-4)
20 Cheese you can knock up by some strange means (8)
23 One way to get money for sea-food (5)
25 Time to give Ellen Head a flower (6)
26 Slept only too soundly (6)
29 Spicy indication of the Speaker's authority (4)
30 Yield somewhat in precedence (4)
31 The little buzzer had a quiet time (4)

114

ACROSS

1 Tossing the caber dance? (8,5)
8 Faithful to the facts (4)
9 He won't waste money on a hedging bet (5)
10 Having no difficulty getting a hearing (4)
11 Clergyman following Di in the top job (6)
14 Educated to remove tie later (8)
19 Given a party when Dante's around (7)
21 Paper in the folder is easily damaged (7)
22 Ring in weekend unhappiness (3)
23 Put me back in the box to burn (7)
24 Put back material with something fancy added (7)
25 In the time of the Mormon saints? (8)
30 Quite good at covering up? (6)
33 Over the eyes it's deceitful (4)
34 Loose talk of extremes of slaughtering (5)
35 Go different ways for a bit (4)
36 Daring form of aerial transport (6,7)

DOWN

1 Animal to put clothes on (5)
2 He's been asked to get us a new arrangement (5)
3 Powerful beam for an idle fellow, we hear (5)
4 Something new in the literary world (5)
5 Number One Wood Street (5)
6 He doesn't do much (5)
7 Gateshead relative looking rather haggard (5)
11 Fundamental redesign of car dial (7)
12 Arrange for some music (7)
13 Passionate departure when there's a violation (7)
15 Imply one can draw a conclusion (5)
16 It's set to be followed (7)
17 Make the artwork moving (7)
18 Part of one's natural abode (7)
20 Live in style at Land's End (5)
26 Not very friendly when a jester turns up (5)
27 Reckoning it ought to correspond (5)
28 Got up like a wild siren (5)
29 It could be the means of getting a rise (5)
30 Follow the old lady as a matter of principle (5)
31 Policemen taking note in the wood (5)
32 Casualty tender (5)

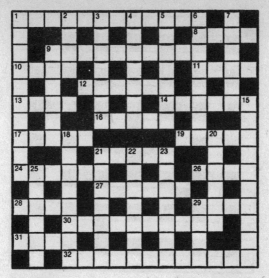

115

ACROSS

1 It might give meaning to building work (12)
8 Things may be made hot for you here! (4)
9 North Sea discovery causing the usual vapours (7,3)
10 No use knocking Ivan about! (4)
11 Vessel holding liquid from the brewery (4)
12 By itself it suggests only gradual progress (6)
13 Gem of a girl! (4)
14 Moves the work periods? (6)
16 Finds out how to lose a pound one works for (5)
17 You'll find them on the news pages (5)
19 Keep out of the saloon? (5)
21 The devil's cuts? (5)
24 Commonwealth capital for adapting saunas (6)
26 Light entertainer? (4)
27 Copy of a diamond? (6)
28 Uncomfortable feeling when one starts chasing after it (4)
29 Sign of something added (4)
30 Unsuitable, ie being ill perhaps (10)
31 Hanging matter (4)
32 Such systems give protection when things get too hot (4,8)

DOWN

1 Things are different after this (10)
2 Bob is able to read (4)
3 Run-of-the-mill defeat in the East (7)
4 Grant of the right to hire a ship? (7)
5 Something to be gained by opening the door (7)
6 Go down quickly after a prominent feature (4-4)
7 There's something wrong here! (6)
9 Quick to push the heartless mob into the river (6)
15 Ruins grips in unexpected fashion (10)
18 Some imp might be up to it (8)
20 Its neck impedes progress (6)
21 Such energy—it's atomic! (7)
22 Transport makes little difference in Wales (7)
23 Putting away nothing in a tie-up (7)
25 To get something done, one takes it (6)
29 Ground for a conspiracy? (4)

116

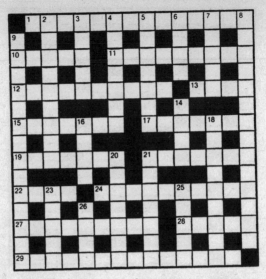

ACROSS

1 No such practice needed for a strip show? (5,9)
10 Very hard in the mountains (5)
11 Having ornamental features of some standing (9)
12 Accepted social behaviour at the assembly? (10)
13 Smart bird to drop Ken! (4)
15 Straightened up for a row (7)
17 Pudding given a knock first (7)
19 Dizzy from dancing? (7)
21 Novelist with a tendency to take in the net (7)
22 Drumming for some bread? (4)
24 He's thoroughly proficient – as a history teacher? (4,6)
27 The fruit that puts flavour first (9)
28 A calf is in deeper than this (5)
29 Victor's such a brave fellow! (10,4)

DOWN

2 One credit may be very little known (9)
3 Some of the nasty leanings fashionable folk display (5)
4 Generally considered to be put in a plant (7)
5 Money given to beggars for publicity purposes? (4-3)
6 Biblical character making a joke (4)
7 Graceful girl presenting a record in shy confusion (5)
8 Was she too talkative about her novel lover? (4,10)
9 Furniture reviewer working at home? (8,6)
14 Bridge of a lifetime? (4)
16 One likely to take a hammering (4)
18 One with a driving ambition to get ahead? (9)
20 He can be helpful when one has a cracked outlook (7)
21 One bird that pecked another (7)
23 Take the railway north to get material (5)
25 A clean-up before going down (5)
26 Dandy personality for a suitor! (4)

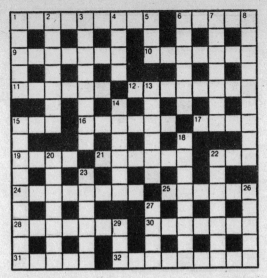

ACROSS

1 Many roaming around right inside in a mountain setting (9)
6 As refreshing a spot as exists beyond the roundabout (5)
9 Coming artist back with a competitor (7)
10 Top of the workshop fashions? (7)
11 Having long hair looking like tobacco (6)
12 Brought in to sort out some dim toper (8)
15 The opportunity's gone if you've missed it (3)
16 Doing a key job in the office (6)
17 It suggests possibilities for the consumer (6)
19 North to a French island in the river (4)
21 Sparkler found in one couple (6)
22 Instrument for amending the law (3)
24 Skilled man using language briefly to upset Ernie (8)
25 Cut a way into the river (6)
28 You might start to make your name with it (7)
30 Central boiler output (7)
31 Not experienced in giving the go-ahead? (5)
32 He can help not having the top job (9)

DOWN

1 They may be brought up to scratch (5)
2 Do they pave the way for raids? (7)
3 Guide the Russian up to the opening (8)
4 Artistic medium for removing soil (4)
5 Former chairman giving the old lady nothing (3)
6 Honour to the chap who is king of the fairies! (6)
7 Lets tea be be thrown around in port (7)
8 The hard stuff to get you warmed up (5,4)
13 People go *down* in the hills? (6)
14 Scope for having a ball (6)
15 Leaving the fairway when supplying fuel? (9)
18 Drinks that have to be dug out? (8)
20 Brown coal to set alight after half a century (7)
22 Morning with a girl in the US (7)
23 Man of the ocean? (6)
26 Time for the other thing (5)
27 The one we have here (4)
29 Half a league into open country (3)

118

ACROSS

1 Careers ruined by that girl looking into things (10)
6 Unpleasant people at the top (4)
10 Finished with an improper girl in Ireland (7)
11 Chorus advice to a bad singer? (7)
12 Bearing the cost of getting things moved (8)
13 Maybe it's the id that makes her crazy! (5)
15 It's not safe to take them (5)
17 Poor experience of Dickens (4,5)
19 Kept up with new arrangements on the aunt's side (9)
21 Artful Dickensian's trick (5)
23 Dot's disturbed about it being the same as before (5)
24 He's learning to include some entertainment in what you pay (8)
27 Most likely to make contact (7)
28 More like a towel than a dog? (7)
29 The exploited groan under it (4)
30 It makes it difficult for one to take the long view (5,5)

DOWN

1 Gert's carry-on can be quite offensive (4)
2 They may expose Walker's supporters (7)
3 Show displeasure at the risk of losing five hundred (5)
4 Ghana revolution after visit by a politician (9)
5 Strange eastern lake (5)
7 That's it, bonehead! (7)
8 Chap giving a hundred to a woman of the town (10)
9 Pretended to be a bit unnatural (8)
14 Cindy peers into a top American's office (10)
16 Given salt from time to time? (8)
18 Such a day—we've heard from Moscow! (3,6)
20 TV returned for check? (7)
22 Trying to avoid going under? (7)
24 Black place for cricketers (5)
25 Flags for a reserve to be put on briefly at half-time (5)
26 Worry about work being a hobby? (4)

ACROSS

1 Brave new set-up in Red pit (8)
5 Intelligent enough to get on at the seaside (6)
10 Good person to help in local troubles (9)
11 Poetic figure getting by with the man in front (5)
12 The stripe that gives a certain style (7)
13 Not much growth left after the harvest (7)
14 One barely seen to take a line? (8)
17 Dig down and find a meal ticket in the river (5)
19 Makes a start with a circle of writers (5)
21 Turn to richer use of persuasive oratory (8)
24 Miss a football club initially to break up evil politics (7)
25 A lot of people at the factory when I get on (7)
27 It's sweet of Rupert to start where Pansy leaves off! (5)
28 Out of date old Comrade in Moscow? (3,6)
29 Make fun of some of the wilder ideas (6)
30 Not the most alert supporters of the line? (8)

DOWN

1 Take no notice of unrest in the region (6)
2 Article sounding a far from full-bodied note (5)
3 Given certain points he can change to increase the value (7)
4 Such a tower is out of this world! (5)
6 Tied up again but may make a comeback (7)
7 The leader of the red-shirts takes the biscuit! (9)
8 Offered in a sensitive way? (8)
9 Keep in a jamjar (8)
15 Society's man of money (9)
16 Capital fellow to spoil his vote with a wild lark! (4,4)
18 Nonplussed by that Chinese soothsayer? (8)
20 Cut to provide a bargain (7)
22 Somewhat inclined to diverge from the Axis (7)
23 Adopts an appealing position (6)
25 Fashion Lawrence started for us to follow (5)
26 A rite that makes us angry (5)

120

ACROSS

1 Take what's coming to you as a conductor? (4,3,5)
9 Flower girl to claim possession of James shortly (7)
10 A prince could start again in Canada (7)
11 Get an officer to cut some meat (6)
14 Something to be said for making the request polite (6)
15 Put back into the warehouse again? (7)
16 Not quite happening to be flat (4)
17 Girl in a singular sort of trouser? (4)
18 Too far away to be friendly (7)
19 One of the king's men on board (4)
21 They might get together for a bite and see a film (4)
23 Pass one learner to become an officer (7)
25 Menace of the rat in trouble (6)
26 A sound to frighten us (6)
29 Does it help the male chauvinist to get along? (7)
30 This couldn't be better! (7)
31 Where one might be taught a healthy lesson (4-3,5)

DOWN

2 Acquit sailors with love difficulties (7)
3 Top person on paper (6)
4 Sole follower (4)
5 Complain that a chap has taken nothing in (4)
6 Bustle about being mysterious (6)
7 Flowers that droop in the centre (7)
8 Eliminate the gap between income and expenditure (4,4,4)
9 Murphy dressed for dinner? (6,6)
12 Precious stone provided by a fairy on the spot (7)
13 Likely scene of a stoppage on the railway (7)
14 He can make quite an impression in his job (7)
20 Wizard fighting grip (7)
22 She takes account of hair at some stage (7)
23 Englishman's dream home in Spain (6)
24 It used to go to Victor's head (6)
27 Zeppelin for instance a matter of gravity to Britain's fliers (4)
28 Catch sight of the place (4)

121

ACROSS

1 Be well informed about music? (4,3,5)
9 Appreciate jazz when you get below the surface (3)
10 He'll go the wrong way in a Paris street, the rascal! (5)
11 Protection for the receiver (5)
12 Join in making a silent turn (6)
13 Find how to play the other side? (8)
16 Condiments may be added at the right time of year (10)
18 What you might eat at a foreign assembly (4)
20 Approval not granted in this corner (4)
21 Are they exposed as smiling deceivers? (5,5)
23 Bishops may move along such lines (8)
24 City girl after some information (6)
27 Anything's better than this! (5)
29 Some of the poor dears coming back seem so dejected (5)
30 Disapproval? You can say that again! (3)
31 Simon Rigdale's way of sapping confidence (12)

DOWN

2 He shows a leg in getting up (5)
3 Just the place for the factory dance? (8)
4 The way man became a robber (4)
5 He does his own thing in Harley Street maybe (10)
6 Somewhere to work after skating? (6)
7 It takes a long time to finish a formal lunch (3)
8 Intimate communication between beaters (5,2,5)
9 Scolding for not wearing posh clothes? (8,4)
14 Put into words something evil about the ring (5)
15 The fiery creature's gyrations cause the Dean's alarm (10)
17 A bit of a romp with Mother gives you the fragrance (5)
19 Has a go at finding a short-term worker up the street (8)
22 You can't get lower than being a weaver (6)
25 Disposed of internally (5)
26 Unfriendly officer taking nothing in (4)
28 Stopper seen to cause rage (3)

122

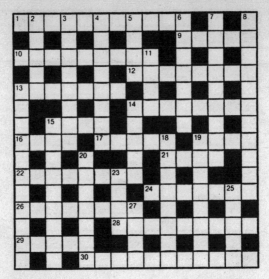

ACROSS

1 It's up to him to spread the product around (11)
9 Sends out at different times (5)
10 Corrupt state of a dude beach (9)
12 Revolutionary way to get rid of money? (8)
13 Black bows where the ships come in? (7)
14 The player hasn't eaten it all! (4,4)
15 With dashes between them one may get the message (4)
16 The horse that threw Nora (4)
17 Give them a drop when you listen (5)
19 Animals brought back by a great performer (4)
21 Drinks that finished off some Africans (4)
22 Capital fellow! (8)
24 Dead body in one of those comedy films? (7)
26 Managed not to fall down on one side (8)
28 Sound humble in a very minor opera part? (4,5)
29 Moved behind a projection (5)
30 Chance to be a knocker? (11)

DOWN

2 One Frenchman identifies the girl (5)
3 Cart turning up and adding some time on for pulling (8)
4 Where one won't be stumped for a rise (8)
5 He's sure different from the man who lets things lie! (4)
6 Put air back economically? (7)
7 Drives mad with diversions? (9)
8 More oil than corn handled here nowadays (4,2,5)
11 Finished being swindled? (4)
13 Where scientists take the long view (7,4)
14 Surplus of fifty for a special friend (5)
15 Not afraid of shifting salt dunes (9)
18 No deviations, honest! (8)
19 He's got what it takes to keep the works going (8)
20 Ran to do a change in a storm (7)
23 They go down when the bingo starts (4)
25 Little hooter (5)
27 Gave an idle performance as an opera queen (4)

ACROSS

1 Getting someone seated in his business (8,5)
8 One for the women obscured by a fine mist (8)
9 He leaves a certain coolness among his customers (6)
10 Coming just before Christmas (6)
13 Fat Tess could be a winner! (7)
14 So reverse a vehicle for the man! (5)
16 Concerning the carry-on after getting a perm (5)
18 I do it differently being a fool! (5)
19 Committed to a union when given a job? (7)
20 Highlights of the entertainment (5)
22 Lessen the effect of what Jack consumed (5)
24 Make a mark in the nick (5)
26 Marchers often want to make it (7)
28 Find a business setback in bad timekeeping (6)
32 Dog a miner almost to the end (6)
33 One might have a shot at the Russian version (8)
34 Going in makes him an outsider to his workmates (6-7)

DOWN

1 Correct me in the final analysis (5)
2 They're privileged to raise the hat to the Head of Establishment (5)
3 Goes on turning like Oliver? (6)
4 In court to give evidence, one takes it (4)
5 Lady from the sanitary inspector's office (5)
6 Automatically thrown out when a crash is imminent (7)
7 Delight in getting there (9)
11 Compete in the heaviest class (3)
12 The money there is in music! (5)
13 Fearful result of getting right into the struggle (6)
15 Convincing information given in bed (6)
17 Hated coming from Rio on to US (9) (9)
18 Girl at home without me in a state (5)
21 Snake with a collecting tin? (7)
23 She gets an agreement from Russia (3)
25 Part of the contract coming up to scratch, we hear (6)
27 Takes a turn at producing food (5)
29 Threat to royalty on board (5)
30 He can teach us to bring the union to some eminence (5)
31 Food brought back from a hamburger bar (4)

124

ACROSS

1 Date for giving you the job? (11)
9 Admission bay? (5)
10 Repeated what's said to be the price? (6)
11 Make up dead fur in a dishonest way (7)
12 Be the one who used to be first (5)
13 Slinks away to return as a top performer (4)
15 Such talk makes Jack seem a toad! (6)
16 You'll feel better after this (4)
17 They get around (6)
18 You'll be sorry to let it fall (4)
20 Not a full description of the house (4)
21 He often gets fagged (6)
22 Get along in one of the new Tridents (4)
23 In which one is in sight but not ashore (6)
25 Workers in a small way (4)
27 The pub's not far away (5)
28 Termini adapted in between events (7)
29 Be there to listen! (6)
30 It makes a change to do so (5)
31 Something to sell? That's the stuff (11)

DOWN

2 She might make me a pal (6)
3 Telephonist providing an entertainment high-spot (8)
4 It might be sickening in its impact (4)
5 Just one more with a walk-on part (5)
6 They have their ins and outs (5)
7 Is it attained when one gets a big rise? (8)
8 Good man speaking with difficulty (10)
10 Employee in digs? (9)
13 Recalls a clergyman satisfactorily with directions (7)
14 Revolutionary means of getting ships out of dock? (9)
15 The talk you'd expect when a new fuel appears (7,3)
19 Give up a top position (8)
20 Allowed pain to continue (8)
24 The big ones sound like VIPs (6)
25 Cause of a fearful awakening? (5)
26 He can teach a trade union to take up some nonsense (5)
28 Not far from Winchester Cathedral (4)

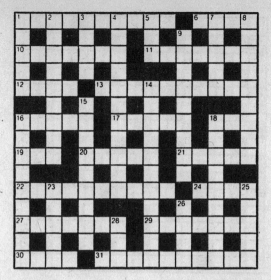

125

ACROSS

1 Last contact to achieve perfection (5,5)
6 Not at all friendly after a knock-out? (4)
10 Pull back the young lady who tends to get behind (7)
11 Dress Martine in a new way (7)
12 People don't like to be in that embarrassing position (4)
13 The dear girl is putting on weight in town (10)
16 Held to be different with one in India (5)
17 Completely without it, to be sure! (5)
18 Girl of some position (3)
19 It might get a thump from an orator (3)
20 Steal a small amount of salt? (5)
21 He certainly gets around, the dog! (5)
22 Providentially dispatched from on high? (6-4)
24 Garment that makes you look like a parcel? (4)
27 Sticky little Violet's keeping company with us (7)
29 He might be able to improve your outlook (7)
30 One comes round to start liking the man! (4)
31 White House office (10)

DOWN

1 It's absolutely unclean! (5)
2 Dark weapon for the sociable? (5-4)
3 Go ahead and take it! (4)
4 Together the bits seem to have a strange finality (4,3,4)
5 See about this creature being made safe (3)
7 Not concealing that we've finished with the West End (5)
8 Do a rotten turn and it will get a big report (9)
9 It shows you've made a name for yourself (9)
14 It used to make dentistry an amusing experience (8,3)
15 Easy not to get up when the fool appears (9)
16 Making things hot for the Cockney's old lady? (5,4)
18 It may be entertaining when the usual road is closed (9)
23 The way to the altar is in the drink! (5)
25 Political get-together – what fun it can be! (5)
26 The conjuror has it in hand, probably (4)
28 Address for a baronet (3)

ACROSS

1 Food for people in a hurry? (6,5)
7 Is Education and Science his department? (3)
9 He mingles with the crowd to get a fish dish (7)
10 One to employ in the kitchen (7)
11 It's obvious it could be soup (5)
12 Warning from the wine cellar, maybe? (4)
13 Get some feet back in exchange (4)
15 Take what you're given (6)
17 A piece of pork to get along with? (7)
19 Lent car for a turn around the interior (7)
21 How sweet Ray and Gus can be! (6)
23 Just a drop of this might be sweet (4)
24 Reversible Arab garment (4)
25 Good enough to have been given a title (5)
28 Smart supporter appearing in neat disarray (7)
29 They're tickled by a jocular pianist (7)
30 Make a point of punctual arrival (3)
31 How small arm can be made to look sweet (11)

DOWN

1 A bit rough when two firms get together in style (6)
2 Nothing in the feature that supports hanging (5)
3 Fruity old fellow making some wine (10)
4 Both troubled about the Royal Shakespeare Company being in the soup (7)
5 It might go down as Scandinavian toast (7)
6 It's of growing significance in food production (4)
7 To compare the soup to this suggests rather bad taste (9)
8 Food for the sailor who wants to pig it? (4,4)
14 Monstrous female finding the French writer some cheese (10)
16 Season for promoting good taste (9)
18 Cut to dispatch round the rock (5-3)
20 Getting into hot water turns one red (7)
21 After a lifetime it's his turn to provide some wine (7)
22 It gives one a lift when another is depressed (6)
26 Refer to the river in an account of the fish (5)
27 A long way but many find fresh food here (4)

ACROSS

1 He's a bit of a rascal about proving the will! (9)
6 Didn't do much when I had played a card (5)
9 Maybe her sort don't go on so long (7)
10 Former journalist in a hurry (7)
11 This Labour lot wouldn't have been much help to Marx and Engels in 1847! (8,5)
14 Probably kicking too! (5)
15 Lacking in friendly warmth (4)
16 Sound return of some of the chosen few (4)
18 Finished nothing in making the final comeback (4)
19 Carry on war for money? (4)
20 Canoe capsizing in a lot of water (5)
22 Don't expect them to be broad-minded just because they've a few more votes! (6,7)
25 Where there's a stoppage somewhere along the line (7)
27 Authority for a person to make an appointment (7)
28 She's the leader of a delegation (5)
29 Something about hospital workers makes them difficult to subdue (9)

DOWN

1 Result of getting nettled by the foolhardy? (4)
2 One not qualified to repair the piano Robert has broken (11)
3 Not likely to be the first to come in (8)
4 Eager to reform and be amenable (5)
5 Conductor of those who were chosen and exercised the horses (9)
6 Charge a little chap with having the wrong gun (6)
7 Be prone to deceit (3)
8 Frustrate expectations of being given the job? (10)
12 Organise into a harmonious group (11)
13 Indians sat around one fighting in Nicaragua (10)
15 Power may depend on what he digs up (4-9)
17 High point reached by tenant payments in rushes (8)
21 A foreigner has it in him to be courteous (6)
23 Man who got on leading a notorious colonial raid? (5)
24 Not so much of the French Nazi force (4)
26 Time to count the years (3)

128

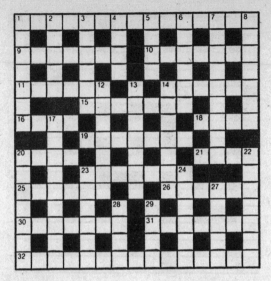

ACROSS

1 People like Uncle Michael Foot dealing with employees? (6,9)
9 Another trade unionist in the family (7)
10 Wonder at Longfellow starting to be a poet (7)
11 Puzzling reference to something full of holes (6)
14 Chance to meet a medical man in a storm (6)
15 One has visions of possibly getting rearmed (7)
16 Self-employed building workers in the mass (4)
18 Inclination towards humbug? (4)
19 He can't be kept inside (7)
20 Establishment of striking sociability? (4)
21 One old turn that is much admired (4)
23 Coal-pit reorganisation relevant today (7)
25 Keep the Territorials in check (6)
26 Mediterranean folk giving classical talks? (6)
30 Cause annoyance when something's burning (7)
31 Accord high status to Ben and Noel for a change (7)
32 Their victory will have a liberating effect (7,8)

DOWN

1 Too generous to be a successful politician? (7)
2 Such an accent as might suggest Norfolk? (5)
3 Sustain to prevent a fall (6)
4 Not well done but it doesn't happen often (4)
5 Having a bad leg is a poor sort of excuse (4)
6 He's as rough as two sailors! (6)
7 Superior to the directors who have fallen in (9)
8 Able to pay for an opening to the sun (7)
12 Love one getting on and eating away (7)
13 The cause is an obsession with him (7)
14 No particular commander? (7)
17 It's under one's very nose! (9)
20 Identification needed if fighting starts in the city (7)
22 Takes in what comes out (7)
23 How food is kept by a man around the pub (6)
24 Push the boat out (6)
27 Fill with one million and fifty out of the blue (5)
28 Time of interment (4)
29 Cover for the head of the French military (4)

ACROSS

1 Bright idea for avoiding corruption (9,5)
9 I catch nothing, being unorganised (7)
10 Plant in the lake (7)
11 Take off in the warehouse (4)
12 Youngster needing a certain pep in his make-up (10)
14 Carried away, perhaps, by shipping activities (5)
15 He can take it! (5)
17 Vessel returning in a channel (3)
18 There it is at last – in the appendix! (3)
20 Expresses surprise at a poisonous afterthought (5)
23 Give a girl a shout which may displease (5)
25 Does he take a lofty view of his responsibilities? (10)
26 It enables the landlubber to go to sea (4)
29 Put your foot down repeatedly to keep it going (7)
30 Bread not available when you leave the ferry? (4,3)
31 Typical patter in severe disarray (14)

DOWN

1 Striking garments? (5)
2 A graduate with true involvement disdaining pay (7)
3 It may be money, one might observe (4)
4 Takes part in the freedom movement (7)
5 Business upsetting Ron in Italy (7)
6 Skilled man going wrong in nice chat (10)
7 Getting what you deserve (7)
8 Not long ago you could depend on taking in foreign money (8)
13 Harsh proposition for the irregular cavalryman (5-5)
14 Liquid obtainable from a tar (8)
16 Advice to the point (3)
19 Exhaust with some hindrance when in deep trouble (7)
21 They go for a spin to catch the unwary (7)
22 There's something in it for a Scotsman, maybe (7)
24 One way by air, then witchcraft and you'll be in Africa! (7)
27 Go through with a gun (5)
28 In one's ear it means dismissal! (4)

130

ACROSS

1 Insincere grief of a column of schoolgirls? (9,5)
10 Get right back before it's our turn in the city (5)
11 Carrying anger to the old Ottoman court (9)
12 Blush to find oneself in a Communist hideout (6)
13 Where one stands before the opening (8)
15 Not quite the perfect thought (4)
16 One might be employed to serve you at dinner (10)
20 Departure of the last King Edward (10)
21 Tear off and leave this (4)
23 Make this to achieve an actressy appearance (8)
26 A power unit returned to nothing in Canada (6)
28 Frank consumed with ambition to be one of the chosen (9)
29 Put a coat on to look colourful (5)
30 Hare in relation to Burke, for instance (7,2,5)

DOWN

2 He could expect cavalier treatment from an opponent (9)
3 You're very lucky to be in it! (6)
4 What a fool to use drugs! (4)
5 Slow and dignified as some of our popular governors (5)
6 Speculate as to how to make a man get up (8)
7 Publicity inclined to change (5)
8 She looks lovely in repose (8,6)
9 Minor trouble resulting from stirring activity? (5,2,1,6)
14 Sailor in the cellar? (4)
17 See if you can understand (4)
18 Exclusive treatment for the unfortunate Miss Cator (9)
19 Time for something to happen (8)
22 Good man getting up or being in a dazed state (6)
24 One might be sent for when there's disharmony in the home (5)
25 Support for one who's not standing (5)
27 Showing average lack of generosity? (4)

ACROSS

1 A piece of cheddar cheese could get over the opening (4)
3 Given the cool treatment (4)
6 Had more than enough sex appeal to get a man (5)
10 Important part of one's intake from one trip (7)
11 One may be expected to rise for dinner (7)
12 Hot stuff to have attained eminence in the Channel Islands! (6)
13 More likely to have a lump in it (7)
16 Any child could lick this little creature! (5,5)
17 Take a drink as it comes back (4)
19 Just what you need when you're as hungry as a horse? (4)
21 Alert women able to supply something juicy (5-5)
24 It makes things easy for the baker at home (4-3)
25 Not much food for a pound according to the code (6)
29 Something strengthening for chaps in trouble (7)
30 The drink that keeps you healthy? (4,3)
31 It happens to be flat before tea starts (5)
32 Quiet not demanded when it's eaten? (4)
33 Sometimes halibut may be caught by what's inside (4)

DOWN

1 Preserve in the form of a small photo (5)
2 Express wonder at royalty preparing dinner (7)
4 With openers they can feed us (4)
5 Shared wish for an arrangement to spare us after-dinner chores (10)
6 Holder of the cup (6)
7 Soft, flexible about payment for confectionery (7)
8 Be careful not to eat too much (4)
9 They have capacity for holding liquor (7)
14 Some little squirt might come out of it (4,6)
15 Put your name down as a subscriber (4)
16 Business talk about a supply source (4)
18 Take possession of what's in No 1 dump (7)
20 It might be the occasion to cause a stir (3-4)
22 Get depressed in a way when food is served (7)
23 Commemorative dinner? (6)
26 It may take a very long time to finish the meal (5)
27 One gets little sleep when there's water all round (4)
28 Stirring soup can be music! (4)

132

ACROSS

1 The crew are company for him (7)
4 Compelled to express gratitude (7)
8 Original make-up? (11)
11 Make sporting use of an instrument (4)
12 It might be used to fix a shoe on (4)
13 Drink firm offering a threequarter-length coat (5)
14 Choose the best (6)
16 Make nothing of what turns a thug on (6)
18 Not at home in connection with getting around (3,3,5)
21 Urge to get Rex hot and bothered (6)
23 It can be pulled out of the chest (6)
24 Whether it's right or not is a matter of degree (5)
25 It's worth a lot to finger a Bondman (4)
27 Silver to the medicine-man can be a bore (4)
28 Small enough to be enveloped in what one wears (6-5)
29 I'm finished with alterations! (7)
30 Encourage when the rep is in trouble (7)

DOWN

1 It enables one to take directions (7)
2 Plaything about the right weight (4)
3 Striking effect of a devilish deed! (6)
5 Comic hero to hit a person? (6)
6 Press to get the lines removed (4)
7 Lower the atmosphere (7)
8 Mayday is one on the air (4,3,4)
9 Brief vision of the future maybe (6,5)
10 Misbehaving? Don't say it! (7,4)
15 React differently and provide food (5)
17 Could it be sanctity your nose detects? (5)
19 Go paler when making a blooming framework! (7)
20 Body of old soldiers or boys (7)
22 Get to grips with the gear (6)
23 Plan to remove one's name? (6)
26 Where Dick has taken a tumble (4)
27 It's a long way down here (4)

ACROSS

1 Current link to get things moving (9)
6 Spells of duty as one goes around (5)
9 Deep-water lads providing the tickets? (7)
10 Calculating creature? (5)
11 There's one between us and the Americans (5)
12 Moral significance of those changes (5)
13 Looking rather grim at the back (5)
14 The rhythm of strikes? (4)
15 Puts into various kinds of category? (5)
17 A little bit of code with fifty added (6)
18 It might come in thumping useful for an outdoor orator (3)
20 Quite a lot of cigarettes (6)
22 Not the type to give up easily (5)
24 Vessels brought back for a break (4)
25 For cooking in cowboy country? (5)
26 A good deal may be hoped for when it's made (5)
28 Give a doctor the wrong fluid to swallow (5)
29 Accommodating way to make the oil go round (5)
30 Made progress a matter of course (7)
31 Oriental lies about a girl (5)
32 Quarries provide the hard stuff on the way (9)

DOWN

1 Get stuck with fake sparklers (5)
2 One doesn't feel too well under it (7)
3 Disturbances at the port when a good man turns up (5)
4 Very rude outward bound from Southampton? (8)
5 He knows enough not to be saucy now (6)
6 Such delight can be quite moving! (9)
7 Suitable uniform for a strip club commissionaire? (7)
8 It cools things down when the situation gets heated (9)
15 Exercise control when verse is up for revision (9)
16 He can soon get a load on (9)
19 An ocean of ink? (5,3)
21 Not the current sources of light (7)
23 Deduce a negative from the amount of heat produced (7)
24 All the nice girls love him (6)
26 Makes a start with a key turn (5)
27 Bird with a part missing (5)

134

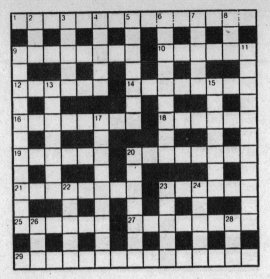

ACROSS

1 Old-timer in pursuit of a performer (5-4,6)
9 Bread masquerading as a cut off the joint? (4,4)
10 Distant meteor breaking up (6)
12 Pursued, we hear, but too virtuous to be caught (6)
14 Ava can so disturb the great lover! (8)
16 He sees the robes are changed before the clergyman comes back (8)
18 Showing affection for French wine – it's in the record (6)
19 Visitor come to give you a shout? (6)
20 Such bearings as a coat of arms might display (8)
21 Order Pat to become a killing animal (8)
23 Mechanically assisted, like a TV woman (6)
25 Having the young one around makes the girl an angel! (6)
27 With Carl and Ivan around we can have a lot of fun! (8)
29 They go in and out to close the clothing gaps (6,3,6)

DOWN

2 Among the prettier male adornments (3)
3 They may provide a grand opening (5)
4 Talk monotonously about not being a worker (5)
5 Military man quite put out if force is displayed (7)
6 Blake's building project for England (9)
7 Bit of a hug for the person who's like all of us (5)
8 The sort of price one pays for being trapped? (3)
9 Instrumental in indicating how small it is (11)
11 Spreading the Gospel might give Eve a calling maybe (11)
13 Acquit the sailor who can find an answer (7)
15 You can still have it when you've given it (7)
17 Half the silver on one piece of furniture – it's true! (9)
20 Dark continental person (7)
22 Wasn't afraid to issue a challenge! (5)
23 It covers one's head in the tube returning home (5)
24 One in sore trouble helping to make baskets (5)
26 Colour with a cry (3)
28 She could be the leader of a dance company (3)

ACROSS

1 Money to be made out of community land in Australia? (12)
9 Quite unexpected beginning with fish (9)
10 She has an air of being past fifty (5)
11 They're made for each other (4)
12 Person of resolution (5)
13 We might have to include a ban (4)
16 Some err badly and show regret (7)
18 Stayed to be associated with Land's End (7)
19 Big enough to be a disaster (7)
21 Zambia and Zimbabwe have it between them (7)
22 Not now found among the Nigerian tribesmen (4)
23 Start damning a Russian for supporting the sitting (5)
24 Make a mess of being top person (4)
28 She might get a nibble at a cocktail party (5)
29 Calling forth the business of the Orient (9)
30 Area of cultivation outside the centre of Hampstead (6,6)

DOWN

2 Beast having nothing to do with Paki agitation (5)
3 That's the King done for, chum! (4)
4 Turn the moose in if it's unpleasant! (7)
5 Could one be a hard-boiled intellectual? (7)
6 Girl ill-disposed to start yelling (4)
7 She's quite at home with the lack of paid work (9)
8 Garter Knight of the Scillies (6,6)
9 Just fancy, people believe it! (12)
14 Line-up of leaders? (5)
15 Vote only for the fat one? (5)
17 Emit grunt that might be difficult to hear distinctly (9)
20 He's nice in a strange foreign way (7)
21 You need plenty to finish off the fanatics! (7)
25 Rosie's willowy form (5)
26 Can Teddy be Russia's creature? (4)
27 Mary's constant companion (4)

136

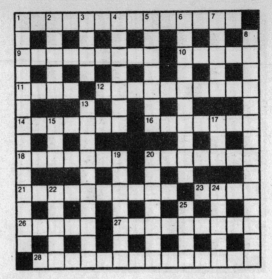

ACROSS

1 Where one makes one's mark in politics (7,7)
9 Unruly animal in revolt (9)
10 Hurried to start chasing cattle here (5)
11 Give a shout in the Shetlands (4)
12 Alan's dream is to become one impervious to fire (10)
14 Put back the mineral after taking a break (7)
16 Peel is wrong about the first letter (7)
18 Writers' work-to-rule instructions (7)
20 Company giving short measure and getting the order (7)
21 The sort of person who lost his head in the French Revolution (10)
23 Pushkin's head preserved in crushed ice, according to the story (4)
26 The bishop might put his head in the joint (5)
27 She might take you in for screening (9)
28 Trade unionists are at war, comrades! (8,2,4)

DOWN

1 Political objectives as to how the revels should develop? (5,9)
2 Local extremists take Lincoln in for identification (5)
3 Lied about not having a job (4)
4 In the mercy of God I am able to smirk (7)
5 Anne got in trouble with all that weight (7)
6 Ground for relief from the shakes (5,5)
7 Had to express pain at the wrong end (5)
8 He found novel ways to entertain Victorians (7,7)
13 Being sent to jail for declared support for the cause (10)
15 Spring is quiet in South Africa (3)
17 Leaves in a steaming vessel (3)
19 He doesn't want to know us (7)
20 Disagreements merit a hundred strokes of the whip (7)
22 Bury one who got the rent adjusted (5)
24 Great Russian character (5)
25 It's hard to smooth matters out (4)

ACROSS

1 Remove imperfections from the tyrant (6)
4 Simple chaps to fight with the Auxiliaries in Ireland? (8)
9 Angelic little beast taking the girl in (6)
11 Marsh is just about correct to cause terror (8)
12 Not happy at seeing a top person in Africa (5)
13 Eager to help Victory inside (4)
15 Quiet scene going forward on the ship (4)
16 They're not yet among the liberated (9)
17 Work with the executive committee fixing fuel prices (4)
19 Fancy tickler in France (5)
20 We all know it's true a team ought to get an award (5)
24 Make it hot for the enemy (4)
26 State a prerequisite (9)
27 Former dictator requiring some examination (4)
28 She's not a union member (4)
30 He gets a man to identify a girl (5)
32 Ready to be cut down beforehand (8)
33 Who could entertain children on TV (6)
34 Rents far out of line bring about a move (8)
35 Dislike giving cover to a Communist (6)

DOWN

1 A tyrant to his secretary? (8)
2 Example of people to follow specially without a friend (8)
3 It's our responsibility (4)
5 A drink at the navigator's side (4)
6 With which the classic rise to riches starts (4)
7 They don't seem themselves when working (6)
8 Some sign that fresh intelligence contributes to strength (6)
10 One of those that rose during the French Revolution (9)
11 The true alternative (5)
14 Not revealed as lacking development (9)
15 Convincing evidence that the printers have been at work (5)
18 Able to get on in law (5)
21 In the Government for a little time and tries to be different (8)
22 Blamed for transgressing the Sun creed (8)
23 The avenger or his horse? (5)
25 Pampered creature always under the driver's feet? (6)
26 Iceman in new-look entertainment (6)
29 A lot of people in the lump? (4)
30 Among those present in the reading-room (4)
31 Girl refusing to go to the Academy (4)

138

ACROSS

1 Helping to keep the salad cool? (8)
5 Angry shot at feeding Lancashire folk? (3-3)
9 Different conclusion making the cake cover look attractive (8)
11 Some incentive for the vegetarian? (6)
12 Unsympathetic egg in a cut loaf (5)
13 Food obtainable from kitchen waste, we find (4)
16 A cheap cut causing some discomfort (4)
17 Staggering example of the baker's art? (5,4)
18 Nothing served with this fish? (4)
20 Eating no beastly food for instance in a vehicle (5)
21 Fight for what's left over (5)
22 Of course she looks different in oils (4)
24 Help yourself to food here (9)
27 Spread not accented for the head (4)
28 Writer Edna not putting on a cheese (4)
29 A dish to gain favour? (5)
32 A taxi coming back with us – you can count on it! (6)
33 Atom-smashing taken to extremes in our salad days? (8)
34 Expressions of love sometimes crossly conveyed (6)
35 Aim at air going round for a drink (3,5)

DOWN

1 Food – the mention of it brings a smile (6)
2 Reduction allowed for meat-eaters (6)
3 Club flavour? (4)
4 Put the stake up to a mountainous height (4)
6 Probably a foreigner providing the wrong loaf (4)
7 There's been a cut in pig meat supplies (9)
8 Edward takes in air when tied up (8)
10 Note decorative work covered with icing sugar (5)
11 One may be turned round to free a bottleneck (9)
14 Sinew-building drinks (5)
15 Like Father having fun with us at dinner maybe (9)
18 Pukka gentleman (5)
19 Panic a sailor into making a pancake (8)
20 Iva's cult takes a nourishing form (8)
23 From the butcher with love? (5)
25 Protection in the mail (6)
26 Aspire to change the old country (6)
29 You'll feel better after this (4)
30 Ascetic bear? (4)
31 As friendly as toast? (4)

139

ACROSS

1 Compensate by putting gear on again (7)
5 Have fun with a good man to provide added weight (7)
9 Out of bed and ready for a disturbance (5)
10 One dropped off that disastrous old airship in South America (3)
11 She's included in the declaration of intent (5)
12 Other people's feathers for your adornment? (8,6)
14 Not a nice person to provide the last of the cheese! (4)
15 Miserly person saving money on fish? (10)
19 It might entitle one to call the Queen Mother (5,5)
20 Feel the absence of a wedding-ring? (4)
22 Position that prevents one sitting down at parties? (6,8)
26 Bungling writer getting back inside it (5)
27 Possible outcome of boring activity (3)
28 Get immersed in a seaside activity (5)
29 One's not at all pleased to fly into one (7)
30 Such means not allowing for anything fattening? (7)

DOWN

1 Big party defeat (4)
2 Dancing is to a great extent a matter of successful exploration (9)
3 Obtain by force—that used to be wrong! (6)
4 Hat for suckers? (5)
5 Country-accent actors on the radio? (9)
6 Not getting any chance favours (8)
7 It sounds time to wake up (5)
8 Getting across poetically in the end (10)
13 It reveals a lot of one's supporters (5,5)
16 This moral conversion takes place in bad weather (4-5)
17 Made to feel unfriendly when a foreigner gets the date wrong (9)
18 Olive is wild when Leo comes round with a flower (8)
21 Could be put away inside (6)
23 Do it up to make a lot of money! (5)
24 Containing a whole range of maps? (5)
25 This sort of thing is almost disastrous (4)

140

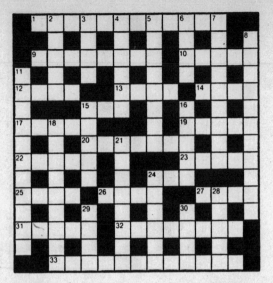

ACROSS

1 Penetrating crash to gain an advance (12)
9 Like a sleuth behind the tractor? (8)
10 Bird to greet in an odd way (5)
12 On and off it makes for quicker crossing (4)
13 It might enable Mac to show a leg (4)
14 This side for Sunderland (4)
15 Permissive time (3)
17 One may be forgotten here (5)
19 Due to there being a circle on one side (5)
20 A writer might dip into it (3-4)
22 Bury a fatherless artist (5)
23 Drunk enough to sleep soundly? (5)
24 So Susie starts giving you the message! (3)
25 Boast of coming back for clothes (4)
26 Get away to make fast (4)
27 Ring enclosure not exclusive (4)
31 This figure is really something like! (5)
32 Having got some degree of instruction perhaps (8)
33 He can solve technical problems on the spot (4,8)

DOWN

2 That's how things are out of town (5)
3 Such a drop might be sweet! (4)
4 Attempt to get round the end of Warwick – it's not easy! (6)
5 Late urge to keep in order (8)
6 Not surprised to be exploited (4)
7 Getting tough maybe in a cooling-off period (9)
8 There may be a lot of fuel in it (7,4)
11 Parade-ground dress for exploratory use at sea? (8,3)
15 She has very little time for rebels (5)
16 Current producers book a good man up (5)
18 They're built to get you places fast (8)
21 One's reek may come from something in the tank (8)
24 Done up by a lynch mob? (6)
28 It's not all the pianist can play (5)
29 Fed up with Tom starting to be clever (4)
30 Most important source of liquid (4)

ACROSS

1 Unfriendly knock that doesn't get you into hot water (4,3)
5 Deceived with German inside offering little scope (7)
9 The thing will look different before tomorrow (5)
10 Reserved for the listener with foreign money? (9)
11 Outgoing narrative that should bring in the money (7,7)
15 The man in the group presents a paper (5)
17 Semi-poet I can be made to sum up (9)
19 Views optimistically a local tax surplus? (9)
20 One going up in flight (5)
21 Do they show what they've got when taking off in finance? (5-9)
25 Not favouring a standstill in pushing sales (9)
27 She has no aim to be different (5)
29 Make a show of putting one on (7)
30 Get a clearer picture from the real gen (7)

DOWN

1 Tricky form of appropriation (10)
2 Record in wooden terms? (3)
3 The big fellow has it in brown (5)
4 Creep around and cause a depression as has happened before (9)
5 Part of an immensely rich collection for a song (5)
6 Old bird laying an egg with mother around (3)
7 Arguing about accepting new shares? (6,5)
8 Old chap with nothing on going round the wall! (4)
12 Claims before the strains appear (11)
13 Overdrawn before our scent is found (5)
14 Tear round the exit going back (10)
16 The number that might be there (5)
18 Paying someone else to take risks (9)
22 Like the new coinage (5)
23 Group of people in the wood? (5)
24 Murphy perhaps appearing at dinner (4)
26 Liquid element of some nations' wealth (3)
28 It's taken in hand when there's a row (3)

142

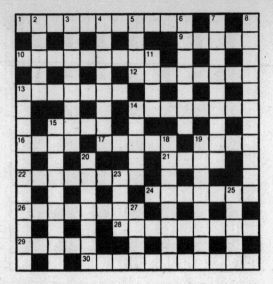

ACROSS

1 Said to be a rather long vehicle (11)
9 A sheep might fetch a couple of pounds in Surrey (5)
10 Insect getting in the crop? (9)
12 Remove from the gatehouse? (8)
13 A blow on it might cause a stoppage (7)
14 Supporters of overhead loading methods (8)
15 Give up a part of the price demanded (4)
16 Bad contrast (4)
17 Do it up to look your best (5)
19 Burn to keep the place clean? (4)
21 Sound a warning both ways (4)
22 The greater part goes on top in the ship (8)
24 The first payment is back in the warehouse (7)
26 It's not his business to help the balance of payments (8)
28 The vessel can include a Russian girl (9)
29 Having had little experience of a hold-up? (5)
30 Note the scope given by opening a Scottish port (11)

DOWN

2 Not an inaccessible part of the river (5)
3 Clothed with the authority of a shareholder? (8)
4 Like the mystery to which one hasn't a clue (8)
5 Old enough to have got along without a man (4)
6 Lower the level in the river (7)
7 It could be a help in night delivery by road (9)
8 Logical location for a London shipping office? (5,6)
11 Girl in a Ruritanian musical comedy (4)
13 It gives an indication of the load that's being carried (11)
14 More than just a healthy appetite (5)
15 Fell down when an officer made a mistake (9)
18 Guidance as to the cheapest of passenger accommodation? (8)
19 The state of the beetle (8)
20 Giving support on reaching land? (7)
23 Smart fellow with a lace ruffle (4)
25 Unsuitable paint mixture (5)
27 Please don't take the ref. away—it might stop play (4)

ACROSS

1 Illumination wonderful for a dance trip! (5,9)
9 Prepared to give you some sort of fit instantly (5-4)
10 Resolve without mine to put people off (5)
11 Work of art of some standing (6)
14 Writer's line giving one a seizure (6)
15 Just finished with Russian money, that's the difficulty! (7)
16 Uncovered an artistic female (4)
18 Do you know you could be naming a goddess? (4)
19 Like one number that's foolish (7)
20 One having a thin time getting plastered? (4)
21 Not taken to be the right alternative (4)
22 One gets an impression of his work (7)
24 The city that takes the cake? (6)
25 There may be a saving when one comes to it (6)
29 Praise for taking part in the Sussex to Lancashire run (5)
30 Coming up in a sound way (9)
31 Good beginning for an undertaker? (9,5)

DOWN

1 The flower of the aristocracy? (5,3,6)
3 Hang about before acrimony starts in Africa (5)
3 Your turn in a race produces a testing performance (3-3)
4 Get this and be gone! (4)
5 Looking sentimentally pretty in between (4)
6 Seated badly but not getting excited (6)
7 Bring in the unknown (9)
8 Not an award of chivalry, but exclusive nevertheless! (5,2,3,4)
12 Obliteration for a time is certain (7)
13 The race isn't finished if you're still in it (7)
14 Slim chance of giving direction to someone making advances (7)
17 It's used with explosive effect (9)
22 School gym class getting fruit over a skirt (6)
23 Responds with another performance? (6)
26 Line of dance (5)
27 The things people do! (4)
28 Not going to extremes of miserliness (4)

144

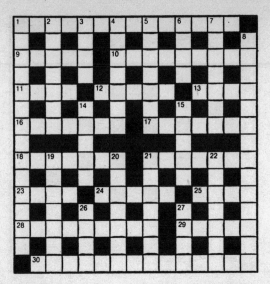

ACROSS

1 It makes a change from a tour of duty (8,6)
9 Perfect order for pie (5)
10 Call for a contest (9)
11 It might give you a chance to get weaving! (4)
12 Something to fight for – and this is the reason! (5)
13 Stone available in the jeweller's shop always (4)
16 It's best to choose one parent (7)
17 Get an extension of time in prison (7)
18 Authority for aggressive bombast (7)
21 Big enough to reform Mr Stone (7)
23 Good stuff for a QC (4)
24 Understand how to get hold of a subject (5)
25 European high spots within range (4)
28 Labourer in a Covent Garden production? (9)
29 Get together to make one (5)
30 Get wind of financial difficulties? (4,3,7)

DOWN

1 Sage suggestions to invest in a necklace maybe? (6,2,6)
2 Get profit out of an oustanding deed (7)
3 Worry about what the Irish might eat? (4)
4 Get back by making a car-mile adjustment (7)
5 Framework for getting Charles to join his sister shortly (7)
6 Not likely to be sleeping in a pantomime? (4)
7 Depth of delight for children (7)
8 Suitable esteem for a keep-fit expert? (7,7)
14 Make a mark as a defamer? (5)
15 He has a name for being straightforward (5)
19 Take over from someone to lessen the tension (7)
20 Such sweet delight in being foreign! (7)
21 Sam lied in order to deceive (7)
22 Having an effect that can be instructive (7)
26 Great build-up in China (4)
27 Its capital is the smoke (4)

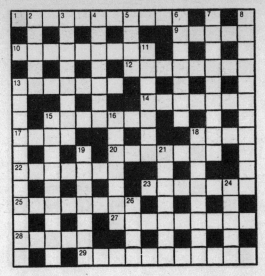

ACROSS

1 Hurl headlong into the rain or snow (11)
9 One so twisted it could strangle a person (5)
10 Thought not concluded, game not started—one begins to guess he's a theorist (8)
12 Tag votes obtainable during dances (8)
13 Friend on the left (7)
14 His criticisms are no great matter (7)
15 Our appearance in confinement shows admirable spirit (7)
17 Jack's cry for attention (4)
18 Just one of those things (4)
20 Meet Rex becoming a reformist in the end (7)
22 Show in a satirical light with nothing on (7)
23 Lay on in painful fashion (7)
25 Musicians take a long time to cover the injured (8)
27 It has reason to elicit the truth (9)
28 Liberate a relative who's lost her head! (5)
29 Giving back what's left before it gets turned in and out (11)

DOWN

2 It communicates a misguided attack on the circle (5)
3 One of the younger element giving voice (8)
4 He's just not the dashing sort (7)
5 At the end of the shift there's warm protection in a basket (4)
6 Feed voraciously on Cheddar? (7)
7 It's assumed something soothing will turn up if the union is behind time (9)
8 Use meter man to show how far things have gone (11)
11 Serious listener at home (7)
13 Keeping party subs low to please the bosses? (5,6)
15 The life we can all lead together (9)
16 When the resolution's changed I'm finished! (7)
18 Relying entirely on what's not said (8)
19 His lordship's old mum inviting you to have a flutter (7)
21 Linger about and start tearing some hair (7)
24 Capital atmosphere in the firm! (5)
26 Sort out some of the issues if the time is ripe (4)

146

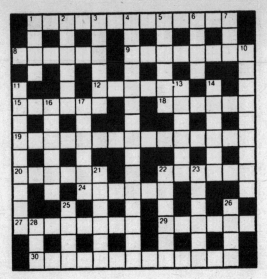

ACROSS

1 Not a colour problem for rational people (5,3,5)
8 Stop trying to earn a living as a bad singer (6)
9 It's a job to find a friend in the same factory (8)
12 Tried to deceive us about the measure briefly raised (6)
15 In which TV sportingly shows it again (6)
18 Learnt to be devious to meet the landlord's demand (6)
19 Being chased by police an unexpected event? (4,4,3,4)
20 Method of presenting a whole set (6)
22 Pelts a group of rollers? (6)
24 Naturalist making a row about war manoeuvres (6)
27 Ship a rep into the blue (8)
29 Admirable worker but be careful of his horse! (6)
30 One lacks contact with the neighbours in it (8,5)

DOWN

1 Let's have a drink at Sheba's place (4)
2 Beastly article on revolution in Lima (6)
3 Like a leading light in the hymn-singing world (6)
4 William Morris' unlocated intelligence (4,4,7)
5 Fighting Communist turning up in prison (6)
6 The girl in the chairman's office (4)
7 Dispose of internally (3)
10 See Wilde's trouble as growing (9)
11 In favour of an employer going round the Channel Islands in a trunk (9)
13 There's something wrong when you leave the party (6)
14 Sat around turning nothing up for an old leader (6)
16 Buff up a foreign language (6)
17 Great chap except as a baker's assistant (6)
21 Mother brings the murderer up to be a madman (6)
22 Grab a bit of music (6)
23 Getting that bronzed look is a bit of luck after Othello's been around (6)
25 You can see that's the place! (4)
26 Try to attract attention at sea (4)
28 Help a rep to get his money back (3)

ACROSS

1 Rap relation badly for being working-class (11)
9 Foreigner with a strange claim to be controversial (9)
10 Some place in Havana, maybe (5)
11 He made a conquest in Bolton or Manchester (6)
13 Rotten things to throw at a meeting - terrible experience when one's fragile! (8)
15 Not relevant to what the garment's made of? (10)
16 High point of a tour of Sicily (4)
18 Look surprised when there's an opening (4)
20 New production of Carmen might be old-hat but brings in trade (10)
23 Vision of agreement among people having a row (8)
24 China, where the estate is redistributed (5)
26 Stocking in two cities shortly (5)
27 A decent cover-up keeps it hidden (9)
29 Officially there's no telling what the Government wants to hide (5,6)

DOWN

1 One of America's Fathers? (7)
2 Take the measure of the resistance (3)
3 Accuse a devil of deserting every single one (4)
4 Can you bear it as a loyal subject? (10)
5 Take advantage of a grim conclusion to put the question (6)
6 The tidiest solution is to have a meal in the home (7)
7 That revolutionary girl of Hargreaves? (8,5)
8 Legislative reform might rile a party man (13)
12 Does something about increasing the list of statutes (4)
14 The Commons as a place of growing inexperience? (10)
17 Bender one of the devout might go on (4)
19 It might be sleep that's disturbed in Scotland (7)
21 Look like a superior copper (7)
22 Compete with a girl's rise in the city (6)
25 Slight advantage of completing what's known (4)
28 Robots' revolting appearance on stage (3)

148

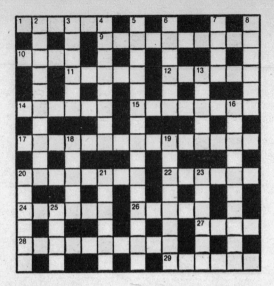

ACROSS

1 Possibly of interest to the consumer (6)
9 Bird having fun in a field? (6-4)
10 Former ruler of various arts (4)
11 Restored harmony when the union gained a different end (5)
12 Amount of petrol causing bitterness when one hasn't finished (6)
14 Respectable lady taking cover with a boy (6)
15 Remain too long in the guest room above? (8)
17 Uncertain progress of a professional draughts player? (9,6)
20 Nothing to pay? Now we're getting somewhere! (4,4)
22 Pass on what's said about fuel (6)
24 A college fellow is such a beautiful young man! (6)
26 Reduce to a more depressed state (5)
27 One might go around with this act (4)
28 What keeps one warm might depend on this (4-6)
29 It's quite usual to give a girl a pound (6)

DOWN

2 Current liberator from work after dinner (10)
3 Don't allow reduced terms in exchange (6)
4 High status accorded to the cardinal (8)
5 One expects it when wronged by a good-looking man (8,7)
6 Have a mind to react with surprise (6)
7 He might benefit from Peter's deprivation (4)
8 Hostelry in heaven for those looking undernourished (6)
13 Not a success in different roles (5)
16 A princess has swallowed one in Egypt (10)
18 May has one for a day (5)
19 Vexed with anxieties about what one's been dressed in? (8)
20 Add a note to a coin in the country (6)
21 You're sure to find a rogue among Aunt Clara's callers! (6)
23 A drink for the man who helps travellers (6)
25 Nothing for the little girl who looks like an egg! (4)

ACROSS

1 Small group of soldiers showing some aloofness (10)
8 Not a company man (6)
9 Meat provided by Adam for Eve (5,3)
11 It's held to improve the vision (9)
13 Deprive of possession in various tiresome ways (4)
15 Lighthearted team to give record backing (4,4)
18 One of the family in hospital (6)
19 Observed the way the wood was cut (4)
20 One doesn't start in the fireplace (5)
21 Implement returned as plunder (4)
23 Bad presentation of a nonsense number (6)
24 He's quite prepared to sell you one (8)
25 Take a meal back for the lady (4)
26 Calling up memories of a vice vote that went wrong (9)
31 Put in a hallowed place the sinner he reformed (8)
32 What a joke the horror film might be! (6)
33 The bad news is just what they expected (10)

DOWN

1 Unhappy if the record's still playing after midnight? (12)
2 Sort of radio strains distorted at a high point (10)
3 Revolutionary hero starting a fight in the kitchen (4)
4 Protection for the post? (4)
5 There's a killer in that huge car! (4)
6 They might be called on for a little help (7)
7 Inclination to compile a catalogue? (4)
10 Protection for a striker (6-5)
12 Night out? That's the style! (7,5)
14 If a car crashed into a land mass (6)
16 Cobbler's drink? (6)
17 Far-away islands where one can obtain teas inside (4,6)
22 There's something to be learned from one (7)
27 Evil deputy? (4)
28 She probably won't be with us long (4)
29 One hopes to gain them at last (4)
30 It isn't us you need here! (4)

150

ACROSS

1 Has a look at the Times? (7)
5 He wants a lot of political change (7)
9 Genuine male of the country (5)
10 He goes below for something valuable (4-5)
11 They come round to give you a quotation (8,6)
15 You might do better to pull them up (5)
17 Case I made for reform in seats of learning (9)
19 He's not by nature an insider (9)
20 Out of this world (5)
21 Something funny about the company apes advertise? (6,8)
25 It goes round where a hand comes out (9)
27 A trick to avoid (5)
29 Man meets bird by design (7)
30 The talk of the country (7)

DOWN

1 Fight over a church in the west country (10)
2 Leaves to get into hot water (3)
3 Pigeon that returns to write poetry? (5)
4 Keep apart from an Easter egg (9)
5 Just a reminder that Eric Askew is about fifty (5)
6 Crazy get-up causing an obstruction (3)
7 Mine not a cat to go around and cause pollution (11)
8 What fun to be an early riser! (4)
12 Does one have an empty time on holiday? (11)
13 Gets to where there's a connection (5)
14 Weighing one's worth can be a taxing process (10)
16 Such a surprise in current circumstances! (5)
18 Taken aback when a dud stone is passed around (9)
22 Long for time to make a point (5)
23 Land of ink? (5)
24 Hands up for an exchange! (4)
26 Arrive simultaneously at an entanglement? (3)
28 Expected to be given to the devil? (3)

ACROSS

1 Count Simbo in fiery form (10)
8 To be expected when the doors open at sale time (6)
9 A sailor gets bad marks if he does nothing (8)
11 Someone from Bray with a job to do on deck? (6-3)
12 Foreigners may be beyond it (6)
14 A hot turn of phrase (4)
15 Openings here for fresh-air enthusiasts (5)
17 The tide you'll never catch at night (4)
20 A rum cafe nut may have the makings (11)
22 Rotten place to leave things (4)
23 Share slightly reduced in proportion (5)
25 Knocks back a piece of the rigging (4)
27 A shot intended to be friendly? (6)
29 Your standing may be raised by it (9)
31 Something explosive among the adverse votes of stooges (8)
32 Entrance money providing a living? (6)
33 Material basis of consuming interest (5,5)

DOWN

1 In which fuel helps a man on the run? (4-6)
2 Quick growth of sentimental rubbish, given the space (8)
3 Custom of the American era (5)
4 Incline to start talking at last (4)
5 Those devilish cuts? (5)
6 Bade Gerry turn round for the old fellow (9)
7 A point the navigator knows you won't identify (6)
10 Test port (11)
13 Possibly elephantine scoundrel (5)
16 Tread on a bird, boy, to make a name in engineering (10)
18 He can give guidance when we're all at sea (9)
19 They might be bright enough to assist 18 (5)
21 The Common Market chap could be a pure one (8)
24 Agreement in the form dispatched (6)
26 Acted as a future officer (5)
28 No doubt it is going to make a fabric (5)
30 Not a steady snack at sea (4)

152

ACROSS

1 Shoot when there's a battle for cooling things down (4,8)
8 One way to acquire a weight of education (4)
9 No need to go on working after this (10)
11 He may push for greater cleanliness in the factory (7)
12 There are things the matter with that last mine reorganisation (8)
13 Run by a chap who's getting old (7)
14 You might find out how to take this record over (4)
16 Up here one may be in difficulties (5)
18 Show dismay when the boss's comeback isn't quite complete (3)
19 Our learned friend is only half qualified (3)
23 Bar that didn't keep you out? (5)
24 People in a hurry? (4)
25 Indication that might adversely affect the royalty (7)
27 It's not planned to use detectives in a very small money matter (8)
29 There may be painful experiences when one puts the ship ashore (7)
31 The last you'll see of a night delivery (4-6)
32 So it may be on board at the price quoted (4)
33 He may have things in store for us (12)

DOWN

1 Sends ahead to be used in hospital? (8)
2 Without a girl one can be unsparing (8)
3 Man of cultivation (6)
4 Morning in a passage of the fullest extent (5)
5 Some indication of quantity sent to north and south (4)
6 No greater change for current production (9)
7 Overseers more confused in the marsh (7)
10 Jerk the end of it when not strong (5)
13 Give me very little time to write a note (4)
15 It enables some twister to get at the drink (4-5)
17 Having called for assistance to secure a footing? (4)
20 Provide refreshments with meat in Surrey (8)
21 Throw overboard from an aircraft it's wrong to get on (8)
22 Island of wine (7)
23 Deduce from one of the finer adjustments (5)
26 Last places you'd associate with wartime atrocities! (6)
28 Load for one of the ferries? (5)
30 Arrange to take note of a Mediterranean port (4)

ACROSS

1 I tried irons but it's different when the goods are sent out again (14)
10 Bound to be leaving port (7)
11 They sound greatest when empty (7)
12 Former cases of oppressive demands (9)
13 Carry to start testing (4)
15 They're associated with rags (7)
17 It might be required after trouble at sea (7)
19 Its role is transformed by people working hard (7)
22 Part of the FBI people in a group (7)
24 This way out at top speed (4)
26 Get a valuation from a Paris pal (9)
29 Carried by Miss Nightingale round the bend? (3-4)
30 It's obvious I would be included in the happening (7)
31 The modern way of dealing with information (4-10)

DOWN

2 A bit taken out of the pamphlet (7)
3 A snooze in it would certainly not be suitable! (5)
4 An outside arrangement can be very slow (7)
5 Puts money in underwear (7)
6 Disturbed by a superior group (5)
7 This won't get you going (7)
8 No directions given in front (4)
9 No shelter in mind for the prince (9)
14 There may be openings to do so (9)
16 Look in the yellow pages (3)
18 Record of a timber supplier? (3)
20 Not allowed to be sick when in charge of it (7)
21 It enables you to come clean at top level (7)
22 It's best to eat late with the technical troops (7)
23 Oriental way behind! (7)
25 In which a trip might be rather pedestrian? (5)
27 A girl gone wrong? (5)
28 It may be held to give a touch of magic (4)

154

ACROSS

1 New sport at the opening of a Naval base (10)
6 Cast around for things to do (4)
10 Get Sam back to entertain the gathering (7)
11 A letter to give one a start (7)
12 First in entertainment from one place to another (8)
13 Not warmly enthusiastic (5)
15 Take that girl out of the champagne set! (5)
17 Get a view of the visionary tourist (9)
19 See the bird gets a smile in opera (9)
21 Do it again in response (5)
23 Eager to conform for a change (5)
24 He seems to lack standing in his occupation (8)
27 It might make painful hearing (7)
28 Falls back again before the artillery (8)
29 Means of attacking a revision of Kant (4)
30 We can see what's been happening in this (10)

DOWN

1 Elgar's circumstantial accompaniment (4)
2 Sounds as if Ivan's in a hurry! (7)
3 Move to get some work done (5)
4 Union official having the instrument for obtaining a new rise (9)
5 Once again (5)
7 Charlie starts a small agitation that will cause serious injury (7)
8 Daily riots can create unshakeable unity (10)
9 Not the man for democratic leadership (8)
14 There's a lot of talk of new laws here (10)
16 A few words may take some time to complete (8)
18 He's quick to assist some fighters (3-6)
20 Greatly pressed in a race not easy to win? (4-3)
22 Declare it's time to be mean (7)
24 Row one might make as part of the act? (5)
25 Organise mates into sporting groups (5)
26 Said to be ready to travel to get agreement (4)

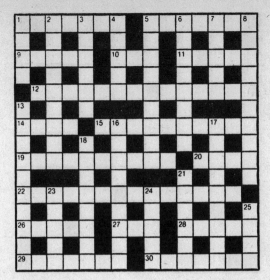

ACROSS

1 Song about us starting to travel in Europe (7)
5 Ape the archbishop? (7)
9 The world of Paris reduced to something sour (5)
10 Man in blue or it may be black (3)
11 Little Tom is always on hand (5)
12 A person one doesn't wish to entertain (9,5)
14 A marvellous job for Victoria! (4)
15 The case for the prosecution (10)
19 All those cross people might choose to speak! (10)
20 Care to come round and see the land? (4)
22 In a state to get excited when pestered (3,3,8)
26 One more in front of the cameras (5)
27 Be human! (3)
28 Entertainment time after work (5)
29 He was against the third crusade (7)
30 Get to grips with the opposition (7)

DOWN

1 Statutory way to lose a supporter, friend! (4)
2 Simple chap with no vice offering the real thing (5,4)
3 One in a hurry to cover the table (6)
4 It can turn out to be quite a caper (5)
5 Standard sum for coming top? (9)
6 Relating in a new way to the whole (8)
7 Bad language used by us in Lincoln (5)
8 Disappointed to be given only beer? (10)
13 In a rage after losing the address? (10)
16 Bare cabin taking on a new look at sea (9)
17 At home with a man when the weather's bad (9)
18 Accepted model for flying maybe (8)
21 Prepare to be pictured again with the rest (6)
23 Drink comes to a pound when you add it up (5)
24 Cast the short line (5)
25 What one's paid to carry on war? (4)

156

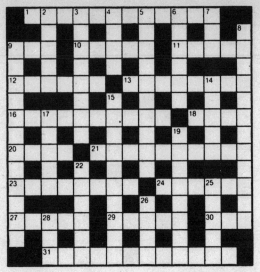

ACROSS

1 Quick resolve to take a break? (4,8)
9 Accommodation for a writer? (3)
10 A fool on the way back but still quite distant (5)
11 Thomas the poet or Bob the singer (5)
12 Run around with the wrong set causing a disturbance (6)
13 Broad view taken by a girl with parents around (8)
16 Another tax on the house? That's not very good! (6-4)
18 Is it good breeding to hold the collar? (4)
20 Girl identified in the normal manner (4)
21 Versatile fellow, the actor! (3,2,5)
23 Just what you need for a change at the seaside (5,3)
24 Link up to form a pair (6)
27 Strongly suggests Reg is troubled at finding us around (5)
29 Barking firm taking on rig repair (5)
30 Smartness causing her to decline (3)
31 What asses we've been all this time! (7,5)

DOWN

2 Repairing the drain – that's as low as you can get! (5)
3 Quietly putting up with flattery (8)
4 Love being given an uncomfortable get-up (4)
5 A breach perhaps but only in part (10)
6 The sort of games rain doesn't stop (6)
7 Nothing but an incomplete line-up (3)
8 Coming down canned or all of a glow (12)
9 The colour of German misery? (8,4)
14 Amend some of the special terms negotiated (5)
15 Clock man's brother? (5-5)
17 Pause indicated before finishing the order (5)
19 Stop a pie being adapted for the purpose (5)
22 Selected to be among the few? (6)
25 Ability to do something shocking? (5)
26 Angry people might be up in them (4)
28 Animal put up to be worshipped (3)

ACROSS

1 Remove from various tough spots (4)
3 Sweets given back by the self-satisfied (4)
6 One in the eye for teacher? (5)
10 One snip that may keep bringing in money (7)
11 High point of a Moslem priest's calling (7)
12 In which one hopes not to look wolfish? (6,8)
14 Turn the doctor out in style (5)
16 Destroy the taxi Peter brought round (9)
18 Given a hard time by those on top (9)
21 Handle as a special favour (5)
22 Can't one be seen after applying it? (9,5)
26 It's a start when you're making a name for yourself (7)
27 Excite the Archdeacon after taking the wrong line (7)
28 Appointment to meet in a Coventry Street restaurant (5)
29 It may be hard to protect the cheese (4)
30 Skills may be useful to a degree (4)

DOWN

1 They don't support the Government work place (10)
2 Common requirement for practical sagacity (5)
4 It gives a person singularly enhanced vision (7)
5 Worn by the person who kicks you in the teeth? (7)
6 Drink that has quite an impact? (5)
7 Antecedents of a great pen, possibly (9)
8 Dead careless about punctuality? (4)
9 Cause to move in different directions (8)
13 It's ten men's turn to display feelings (10)
15 It shows how wicked one can get (9)
17 Net result of needing a small bag (8)
19 One learns to take a short break when Mark's around (7)
20 Brown having gone wrong is in confinement (7)
23 I do it wrong—what a fool! (5)
24 Slippery youngster (5)
25 It could be useful when one needs a rise (4)

158

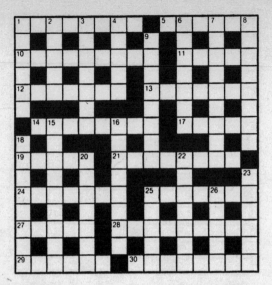

ACROSS

1 Bet on a local government division not to be too progressive! (8)
5 Something to be gained by an open-door policy? (6)
10 In Africa if not in Wiltshire (9)
11 Go in for chips without fish (5)
12 Given the sweet treatment (7)
13 Snobbish chap taking on something slippery (7)
14 Big Laura's conversion in the Socialist world (8)
17 It's water under the bridge at Cologne (5)
19 They're paid to keep local government going (5)
21 Sheer anguish of soul in an erratic beat (8)
24 Military man with sex appeal knocking back drink – first-class! (7)
25 Agreement to keep it small? (7)
27 Not beginning to be defeated by cannibals (5)
28 Easily persuaded by religious propaganda? (9)
29 Lessen the impact of one's rage (6)
30 Offered by a sensitive soul? (8)

DOWN

1 Cut the piece about dry wine (6)
2 Commander getting on to interrupt the sentence (5)
3 Coming clean about the American Government's lack of weight (7)
4 A slice on the golf-course? (5)
6 One might improve the look of the place (7)
7 Revolutionary enough to want to cut out the middleman? (9)
8 He seems in no hurry to do his act (8)
9 Look at a drink that might improve one's vision (8)
15 The last word in governmental tough talk (9)
16 They have no illusions about disturbing Ali's rest (8)
18 Hope for the future we can see before us (8)
20 Odd to encounter a venerated figure on the mountains (7)
22 Restricted cover protecting a child (7)
23 Be there for a race at last! (6)
25 Box the unfortunate Carter endlessly (5)
26 Heroine of light fiction (5)

ACROSS

1 Fair credit exchange might prove fatal to a brother (10)
6 Top man taking part in the tyrant's armed repression (4)
9 He looks after your rise when you go up the river (4-6)
10 See, the ship is a wreck! (4)
12 Artist leading politicians into swindles (5)
14 Reforming a policeman might be nice sport (9)
15 Drives to a joint in which one can't get steam up (5-4)
18 Anger has points for the peace goddess (5)
19 Make repeated applications to clean up (5)
20 Basis for workplace representation (9)
22 Add details of the package brought back before you speak (9)
24 Heath the artist has a certain value (5)
25 This is the beastly end! (4)
26 Where you might look in to get the wine you shouted for? (4,2,4)
28 It sounds the proper ceremony (4)
29 Not much of a consumer (10)

DOWN

1 There's a basis for exerting leverage at this point (7)
2 Light on a car crash (3)
3 Dissolute characters have their inclinations (5)
4 Takes good care she distributes riches all round (9)
5 Line up for cover (5)
7 Got rid of any difficulties creases might have caused (8,3)
8 Shyness caused by not quite making the team? (7)
11 Easing the strain of half a life amid the rocks (6)
13 Man of the cloth? But he's quite unspiritual! (11)
16 It goes with a medal for endless robbing and twisting! (6)
17 Is he marching in favour of a trial that's been refused? (9)
19 There's protection here for the homeless (7)
21 Warning of danger – Labour on the move! (3,4)
23 Float around overhead (5)
24 Weapon that might cause a flier to crash (5)
27 Fighting man doing a bit of a line (3)

160

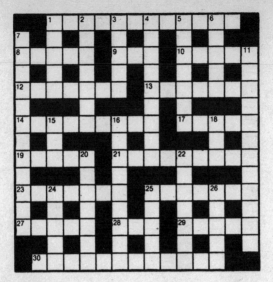

ACROSS

1 It's put in to make the port work (12)
8 A last letter from some gallant sea captain (5)
9 Don't deny you're a proprietor! (3)
10 Where ships can anchor while carrying vehicles? (5)
12 Having an inclination to provide a catalogue? (7)
13 Eat rope if it will make you work! (7)
14 Not the best market for coal (9)
17 The animal's all right when a picture is begun (5)
19 Be quiet and polish the plant! (5)
21 Silent sea change of crucial importance (9)
23 Letters being despatched to one of those far-flung offices? (7)
25 Two heating fuels in one? (4-3)
27 Takes a poetic form (5)
28 The girl in the blue velvet gown (3)
29 Not the first time there's an improvement (5)
30 Fuel needed, maybe, to deal with these cargoes (3,9)

DOWN

1 Turn aside to provide thoughtful results (5)
2 The power to postpone a stoppage (7)
3 Get this way and you'll make progress (5)
4 Capital characters (9)
5 Destructive tube traveller (7)
6 Nothing for Mother to laugh at in America (5)
7 Contribution to getting things moving on the railways (7-5)
11 As a constable I entertain by doing one thing well (12)
15 Big trouble isn't entirely a drawback (3)
16 It may be needed to provide better feeling (9)
18 He takes a bit of a line in the Middle East maybe (3)
20 Ship in splendid condition bringing promise of fruit (7)
22 Falls between Canada and the USA (7)
24 It may go to the lady's head (5)
25 It's obvious which vehicle has the French in it (5)
26 Gets a grip on some cargo transfer problems? (5)

ACROSS

1 Dismiss for drinking? (4)
3 Striking means of inviting people to dinner (4)
6 He might provide notes for haggis eaters (5)
10 Get up to take in the sun and have something to eat (7)
11 Not quite so noble as a baron of beef? (7)
12 One whose outpourings can be quite refreshing (6)
13 Chicken going right into hot water (7)
16 Juicy offering from Ivan? (3,7)
17 Where drinks are taken on the premises at some points (4)
19 A dish to avoid? (4)
21 It's Crimeville when this food's badly prepared! (10)
24 Lettuce in sticky stuff for a sweet? (7)
25 Had a shot at making a meat paste? (6)
29 Sweet to provide transport before arranging a meal! (7)
30 Flowers that give wine its perfume? (7)
31 Make the crab look decent? (4)
32 Appointment that might be fruitful (4)
33 Drink of no importance if it's small (4)

DOWN

1 Small fish for a lean consumer (5)
2 Swore vehemently, one might say, when given sweet covering (7)
4 Where headless witches can make things hot for you (4)
5 Dwarf swallowing stewed roast is a good judge of food (10)
6 Not quite pulling off the road for gingerbread (6)
7 Something in the food that may be not ripe (7)
8 Covering part of the war in Denmark (4)
9 Shy objective at the fair (7)
14 Food prepared by one with no experience of tomatoes? (5,5)
15 It's a turn-up for drinkers! (4)
16 At length Gert can get quite nasty! (4)
18 A month's work producing seafood? (7)
20 Care to mix oil in for energy value? (7)
22 Sounds like a suggestion that we have some salad (7)
23 The rascals find temporary accommodation in a ship (6)
26 Put off the cleaning gent (5)
27 Seen not to be about when cold (4)
28 Help to find a junction beyond Lincoln (4)

162

ACROSS

1 In a business take-over the short answer is to give you the bird! (9)
6 All the wives start getting Eve into trouble (5)
9 Noted entertainment (7)
10 When church starts it's not quite the right moment to criticise (7)
11 Peer taking an opportunity to roll back into office (4,10)
14 A bad actor gets nothing back in America (5)
15 It's a mistake to let things slide (4)
16 Where to start a grand tour in India (4)
18 Face the other way when put down (4)
19 This is the place (4)
20 Pop creature not starting to give support (5)
22 Take the walk that's laid down by law (14)
25 It shows who's brought a book out (7)
27 A Northern Ireland policy that changes colour (7)
28 Those chosen to provide the votes (5)
29 Pert Ellen can turn quite nasty! (9)

DOWN

1 Start mine again, girl! (4)
2 Give the others a speech that will bring the King back (11)
3 Simple and innocent like a Roman Catholic conversion of Diana (8)
4 Airy spirit of a successful slimmer? (5)
5 Direct one to become obscure (9)
6 Striking feature of a Russian device (6)
7 Regret taking part in cruel sports (3)
8 Economically orientated to an important degree! (10)
12 The sort of body that wants to lay down the law (11)
13 Beggars' co-operative society? (10)
15 He can see something's happened to the poet's cart (9)
17 Albert has one in Kensington Gardens (8)
21 No laxity allowed when little Diana leaves the area (6)
23 Wanderer getting right up and becoming a politician (5)
24 Striking progress for the fuzz? (4)
26 Writer, yes, but not quite a poet, perhaps? (3)

164

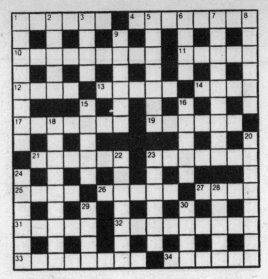

ACROSS

1 Story of how the money goes (7)
5 The elder MD could be the interfering sort (7)
9 They're shaken at a friendly get-together (5)
10 It's a little boring for the shoemaker (3)
11 It sounds as if you've smelt something (5)
12 The novelty of it won't last a fortnight (4,4,6)
14 Body of soldiers from the ammunition depot (4)
15 Work taking place where there's some hostility (10)
19 A meal without a first course just isn't in the running! (3-7)
20 Land at a Crusader port? (4)
22 Jumping to do a thorough sprucing up? (6-8)
26 Bury the fatherless artist (5)
27 Put to work in various endeavours (3)
28 She may return a bad ring (5)
29 One of the gang following pop performers (7)
30 Storm when a short-term worker joins the wrong set (7)

DOWN

1 Painful accompaniment (4)
2 State a prior requirement (9)
3 The province of the coat-maker? (6)
4 It gives the lady a high level of sparkle (5)
5 Man with sound quantity seen by the way (9)
6 Tyrannical diet cops ordering change (8)
7 The one with fat all round has land in Scotland (5)
8 Allusions to former employers perhaps (10)
13 Supplying what the empty room requires (10)
16 It lets one down lightly in a high-level emergency (9)
17 In money I have found a reason for working (9)
18 Cutting short what's grown at school? (4,4)
21 At one's best, you can tell (6)
23 Not a full share, just a proportion (5)
24 Put up before being caught short (5)
25 Administer punishment all round? (4)

166

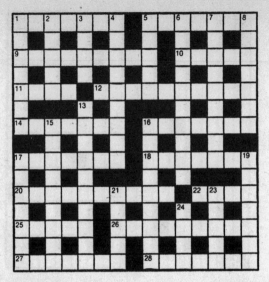

ACROSS

1 A lot of gas holding something up (7)
5 Reclaim the difference—it's almost unbelievable! (7)
9 High-scoring area on board where two might lie (6,3)
10 Make a big hit as a demolition expert (5)
11 Not quite happening on the level (4)
12 A topic mild enough to be changed by the tactful (10)
14 Make a mark as one that won't run (7)
16 Getting across some sort of original thinking (7)
17 Work with journalists to treat with cruelty (7)
18 Rebuked for taking months coming back to bring in the aged (7)
20 Trade unionists are at one in this (10)
22 Round on a friend for being rather precious (4)
25 The Queen succeeded in starting it (5)
26 Lying about how one might repair a place (9)
27 First principle of a proper medium (7)
28 Taken on to reform a small department after some fuss (7)

DOWN

1 Speech requiring publicity coverage (7)
2 Use the outer roundabout this way (5)
3 Incredible what a big, awkward chap he is! (4)
4 Announces new books for sale (9)
5 One might sit to provide a small-scale pattern (5)
6 Fresh start concerning money available at a different point (10)
7 Hired to look as if granted royal privileges (9)
8 Halt ice re-forming—that's good! (7)
13 Being there some time when you can take steps (10)
15 Disgusting perversion of pure lives (9)
16 A liner sunk by a U-boat (9) (9)
17 Say what you see? (7)
19 Held up action about a song (7)
21 Send what's right when time's up (5)
23 Colourful coat to put on (5)
24 Old man with nothing on going round the wall (4)

ACROSS

1 The lady in red having a dubious reputation (7,5)
9 Give me a certain length (7)
10 Time in custody can be extended (7)
11 Comparatively unfeeling when there are as many as this (6)
14 It enables the traveller to get tanked up (6)
15 Standing instruction to the highwayman's victim (7)
16 It has its points in assisting the consumer (4)
17 Pleased to see the old statesman has lost weight (4)
18 Make an assertion that may be cleared (7)
19 A penny off the fruit for every customer (4)
21 Over your eyes it can be quite deceptive (4)
23 Talk of something to throw at Sally's head (7)
25 Go quietly if you don't want to put your foot down (6)
26 Say what you like, it's free! (6)
29 Here's that old film again! (7)
30 The state of the Grand Canyon (7)
31 Is he bugged by his studies? (12)

DOWN

2 Cleaner to see me right – delightful person! (7)
3 Defeated away from home in colour (6)
4 We turn up and give the Queen a jug (4)
5 You were here on a postcard, for instance (4)
6 Shout if it's blue! (6)
7 Not flat as you might expect (7)
8 Had a pile to distribute with the fluter in the city (12)
9 Writer employed by the post office? (3,2,7)
12 Fancy a clergyman being on the lake! (7)
13 Diana and Alexander shortly starting to talk in regional speech (7)
14 Being titled she has letters in the papers (7)
20 Turn over to determine whether the headgear will fit (7)
22 Heavy one turning sour (7)
23 Find somewhere in England or settle in America (6)
24 Time for some fresh water (6)
27 This time it's the limit! (4)
28 We don't believe this bird turned up (4)

ACROSS

1 He's got something that makes him one of the haves (8,5)
8 Attractive as an employer in need of more staff (8)
9 Reach a turn in the river (6)
10 Extremes of scholasticism causing disagreement in church (6)
13 Handcuff a chap able to come back inside (7)
14 Try to show discrimination (5)
16 Query the position of the lady when we come round (5)
18 Not keen on a new diet around Peterhead (5)
19 Line-up on the classical front (7)
20 In which people learn their place in society? (5)
22 It's hard to express disgust (5)
24 Could the expert be made to investigate? (5)
26 One day's stadium takings could give us a ship (7)
28 Establish as top man – with knobs on? (6)
32 Time of considerable importance (6)
33 She has an old-fashioned remedy for those who lack top protection (8)
34 Put down the receiver to avoid taking sides (3,2,3,5)

DOWN

1 Fear to put a god in charge (5)
2 All right to provide a piece of pie for an animal (5)
3 How Meg and Ian got involved is a puzzle (6)
4 Classical Roman cover-up (4)
5 Where D-Day Americans could go to town (5)
6 Doubled up at speed to tell a story (7)
7 When going round with a stuck-up boy-friend French wine makes a good start (9)
11 He goes round the roundabout at Plymouth (3)
12 Moves of a progressive nature (5)
13 Give me a team to get the firm nationalised (6)
15 Take off to the east in line (6)
17 Funny as the year's first session in court? (9)
18 A drink gets me up the pole! (5)
21 The part that gets men into trouble (7)
23 High-class Foreign Office sighting of a flying saucer maybe (3)
25 Divide by two on this account (6)
27 Just like him to suggest a shipwreck! (5)
29 The philosopher at the breakfast table (5)
30 Scientific energy starting to cause a row (5)
31 Feeling the need to come up to scratch? (4)

ACROSS

1 Pours ice as if it were valuable (8)
6 Means of conveying liquid in smoke (4)
10 Possible TV choice for shipping? (7)
11 One of the GPO letters (7)
12 Girl with very little time for violent Irishmen (5)
13 It could throw some light on the screening process (9)
14 One mind is distorted to some extent (9)
16 Give the girl no return as a flier (5)
17 Right on top when one isn't a settled type (5)
19 Bit on the crest of the bird (9)
21 Old-fashioned pulling power upsets the orchestra (9)
24 She's quite taken in by His Excellency! (5)
26 Work on a shipping route looking delicately white (7)
27 Magnate in trouble supervising the opening (7)
28 Don't go when support is needed! (4)
29 Posed in front of the old city one time this week (8)

DOWN

2 Is in the country, displaying no illusions (7)
3 There may be something in it (9)
4 Low down in the shipping world (5)
5 He's got a floating asset (9)
6 The arrogance of those lions! (5)
7 Artist providing a possible tie-up (7)
8 On top but not the best people (4)
9 The old duke's carriage (8)
14 He knows which way the business ought to go (8)
15 Their suppliers are alien to us (9)
16 Combine to get the ravers on the move (9)
18 It's not quite the same thing (7)
20 Cover up with a girl in a predicament (7)
22 Very difficult because of all the locks? (5)
23 Quite enough for a row (5)
25 One of those dressing-up numbers? (4)

170

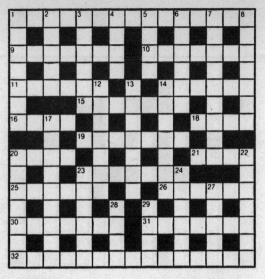

ACROSS

1 Lawyer and military man in the Government (7-7)
9 Ran Gaul the wrong way, not being smooth (7)
10 In which one might be going places in a small way? (7)
11 Close-up trial for the one with the most girlish appeal (6)
14 Half the list gets close to being one-dimensional (6)
15 Oh, a riot when Nelson's around! (7)
16 Not very far to pull the cart back (4)
18 Shut a lord in the privy? (4)
19 We aren't paid for this sort of work (7)
20 Intend not to be generous (4)
21 Get hold of something smashing? (4)
23 Period certain of obliteration (7)
25 Fliers taking part in another onslaught (6)
26 Savoy heroine suggesting good taste (3,3)
30 Chap with different gear in charge (7)
31 Old ones can find themselves in the soup! (7)
32 Bloated estate owners and what they live off? (3,3,2,3,4)

DOWN

1 Any char around can get rid of government (7)
2 Too drunk to be liberal? (5)
3 Part of the quarrel is how to find enjoyment (6)
4 Do what's necessary to make the job pay (4)
5 Quite prepared for some sport (4)
6 Sister joining an American union body to represent the Pope (6)
7 Not one of those quiet swindlers (9)
8 Steel enthusiast? (7)
12 They work hard to get fuel in conditions of disturbed rest (7)
13 Try to get votes for a tent-maker? (7)
14 The reader has his place here (7)
17 Back over the mountains to make new dispositions (9)
20 The prophet might confuse them with Mao (7)
22 Confused to be given inspiration? (7)
23 Something puzzling in game scrum (6)
24 There's some amateur opera in our part of the world (6)
27 Song turning up to give thanks for a wartime meeting (5)
28 One needs a couple to make it (4)
29 Carry on needling (4)

ACROSS

1 Take off with the fish, boy (9)
6 Divine darts-thrower (5)
9 Thinking to make Eve spin around (7)
10 It's burdensome when a person turns sour (7)
11 It's water under the bridge at Avignon (5)
12 An age of celebration (6-3)
13 Dispatched with people in it showing feeling (9)
15 Time after work for entertainment (5)
16 Day to day occurrence (5)
18 On the level at the seaside (9)
20 Something growing out of tangled garden hay (9)
23 Note the file in one's hold (5)
25 Feel a thrill of fear (7)
26 Fancy I am taking a drink on the way (7)
27 Boat upset in an ocean storm (5)
28 Not a sound typewriter? (9)

DOWN

1 Very good at suggesting a senior policeman (5)
2 Be quick with the cereal in Cheshire (7)
3 It sets out the charges for taking things (5-4)
4 Clumsy writer standing up in it (5)
5 Carry on like a foolish creature on parade (5-4)
6 He's in court briefly holding the treasure (5)
7 Suggest a permanent get-together (7)
8 Reckless peers taking a tumble in time (9)
13 It's not natural! (9)
14 Holly, for instance, is always giving the go-ahead (9)
15 Royal Dutch drink? (9)
17 Pin dug up and gone astray (7)
19 It shows greed for a girl to take food (7)
21 Get along like a doctor in drink (5)
22 Defence of an absentee (5)
24 Apply force in the papers (5)

172

ACROSS

1 One who counts votes to bring about secret ruin (10)
6 What we have when we've finished our labours (4)
9 Eating with Rita turns out to get one into favour (10)
10 Move very slowly—like an outsider? (4)
12 Every man has one in a corrupt Government (5)
14 Novel occasions of some difficulty (4,5)
15 Ecstatic about the strike the union nearly rouses (9)
18 The man in possession (5)
19 Materialism of the clergy (5)
20 They put us in competitive situations (9)
22 Having too much on (9)
24 Follow the master in a matter of doctrine (5)
25 It might be better if an abstainer got stuck into it! (4)
26 Cut in the allocation of frippery (10)
28 She might get less unsparing (4)
29 Opportunity to swagger back as one of Thatcher's men (10)

DOWN

1 One makes an error going on foot (7)
2 Man taking part in a bigger comeback (3)
3 Rated differently when one has a skill (5)
4 Next door to being Christian's loved one (9)
5 Don't accept exclusion as a competitor (5)
7 Not asking you to make much effort (11)
8 Poet in the corrupt PR sense (7)
11 Get along like a wandering actor (6)
13 Things will be better after this (11)
16 Give support in carrying the banner maybe (6)
17 Happening to be seen around in youth (9)
19 Make a hit with what you wear? (7)
21 It might cause a stoppage in the works (7)
23 Hated to be different in the end (5)
24 Man leaving the plant to become a famous bowler (5)
27 Indisposed after church in a man of war (3)

ACROSS

1 A hundred on deposit provides the money (4)
3 Record one note for a story (4)
6 Go back in a vehicle that's not what it seems (5)
10 Sweet and nutty academy president on the mark (7)
11 Natives of Whitstable maybe (7)
12 Not at first to be believed that you could eat it! (6)
13 Traditionally a quick sale food item (3,4)
16 No-one makes a killing catering for him (10)
17 One of those put on by the unwise consumer (4)
19 In local society as well (4)
21 All the better to eat you with, honey! (5,5)
24 Has ring altered to decorate a dish (7)
25 One in a position to provide fish (6)
29 Portion of food served to those on assistance? (7)
30 Occasion for some steamy outpouring (3-4)
31 The name of the champion (5)
32 Very fine but not often seen (4)
33 Possible basis for breakfast in bed (4)

DOWN

1 Police make an excellent start in the wood (5)
2 Preventing air getting to a fish under water (7)
4 Strip off in fruity style (4)
5 Crooked coach stole confectionery (10)
6 Cut the part about shortage of time (6)
7 King going mad about the girl and getting in a pickle (7)
8 It may go round the waist or in the window (4)
9 The big rise allows food to come from the interior (7)
14 Dusky sweetheart from Demerara? (5,5)
15 He has made a hash of being top man (4)
16 Some of what you save always provides the basis of a meal (4)
18 The sort of wine you might drink with spaghetti (7)
20 Include everything in an attempt at a salad item (7)
22 When the biscuit man's around I become a great actor! (7)
23 People without a head go down into the plant (6)
26 Yemen elements deployed on the other side (5)
27 A question of substance (4)
28 Move to spread some sweetness possibly (4)

174

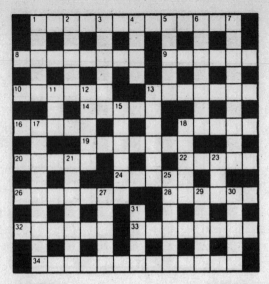

ACROSS

1 Ale stinks, mate – but you'd be wise to put it differently! (13)
8 Mark has the measure of a Yorkshire coalman (8)
9 Live in some style (6)
10 Is the venerable egghead able to identify the lady? (6)
13 Food to gorge? (7)
14 Calculating creature, we can assume (5)
16 Grim to the last? (5)
18 Not the best man to prepare for stardom, maybe (5)
19 Someone in digs will see the dog right (7)
20 It's the custom to give America time (5)
22 On the look-out for changes later (5)
24 Good enough to make it big (5)
26 Noble band of those who look their years? (7)
28 Obsession with reforming the family income supplement shortly (6)
32 Wrong about teacher? (6)
33 Minister for upholding the rule against blacks? (8)
34 Dominant figure, maybe, in the class struggle (13)

DOWN

1 Pull them up for improved performance (5)
2 March past (5)
3 Sent away for former idle turn (6)
4 Drink that might come to you in a round (4)
5 One way out of Devon or the south coast (5)
6 The man they couldn't keep out (7)
7 Try to finish first (9)
11 A person referred to in telephone conversations (3)
12 Caper one may be led to find vexatious (5)
13 Groups of sailors one hears about at sea (6)
15 Downfall of the Pompadour's following (6)
17 Sat up without seeing television on board – how insipid! (9)
18 Sounds a terrific basis for a warm-up! (5)
21 Sharing around the food decoration (7)
23 Indelicate person (3)
25 If a car crashes it will be south of the Mediterranean (6)
27 Find a man to express enjoyment (5)
29 They might get together for a bite (5)
30 The case for giving people a rise? (5)
31 Taunt with being a fool (4)

ACROSS

1 Opening for a member (7)
5 Meaning almost unadulterated wine (7)
9 Small retreat in Cornwall (9)
10 One isn't committed to sit on it (5)
11 No setback when money is provided (5)
12 Liked better than some others (9)
13 Too mean to be open-handed (5-6)
16 Plymouth gardener's aid (3)
17 Keep on complaining in the manager's office (3)
18 In which you might have to make snap decisions (11)
20 Big enough for Loch Ness? (9)
22 Credit a fool with being stupid (5)
24 Not so if it's any good (5)
25 Mum, Norah and I involved in making music (9)
27 He's got the museum to look after (7)
28 Record of transactions by TV's Robin? (3-4)

DOWN

1 Where a girl can turn up star information (7)
2 A horse to get on (5)
3 Do too much unconscious lying (9)
4 Oriental attempt to identify self-esteem (3)
5 Claiming great merit in super tote turnout (11)
6 Search with a gun? (5)
7 Proprietor's joint possession (9)
8 Put your foot on it to get something going (7)
12 Someone between a guide and a friend (11)
14 Union official to arrange the music (9)
15 The book of Numbers (9)
17 Con maid into wandering around (7)
19 It conceals certain features of Eastern womanhood (7)
21 Appointment to irritate the good man (5)
23 A motorway departure for our foreign friend (5)
26 It makes one angry to see it (3)

176

ACROSS

1 What he's got he spreads around (11)
8 Defence of one who wasn't there (5)
10 Thought of something patently new (8)
12 Given an order to go a certain way? (8)
13 Cautious about it being a good cause (7)
14 Doesn't like to see Red Poles disturbed (8)
17 There's such a region in the far north (5)
18 Almost panting for a bird (6)
19 Weaken a little fellow taking breath (6)
20 It would be a help if she came back (5)
21 Expatiated on the expansion programme? (8)
23 Wind causes some obscurity when the rally starts (7)
25 Going beyond the limit (8)
28 Having an inclination to suggest a certain angle? (8)
29 Payments required to dispose of tears (5)
30 Such activity certainly isn't reducing the size of a building firm (11)

DOWN

2 Qualified to enter the parlour? (5)
3 There's one in the singer's town (6)
4 Starting a fire to get things going? (8)
5 Accustomed to be sworn at if following a sailor (4)
6 Care to come round in a hurry? (4)
7 Two boys together can be so old-fashioned! (9)
9 River test of some kind of revolution (10)
11 He often gets immersed in his job (5)
13 Machine for redistributing Rome's crops (10)
14 Star king (5)
15 Where the mail went astray in South America (4)
16 They may be the outcome of industrial activity (9)
17 It takes you out to sea with never a roll or pitch (4)
19 They may identify an office-holder (8)
20 Swift and others? (5)
22 Not allowing any slackness here (6)
24 Gas is included in a special cargo nowadays (5)
26 Provider of all-round entertainment (4)
27 Too much of a good thing! (4)

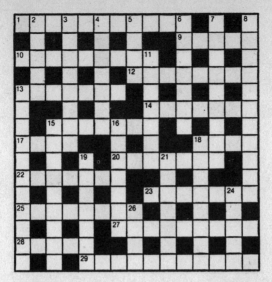

ACROSS

1 There's not enough to live on under here (7,4)
9 Having an odd flair but lacking strength (5)
10 Chips can go in after the fish (9)
12 Julius Caesar's twitch might make some sort of story (8)
13 Intend the German not to go straight (7)
14 Furniture needed to provide cover (7)
15 Make healthy again with a break for a mineral (7)
17 Wrongly suggested the little devil had gone (4)
18 Revolutionary music maybe (4)
20 He rather overdoes the enthusiasm (7)
22 Supreme protector of the worker? (7)
23 One mist that might cause dampness (7)
25 Some of the Americans bring a hoax into town (8)
27 Name as appointed but not yet installed (9)
28 When the dog returns he can display something frilly (5)
29 The one who devises those breezy plans? (11)

DOWN

2 Speak of nothing but speed (5)
3 Given a bigger area (8)
4 Brown finds a man to give the line (7)
5 Stagger up and have a look (4)
6 Rubbed out a sound letter when unable to return service (7)
7 I can't fast, strange as it may seem! (9)
8 The person to solve our current problems (11)
11 Dear one out to produce educated young ladies (7)
13 It takes a lot of money to make him what he is (11)
15 Allusion to what might be helpful to the job applicant (9)
16 Get rid of stuff that's been transported (7)
18 Doesn't agree to be dispatched into a Norfolk town (8)
19 Having a narrow part that sounds undernourished (7)
21 Has boil treated to do away with it (7)
24 There's more to be won from the next race at Windsor (5)
26 Chaps who are high-class are given a choice of food (4)

178

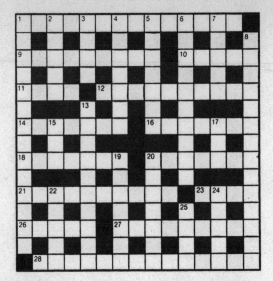

ACROSS

1 Causing workers to arrive at different times, to their great surprise? (9,5)
9 Letter from some sort of actor (9)
10 You might get one by breaking this wood (5)
11 Taking part in an East-West meeting once more (4)
12 Likely to go off if not taken in soon (10)
14 Make exclusive use of the door (4,3)
16 Don and Olga having a tumble in the boat (7)
18 Sound as a bell before the artist reveals the monster (7)
20 High point of Cleo's needling (7)
21 A satirical turn soon starts to expose believers in blood (10)
23 Mark of a one-way vehicle (4)
26 Said to have followed a religious pamphlet (5)
27 The joy of getting somewhere? (9)
28 Person ordained to be in office? (8,6)

DOWN

1 Unhealthy responsibility of a minister? (6,8)
2 Not closing one's eyes to the possibility of a funeral gathering (5)
3 It's in a box in the car (4)
4 Go back and stand another round? (7)
5 You could put on weight in County Durham, love (7)
6 Generous enough when one's lost one's grip? (4-6)
7 Rob HM so as to get a diamond, perhaps (7)
8 He might rouse the workers in a royal enclosure (4,4,6)
13 He predicts the core will break up inside quicker (10)
15 Among the ludicrous fiascos of Rhodesia (3)
17 Don't start desert witchcraft (3)
19 Act I is a transformation in the Eastern manner (7)
20 It could be the end of all that piping (7)
22 Be obsequious during a go-slow? (5)
24 Underworld character associated with the bishop (5)
25 Foreign capital in Czechoslovakia (4)

ACROSS

1 Hit the one who's doing the damage and causing a scab (6-7)
8 Go on talking about a bad player (6)
9 Fought back for new rises with a man (8)
12 First person to doctor the ale and cause a Communist comeback (6)
15 Everybody starts to charge what hasn't been proved (6)
18 Too far off to be friendly (6)
19 What the fake bishop gives is not as good as you might think (7,8)
20 More likely to get a hearing (6)
22 Put in with a bird to restrict freedom (6)
24 Lower the status of a churchman by letting me in (6)
27 Heaven is being in a demonstration! (8)
29 Comes up after minutes perhaps (6)
30 All-out show of strength for new donation terms (13)

DOWN

1 Not the real way to get something cured (4)
2 A bit of your own back (6)
3 Pretty fish container (6)
4 Down where it's cheaper (7,8)
5 Time of rising in Ireland (6)
6 Make a contact show affection (4)
7 Eggs for a buck (3)
10 Man in the depths and non-worker going different ways (9)
11 Enabling one to get to grips with goodwill (4-5)
13 Why, this is it! (6)
14 Bobby's one of them (6)
16 It's hard work having a party! (6)
17 Given protection for the hands (6)
21 One rig to repair in the area (6)
22 Tribal conference in a bad trouble (6)
23 Thanks to a strike I am seen in the Pacific (6)
25 Warmongers starting to get a bit heated (4)
26 Head vegetarian? (4)
28 First requirement after the accident (3)

180

ACROSS

1 Move to take the birds on and make a name in railways (10)
8 That's as far as you can go (5)
9 Bird on the edge of the water where ships dock (9)
10 It's oneself one is thinking of here (7)
13 By no means unsavoury shipping character (4)
14 Get along without power (5)
15 He made a conquest a long time ago (6)
16 Slap into the mountains! (4)
18 Coast irregularity giving place to races (5)
20 Disposed of old Bob – he's getting on (4)
21 Burden of a boy who's swallowed nothing (4)
23 It might be written in Mrs Miniver's engagement book (5)
25 She's said to be thinner (4)
26 Star twins (6)
27 Black singer (5)
29 Inclination to write everything down? (4)
30 Disturbed to see a trump put down first (7)
33 He's possessive where the estate is concerned (4-5)
34 He can study a shipping problem in depth (5)
35 It's by no means certain his enterprise will succeed (10)

DOWN

1 He's responsible for finding the customers (5,7)
2 Hides even slop perhaps (8)
3 Difficult to avoid being sloppy (4)
4 They may be in the soup, the fools! (7)
5 Provided possible fuel cover? (5)
6 Not just relying on words (9)
7 One way for a boy and girl to meet (4)
11 The sort of men one associates with ladies (6)
12 He's got it made! (12)
17 The hard stuff causing things to get heated! (5,4)
18 It might be conveyed in a note (6)
19 Low character among the security guards (3)
22 He may decide the shape of things to come (8)
24 Something might be said to break it (7)
28 I had gone first but didn't do much (5)
31 Just one of those things (4)
32 Drink when not at sea (4)

ACROSS

1 Parliamentary manoeuvres by the Energy Minister? (5,8)
8 Leading to spending very little time among the trees (8)
9 One might be excited at getting into it (6)
10 By itself only gradually significant (6)
11 He hopes a new order will be an improvement (8)
14 Lady artist joining the party (4)
16 Dear person (3,2,5)
18 Pleased about one's own achievements (10)
19 Not this side for a musical story (4)
21 Left high and dry in London? (8)
24 Used to change being thrown out (6)
26 No sex please, just a human being! (6)
28 Daisy's lover couldn't afford one (8)
29 No place for working people (7,6)

DOWN

1 Condition favouring six this way (7)
2 Take away by force what's right in the way (5)
3 Where all the Reds are chickens? (5,6)
4 Creature not starting to totter (5)
5 Good alternative (3)
6 Weave together from a neat relic (9)
7 Bit of a drama when you make one! (5)
12 No. 1 links for starters (5,6)
13 Send to one side before time's up (5)
14 Dodges an endearment (5)
15 A friend about to cause trouble in Paris in one estimation (9)
17 Coming through it is something to sing about (3)
20 Trick to keep the French in view (7)
22 They could get together for a bite (5)
23 Things certainly aren't getting better in this (5)
25 There's gravity in bringing up oils in Ireland (5)
27 Agree to drop off? (3)

182

ACROSS

1 Fought for industrial waste? (8)
5 Society Island (6)
10 Having taken on a cargo of fifty at a foreign port (5)
11 It could hold freight or ancient trouble (9)
12 Traditionally not a collier's port of discharge (9)
13 Worry about decorative work? (4)
16 In debt all round for flying (5)
18 Road speed altered by a madman (9)
21 Contrives a machine to make uncertain noises (9)
24 Bonus provided at X rate of exchange (5)
25 Prison for making a cut? (4)
27 Clothing is nothing to me – it's so boring! (9)
31 Most likely to win a tough contest (9)
32 Animal given ten in proportion (5)
33 Weapon returned before you start to be sleepy (6)
34 After a century Michael undergoes some sort of transformation (8)

DOWN

1 Old Bob gets a beer when prices are reduced (4)
2 Beginning to look flush? (9)
3 Fear of Father not being quite nice (5)
4 Cut by the revenue men? (7)
6 Get this and be gone! (4)
7 Not quite a meal but a good shot all the same (5)
8 Trial on air not making sense (10)
9 Tries to make catches in corners (6)
14 Made to change in a new way (10)
15 Just a stretch of water? (4)
17 This way to get on board, friends! (4)
19 Do the human thing (3)
20 Self-operating car giving the old lady a twitch (9)
22 Vision allowed when there's a hole (6)
23 Extend the time in prison (7)
26 Shipload of motors? (5)
28 The good man needs a drink to play the guitar (5)
29 We have the responsibility (4)
30 Payment might amount to a couple of pounds (4)

ACROSS

1 Making progress in avoiding criminal deviations (5,8)
8 Manage to put something over the bishop? (4)
9 Put your finger on what to do with the garden? (5)
10 After taking direction a bad actor doesn't seem real (4)
11 Take belated revenge to determine what was sportingly achieved years ago? (6,3,6)
15 Back with one's name (7)
17 Occupied in preparation for marriage? (7)
19 In a Hampshire town one may appear a beastly female (7)
21 Like Tennyson's stories of King Arthur (7)
24 Flying fortresses? You just imagined them! (7,2,3,3)
29 Programme for feeding people with a high-class following (4)
30 Sign that the number is about to be all right (5)
31 Nonsense to disclose a secret, blow it! (4)
32 He wants people to give him his due (4,9)

DOWN

1 The world of Shakespearian theatre (5)
2 Clumsy way to catch a writer up in it (5)
3 She's one of the legendary immortals (7)
4 Got leg wrongly placed – it won't go through the hole (6)
5 Skill is an aspect of the mechanic (7)
6 Enjoyment of a blow over nothing (5)
7 The business of the union? (5)
11 The girl to call up to provide some cover (7)
12 Do use it as a change from the snappy (7)
13 Royal holdings destroyed in the rail age (7)
14 He encourages one to do the wrong thing (7)
16 Regret finding oneself in a Paris street (3)
18 Chap to give steady support in camp (3)
20 Not an easy person to convince (7)
22 Throw camping gear in the river by way of easing strained relations (7)
23 A few cents' worth of metal? (6)
25 Forward as a top person (5)
26 Little Tom may be up for approval (5)
27 Time we had a meal, say (5)
28 Not so good at first, one might deduce (5)

184

ACROSS

1 A national leader would be quite wrong to stir up the Croats (6)
4 One who fights for what's outworn to be dumped? (8)
9 Basis for much boring activity (3-3)
11 Bird beginning to follow a Communist (8)
12 Giant-killer seeing Father about six (5)
13 Not much to pay for entertainment? (4)
15 Not again! (4)
16 The way workers go under (4-5)
17 Cough with an edge to it (4)
19 Provide some financial return (5)
20 Food for someone who's quick? (5)
24 Fancy not starting when you've all that paper! (4)
26 Greeting from someone with the jitters? (9)
27 Original Bobby in the Isle of Man (4)
28 Genuine reference to Madrid's footballers (4)
30 When they have a row it doesn't amount to much (5)
32 He'll do better with experience (8)
33 Like the look of one who has been at the booze? (6)
34 Copper for man besotted with greed (8)
35 The businessman who gives you your cards (6)

DOWN

1 It might be hit when the shooting's too high (8)
2 Just the thing for the gunman who wants a quiet death (8)
3 Right to help when there's an attack (4)
5 Signalled to get saved at last (4)
6 Alison not giving in as well! (4)
7 It's obvious Tom's starting to express a grievance (6)
8 Bad time after some nonsense (6)
10 Old Redshirt who took the biscuit? (9)
11 No cotton-picker, this old man (5)
14 Going down among the psychiatrists? (9)
15 Proposal for price reduction (5)
18 Encountered Capone and got lead maybe (5)
21 Backing a clergyman to embarrass the earls (8)
22 You'll have a job to find one (8)
23 Do it up and you'll feel better (5)
25 Time to make a comeback possible (6)
26 Having a fibre that gives an edge over the writer (6)
29 Some little squirt at the bar (4)
30 Light support? (4)
31 Said to be in no hurry to make gin (4)

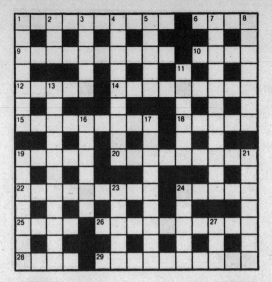

185

ACROSS

1 Aristocrats lost their heads when it came down (10)
6 A man who takes him in must come from the States (4)
9 Property is able to produce this for those who have it (10)
10 Carry on the struggle for something to live on (4)
12 Force a little chap to take on the Spanish (5)
14 Taxed too highly by the council – it's not *that* valuable! (9)
15 A nice star turn in the narrow sense (9)
18 The basis for shop action (5)
19 Outline of a medical man at the back of the ship (5)
20 Lordly attendant to tell you what's inside? (5-4)
22 Before putting in a bid as a claimant (9)
24 A chap has nearly everything – like the Queen (5)
25 Take off in the back garden (4)
26 It's his job to carry out a stick-up (4,6)
28 Let us know about the Swiss hero (4)
29 He's not an outgoing sort of person (4-2-4)

DOWN

1 Yes, pigs make a difference when people are on the move! (7)
2 The Italian circle as an international body (3)
3 Turnover of material that suits one (5)
4 Freedom fighter as seen by the ruling regime (9)
5 Chemical effect of one rent adjustment (5)
7 Don't expect him to support progressive moves (11)
8 Red Chad disturbance in the gorge (7)
11 Just a little bit sweet maybe (6)
13 More than one item in the wrapping business (7,4)
16 Song of the man with capacity for change (6)
17 North American union get-together just as you'd expect (9)
19 Something to pay and that's not all! (7)
21 Make a bigger contribution to our understanding (7)
23 After the fall, that's the general idea (5)
24 It's ruled by some cocky character (5)
27 One thing and another (3)

186

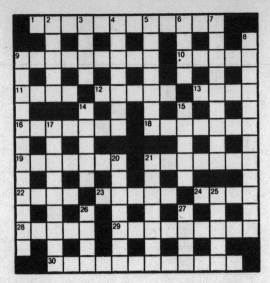

ACROSS

1 Noble of them to sit without being elected! (5,2,5)
9 Building in the green belt urged by Blake? (9)
10 Grieve to have little time with the ashes (5)
11 Communist leader to demand a lot of drink (4)
12 What fun to be in politics! (5)
13 Lucky it's attached to a horse! (4)
16 Take off and do something similar (7)
18 Bad oil circle making move in devilish game (7)
19 Work on newspapers to keep the people down (7)
21 Colonial boss of growing ambition (7)
22 All the people all the time? You can't do it! (4)
23 Here, this is in the next world! (5)
24 Help to provide a chance to win money (4)
28 Wood where the police are said to be (5)
29 It's a relic that can look quite convincing (9)
30 Get-together of people who've got together (5,7)

DOWN

2 People are afraid of them in the progressive movement (5)
3 One might be given an order to wear it (4)
4 Cattle food for the fuel consumer? (3-4)
5 Cover round a little creature restricted as to company (7)
6 Inclination to swindle? (4)
7 Posh tutor out of place in Merseyside (9)
8 Like an American Republican or any other enemy of the people (12)
9 Self-important official giving a lift when he's got the job? (4-2-6)
14 There's a new one on the Sussex coast (5)
15 Sex appeal makes a youngster good enough to eat! (5)
17 One wasn't prepared to make such a speech (9)
20 The colour of a cake? (7)
21 Get ready before you make cuts (7)
25 Continue facing the bowling and get some stick! (5)
26 Some of these might lack complete detachment (4)
27 Inclination to sound like a composer (4)

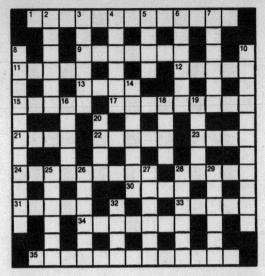

ACROSS

1 Misunderstandings of what zebras are for? (5-8)
9 Rip lace in making a copy (7)
11 Very old and very cold speech (5)
12 The general idea is about right for the mill (5)
13 Copied in a beastly way? (4)
15 The Queen's country (5)
17 One of the submerged and one of the toffs going different ways (9)
21 In the programme it gives me a setback (4)
22 There's nothing to mark the man (5)
23 Shut up an animal (4)
24 Does he make savings as a scientist? (9)
28 Draw near at last to see a swimmer (5)
30 Lucky it's attached to a horse! (4)
31 One wasn't there to give a defence (5)
33 Demand to shut up about one (5)
34 Tearing around for the hard stuff (7)
35 Where trees touch and members get together (6,7)

DOWN

2 The Queen in Canada (6)
3 Current worry for the master (6)
4 Beaten by the time signal? (6)
5 Bar for travellers (4)
6 Ass putting on wrong gear (6)
7 Cut for the tax man (6)
8 More money to be going on with (8,3)
10 One can live here in grand style (7,4)
14 Talk about having something to throw to old Bob (7)
16 Something yellow in the little monkey's paw (5)
18 His lordship will start yawning soon (4)
19 You'll enjoy eating with this! (5)
20 A piece of paper to fill in—the usual procedure (4)
25 More demanding character (6)
26 Beginning of a revolution in Rio over drink (6)
27 Do well in the Forth River race (6)
28 Modern about money (6)
29 Lady fighter of South America (6)
32 Clean-up in the city (4)

188

ACROSS

1 Bit of unfamiliar characterisation causing a hold-up (4)
3 Lovely girl making a cad what he is (4)
6 It means something to know in Scotland (5)
10 Food in a flap (7)
11 Not the mixture for vegetarians (4,3)
12 Corrects some of them before the finals (6)
13 Finish with a saint for salads (7)
16 It weakens the spirit but bucks one up (5,5)
17 Sure to make a difference for an employer (4)
19 Ready to drop off (4)
21 A redhead's sleep takes the biscuit! (6-4)
24 Joy's sweet, being Turkish (7)
25 Food formality? (6)
29 It may come in handy in the kitchen (7)
30 Even USA are affected in some ways (7)
31 Patch something up in a sweet way (5)
32 Forced to return for some cheese (4)
33 Enrolling of men to pay a tax? (4)

DOWN

1 It's big for New York! (5)
2 Cutlery and where to use it (7)
4 It might just occur to you (4)
5 Dish a bad actor with messy missiles (3,3,4)
6 It's sad to see a soldier in the cart going up (6)
7 Breakfast offerings for those who are asleep (7)
8 Poverty the trouble in Eden? (4)
9 Fish to be obtained on the wharf (7)
14 Something tasty from the Continental pornographer? (6,4)
15 Just a little bit of a fall (4)
16 Sweet and sour? (4)
18 Waste a piece of fruit in batter? (7)
20 Make a rather unreal claim? (7)
22 Care to alter the true run? (7)
23 A lot of lies in the paper? (6)
26 Hurrying to make a pudding (5)
27 — But no good at it? (4)
28 Coffee island? (4)

ACROSS

1 Where a Sussex man might belong (10)
6 Hang about for some bread (4)
10 Found fault in a small way (7)
11 Armed force in church? (7)
12 Not done, perhaps, if nobody's hurt (4)
13 Service I have provided in a big way! (7)
17 Navigation warning carrying no great weight? (9)
20 Cut thus to make a getaway (5)
21 I leave Nellie to come back a different girl (5)
22 Act as agent in connection with a gift (9)
23 Worker in a heap on the roof (7)
25 Something shady in a city street (4)
30 Go down as the man who started the business (7)
31 He may have been selected to conceal the principals (7)
32 Inclination to be a dashing fellow? (4)
33 Trying hard to change its present form (10)

DOWN

1 Gain for a London team in Sussex (10)
2 Drink in royal get-up (5)
3 Man in the Irish Sea, for instance (4)
4 Guide to religion for the young (9)
5 There could be a stoppage here in the desert (5)
7 Leave out the award that goes with it (4)
8 Get a touch of emotion (4)
9 He seems to be getting somewhere (9)
14 Levels of attainment that justify flying flags? (9)
15 Animal to protect the harbour? (4)
16 Colony for people getting out of debt? (10)
18 Source of a warm stream (4)
19 They're bringing North Sea gas to Britain (9)
24 More than is required for company (5)
26 Scope for mountain climbing? (5)
27 A long way off in an East African safari (4)
28 A great amount of material is carried in it (4)
29 A politician's current measures (4)

190

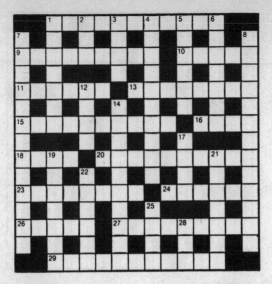

ACROSS

1 Has a job with an expedition when the factory's shut (5,6)
9 Did something theatrical (9)
10 Move to show pride in giving support (5)
11 One doesn't remain after an attack (6)
13 Expert getting fifty if in charge of fertility (8)
15 Take in at a missile explosion (10)
16 Only a stretch of water? (4)
18 Move unsteadily to music? (4)
20 A French comedian about to refuse what's not profitable (10)
23 Protectionist newspaper (8)
24 Make a safe start with poems in Russia (6)
26 Could be real strength! (5)
27 Meaning to distribute tin at last (9)
29 Hangs on to powerful fortresses (11)

DOWN

1 Frets about starting to ride in possibly worse surroundings (7)
2 Disastrous old airship losing one in port (3)
3 Turn us over to a politician where oil is found (4)
4 Reckon dust must be disturbed if you don't keep enough for the customers (10)
5 Short measures last month amounted to abuse (6)
6 One might find it easy to overlook things (7)
7 Don't expect a soft life under the old Greek system (7,6)
8 The usual give-and-take when dealers get together? (5,8)
12 She might make some of them marvellous meals (4)
14 Doing a stretch (10)
17 Eat up, girl! (4)
19 Rushes into making accusations? (7)
21 They get high on religion (7)
22 A top person on paper (6)
25 There's irritation when Ken leaves the room (4)
28 Nothing but an endless river (3)

ACROSS

1 Not a Labour leader of any substance? (6,8)
9 By no means simple to speak after the way Labour is cut short (9)
10 Decree that may be cited (5)
11 It provides some cover for a clansman (4)
12 Machine for copying the strange court plaid (10)
14 Determine to find the answer again (7)
16 There's nothing to be said for it (7)
18 Sounds as if the old historian should get a place up north (7)
20 Big seven in the oil business, relatively speaking (7)
21 Person's ire stirred by being kept down (10)
23 Cause a storm in a teacup (4)
26 Sign up some of those keen roller-skaters! (5)
27 Hate to bemoan ITA carve-up (9)
28 Dealing informally among Quakers? (7,7)

DOWN

1 Get an oratorical angle on Hyde Park (8,6)
2 Help to make a girl almost sick (5)
3 Producer of notes from a study of American hoboes (4)
4 Does it show the extent of the law? (7)
5 Penetrating points that are not quite without utility (7)
6 Nothing to be said for having no address? (10)
7 Exercise landlord power in the Victorian manner (5)
8 Under which discipline is beginning to affect runners (8,6)
13 Some mate like Shaw or O'Casey? (10)
15 Dear correspondent (3)
17 Said to be close to a dead Labour hero (3)
19 A man you might somehow cut with ease (7)
20 Give a display even though the entertainment has been cancelled (4,3)
22 Turn up with crazy Reg to remove undesirable elements (5)
24 Instruct along the lines laid down? (5)
25 Good sound greeting if turning up (2-2)

192

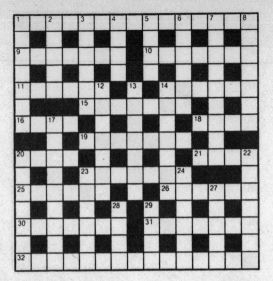

ACROSS

1 Where London students learn about the days when Britain ruled? (8,7)
9 One going across for a tool? (7)
10 Cave where the tea might run out? (7)
11 River band taking a couple of points (6)
14 Ever in trouble about giving approval to cancel (6)
15 Like a clockwork soldier? (7)
16 She won't be in office long (4)
18 Last thing you'd expect a pacifist to show! (4)
19 Cold meal taken in for the anti-crusader (7)
20 A fine whisky to put in the beer! (4)
21 All that's left when you've paid by cheque (4)
23 Up-to-the-minute coal-pit reorganisation (7)
25 Socialised transport in Cleveland? (6)
26 One person who's ready to make an advance (6)
30 Strong advocate of taking a job when there's beer around (7)
31 Anger at expulsion – it's a scandal! (7)
32 It shows how long one can carry on (4,2,9)

DOWN

1 Understanding how to get a look-in? (7)
2 Obviously it's not worth twopence! (5)
3 One in a hurry to climb a pole? (6)
4 Air of a woman who has lost her head (4)
5 It's just like what they write in the ads (4)
6 What a mess the young can make! (6)
7 The money man sees one company go bust and ends in a bit of a fog (9)
8 First principle of resistance? (7)
12 One star turn in Congress (7)
13 Crazy about a possible space flight aim? (7)
14 He wants a lot of change without revolution (7)
17 Elm disease is unpleasant but sounds agreeable (9)
20 Mr Donat could be quite biting (7)
22 Asian polish-up that might seem to be different (7)
23 A lot of needling and you get the picture (6)
24 Permissive missive? (6)
27 Row about an artist in the gutter (5)
28 This place will do for the present (4)
29 Good comparison (4)

ACROSS

1 Key date of the theatre season? (7,5)
9 Moving house? (7)
10 Keep away from sea toil (7)
11 Small turnover in the coat trade (5)
12 Trying to get one to do the wrong thing (8)
14 Man of endless whiteness (4)
15 Jottings from the bank? (5)
16 Follower of the dead (4)
17 Is it Una seen around in Africa? (7)
20 The Scottish landowner hasn't finished the beastly place (4)
22 Same again please (5)
24 Made to go back for the cheese (4)
25 Spill the old lady's fragrance? Never, lad! (8)
28 Creature carrying very little weight (5)
30 No Times around to put a dampener on things (7)
31 It's monstrous to put that man in the wrong race! (7)
32 It's almost too late, except for light refreshments (8,4)

DOWN

2 Wall as a protection from an airborne mascot (7)
3 A writer is first with what's new (8)
4 Morris men's number (4)
5 Number one on the Stock Exchange-must be sound! (5)
6 The clique that won't quite grow up (5)
7 Occasion for afternoon drinking (3-4)
8 Is it considered poor entertainment? (7,5)
9 Rather a gasbag, the old reactionary (7,5)
12 Railwaymen's instructor? (7)
13 Doing imitations makes her cry (4)
18 Nothing new about being exploited! (4)
19 Simon had somehow to deliver a rebuke (8)
21 Well able to sing the delivery details? (7)
23 One aunt can be put in the back of the car (7)
26 In addition it readily produces salt-petre (5)
27 The premium choice is his (5)
29 The last you'll see of a hare (4)

194

ACROSS

1 A beer toll may be not too bad (9)
6 Eat like a winner (5)
9 Fundamental like church music? (7)
10 Style of vessel giving discomfort (7)
11 Alienate the wrong set on the mountains (8)
12 Retain difference of vision (6)
14 Something to eat in a foreign assembly (4)
15 Significance of earnest theatre-going (10)
17 Campaigner Mary finds a home for a top politician (5,5)
19 Run away with some cloth (4)
22 Not entirely elevating fruit (6)
23 One doesn't forget that White isn't wanted (8)
26 His work can be seen in the window (7)
27 In the US claiming to be Heath (7)
28 It's water under the bridge at Nottingham (5)
29 Name an attendant in the forefront of literary work (5-4)

DOWN

1 They are over there (5)
2 He gets what's left (7)
3 For those in a hurry to take off (6)
4 Having returned with the bacon for a game (10)
5 Catch sight of an Oriental snooper (4)
6 A bridal couple can be spotted with this (8)
7 Old bridge sale? (7)
8 Most common before little Virginia achieves fast time (9)
13 He's there for the asking (10)
14 Utterly declined to take privilege (9)
16 One for the women (8)
18 Do something that makes copy (7)
20 Childish means of making music (7)
21 She and a rep form a social circle (6)
24 Find just a little bit left (5)
25 Worry about decoration (4)

ACROSS

1 Just the dish Buck Jones might offer? (5,6)
7 Snake feathers? (3)
9 Praise what dieting has done for your figure? (7)
10 Group about to butcher for the pot (7)
11 There's time for it at the end of the morning (5)
12 The sort of sandwich you might get in Copenhagen (4)
13 Give the amorous eye (4)
15 Quite a stew when a piece of cloth is removed! (6)
17 Points into joints (7)
19 Fruity pair entangled on the bed (7)
21 Possibly arresting material for a kettle? (6)
23 Depressed by a little bit of fluff? (4)
24 Man of the church soon to lose his head (4)
25 One intending to be the first arrival (5)
28 Things were hard in those days! (4,3)
29 Send round pure ice for a person of discrimination (7)
30 The way some like it (3)
31 It forms the basis of many a good meal (6-5)

DOWN

1 Talk vaguely of making a batter cake? (6)
2 Take instruction from dear little Arnold (5)
3 Heated some chips, added stew with some chips again – it's quite a mixture! (10)
4 Let the wine breathe where down-to-earth procedures may be looked for (7)
5 Do they hamper those who carry them? (7)
6 One of two contemporary arrivals (4)
7 How the people of Sausage Town like spaghetti! (9)
8 Try cases in showy, stagy way (8)
14 The after-dinner chocolate flavour (10)
16 Pointer to an underground growth that could be nutritious (9)
18 Something to eat between rounds (8)
20 The abbey colourist has a point (7)
21 Unable even to be poetic in an eating-place (7)
22 Don't move if you want to keep food! (6)
26 Not much left after the slicing (5)
27 Fat ingredient of a popular dish (4)

196

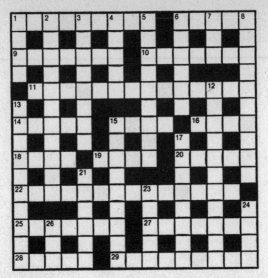

ACROSS

1 Bring in a worker of some significance (9)
6 A stupid person to bring back and so unfriendly (5)
9 Many jumped when given the axe (7)
10 Pippin not returning with the bones (7)
11 Late abode of a marching soul (4,6,4)
14 A quick word that can be cutting (5)
15 Break for something to eat (4)
16 This side for those on the left (4)
18 The end of all that waggery (4)
19 I'm all right—just wild (4)
20 They sound like imperialist ways (5)
22 Exploited country where a split might be expected? (6,8)
25 Ran road around the principality (7)
27 We and the French have it between us (7)
28 Fear of Red revolution when Christianity has been established (5)
29 Scattered enchantment and expired outside (9)

DOWN

1 Not far from a certain Chancellor's door (4)
2 Favouring the standpoint put forward for consideration (11)
3 Regretted being confined inside the plant (8)
4 Lead astray right into a tree (5)
5 Reversion to an earlier type of undersized fish? (9)
6 In which troops are in for a striking surprise (6)
7 Choose from among the top ten recordings (3)
8 You don't look yourself at this sort of dance (5,5)
12 In action in the theatre? (11)
13 Rolls to take a youngster around (10)
15 End of the golden road in the Uzbek Republic (9)
17 The art of copying cards? (8)
21 The girl in the network (6)
23 Gets ready to travel for peace, we hear (5)
24 Pleased to drop the old politician's burden (4)
26 Proper gift to the devil? (3)

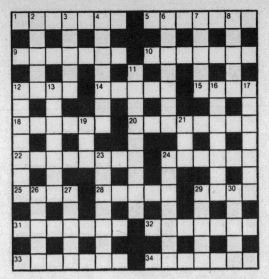

197

ACROSS

1 Not too well after the car accident? (3-4)
5 Time for musicians to cover the wound (7)
9 Bird thankful to be between a vehicle and the road (7)
10 One might miss one's footing on a day out (7)
12 Fight and get some knocks returned (4)
14 It provides coverage of the home front (5)
15 Accommodation for some of those revivalist enterprises (4)
18 Very small member of religious group? (6)
20 What a boon Boris starts before Doris the writer! (8)
22 Firing from a distance can be rather a gamble (4,4)
24 Grow up fast in Brussels? (6)
25 Don't expect us to finish the sacred song! (4)
28 Notch up twenty points? (5)
29 Chapter-head (4)
31 Having a preference that's not wholehearted? (7)
32 Hit back with the capacity to give a story (7)
33 Makes jokes about one's breathing difficulties? (7)
34 Not favouring Eva's Red revolution (7)

DOWN

2 Wrongfully assume little Prudence will shortly come up after us (5)
3 Discourage in wide terms (5)
4 Arresting document (7)
6 Hurried in the wrong gear to get something organised (7)
7 The point about a record warehouse (5)
8 Inviting one to go ahead without experience (5)
11 Testing time for supervising an offender (9)
12 Vessel that might cause death in the group (7)
13 It's noticeable about those who aren't with us (7)
16 It happens there are 10 speed changes (7)
17 Put on the pressure to get drunk? (7)
19 Childish reason for ordering salad? (3)
21 Try a little just to end the talk! (3)
23 Army taking a long time to find a prisoner (7)
24 Winner of a shop election (7)
26 The man with the wrong hat is a Tory politician (5)
27 The poet's feet (5)
29 Man leaving the plant to see a bird (5)
30 A last turn in the mountains (5)

198

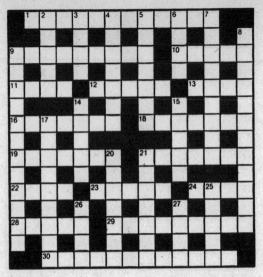

ACROSS

1 Mechanical picker proving rather a gamble? (5-7)
9 Colonial spot of rock (9)
10 Sound money hiding-place (5)
11 Some of the mercantile class in opposition (4)
12 Takes off in reverse to get the rest (5)
13 It's insulting to speak so indistinctly (4)
16 Lily's relative killed everybody inside (7)
18 The rate has to be adjusted at that place (7)
19 Result of using the exit? (7)
21 Indication provided by a dog (7)
22 Everyone getting to drop what goes round (7)
23 Russian agreement in the light of a Democratic Republic being formed (5)
24 Story of a southern chief (4)
28 Peculiar charm returning in a tram or a bus (5)
29 Strong dislike of the aim Tony is bringing about (9)
30 Isn't it dangerously late for morning refreshment? (8,4)

DOWN

2 Plunder some of the others for the machine man (5)
3 Terrible one at the front (4)
4 Sailor giving his friend everything (7)
5 Stream now in action? (7)
6 Cause one to give a scratch performance (4)
7 Very good at getting out of prison accommodation? (9)
8 There's no telling what's agreed in it (6,6)
9 Item of Liberal luggage? (9,3)
14 One's aroused when it's up (5)
15 At the end of a season it becomes a virtue (5)
17 Skill I suppress to provide something to eat (9)
20 Do better than a bird after a time (7)
21 Doing his best not to get shot, maybe (7)
25 Goodbye to all our French friends (5)
26 Carry on war for something to live on? (4)
27 That's all, just the two of them (4)

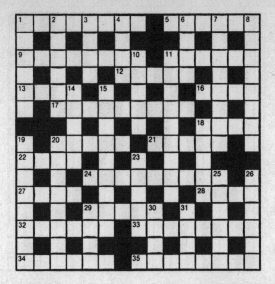

ACROSS

1 Try every one inside the drink box (3-5)
5 They could be pressed to provide the wine (6)
9 Better pair of spectacles mixed in a salad maybe! (8)
11 Plenty to eat in store for you here maybe (6)
12 Attempted to get the case disposed of (5)
13 A bear without a head will go round and round (4)
16 It might be offered as half-time drink (4)
17 There may be a clear reason for employing it at dinner (4,5)
18 Do up shoes to look decorative? (4)
20 Good man needed to catch fish—it's very hard! (5)
21 Swing wildly when I fall about (5)
22 Scene of a clean-up in the city (4)
24 Cement I am transforming into something edible (9)
27 Paddy's food offering (4)
28 Fish tea? (4)
29 Make a mistake by going round for some fruit (5)
32 Throws out a kiss in the course of disturbed sleep (6)
33 Writer of new oven catalogue (8)
34 Crazy Margaret provides a certain spice (6)
35 They go down enjoyably with beer (8)

DOWN

1 Sets of figures in support of meal provision? (6)
2 Reforms people found in sad disarray (6)
3 Unlucky cheese? (4)
4 Just a little when you find the place! (4)
6 See what the characters say (4)
7 Basis of deep trouble sprinkling salt around (8)
8 They pack in close when they're canned (8)
10 Good to eat with onions? Rubbish! (5)
11 Joint supporting Mary's follower (3,2,4)
14 You start thinking of a time that will never return (5)
15 Different ones are satisfied by varying the menu (9)
18 Call up about one, flower! (5)
19 Where Angus might go for a steak? (8)
20 Merchandise on the vessel where soup is made (5-3)
23 Express contempt when the salad starts with maize (5)
25 So exciting it gives you the shakes! (6)
26 So these cases make the philosopher's name! (6)
29 Miserable flower without a bell (4)
30 Yellow in white (4)
31 Advanced before Easter? (4)

200

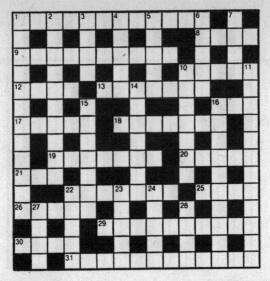

ACROSS

1 School for shippers? (12)
8 It may be instrumental in getting the loot back (4)
9 Press-button processing (10)
10 Any departure from the North Pole heads this way (5)
12 Since nationalisation, yours too (4)
13 They keep things moving in the road haulage business (7)
16 Shining foreign coin? (3)
17 Accessible part of the river? (5)
18 Nine vehicles started for the old city (7)
19 A prayer for door-to-door service? (7)
20 Cover some of the riots in the Mediterranean (5)
21 Always prepared to be agreeable (3)
22 Defeat after changing gear? (7)
25 Getting by when the food is dirty? (4)
26 Describing the possessions they have (5)
29 Dockland character finally on hand (10)
30 Vaguely indicate a disturbing sea phenomenon (4)
31 Treated very coolly with deliberate intent (12)

DOWN

1 He helps to keep the home fires burning (4,8)
2 Being there at a certain time to have some fun (10)
3 No longer wild, thanks to me (4)
4 Not the whole issue, just a proportion (5)
5 You may sniff but it could be sanctity! (5)
6 The spirit of those who are different (5)
7 One-sided point of departure? (4)
10 Religious ceremony to start court action? (7)
11 Old house not entirely of brick (4-8)
14 It makes singular progress along certain lines (4-3)
15 To avoid the storm, one takes it (7)
16 He helps to make the vessel go one way and no mistake! (10)
22 Old man going to sea (5)
23 One might be quite put out by it (5)
24 Not the gesture of a responsible person (5)
27 Part of the attraction of a good fire (4)
28 It's not moved to take you out to sea (4)

ACROSS

1 Pain? Maybe it's that long loaf! (6,5)
7 Sort of blonde like Hilary's head (3)
9 Trooped around causing damage to a vessel (7)
10 Sort of helping you can expect when a politician is host? (7)
11 Spirit of those that have been converted (5)
12 Rendering of part of a popular ditty (4)
13 Due to ring one day (4)
15 He can let you have food in what sounds a bigger way (6)
17 Saving of a firm when there's bad money about (7)
19 Explosive biscuit? (7)
21 Suitable sort of meal for the athletic type (6)
23 Before coming among the Canterbury pilgrims (4)
24 Tinned food puts a girl way in front (4)
25 Risked death getting the vegetables chopped? (5)
28 Use air to adjust her beat (7)
29 Oriental reason for exciting feeling (7)
30 Getting in is just like him! (3)
31 Sea-food certainly not eaten in strips? (7,4)

DOWN

1 Having had a swell time eating? (6)
2 The high cost of soil? (5)
3 Alluring picture of a tart? (10)
4 Railway lubrication man – is he chicken? (7)
5 Make a big change (7)
6 Experts at providing lumps of butter? (4)
7 Pointer to the hidden part that's nutritious (9)
8 Take time off for a shady oil manoeuvre (8)
14 Such dishes are different in degree (3,3,4)
16 Traditional food makes a change from boar's feet (5,4)
18 Hurry to provide an egg dish (8)
20 Had more than enough of mad Peter with the French inside! (7)
21 All that picnic food gets in the way! (7)
22 'Buy' is the most usual one – and it tells us how (6)
26 He doesn't seem pleased to tell us the town's news (5)
27 Keeping one's collar on shows breeding (4)

202

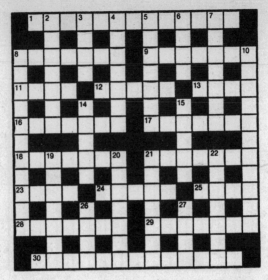

ACROSS

1 It's made a point of breaking away (8,5)
8 So great a change in warehousing (7)
9 A classified road walk has its points (7)
11 Prepared to let the outsider in (4)
12 Room at the top (5)
13 Complain of a vessel leaving the vehicle enclosure (4)
16 Starting to play tennis in church? (7)
17 Prepare to exercise pulling power (7)
18 The region that might be nearest (7)
21 Build-up of good wine? (7)
23 A route not taking one home (4)
24 Ruling faction taking most of the month giving thanks (5)
25 Baby Doll will call for her if pressed (4)
28 The German swallows the ice when he tipples (7)
29 It's made to undertake a future performance (7)
30 It's wonderful what he can do in a job (7-6)

DOWN

2 Among the first of the Army diggers? (7)
3 One vehicle might be Russian (4)
4 Supporter of the board (7)
5 Nonsense of an abrasive tendency? (7)
6 Basis for travel (4)
7 One's not at all pleased to take it (7)
8 Spokesman on the floor (4-7)
10 Turn up late to sex protest (11)
14 Bird with a pool in the city (5)
15 American woman taking the water in Norfolk? (5)
19 His wail might be interpreted (7)
20 Person with no side (7)
21 Slight breeze when one is used? (4-3)
22 Look at a former coal establishment (7)
26 Bird said to get stuck into the joint (4)
27 Time I left the nymph (4)

ACROSS

1 Delicate move of the belt after America suffers a reverse (6)
4 The King or one of his defenders on board (8)
9 Poland and Sweden have it between them (6)
11 Stop Parliament meeting for a time on behalf of some crook (8)
12 Make a bit of room on the island for a capital chap (5)
13 Not now a part of the authentic collected works (4)
15 Shut up to indicate approval maybe? (4)
16 It might make a difference to what's proposed (9)
17 Leg broken on the way between the hills (4)
19 Having a lot of points of crazy significance? (5)
20 Very good at suggesting something better (5)
24 Check about getting inside (4)
26 Whistle-blower or cause of obscurity, he's no revolutionary (9)
27 Occupied in displaying different colours (4)
28 As simple as Simon might be? (4)
30 It's a relief to let it off when your mates come round (5)
32 Not many people share power with him (8)
33 The place where the planes crashed (6)
34 Thrilling sensation provided by the bellringer? (8)
35 Port authority detectives aren't excited (6)

DOWN

1 Wrongly boast of taking time to cause damage (8)
2 Took on trust a bit of a line given by a girl in bed (8)
3 Retreat of the wild one (4)
5 Cape instrument? (4)
6 The kind to get things into order (4)
7 Get man a new look that's quite attractive (6)
8 It keeps going in when the sewer is working (6)
10 Uproar when a Communist starts to make a proposal (9)
11 Put on a colourful cover (5)
14 Dumb mason having a fling as the scourge of bureaucrats (9)
15 Express contempt at Rene's conversion (5)
18 Well known to have been set to music? (5)
21 No Queen can rule this country (8)
22 Made angry by something burning? (8)
23 Not one of Zimbabwe's black workers (6)
25 Grow like a vegetable (6)
26 Put your name down again if you want a get-out (6)
29 Means of transport held up by sleepers (4)
30 Read about the end of a monk (4)
31 Post for personal protection (4)

204

ACROSS

1 Nothing hollow about this! (8)
5 It takes a month to get a politician to go (6)
10 Bar everybody going behind the trees (9)
11 Is use to be made of the girl? (5)
12 Give a lift to an American (7)
13 He can cause a stoppage just by whistling (7)
14 Noted personality among leaders of a march, maybe (8)
17 Return visit about one tree (5)
19 Where a top person might live? (5)
21 The gallery for the citizen? (8)
24 He puts a word in for the opposition (7)
25 The chap in charge, it seems, can't read everything (7)
27 Try to find at least a vestige (5)
28 Finish taking a miner around in the gallery (9)
29 The sort of shame that makes you weep! (6)
30 Giving miners no cover (8)

DOWN

1 Ameliorate when there are some signs of tension (6)
2 Big round of lager (5)
3 Throw away something one has in hand (7)
4 A skill to exchange (5)
6 Quiet revolution in sea fuel distribution (7)
7 Diggers have got down under here (9)
8 Coppers about to make a brief return by deception (8)
9 Certain to be worried about starting to learn an instrument (8)
15 A ruler is on his own in one (9)
16 In which most people disagree with you (8)
18 That epic may be quite touching (8)
20 The company take poor Ellen to be Irish (7)
22 One might be held after being given to someone else (7)
23 Wanted in a hurry by an old city person (6)
25 Throw away a small piece (5)
26 It might be any place in Spain (5)

ACROSS

1 Try this instead (10)
6 Hang about to serve the consumer? (4)
10 Previous to being a religious head (5)
11 Counting feet possibly ruins game (9)
12 Having more than just enough (8)
13 Cause annoyance to superior people (5)
15 Hand-out for information (7)
17 Give her a mixed beer and she'll end up like the Queen of Malacca! (7)
19 He's made it out of a damaged reactor (7)
21 Clergymen's signals about vermin (7)
22 Shrewd enough to dress well? (5)
24 Blue lava could be worth a bit! (8)
27 It appears with dignity in a Landseer painting (9)
28 Not starting to get thinner in the middle (5)
29 Wine to pawn? (4)
30 Where eaters can take it easy for a start (10)

DOWN

1 Part of the tribe finds a month quite short (4)
2 Paper carrier not long in court? (5-4)
3 Some of the pretty rolling country in Austria (5)
4 There's a storm when the casual worker joins the wrong set! (7)
5 One may have a lot of pull in farming circles (7)
7 Otherwise known as a follower of Mohammed (5)
8 Where a girl in a smart dress might feel the pinch (5,5)
9 It seems very cool in our salad days (8)
14 African with a common name wielding the hammer (10)
16 Make allowance for distance from the equator (8)
18 Only one pussy in this part of Spain? (9)
20 Money received in connection with the meeting place (7)
21 Offertory prayer? (7)
23 Like a small picture of some jelly (5)
25 It's goodbye to the French Ambassador (5)
26 It's holy in the scriptures (4)

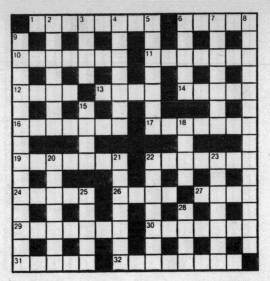

ACROSS

1 Agreement to get smaller? (8)
6 After a dull start an animal makes money (5)
10 Gets rid of the transport burden (7)
11 Get back and make a new demand (7)
12 Timber trade records? (4)
13 Where the mail is diverted to provide foreign capital (4)
14 Something revolutionary in the engineering workshop (5)
16 News of the rise and fall of water? (7)
17 Contributing to the music of fuel distribution? (3,4)
19 Cab seen not to be around here (7)
22 Shelter at the end of the passage (7)
24 Tempestuous spirit (5)
26 Weapons put back to be comfortable (4)
27 It might bring one up to scratch (4)
29 Cargo from a different seaport (7)
30 The talk of Rome (7)
31 Bright spot for a coal merchant? (5)
32 They're kept going by fuel deliveries (8)

DOWN

2 Forced to make big dole changes (7)
3 It's hard to get from tropical forests (4)
4 Attacks when a lass is in trouble (7)
5 Nora and Dot might give sailors rough time (7)
6 Describing Prince Philip in terms of Edinburgh (5)
7 Associated with a party hiring a ship (7)
8 He can provide what may be needed for a build-up (6,8)
9 Order to move fast under pressure (4,5,5)
15 Soon to be briefly unknown (4)
18 Pay rent to him if he's got land (4)
20 Does he run off when he should be on the bridge? (7)
21 Relax when comfort is not on the menu (4,3)
22 Man with some pull in the transport business? (7)
23 You might get a look-in from here (7)
25 It might convey something on the road (5)
28 Germans agree to start vacating the island (4)

ACROSS

1 People in partial confusion governing us (10)
6 It's our responsibility (4)
10 Think how to make a light return (7)
11 Railwaymen might cause a stoppage here (7)
12 Truth as to evidence of debts causing party dissension (8)
13 The ones to give direction to a doubter shortly (5)
15 Scope for shooting in the mountains? (5)
17 Not interested in arranging a mail trip (9)
19 Ship about to be taken in by an aircraft (9)
21 Classical means of communication in South America? (5)
23 Mark is bad about expressing gratitude (5)
24 Likely to turn Bob paler (8)
27 Make one's mark by claiming to be a journalist (7)
28 Time to be unyielding (4,3)
29 Require to get the French off the point (4)
30 Like a space traveller lacking in gravity (10)

DOWN

1 Drink to the Left! (4)
2 Brief allusion to the weather in chorus (7)
3 Having no skill in taking a pet round (5)
4 He finds a way of being first in chapel (9)
5 Homes for lay performers (5)
7 Baron involved with eleven in Africa (7)
8 Separate country in the North-east (10)
9 Poem going beyond speech, it seems (8)
14 Calling for a declaration? (10)
16 Little England has Ernie rattled as a skilled man (8)
18 Keep repeating that there must be a poll (9)
20 This used to be quite enough for instance (7)
22 Farming carried on up to pension time (7)
24 It's a bit sticky if the sparklers aren't real! (5)
25 A fight that's going round (5)
26 Brown girl taken around by an old soldier (4)

ACROSS

1 Vegetables discussed with kings (8)
5 Poor performer at making a pie maybe (6)
9 It may hold tea for a scantier brew (8)
11 Not quite space to leave the car when cake's wanted (6)
12 Chair material? (5)
13 Give Heather some fish (4)
16 We're pushed around and put in jug! (4)
17 Fruit and vegetable (9)
18 Endlessly fat fruit (4)
20 Money not earned by making the joint juicy (5)
21 One of a pair involved in a row (5)
22 The man with the editor shortly gets attention (4)
24 Celebration meal for runners? (9)
27 No water added to mess it up (4)
28 Make a mess of the left-overs (4)
29 Plant as basis for a stew? (5)
32 Just a little bit sweet? (6)
33 Contents of a New Year's cup? (8)
34 Business time and trouble (6)
35 Isn't rare mixture but gives a clear cup (8)

DOWN

1 Wrinkle like a shellfish (6)
2 One of the bunch making a sweet split (6)
3 Split peas in the recess (4)
4 They may give a vision of Oriental compliance (4)
6 You can include him in a balanced diet (4)
7 Make a tart the Derbyshire way (8)
8 Must rant madly in rages (8)
10 Scope for old-fashioned cooking? (5)
11 One of those who are eating out (9)
14 Maybe a railwayman will protect you (5)
15 It's laid out to receive a food drop (9)
18 Shove a pound inside for material luxury (5)
19 Refreshment for the Cockney's mate? (5,3)
20 Blasting food substance? (8)
23 Nero's head in a bag as something to eat! (5)
25 There's one in town for the singer's love (6)
26 Drink after drink (6)
29 Glided way over the top (4)
30 It enables one to see a Scot's supporters (4)
31 She might make a comeback in Handel's *Messiah* (4)

ACROSS

1 Last time for Napoleon, first time for the Wilson Government (7,4)
9 Offensive old boy refusing to let the Sioux change ends (9)
10 The panic ends when Dr Zhivago's girl is given a new name (5)
11 One direction is quite enough to try (6)
13 Set forth why you're in favour of sterling (8)
15 Social Conservatism early in the week (6,4)
16 Unpleasant person one might put one's foot on (4)
18 Absorbed in getting a parcel done up, say? (4)
20 Laundry not returned is in a state! (10)
23 Put too much on the table? (8)
24 From which one might get beer or a shot (6)
26 Active as one might be when up (5)
27 Talking like Jack the toad? (9)
29 It's his job to manipulate the hard stuff (11)

DOWN

1 Government killer whose work is suspended (7)
2 Ex-president not getting on – that's nothing! (3)
3 Entertaining spot for a fiddle (4)
4 Mad to be first to get stuck into the beer! (10)
5 A small capacity for excess profits tax, one may take it (6)
6 Say something about the old city height (7)
7 They're produced for us to buy, not necessarily to eat (8,5)
8 Old man with extensive support able to take to the air (5-4-4)
12 Go-ahead folk take it, laggards swing it (4)
14 Happening now and then to describe a table (10)
17 In certain cases he was able to rule (4)
19 Bond's incentive payment (7)
21 Starting at the bitter end, the dog! (7)
22 Get down for a match? (6)
25 He gets a bit of grub out of the cave (4)
28 Beast of American clubman (3)

210

ACROSS

1 Saw one of Tom's friends taking plum du.·f (7,4)
7 Make·a hit in glamorous set-up (3)
9 Double the business with some crazy milk container (7)
10 Not pleased to be getting unemployment pay (7)
11 Eager to make adjustment to achieve harmony (5)
12 A little bit of a cat? (4)
13 Stale stuff, this cereal (4)
15 Reduction allowed for the meat eater (6)
17 Demonstrators in difficult weather conditions? (7)
19 Sea-food you pay the postman for? (7)
21 Spend a lot on soda-water? (6)
23 Atmosphere you find in a French restaurant (4)
24 Song girl losing her head (4)
25 Make an impression when you score (5)
28 Such a trite remark, I'm bored to distraction! (7)
29 One politician can go around to make things better (7)
30 A member of the Welsh flock (3)
31 Room to prepare meals in a small way (11)

DOWN

1 Gathering for the gregarious (6)
2 Zero mark for film quality (5)
3 Offer a lion chop as meat! (10)
4 Take away from trade distribution when caught short (7)
5 Not the place for an alfresco meal (7)
6 King getting beer from the greengrocer (4)
7 Little creature among enthusiasts for surplus food (4-5)
8 The quality you don't get in bitter beer (8)
14 It enables one to put pressure on in the kitchen (7-3)
16 Given low treatment by the chef? (9)
18 Hurry to take a science walk (8)
20 Take in what's come up (7)
21 After a lifetime it's his turn to produce a sort of omelette (7)
22 Food said to raise a smile (6)
26 Our trouble in a race for fish (5)
27 Go down where the washing-up's done (4)

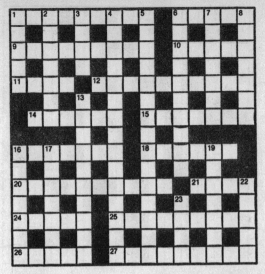

ACROSS

1 The weaker sex stop the stronger sex (9)
6 Fish like endings (5)
9 Adjective for set hours of prayer (9)
10 'More in sorrow than in —' *(Hamlet)* (5)
11 Before the North Spring Bridge (4)
12 Woman's under and outer garment make one for the farm (5-5)
14 He stinks! (6)
15 Acted like a ham (7)
16 The funny chap is one for an Indian game (7)
18 Forsaken in the South East, returns and registers (6)
20 A poet's circle is taken aback by your old-fashioned manipulation (10)
21 Hurt in the Spanish Armada (4)
24 Fish half of it right out (5)
25 Unfortunate girl returns to one egghead in the end (3-6)
26 In a possibly rude situation, a number raise objections (5)
27 Odd Eric holds a dollar (9)

DOWN

1 Hamlet's twisted threads (5)
2 Stamp the label and put what belongs to me outside (7)
3 In undergoing interrogation, in extremis, the cardinal is . . . (4)
4 . . . not telling anybody anything (15)
5 Maybe old, maybe choice, maybe Caliph, but is certainly long-headed (15)
6 They have achieved their driving ambitions (10)
7 Domestic pet would hear the name of Wild Cherry (7)
8 'As the hope-hour—its sum' *(Hardy)* (7)
13 There's a priest (Christian) in her flying machine (10)
16 Planned by boy underground (7)
17 The caterpillar that gives a wound to another crawler (7)
19 Student—his plate might be nearer (7)
22 After me, the fish is served up with wine (5)
23 'And "—" Stuck in my throat' *(Macbeth)* (4)

212

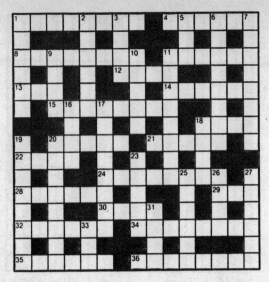

ACROSS

1 A film about the wood is badly distributed (8)
4, 10 down. But it isn't when it is sung (6,5)
8 Market town where it's the fashion to follow five in a row (8)
11 Father's attempt to make a top for mincemeat (6)
12 Leaders of pantomime in London's Lyceum having a little ball (4)
13 'They will — like wolves and fight like Devils' *(Henry V)* (3)
14 Fasten the account in that odd arrangement (6)
15 Drug and ship abroad (8)
18 The position of one toy (4)
20 It can't be explained but the Wise Men note . . . (5)
21 . . . the bright light and eastward look (5)
22 Bird makes love in bed (4)
24 Measure last for shoes, e.g. (8)
28 Composer orders transport at one (6)
29 One to two pounds are bad (3)
30 Choose a roll (4)
32 Handsome street greeting to French nude (6)
34 Wild ass – see – it's going about in a natural manner (8)
35 See 31 down
36 The Magi's star seen in the window? (8)

DOWN

1, 23 Pantomime Fairy Queen gets the bird (6,5)
2 Mistakes made in baking smaller ratafia biscuits (6)
3 A bit of Christma. decoration puts up the stakes (4)
5 She gives aid – of a sort! (3)
6 Enter cat – for the interval (8)
7 Do they stock up as stocking fillers? (8)
9 Critically examines the surgeons (4)
10 See 4 across
11 Pilot saw ruined East End district of London (8)
16 The vehemence of the attack! (4)
17 Sloth, with left foot in the river, gets the instrument (4-4)
18 Put up a time – space result (4)
19 Harbinger of snow? (3,5)
20 Doctor Spike is about to employ a soft-leaved plant (5-3)
23 See 1 down
25 Spying the mince pies, the little boy finishes them (6)
26 The title goes up, and it's 'Hoar-frost' (4)
27 Small private room near the top (6)
31, 35 across. Speak bluntly about what might be for dinner (4,6)
33 Treat us to the Third (3)

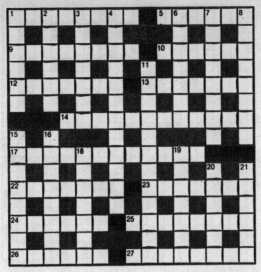

213

ACROSS

1 Town is against dividing the food (8)
5 Fighting and saying it's capital (6)
9 Light carriers (8)
10 Not just an amusing occasion that hasn't got started (6)
12 'And wisely tell what hour o' th' day The clock doth strike, by ---' (Butler) (7)
13 Girl leader of toll-gate wreckers (7)
14 Royal husband has seven letters in print (6,6)
17 He travels round with a horse (5,7)
22 Foolish fish (7)
23 Mean girl found in time (7)
24 Those who worship or those who work (6)
25 Studying student, and being paid for the job (8)
26 By the sound of it, indulges Oriental creatures (6)
27 We hear Cockney's description of flood, in tears (3-5)

DOWN

1 He needs one more for his sweet wife (6)
2 No cardinal is over age and under age (6)
3 From one who drinks, I am to take a bribe? How awful! (7)
4 Novel fashion in ridiculing (3,9)
6 The beautiful Miss Lee (7)
7 Stiff way of presenting the cards (8)
8 Tirade interrupts cautious act of protection (8)
11 Orestes, eg (5,7)
15 Sect governed by Father Time (3,5)
16 Wagon carrying rope and leather (8)
18 Eleven (7)
19 'A woeful ballad made to his mistress' — *(As You Like It)* (7)
20 In days gone by, a dutiful Catholic (6)
21 'Being holiday, the —'s shop is shut *(Romeo and Juliet)* (6)

214

ACROSS

1 The coldest part of the Atlantic Yacht Race (3)
5 It sweetens the gentlemen in black velvet, having swallowed 14 (8)
10 In rising, priest gets the next man confused (6)
11 Many found at a sale (3)
12 Caterwaulers back strict censor with musical direction (8)
13 Carpet for a stately home (6)
14 'Methought I was enamour'd of an —' (Midsummer Night's Dream) (3)
15 Made fun of the money put back (4,2)
18 York hobo goes to pieces beside the bishop's staff, rightfully or wrongfully (2,4,2,2,5)
21 Two articles in underwear, not up to much (5,3,7)
25 He suits the comparatively healthy (6)
26 Shorten the strike (3)
28 Author, one with very long arms (6)
29 Public performances where claret is served very freely (8)
31 Wanton dress (3)
32 This should smooth things down at a fight (6)
33 Discovered, the little boy shed tears (8)
34 Directed plummet sounding (3)

DOWN

2 Birds, and noises of birds (5)
3 They've never been seen yet on an island (5)
4 Drink to one taking care of the colonnade (7)
6 Not in love, note! (3)
7 One Special Constable is to summon up a hermit (7)
8 Sound to drive away a politician coming in for a wash (7)
9 A smoker, he could be a snob (9)
16 Bends the Spanish fiddlesticks (6)
17 Hut with one room, or one and another, that is! (6)
18 A number under the bed outside made a bad mistake (9)
19 Poem—do half of it in Old English (3)
20 Sailor has to climb to desert doomed ship (3)
22 Fed up with silly little detectives' faults (7)
23 It moves like a wheel up and down (7)
24 A student, a cheat and a flower (7)
26 She puts many to the test (5)
27 'The hour is ill Which severs those it should —' (Shelley) (5)
30 Half the German songs give a wrong impression (3)

ACROSS

1 Fate that is fixed before scoring a goal (14)
9 'Love on the Dole' speech (7)
10 French city with another word for 'fewness' (7)
11 'O noble English! that could — With half their forces' *(Henry V)* (9)
12 Boy secretes a bottle (5)
13 Insects that spit up round the hour (6)
14 Has funny coloured leather (8)
17 Briefly admitting you and me and M (8)
19 Dreadfully sad foreign soldier in a vehicle drawn backwards (6)
22 Take possession of Queen Teresa's heart (5)
24 Found his stable in ruins (9)
26 Gold people love a lover (7)
27 Adjective for splendid cast (3,4)
28 Not being noticed enough, it's put below (4)

DOWN

1 To pair, one is naturally disposed (5)
2 He once performed and now he claims his rights (7)
3 Perhaps GI is put out by these mottoes (9)
4 Japanese poems written by one among the army vehicles (6)
5 Drug-yielding plant (8)
6 A good card for a good fellow (5)
7 It's a rotten refrigerator if icebox conceals a small opening (7)
8 Three hundred and one only delivered in whirlwind fashion (8)
13 Where do the Everest climbers hope to go? (2,3,3)
15 Reforming a bad girl, I rebel (9)
16 Where one waits along with worker, Queen and Dutch uncle (8)
18 Coming in with the Doctor to lance the bird (7)
20 Gleam of light, it's possibly in the valley (7)
21 'You would — to the divine perfection' *(Longfellow)* (6)
23 Stretch of open country is strange with no street (5)
25 Engineer coming in had hurried (5)

216

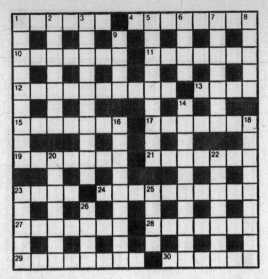

ACROSS

1 He precedes dainty character in Shakespeare (6)
4 Something to be tacked on (8)
10 'While I stand on the — or on the pavements gray' *(Yeats)* (7)
11 Carriages with second strips (7)
12 The unlettered one should get into another form, with note (10)
13 Money left to rebel army (4)
15 The answer to why . . . (7)
17 . . . town carriers get very warm (7)
19 Blue-back footwear – look! (7)
21 Oriental tangle has become neat (7)
23 Fellow with vehicle marked for test to come (4)
24 See Mrs Dark, perhaps, or Madame Mantalini, maybe (10)
27 Lifting fruit by string (7)
28 'The bird of dawning — all night long' *(Hamlet)* (7)
29 Two of our features in one (3-5)
30 Finishes palindrome on piano (4,2)

DOWN

1 Gun with oddly square hub (9)
2 'I seem to tread on — ground' *(Addison)* (7)
3 Poor Sue's gone under, though shortly about to possess urban property (4,6)
5 Pretend boy is up to collect (9)
6 Some of the 'free' were in jug! (4)
7 Shark, from the animal angle (7)
8 Corruption of master, married to assistant secretary with sex-appeal (5)
9 War-god has nothing for the beginner (4)
14 More than one compact way of serving meat and greens (10)
16 The old brother among the crew makes a bloomer (9)
18 This could be short to one in a put up job (9)
20 Running dogs I have put below (7)
22 Low ornaments from some joint over a back street (7)
23 Evil twenty minus four (5)
25 Another ornament – made of southern wood (4)
26 National leader has nothing on the horse (4)

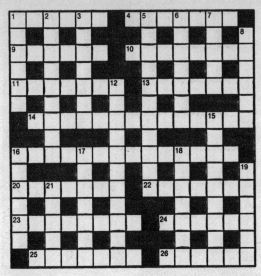

ACROSS

1 He thinks himself superior to others (6)
4 Make a hole in the carrier (7)
9 Norma and Sir John in Love, for example (6)
10 Food of the gods laid out by Sambo with a curious air (8)
11 Something to do with nature study (7)
13 'He purchased—and forebore to pay' *(Kipling)* (7)
14 'Panorama'—a sight made into a series—they're fantastic! (14)
16 Tom, Dick *or* Harry (3,2,3,6)
20 Being rather old-fashioned, I am at first at a complete standstill (7)
22 Gets rid of boy, hiding irritation (7)
23 Sound receivers (8)
24 Girl embracing Prince from the mountains (6)
25 Before and after the proper time for a clergyman (7)
26 More than one saw this sad, sad age (6)

DOWN

1 Lozenges round in the middle (6)
2 In a panic, left China with a divided facial feature (5,4)
3 'On the green banks of —, when Sheelah was nigh' *(T. Campbell)* (7)
5 Dim composer composed again and made a concession (11)
6 Handing over the vase in the ring (7)
7 The material that is left is the French (5)
8 Hymn in the German translation (6)
12 Dispersing them, Charles gains protection (5,6)
15 Sounding for at least the third time (2-7)
16 She has stuffed him with fish (6)
17 Opening numbers, lit up about right (7)
18 What Tweedledum and Tweedledee became? (7)
19 Flowers seen at Harvest Festivals and in Easter services (6)
21 He diminishes the fruit little by little° (5)

218

ACROSS

1 Spendthrift poet (7)
5 Food or fog? (3-4)
9 Marine commander, sheltering in rock, warning of bad weather to come (5-4)
10 Swimmer coming round specifically for support (5)
11 In turning a deaf ear, Don is obviously frightened (6)
12 The Spanish, surrounded by letters of credit – all abandoned (8)
14 Botanist at the mountain is in the New Testament (10)
16 Adjective for certain district and dwelling (4)
18 Grim party goes to the old town (4)
19 Facial feature of one Pinch in 'The Comedy of Errors' (6,4)
22 Everyone in front gets neuralgia (8)
23 'And Jacob — seven years for Rachel' *(Genesis)* (6)
26 Book of Psalms without any Psalms? It makes for change! (5)
27 Removes some of the restraining harness (9)
28 Complicated studs into which the French struggled (7)
29 Afternoon departure of a dark lady (7)

DOWN

1 It's a shame about us providing support (7)
2 Call up is all right in the evening (5)
3 Crystals from a dreamer (8)
4 Mauretanian rising up into space (4)
5 Capable of grasping her in sleep, perhaps (10)
6 Third man overlooks two directions leading to willows (6)
7 Doggedness – or mulishness? (9)
8 Board for the painter (7)
13 Follower with temperament and drive (10)
15 Lops head of Titan, scattering centaurs (9)
17 'Trip no further, pretty —' *(Twelfth Night)* (8)
18 Bold boy is in a clever position (7)
20 It's sad being ordered about by society perverts (7)
21 The bay that provided shelter for Daphne (6)
24 Uranium in the valley fetches a price (5)
25 Ring Academician in the battalion for the port (4)

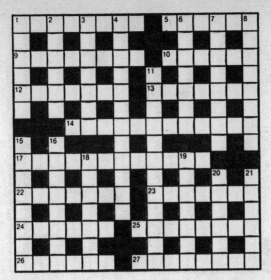

219

ACROSS

1 Demure girl in league with conservatives (8)
5 Chestnut backed by simpleton (6)
9 He works a tragic affair at a height (8)
10 'Time, a — scattering dust' *(Tennyson)* (6)
12 Peter MP is secure as first comer (3-4)
13 It goes round, forward and back (7)
14 Vegetables? Well, they are part of the course (6,6)
17 London playhouse song – 'Out at Three' (5,7)
22 Many grow old, in spite of it (7)
23 Sturdy daughter, one before the Queen, is the more staggering (7)
24 One-eyed pointer (6)
25 White heron (8)
26 'The heavens rain — on you' *(Twelfth Night)* (6)
27 Cards dealt out to a pupil teacher – he needs spades (8)

DOWN

1 One side of stage suits concert piano to a T (6)
2 Skating attendants put me in a nice outfit (6)
3 It shows where the driver might be going (4,3)
4 Not being able to see the horizons Codlin's partner saw (5-7)
6 A snob's model or a Shelley poem (7)
7 Fisherman's assistant takes a dram, supposing that the canvas is up (5-7)
8 Sweet girl, not of one's family (4-4)
11 Coketown matron (3,9)
15 Dance company, after 'The Roman Priest'. . . (8)
16 . . . do well with 'Love, the Magician' (8)
18 Overall creeper (7)
19 Random character takes stick to boy (7)
20 Composer scores six, up to half time (6)
21 Chaldee to take precedence (6)

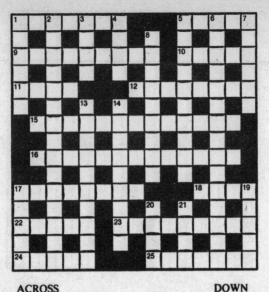

ACROSS

1 Song composed by a nymph (7)
5 'O sweet Fancy! let her —'
   (Keats) (5)
9 Musical trifle (9)
10 Happen the dog follows the
   commander (5)
11 Girl going right, boy going left (4)
12 Film made by a busy person, going
   with a swing (8)
15 He poured oil into a man's wounds
   (4,9)
16 This is *more* than the limit! (6,3,4)
17 This is not true, but it's about the
   right rubbing (8)
18 He ought to succeed, he has one
   right (4)
22 Box is to take the French racehorse
   (5)
23 One parent is in a fit theatrical part,
   very long and rambling (9)
24 Outfits wrapping oriental birds (5)
25 'If you wish in the world to advance
   Your merits you're bound to —'
   (Ruddigore) (7)

DOWN

1 Cottages and carriages about one
   inch! (6)
2 One way of getting out of creek—we
   leg it like mad round the harbour
   centre (3,6,6)
3 One way in eight (4)
4 In Leo's London Town (4)
5 Be quick! (4,6)
6 Funnily enough, on a columbine,
   one can be very rarely seen
   (4,2,1,4,4)
7 Infuriate, eg, the musical composer.
   Turn everything upside down! (6)
8 A cheap way of sending messages (9)
13 'Skill of a doctor with broken noses'
   —put it in (10)
14 Denry Machin on the council sends
   some packing! (9)
17 Loud, long and limp side (5)
19 Magistrate is about to meet the
   woman (5)
20 G.I.'s expression for a couple of
   curves? (4)
21 When it is hard, it is ready (4)

ACROSS

8 Queen's Latin coin possibly irrelevant (15)
9 Slave, eg, making a border (7)
10 Drag the leg that's drooping (4)
11 Keep front half of taxi in control (6)
12 Fibre obtained from whistle-fish (5)
13 The elegance of a young thing, we hear (4)
14 Expert style, we hear, catches a little grebe (8)
16 Failure to follow suit (8)
19 Foundation of many sauces (4)
21 Seize returning man for the VIP (5)
22 Flags and flowers (6)
24 Palindromic essence (4)
25 Short honourable love song sent back by girl (7)
26 He pops her sconce for a natural light (15)

DOWN

1 'When pain and — wring the brow, A ministering angel thou!' *(Scott)* (7)
2 Eye-catching quality of one's cousin's cups (15)
3 Being cut off is nothing, tail on somehow (9)
4 Adjusted the pattern you are looking at (7)
5 Palindromic musical composer (5)
6 First aider (9-6)
7 Vehicle No. 501 AC offering cordial! (7)
15 Rude manners of the Rabbi's ram (9)
17 Taking care to rise about one, he causes pain to the listener (7)
18 '—d with flowers, I fall on grass' *(Marvell)* (7)
20 It's not fastened – by gum! (7)
23 Palindromic Eastern Kings (5)

ACROSS

1 Fatty suet is cut up for the fat container (7,6)
9 One in deep trouble in the next sorry shift (9)
10 Ban also incudes a Baron (5)
11 'War's —s will cloud into night' *(Hardy)* (5)
12 Bears wreck to each inroad of the sea (3-6)
13 Animal, with one on or off, he's the same (3-4)
15 Chirping of a nitwit, terribly nervous (7)
17 Town article written by a cad (7)
19 Ironing out time (7)
21 Telling this on oath amounts to perjury (9)
23 Philosopher holds film class in town (5)
24 Incur fury of Scandinavia (5)
25 Viking eg takes number on to work passage (9)
26 Red setter (lady) spoilt the holidays (3,6,4)

DOWN

2 The one who gets support is the worker with a hangover (9)
3 In fact, he's ripped a ligament of the foot (5)
4 Relation on *Below Stairs* (7)
5 Abstainer holds up menu for a bit of sponge (7)
6 Grave of Roman god, in English (9)
7 Riotous rumba casts a shadow (5)
8, 20 Fairy Queen gets the bird in Pantomime (6,5)
9 Bad mark given in the same bad tests (5)
14 I notch one to California, all the same! (9)
16 Art ruby, it can be paid in tribute (9)
17 Stick to Latin in this locality (6)
18 Sound fruit suits me to a T (7)
19 Heighten the measure over the arc (7)
20 See 8
22 'And the hopeless — was laid in rest' *(Chesterton)* (5)
23 Primate, reverse of religious, when in bed (5)

ACROSS

1 The one of Italian is It! (12)
9 Less than half this number (4)
10 One not free to write dreadfully bad novels (9)
12 'I'll speak in a monstrous — voice' *(Midsummer Night's Dream)* (6)
13 Critical Miss Dench meets the returning layman (8)
15 Company and Monsieur engage to settle by mutual concession (10)
16 Considers the oceans sound (4)
18 Where to keep 27 after a shuffle (4)
20 I do elegant anagram for deputation (10)
23 The art of writing advertising copy (8)
24 One gets up to display flags (6)
26 Seize by fear (9)
27 Unusual case for cards (4)
28 To which a girl belongs (3,6,3)

DOWN

2 Larry has the bug badly, making a nightly entrance (8)
3 Girl who may sparkle in print (4)
4 Defeated leaders in Paris who fell off (10)
5 He comes from the South and also from France and the East (6)
6 Just fancy! (7)
7 No necessity to set south between the rocks and the headland (12)
8 Mr Thumb and Mr Tiddler's drum (3-3)
11 Dirty dog, right in front of worker, gets the fruit (5,7)
14 I am a triangular structure and an obstacle (10)
17 There was no stylish one for Daisy Bell (8)
19 Adjective for certain hats and houses (7)
21 It has an arch to show how the army should march (6)
22 In this place, the superior County stick together (6)
25 Not used in Mid-Lent (4)

224

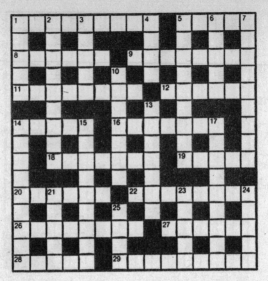

ACROSS

1 Mix the cocoa, and with a bit of luck, make a hot drink (9)
5 Refuse to banter (5)
8 Magnates get the heavy lazy fellow to go back to the doctor (6)
9 Biblical scourge and Hebrew measure quietly secreted in a Biblical Mount (8)
11 Scheme with Italian at summit (8)
12 Might be a box for the films (6)
14 Take steps to discover these troublesome creatures (5)
16 Leave one belt on (7)
18 He faces the facts concerning one border (7)
19 Priest seen in a Roman Catholic survival of the past (5)
20 The right swimmer is the wrong sort of man (6)
22 Foretold before the artist's return (8)
26 Sam returns to fellow creature (8)
27 Adjective for certain beads and books (6)
28 Guide the young animal (5)
29 Obsolete coin (9)

DOWN

1 Picture paper (5)
2 'Is the Queen to follow the music-maker?' writes one of the co-ordinators (9)
3 The game's up – right in the middle deck (5)
4 Reproduce part of the sketch (4)
5 Plant with spicy seeds (9)
6 'I — from dreams of thee' *(Shelley)* (5)
7 Enthusiast almost static; that's queer! (9)
10 Song about a bounder in Paradise (7)
13 After the Yorkshire pudding, we hear why some hens are kept here (7)
14 Girl dividing Father and Mother's pictures (9)
15 Entrance for those who may well entrance (5,4)
17 Fruit retailer among the stalls and boxes (4,5)
21 Smack, in a sense (5)
23 Band breaks up (5)
24 Town hat (5)
25 Eat between meals (4)

ACROSS

1 They pull out the footboards (10)
6 Tailor and executioner, drink to audience (4)
10 'Fear wist not to —' *(Francis Thompson)* (5)
11 Pain breaks the rule again (9)
12 Heap of stones beside mine, making 16 (8)
13 Choose a cut, we're told, for this meal (6)
15 In USSR, John gains a brief advantage (4)
16 Manor Wight (4)
17 Job was finished before he began (5)
20 'Kitchen —s and nursery-mishaps' *(Crabbe)* (5)
21 Pair taken from pretty artist (4)
22 Miss Elliot's worthless admirer departed (4)
24 River pests! Call the coppers! (6)
26 Claim as one's own town in Yorkshire, not the capital (8)
29 Clean woman – to a certain degree, she was the cause of her husband's death (9)
30 Mathematical poisoner (5)
31 Eagle-eyed in spotting the Lesser Nelumbo (4)
32 Rod taken with care for minister in ward (5,5)

DOWN

1 Soak, he half kept in step (5)
2 Cook to beat the boar's head main course (5,4)
3 The curse of Pindar, for example (6)
4 Diana's German plaits (10)
5 A right round-up for sale up north (4)
7 It carries ideas of Swedenborg and others (5)
8 Coconut, an oddity as an interim payment (2,7)
9 Dog teeth (7)
14 Term for a wife (6,4)
15 Peruvian Prince, climbing island, is drunk (9)
18 He needs more than a cod-piece (9)
19 As clues go, this is a sweet anagram (7)
23 Ethel said Mr Salteena's was stuffy (6)
25 'Nihil rei' meant nothing to him (5)
27 Home in the highlands (5)
28 Welsh gilt edged strip of leather (4)

226

ACROSS

1 King and Prince finish up in a peculiar Gothic style (13)
9 Graceful turning of a neat leg (7)
10 Adjective for a certain language and lantern (7)
11 Lace for Iris (5)
12 Warm covering given back to barbarian (9)
13 Possibly cold and certainly strict (5)
15 'The answer lies between right and left and is put in the gallery.' Interpret this! (9)
17 Underground dwarf heard the time-keeper (9)
18 Look round, silly—and catch! (5)
19 He is cruel, putting the chaps between two rocky heights (9)
22 Cast of unusual worth (5)
23 Man's fourth age, according to Shakespeare (7)
24 Liked putting letter in a tree (7)
25 He is morbidly anxious about dry coach—hop in! (13)

DOWN

2 Look intelligent, Euphrasia! (9)
3 Snap up about fifty ideas (5)
4 This is not an honour for Nick (5)
5 'A largess—, like the sun' (Henry V) (9)
6 Warning beforehand and possibly later, too (5)
7 Playwright who plays on our emotions (13)
8 Hockey's 'mid-on'? (6,7)
10 Get coat altered for country residence (7)
14 Book two players on the first of December, a short month (9)
15 Part of a pig or horse (7)
16 A USA trail at fault, but Sydney's there (9)
20 In general, lying down helps one to recover (5)
21 Epitaph on city (5)
22 In fact, a piratical animal (5)

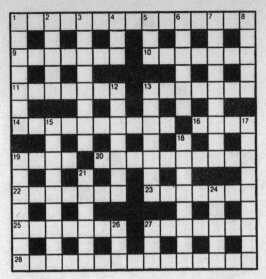

ACROSS

1 Part of the ship where fellow left snake (9,6)
9 Lachrymose (7)
10 Honour you can carry off, one takes it (7)
11 Doubter may be unduly thrust forward (7)
13 Visionary Doctor, a mere lunatic (7)
14 'Hearts just as pure and fair
May beat in Belgrave Square
As in the lowly air
Of — —!' *(Iolanthe)* (5,5)
16 One container is open (4)
19 Mass for a corpse (4)
20 Musical instrument for a large tea-party (10)
22 Very many fellows in one bed causes a remark (7)
23 Poem by Swinburne (7)
25 The French note the Monarch is without (7)
27 Bishop of Barchester (7)
28 Note journal shows general placebo has got approval (11,4)

DOWN

1 Beds containing heavyweight materials (7)
2 Foolishly met an intended (5)
3 Inflowing stream of wealth (8)
4 Wicked Willy's heart (3)
5 Grub's up – that's the point (3)
6 South wind brings the flower out about the middle of January (6)
7 Mix jorum dram, sergeant! (4-5)
8 Rubbish or revolver? (5)
12 Plain fish is supplied in the contingency (7)
13 Reduced the strength? The instrument inside did! (7)
15 Pocket-companion (4-5)
17 Food and drink on the piano takes some rearrangement (4-5)
18 The first half is heard if the second half is pulled (4-4)
19 Rustic, but endless, flatulence (7)
21 I'm wool and cotton – iron me out! (6)
24 Girl in gold coming up for broadcast (5)
26 Servant who might be a cheat (3)
27 Some of the group eat a little vegetable (3)

ACROSS

1 First get round the man in command (6)
4 Bird with forehead, and crown (5,3)
10 Title: 'Saloon' by Lovelace (7)
11, 28 Departing with law, rewritten by ruler of note (7,3)
12 Hard cash – cause of strike (4)
13 Ringer needs the whip for risky job (4,3,3)
16 It's hateful upsetting the party with admissions of debts (6)
17 Field of view shows Queen in conveyance (7)
20, 21 Cathedral murder victim (6,1,6)
24, 26 Thoroughgoing punter, drenched in a storm (7,3,4)
25 Part of the idiotic auditory (4)
27 Little holes seen in the rug in the porch (7)
29 Now is the time for a gift (7)
30 'For — she and sweet attractive grace' *(Milton)* (8)
31 Iris's part in 'The Tempest,' amended suitably (6)

DOWN

1 Little Robin's infancy? (8)
2 Musical instrument producing endless harmonies with some measure of sonority (11)
3 Saint Mark in the kitchen (4)
5 We wandered outside, getting pricked (8)
6 Some claim their dragging for information would be useless (4,6)
7 Witchcraft turns Nigerian upside-down (3)
8 Deputy left the English channel (6)
9 'Farewell the neighing —' *(Othello)* (5)
14 The best part is about the ticket torn up by the eleven (7,4)
15 'Books, and my food, and — —' *(R.L.S.)* (6,4)
18 What motorists did with second hand goods (4,4)
19 Town post suited to people of fashion (8)
22 Essays the quarter-sessions kirk (6)
23 It should be kept strictly by musicians (5)
26 See 24
28 See 11

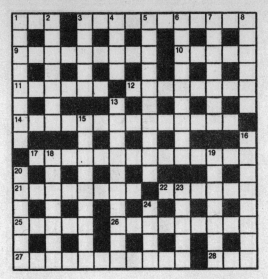

ACROSS

1 Bird served as main dish (3)
3 A backward county, in short, gets a tangled mass or mixer (11)
9 Laurel, perhaps. Hardy, certainly (9)
10 Peaceful message from lunar module (5)
11 They have arms in church (6)
12 In mistake, Rose nearly gives us the stuff to burn (8)
14 Bird tears red ribbon to pieces (5-9)
17 Brighton has taken in the old railway, restoring its old name (14)
21 Take two off here (8)
22 Dancer gives decoration in exchange for money (6)
25 They are much admired fish, love, by the French (5)
26 'As if his whole vocation Were endless —' *(Wordsworth)* (9)
27 Out of mourning—see—the Dauphin! (11)
28 Gold coin or note (3)

DOWN

1 President is cut short with a certain strong demand (8)
2 'The poor man had nothing, save one little—' *(Samuel)* (3,4)
3 Messenger gives us a leg up (5)
4 Drinks made from apples, not very soft (4)
5 Begin with Reger composition, some call it 'pop' (6,4)
6 A grand place to be buried in (9)
7 Some of these clues? (7)
8 The garment for a tomboy (6)
13 Being anxious about the plumage (10)
15 Right name, wrong dream (9)
16 'Hail horrors, hail—world' *(Milton)* (8)
18 Where a cricket score goes against the grain (7)
19 There's nothing in this unusual script about 'imaginary circles' (7)
20 Unstable in business (6)
23 Robin of song (5)
24 Child gets the time wrong (4)

230

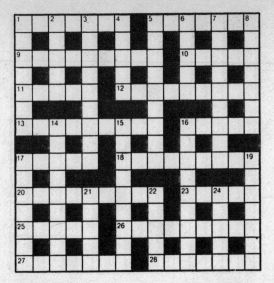

ACROSS

1 Stow away before sweet, in case of a navigational hazard (4-3)
5 They are barely seen (7)
9 'Like dull —, numbing pain' *(Tennyson)* (9)
10 Motor-cycle went with very little spirit (5)
11 Scene in which we are naturally interested (5)
12 It lights up the scene of actor's torment (4-5)
13 Involving giant line out (9)
16 Exclude this arrangement of sliced bread (5)
17 Tear-jerker (5)
18 Handel composition of three notes, with one repeated at a certain time (4,5)
20 For example, crabs are cactus – this is very odd! (9)
23 Sedate robes refashioned (5)
25 'Are not — and Pharpar rivers of Damascus?' (5)
26 Inhabitant of India meets a Dickensian character (9)
27 Hide nothing in the bureau at home (3-4)
28 Poet and essayist (7)

DOWN

1 Descend horizontally (7)
2 Cut right inside the hollow (5)
3 Is love nothing in Latin seclusion? (9)
4 Gives out a second after time is up (5)
5 Giant, also, could be longing for the past (9)
6 Perishes, with a thousand pocketed coins (5)
7 Hot ash put under a fence for a time (9)
8 Leather worker, senior, about 22 (7)
14 Grind to a powder (9)
15 Pipe the King's daughter into the pub, as a prelude (9)
16 Stop an unseemly display from the Syrian capital (9)
17 Feature of cider country or town in Somerset (7)
19 Greatly pressed (4-3)
21 Ironically blame the shape of TV aerial in the army vehicle (5)
22 Muddled theologian, in drink (5)
24 Accounts for the hatchets (5)

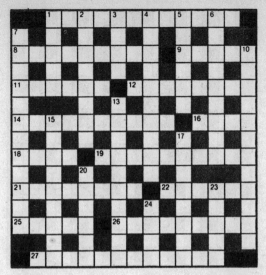

ACROSS

1 Senior, pleasing a Dickensian character (8,4)
8 Irritating habit (4,5)
9 Filthy lucre, a continuing source of evil (5)
11 Lionel's letters in metal work (6)
12 16 lines at least to re-list in another order (8)
14 One of a pair, nobly titled (10)
16 Her uncle married her and made love (4)
18 King – and founder of the Samaritans? (4)
19 Local Queen with gentle spiritual illumination (5,5)
21 Girl, not so much the end, as unresponsive (8)
22 Designed for being drawn, it needs 12 feet (6)
25 It is in the rent-charge (5)
26 How the decimal system works – on this I have concentrated (9)
27 Far removed from the Cheshire Cat, who would love it (7,5)

DOWN

1 A sort of thing in the Red King's dream? (5)
2 'Their aid I thus —, Though I forget their name!' *(Princess Ida)* (8)
3 Banter from the bar (4)
4 Rare oil set into very small tubes (10)
5 Check up on first county . . . (6)
6 . . . putting it up in short for England after OK labelling (9)
7 Unhappy hunting ground of the Red King (3,3,9)
10 Came up often to sound a note for the song (4,2,6)
13 Since evil rises, convulsions put an end to the art of prize fighting (10)
15 Rather slow river in the French Jewish quarter (9)
17 Duke with his own carriage (8)
20 Made from a tree growing up among the crimson red lance-woods (6)
23 One chimney, one among the topless towers (5)
24 Pertaining to the ear of the Indian corn initially (4)

232

ACROSS

8 Where the wet typist comes from? (4)
9 Nightwatchman or storeman perhaps? (10)
10 Two comic cats coming in so abruptly (8)
11 It is hard there is no race in Kentucky! (6)
12 Old gipsy cheers up, heart and soul (6)
13 Scholastic union is to bring out of the egg—a bird! (8)
15 Wild nymph's cry, once, to music (8,7)
18 Animal cut in two by a trap—it's not fair! (8)
20 Can not back the Swiss division (6)
21 Eg Witch goes round in the end (6)
23 The true note first—it is heavenly! (8)
24 Strange aim—to study animal growth and vegetable growth (10)
25 Returned objections—'It is blunt,' 'It is stunted.' (4)

DOWN

1 Prophet wraps up remark in something comforting (10)
2 Bird of ill omen (8)
3 A fierce person to protect the silver within (6)
4 Law officer summons solicitor and soldier (8-7)
5 Bird is male and adult as well (8)
6 A croon composed for a floral trumpet (6)
7 Undiluted bull! (4)
14 Play that disturbs cool air at sunrise (10)
16 I shut one in order to excel (8)
17 Put black against white, eg (8)
19 Lunatic and I as nymphs (6)
20 Fish given to the right band of warriors (6)
22 Cleopatra's attendant gives up the garment (4)

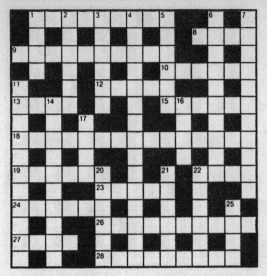

ACROSS

1 Wrongly positioned Motorway ran round French lake (9)
8 The French look for a French composer (4)
9 Afterwards, in a test, this becomes three-sided (10)
10 '—, unhonour'd, and unsung' *(Scott)* (6)
12 Healthy report (5)
13 Morning letter expressing assent (4)
15 Festival held in a temple – as term implies (6)
18 Hyphened, like Baden-Powell (6-9)
19 Cavalryman from America in rash retreat (6)
22 God of marriage has no Eastern song of praise (4)
23 'A countenance more in sorrow than in —' *(Hamlet)* (5)
24 Extremely uncommon artist precedes all the others (6)
26 Too narrow-minded and misguided to train Len (10)
27 Hawk easily taken from the spinney, as it is very young (4)
28 It is part of our system to strengthen part of the prison (5-4)

DOWN

1 Evangelist and his cross, possibly (4)
2 Dark girl meets us coming up (6)
3 Note catalogue given out by the instrumentalist (6)
4 Eg, Puck could be in our magic Act V, right at the finish (15)
5 Deceive the townee about the Spanish (6)
6 Friend understands Father as one having seniority (10)
7 Travelling under direction in old Yorkshire (5,6)
11 Undesirable player (4-7)
14 Queer saint queerly mounted (10)
16 Cuts, reducing taxes by a fifth (4)
17 Possibly a leaf-insect (4)
20 Desert one on a fixed allowance (6)
21 Young swimmer from the lake, in French grey (6)
22 There's often a body in the body of this car (6)
25 Dye extracted from vanilla (4)

234

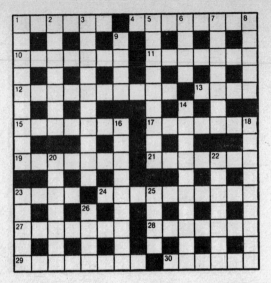

ACROSS

1 They came from China and kept in step (6)
4 Empress has a Society accent (8)
10 To agree entirely (7)
11 Re-write list in the Scottish Order (7)
12,23D Classic building causing Scottish ire (10,5)
13 Making love to a girl, he practised birth control (4)
15 A putrefaction causes freedom from blood poisoning (7)
17 Near it, I might show disinclination to move (7)
19 Letter written by philosopher-saint brings to light . . . (7)
21 . . . a more vigorous measure, embraced by leader of Women's Lib (7)
23 Record slipped in as 'High Spots' (4)
24 Odd places, part barrows (5,5)
27 Lay broken tile and give a name to . . . (7)
28 . . . coin I half seized for a Russian flower (7)
29 'The music, — like a god in pain' *(Keats)* (8)
30 Grew a flower in a pollen-basket carrier (6)

DOWN

1 Goddess sheltered by a powerful Prince (9)
2 The object of the Infanta's visit (3,4)
3 'A dreadful fate You'll suffer — — — *(The Mikado)* (3,3,4)
5 Adopting the name of a Sunday (9)
6 He succeeds with her, and one is introduced (4)
7 Stuff money into the crooked seat (7)
8 'O Caledonia — and wild' *(Scott)* (5)
9 Perhaps only one herald (4)
14 Combine two scenes in the last one of all (10)
16 Silly pansy, he is like a doomed Corinthian (9)
18 Come round the new set, it's likely to be a show-stopper (9)
20 'New Foes with an Old Face' (7)
22 Italian girl rises like a mermaid (7)
23 See 12
25 Produces egg covers (4)
26 Blow the heads up! (4)

ACROSS

8 Decorator's warning (3,5)
9 'Art remains the — — possible' *(Browning)* (3,3)
10 Cancer, for example (6)
11 This is a colouring matter (8)
12 How oddly she clued the programme (8)
13 Food coming in instalments, the listeners might think (6)
14 This falls between the Ides of March and All Fools Day (4,3)
16 Semi-bib designed for drinks (7)
19 This is functionless in the gate, so it opens backwards! (6)
21 Chum is only partly adept as a fence (8)
23 Purple thyme oddly planted in a street (8)
25 Dog has eaten dog-collared one! (6)
26 Silent characters made to enrol (6)
27 Restrained, or it might become clean mad! (8)

DOWN

1 Introduced Richard to the Saxon in *Ivanhoe* (6)
2 'This — is, as I take it, a kind of lethargy' *(King Henry IV, Part II)* (8)
3 Damp record on our generation (10)
4 Representation of a unicorn's head in good condition (6)
5 Doctor on 'The Mother of Nokomis' (4)
6 Counsellor takes chaps to west country hill (6)
7 Bearing a vehicle (8)
13 Smug little compositor with odd issue of 'The Lancet' (10)
15 In any case, an Athenian drug (8)
17 Train made from tin crust (8)
18 Summary of book 'Under the East Philippine Islands' (7)
20 The last of the beef (6)
22 Spotted little girl meeting little boy (6)
24 Even *one* is abominable! (4)

236

ACROSS

8 Lord of the Marbles (5)
9 Government officer came awkwardly into the scheme (8)
10 Scanty food, but sweet (10)
11 Team with a pretentious air (4)
12 Where to make the answer stick (6)
14 Qualified Doctor passed over on condition it is included (8)
15 Independent worker with a skin disease (4)
16 Britannia, eg (5)
18 Royal suicide (4)
20 Rich lode producing a bleaching agent (8)
23 Engineer, drowned in the bath, showing a sign of life (6)
24 'Scots, wha hae wi' Wallace —' *(Burns)* (4)
25 Supporter of dictatorship with a broken sob introducing the musician (10)
28 It's not right to approach the team (4,4)
29 The composer in contact with it is shortly coming back (5)

DOWN

1 Operative given honour in New Cinema (8)
2 This is in the German tongue – what a bore! (4)
3 Barmy Beys born with a false sense of values (8)
4 It takes place in the Whitsun, or perhaps, Easter recess (4)
5 Frank is able to overlook palindrome (6)
6 The flippancy of some literature about fliers coming to grief (10)
7 Two old pennies in a Cheshire town procures a cut of mutton (6)
13 My red robe casually enshrouds one contriving pretty needlework (10)
14 Dark spot in crystal staff left inside (5)
17 Rewrite heartless 'Tale of a Tub' and reduce to a synopsis (8)
19 'Merely corroborative detail, intended to give — verisimilitude' *(The Mikado)* (8)
21 Reduced by 50%, a number inhaled (6)
22 Not an upright type (6)
26 Adjective for certain beds and boxes (4)
27 Try a match (4)

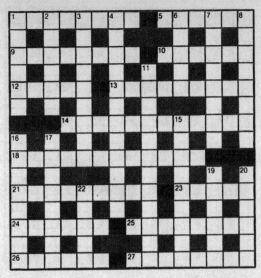

ACROSS

1 Author is sympathetic about the Queen (8)
5 Vessel made of wood and tin (3-3)
9 Drive with a string for the seaweed (8)
10 Inca leaders become giddy in rotation (2,4)
12 'Doing nothing with a deal of —' (Cowper) (5)
13 They hinder the observers going round the ruined castle (9)
14 What the fiddler may do to show he has some guts (4,3,5)
18 'Subject to the chances, the —s of existence' (Henry James) (12)
21 Primate in right school recess finds corresponding material (4-5)
23 Broken horse prop (5)
24 Plate of bone given back for the dog perhaps (6)
25 Tea-time's altered for the judging (8)
26 The bird is heard and the seal is seen (6)
27 His cohorts gleamed in purple and gold (8)

DOWN

1 The least feminine Oriental goes to the Occident (6)
2 Cut short the felicitations. Head must leave and get out (6)
3 Pub visit in mind? Ring a neighbour (5,4)
4 The English, in straits, covering dicey way out (6,6)
6 Girl's upside-down plant (5)
7 (8)
8 Unique press (8)
11 Foolishly, he apes sister and denies right of private property (12)
15 Low limb in New York is naturally lit (9)
16 Injuries inflicted by Backbite and Co. (8)
17 Leaving out nothing, I'm coming up to Tooting, minus a pair of spectacles (8)
19 One Republic therefore joins another (6)
20 It has a tunnel cut before noon (6)
22 Quiet slow race (5)

238

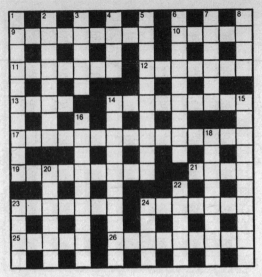

ACROSS

9 'Glossy purples, which — All
   voluptuous garden-roses'
   (Tennyson) (9)
10 Place below (5)
11 Letter posted inside seemed badly
   written for the manor-house (7)
12 Longfellow provides
   accommodation (7)
13 Who has one at the request stop? (4)
14 All get on splendidly with
   Veronica (9)
17 Brownie gets the bird. Well done,
   mate! (5,10)
19 Held back the side at scrum (9)
21 Relation seen in the haunted room
   (4)
23 Since coming round, the French
   make no noise (7)
24 Kipling wrote of these years (7)
25 Very severe plane crash (5)
26 It's only paste (9)

DOWN

1 Poet's media overvalue the poet (10)
2 It destroys two riotous mobs at first
   (4,4)
3 Coupled by Miss Austen with
   sensibility (5)
4 Tool which cuts into a bad zecchino
   (4)
5 Race with the girl in front finished
   with no one to see (10)
6 The very young have squandered the
   fund, and strip inside (9)
7 In this dithyramb, let us go as fancy
   leads (6)
8 Carriage one enters warily reluctant
   (4)
14 One of summer's drawbacks, as
   mentioned in a Shakespeare sonnet
   (5,5)
15 Game poaching is legal here (4,6)
16 Quaintly saintly and heartlessly not—
   possibly both at once! (9)
18 'Strew the — hearse where Lycid lies'
   (Milton) (8)
20 Aline's turned into another girl (6)
22 Adjective for kleptomaniac's palm
   (5)
23 Springs up to put down the students
   (4)
24 Dress up the object exciting pride (4)

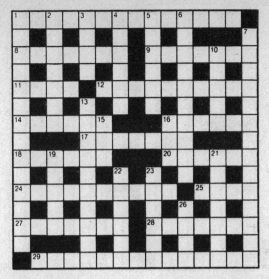

239

ACROSS

1 Typical figure – is it back to a hundred? (14)
8 One is given the sack with retrospective regret, totally unprofessional (7)
9 James, perhaps, given 'time' – ie, captivity (7)
11 Adjective for certain wheels and whiskers (4)
12 Arrangement for sinking (10)
14 Nothing written by the French about the theologian being sat on (6)
16 Put feathers on top of further shelf (6)
17 First class return to flower country (7)
18 New depots, as advertised (6)
20 Ten about to snatch the catch (6)
24 Doing river turned out to be more important (10)
25 Capital harbour (4)
27 Inactive state? One might be near it (7)
28 Wine served with the right bird – his is bad (7)
29 'There is room here for only — — — Americanism' *(Roosevelt)* (7,3,4)

DOWN

1 150 work at hot plate in Austria producing an awful sensation (14)
2 Conflict that takes the mutilated dead around for granted (7)
3 The last word is one given to the servants (4)
4 The sailor to receive a shield (6)
5 Automatons with right and wrong boots (6)
6 At 'The Red Rising Sun' first deposit the port (10)
7 He should know which way the wind is blowing (7,7)
10 Chaps put in a small advertisement – 'Repair Needed' (5)
13 The soft Oriental lace is overvalued, and also seen through (10)
15 Pheasant's brood is kicking up a row! (3)
16 '—, my lord, —! a soldier, and afeard?' *(Macbeth)* (3)
19 Beleaguering a company of herons (5)
21 Rebel leaders grudge the postponement (7)
22 All imagine there's some fish at the end of the queue (6)
23 Wind round three quarters – a sharpish blow (6)
26 King and Poet (4)

240

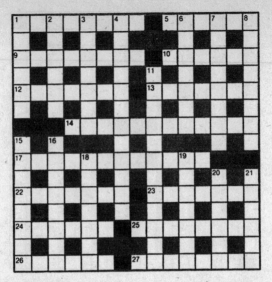

ACROSS

7 Cook takes a long time to make soup (6)
8 Animal food for a Shakespearean character (8)
10 Return game on the Sabbath is Bridge (4)
11 Elastic contrivance; give it back to me for a season (10)
12 Mongrel, not off his meat (6)
14 Odd noises made between two Poles causing curiosity (8)
15 Little notice is given to the rhyme, it is unfavourable (7)
17 'His glassy—, like an angry ape' *(Macbeth)* (7)
20 Benjamin and theologian now oddly lower themselves (4,4)
22 Drink that suits the bobbies to a T (6)
23 Fellows pass before many miles (10)
24 Look both ways (4)
25 Party leader who covers the country home? (8)
26 Send out a meal about one (6)

DOWN

1 Settle for an enclosure around the house (8)
2 Fine material for an open space (4)
3 The third one might be it (6)
4 Loving the fuss that's made over the pledge of betrothal (7)
5 Possibly nine secret police in Jersey (10)
6 Confines a number of loose women (6)
9 The first book production (7)
13 It will take measurements ie, do the lot somehow (10)
16 Briefly, Thomas and Charles are much engaged in getting a bag for food (7)
18 Trust the old politician on the Council of Europe to understand credit (8)
19 Ask where they used to sing (7)
21 The times of the obscure Cheops (6)
22 Plague the French for a pound (6)
24 He brings down the curtain, we hear! (4)

242

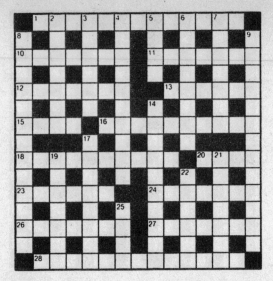

ACROSS

1 Men and porter chap bring about a renewal of cordial relations (13)
10 Sudden spate destroying our huts (7)
11 One little piece, only half of it is liable to fall into pieces (7)
12 Inhabitant of ancient France, and his awful French! (7)
13 Listeners may think it's a vendor in the room below (6)
15 Loosen some of the ground on the top (4)
16 Unfortunate combination of poor leading actor with a revolutionary (3-7)
18 Autumn account with acknow-ledgements of debts is all wrong (10)
20 A French gentleman with half inch old ruler (4)
23 My reed somehow effects a cure (6)
24 What one may wear in very early life (7)
26 What one may wear for very informal occasions (7)
27 One who experiments with odd prime numbers (7)
28 Mistakenly, I march in front with liturgy written by an abbot (13)

DOWN

2 'These thoughts may startle well, but not —' *(Comus)* (7)
3 Drag in Peg to complete the circuit (4,2)
4 Concerning the eyes of a number understanding the work on high tension straw (10)
5 Literary drudge scores a notch (4)
6 Animal feature in a soft-leaved plant . . . (5-3)
7 . . . and what that animal often is (7)
8 Patient enduring protracted painful illness (4-9)
9 Doctor Henry first of all takes many up into a queer disco to make a study of liquids in motion (13)
14 She once cut out a shield (10)
17 Forbidden food, by the sound of it, put down for a Mediterranean swimmer (4-4)
19 I'm coming up, taking a drink out for the cripple (7)
21 Shrew puts out bits of a rusk in the mean time (4-3)
22 John Gilpin's trade (6)
25 Isle of Man Royal Marines (4)

ACROSS

1 Palm this affair off! (6)
4 Small coin, farthing, to hand for some fuel (8)
9 Assuredly there's nothing in this burlesque (6)
10 Position in name only secure in a reshuffle (8)
12 Pot plant tender is a girl (8)
13 Trial or treatment? (6)
15 'O make this heart rejoice, or ---' *(Cowper)* (4)
16 Cart back the rods, they're not metric (10)
19 Peltasts get the bird put back among the sailors (10)
20 Trade on the coast (4)
23 Free nutcrackers, that is, to a Duke (6)
25 Make rough and tumble separate (8)
27 One way of making local calls (3,5)
28 Ostrich has no love for Owl (6)
29 'Guys and Dolls' location (8)
30 There's nothing here to rank with a Royal family (6)

DOWN

1 Re-fold facsimile (7)
2 Meet forgot old girl (9)
3 Tru'y poetical country upriver (6)
5 Galatea's shepherd (4)
6 Correct errata, including 'be deviate' (8)
7 Phil's instrument (5)
8 'Eyes have they and see not' *(Psalm CXV)* (7)
11 'The justice of it —' *(Othello)* (7)
14 Speech given by old copper in a uniform (7)
17 Burning Haydn's work, half the MS is hidden (9)
18 King, he cares about the investigation (8)
19 Trunk call (7)
21 Chinese fruit (7)
22 'Thou unnecessary —!' *(King Lear)* (6)
24 Stick up by an old maid (5)
26 Hands up for a change (4)

244

ACROSS

8 Bass line with Italian madly in and out (8)
9 Monkey rushes about (6)
10 Animal, a tame one, in old Siam (6)
11 Heavy book about fuels is heavy going (8)
12 Castor or Pollux, eg (4)
14 Inclination to bestow a gambling piece to the centre (8)
16 Putting off patricians or not, is out of order (15)
18 Land army gets into a state (8)
20 Adjective for certain rags and rings (4)
22 Guide the nail on to the wood (8)
23 Dance with two mugs (6)
25 Have nothing to do with the row about the animal (6)
26 'Stain the white—of Eternity' (Shelley) (8)

DOWN

1 Built by Romans, yet somehow the brothers live in it (9)
2 Swelling style with no Latin in it (4)
3 Half recommending the closure (6)
4 Mimsy or slithy, eg (11,4)
5 This successful result might be the ruin of it (8)
6 Boy is to give song to North London district (10)
7 Strange game (5)
13 Dicky relation appears to be an actor (10)
15 Lady of the Lake? (9)
17 'Consider—, only don't cry!' (Through the Looking-Glass) (8)
19 Period that sounds rotten (6)
21 Artist comes in to make an offer for the embroidery (5)
24 Tidy cow (4)

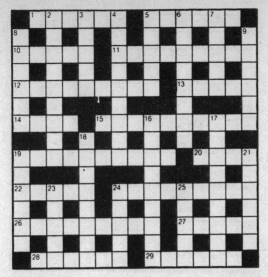

ACROSS

1 Let me trip about (6)
5 Tell about the deceased (6)
10 'Where'er you —, the blushing flow'rs shall rise' *(Pope)* (5)
11 Horrifying experience near one of the moon's areas about the end of August (9)
12 What competitors should do, even at the top (5,4)
13 Girl introducing Australian port (5)
14 Tax that which is due (4)
15 Figure written in pencil, 50, in the end denotes the germ-killer (10)
19 Pointing out a large number in India, it returns a lesser number to the East (10)
20 Cards . . . (4)
22 . . . often this (5)
24 Abnormal narrowing of a passage (9)
26 Heavenly food (5-4)
27 Delius's Fair in Lincolnshire (5)
28 Adjective for certain fish and furze (6)
29 Mine props two letters against some stones (6)

DOWN

2 Irregular trade, even, is weakened (9)
3 Boy comes up to me with a decoration (5)
4 The most delicate trees tend to go wrong (9)
5 Just Conservative (5)
6 Seducer wrapped up in a tablecloth – a riotous affair! (8)
7 Possibly rated as traffic (5)
8 Unemotional and hard about the end of Pat (6)
9 Stay where you are – Mother's in control (6)
16 Author in the beginning takes ship for town on the firth (9)
17 Giving the address from Uncle Trig's letters (9)
18 Sunk by a Dickensian Captain in South Dakota (8)
19 Adjective for certain club and corn (6)
21 Hammer left hidden in natural growth (6)
23 'For e'en though vanquish'd, he could — still' *(Goldsmith)* (5)
24 Post the prize (5)
25 Pole takes a public carriage to the Queen (5)

246

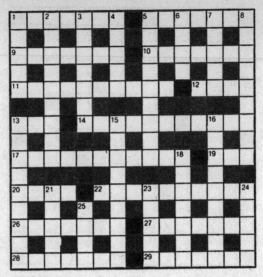

ACROSS

1 Lovable modest query (7)
5 Managed to get everyone taken separately in colour (7)
9 Ordinary one born in the end to become one marked for the Church (7)
10 Part of the ship adding up to over 2m (7)
11 Where to choose a bag, they say (10)
12 Phantom fish with two parallel tails (4)
13 Little girl scores a hit (3)
14 Am in love with island district – it relieves pain (11)
17 Boy monk with secret X marking religious area (11)
19 Game needing the backing of a monkey (3)
20 Smack, with two masts (4)
22 Part of car park lent to lunatic (6,4)
26 State of faulty airstrip (7)
27 'Convict in loathsome situation (Hamlet) (7)
28 'All for your —, we are not here' (M.N.D.) (7)
29 Permissive characters (7)

DOWN

1 Behind one, down river and up river (5)
2 Guide for the honey bee (9)
3 Printed material has a place in the British Academy (7)
4 It has a fragrance which has been written up in timeless verse (5)
5 We hear two boys rode the easy way (5,4)
6 Flower song, by Shakespeare's Bottom (4)
7 To amass is difficult? There's nothing in it! (5)
8 Dead runner left money for medicine (9)
13 Planking down food, and more food (4-5)
15 Clumsy Lenin Gate – alter it . . . (9)
16 . . . and please to make a space for driving in (9)
18 Plant down a thousand and two Biblical characters (7)
21 Motionless apparatus (5)
23 Bar served up a feast (5)
24 Plausible set up of boats (5)
25 String underwear for someone in Lear (4)

ACROSS

1 Stacks a hundred lights (6)
5 Triangular structure is a shed, and there's money in it (8)
9 The locks of young 25 (4,4)
10 Stands drinks all round in the crush outside (6)
11 Little Albert and I divide the routed terrorist army (12)
13 He has a warm coat, but sounds naked (4)
14 Good man in miners' churches (8)
17 Search one on interrogation (8)
18 Scrape this fruit (4)
20 Terribly raw golfer comes to study a colourful plot (6,6)
23 This can show where the speaker came from (6)
24 These are made in a tray for drinks (3,5)
25 'John—my jo, John' *(Burns)* (8)
26 'Woodwind' author with manuscript (6)

DOWN

2 He is not to be relied upon to put up the guard (4)
3 Lay down conditions or frame the charges (4,5)
4 'Cloudless climes and—skies' *(Byron)* (6)
5 Extraordinary pearl in a Martian Roundhead (15)
6 Get off the Hell Hill! (8)
7 I ramble up and race down (5)
8 Irritation produced by the antlers (10)
12 Member of the party gives note to the old tax collector (10)
15 Territorial Army contains possibly natural spinner (9)
16 Only a fool esteems such fertilisers (8)
19 Venomous computers (6)
21 Women's possible answer to this question (5)
22 Cartload of grease (4)

248

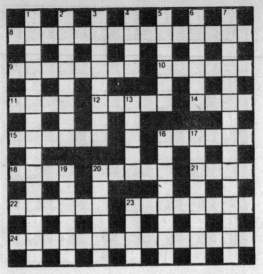

ACROSS

8 Funny! A lame horse put in place of a legislative body! (10,5)
9 He starts putting spirits into the beer! (8)
10 Old penny boiler (6)
11 It may jut out the odd inch (4)
12 Town that hid Polonius (5)
14 Out-and-out row (4)
15 Consented to a deadly sin (6)
16 Unpleasant character is sorrowful first and repentant finally (6)
18 Sweets returned by the offensively complacent (4)
20 'In modest or most seemly fashion' *(The Tempest)* (5)
21 Awkward boor is left out (4)
22 The way in which a Master embraces a girl (6)
23 Game where we may see a player in a huff (8)
24 After tea, Mrs K. has somehow to begin again (4,1,5,5)

DOWN

1 Let the cat out of the bag and made a present of the bag (4,3,4,4)
2 Allegiance without, eg, a treaty (8)
3 Where you may see some creatures writing out a yarn in Shakespeare (8)
4 'Where each second Stood — to the first' *(Othello)* (4)
5 Lots of flowers (6)
6 Tomboy garb (6)
7 Very eager girl sums up the sailor requested to go outside (2,4,2,7)
13 Boy given the keynote for sonata's last movement (5)
16 Fellow feeling caused by heartless story about my upward course (8)
17 'These violent — have violent ends' *(Romeo and Juliet)* (8)
19 A number on horseback overturned by a flier (6)
20 Saint on current contest (6)
23 Cooks some hares and some rabbits (4)

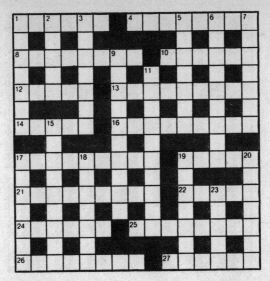

ACROSS

1 Brother with school hat (6)
4 Eggs on county runners (8)
8 Steward making a conservative investment (8)
10 Shakespearian servant, one in three (6)
12 A book: *I Excuse* (5)
13 Cut herb for a vulnerary (9)
14 '— is Heav'n's first law' *(Pope)* (5)
16 Paris worker has name in odd *Time and Tide* (9)
17 Three directions point to a road that's cleared (5,4)
19 Student gets two notes in the whip round (5)
21 'Fitted for — and nearest prose' *(Dryden)* (9)
22 Robin with two note song (5)
24 Fly, vulgarly (6)
25 'Turn it up!' as the hen said to her mate? (4-4)
26 'With some sweet oblivious — Cleanse the stuff'd bosom' *(Macbeth)* (8)
27 Novel hat (6)

DOWN

1 Duck not a duck (7)
2 Showing weariness in the backing I unnecessarily give (5)
3 The ego obvious in a Dickensian character actor (7)
5 Steal up to the all-wise musician (7)
6 Red cotton has got twisted (9)
7 Dutch uncles come up with the rare iron (7)
9 They cause a shortage of greenery (10)
11 The most respectable clothes are altered by us, and then set out (6,4)
15 Attire to draw all hearts, maybe (5,4)
17 A cover up in the main part of the chancel (7)
18 Fluted and ornamented round top of turret (7)
19 He applauds important part of *The Chimes* (7)
20 Point disturbing country jailer (7)
23 A sound round island (5)

250

ACROSS

9 Nothing served at dinner—only ground-up seeds (7)
10 Summary of the 'Pie' Anagram Book (7)
11 The map that suits Mrs Mopp to a T (5)
12 Sign as I do for identification (9)
13 Bit by bit, bit the food (9)
15 Poisoner, dividing the guineas, produces signs of astonishment (5)
16 It may run into a river, one enveloped in mist (6)
18 King Charles' secret fondness for a flower (6)
21 Establish by a law written in nineteen fourteen actually (5)
22 Fractional feature (9)
24 It's displayed by the well dressed and 29 (4,5)
26 Guide a number into the vessel (5)
28 Floating sheet (3-4)
29 See 24 (7)

DOWN

1 Make, after thought, a surgical instrument (7)
2 Dangerous high spot (4)
3 Place the chess pieces on top of the table—this is the arrangement (10)
4 On the shelf is a power gauge (6)
5 Curiously calm tile like gold, perhaps (8)
6 Ensign has no measure to put his name to (4)
7 Sister, quietly happy about uniform (10)
8 Stripes, unfortunately, continue to exist (7)
14 Additional screen in the cricket field (5,5)
15 George has diagram number about the globe (10)
17 Patriarch has names wrongly written (8)
19 Put up 9P, including a guinea, for the bird (7)
20 Number under summons, put down in black and white (7)
23 '---, my lord, can look as swift as yours' *(The Merchant of Venice)* (2,4)
25 Sounds like the end of an animal story (4)
27 Praise this Archbishop (4)

ACROSS

7 Policeman or stripper? (6)
8 Walking with a politician through the market town (8)
9 Flat earther? Only on paper (8)
10 Animals that carry one into a humble retreat (6)
11 'Think on me, That am with Phoebus' amorous pinches —' *(Antony and Cleopatra)* (5)
12 Lucky at breaking and entering into a wealthy pile (9)
14 They vary according to where the capital is (8,3)
16 Place between Bury and River, south east (9)
18 The old car comes first by finishing in top gear (5)
21 Good man having a loaf or leisurely walk (6)
22 Activity needed to put back Number One and Ten in a tree (8)
23 Motherly mother bird, with one left (8)
24 'Ocean's nursling, — lies' *(Shelley)* (6)

DOWN

1 Disclose the Academician in the Festival (6)
2 Fisher companion to a witch (5-3)
3 Queen leaves brother some soup (5)
4 Conservative with a heart all stone? It's incredible! (4,5)
5 Physical overstrain puts the artist in a whirl (6)
6 Digs up the urn, as it comes to pieces (8)
8 Cat, a slow mover over the frail boat (8-5)
13 As anglers do, request news from a distant friend (4,1,4)
14 One meets irritating creature with an article belonging to an ancient Bishop (8)
15 Believing the ring to contain some injurious influence (8)
17 Bit of fishing tackle found in upriver location, very much the worse for wear (6)
19 Open up the blackfish (6)
20 Pull up the man with a word of welcome (5)

252

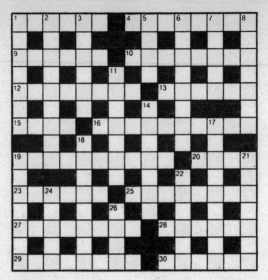

ACROSS

1 Sailor's potted sermon (6)
4 Social worker with secret task for recluse (8)
9 Confidential information re insect (6)
10 About noon, Ulric gets turned into a jester (8)
12 It sounds naughty returning money belonging to sailors (8)
13 'Falls —, or hearing die' *(King Henry VIII)* (6)
15 Adder of notes to the works of Shakespeare (4)
16 Pants suitable for hill climbing (6,4)
19 Spider that goes like 25 (10)
20 Parking, too, for the dog (4)
23 Prophet disturbed by old town affairs (6)
25 Order braided button for a large jumper (8)
27 Amateur soprano tells how she demands a sweet (3,5)
28 Flier might use illegal method (3-3)
29 Plumbago fruit cut in two by a single shot (8)
30 This port doesn't upset (6)

DOWN

1 Her elders were not her betters (7)
2 'Some — blackness, mothy and warm' *(Hardy)* (9)
3 Miss Sedley Lamb's confession (6)
5 Two or three possible answers to 'What is your name?' (4)
6 Ample head of hair – and then some! (8)
7 Haul in two rivers (5)
8 Statement is up – there's nothing in it for the soldier (7)
11 Chooses to wear party colours (7)
14 Six hundred Greek feet, where they ran (7)
17 Detestable sourpuss follows river over half a mile (7)
18 'Holy Mike!' as the giraffe might have said to Noah (8)
19 Good man taking a very thin slice (7)
21 Occupied Old England first (7)
22 Acquits the poet in the Civil Service (6)
24 Dido and Aeneas work overtime (5)
26 Actors take a squint (4)

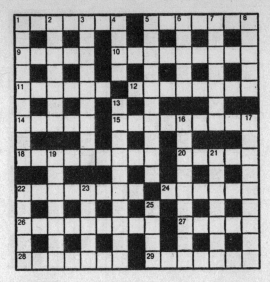

253

ACROSS

1 Town success due to chance this time
—what a relief! (7)
5 The Woman in White? (7)
9 Composition result of 3 down? (5)
10 Semi-dotty signs in the Walrus and
the Carpenter's initial verse (5,4)
11 'Crowned with rank fumiter and —
weeds' *(King Lear)* (6)
12 Grave situation revealed by
effluence meter yesterday (8)
14 Bitterly feels the result of
incorporating Liberal principles (5)
15 With goose being cooked, what is
the position now? (3,4,2)
18 Heir presumptive has seen to LSD
being wildly distributed (6,3)
20 House, sixteenth century, where
assemblage returns, including
daughter (5)
22 Small holder is in an easy gallop (8)
24 Being in love, subscription is
returned by composer (6)
26 Low story (9)
27 Old chap pockets a pound for the
sword (5)
28 Sportsman—where and on what he
may stand (4,3)
29 Davy's assistant (7)

DOWN

1 Liberal and pro-Church Army (4,5)
2 Principal coin with head of Regina,
one pound (7)
3 Actual disadvantages of the trawling
industry? (3,6)
4 'This teeming—of royal kings' *(King
Richard II)* (4)
5 Drink, as ordered by beery in-law
(6,4)
6 Keeper of sheep by oriental tree (5)
7 Henry and Joseph are cask makers
(7)
8,17 An alien tract, possibly Yemen
area (5,9)
13 Spreading rumours, the old reformer
is interrupted by reformed sniper
(10)
16 But our men somehow achieve
majority (9)
17 See 8
19 The occupant has a Buddhist
understudy (7)
21 Doctor, with pair of spectacles, was
in front and drivelled (7)
22 Part of the caravan arrived and then
left (5)
23 Accomplice completely understands
the Saint (5)
25 It may well change colour later on in
the pale afterglow (4)

254

ACROSS

1 Whereto the broad way leadeth (11)
9 Even Dinah, unfortunately, has the right to eat a square meal (4,6)
10 Country one has invaded before (4)
11 Insects served with vegetable – the French finish it! (7)
12 Provision merchant has career ruined, and about time too! (7)
14 Part of a Saga interpreted anew (5)
16 Saint in 'The Blue Lion' drunk? It's inexplicable! (9)
19 Chalk in green taken initially for drawing (9)
20 Hemlock inflorescence, eg (5)
22 Like the last season's success, try including Elgar's Introduction (7)
24 Note a certain bar of music (7)
27 The middle of the propeller is white (4)
28 'The — who banks with Coutts' *(The Gondoliers)* (10)
29 Morality men all upset for just a second! (11)

DOWN

2 The chosen railway – supposing that it comes between to adapt to a comparatively modern motive power (9)
3 Three-legged pot race round Split (6)
4 'Like hidden lamps in old sepulchral —' *(Cowper)* (4)
5 Characters in 'Il Trovatore' adore a character in 'Carmen' (8)
6 Fat, round, wild bees (5)
7 Look! Football played at Wimbledon! (4)
8 Loyal learned Conservative (4,4)
13 In a line with some of the permanent way (5)
15 No knight to banter climbing up the fortress (8)
17 'Let no such man be trusted' (according to Lorenzo) (9)
18 In line for a profit (8)
21 More successful gambler (6)
23 The trunk of an elephant, or so they say (5)
25 Duck flew round the bay (4)
26 Lean over to hear the composer (4)

ACROSS

8 Self-confessed father of powerful unit (6)
9 All is soft, sweet pepper! (8)
10 Ascertained the amount of drink outside the safe (8)
11 Eddy has a bit put in to annoy (6)
12 Half of it, by mistake, causes extreme fear (6)
13 Claim, unduly coming from town with no aspiration (8)
15 Half a mo! (4)
16 Conservative or adult woman (4)
21 Faithful Conservative (4,4)
23 Superhuman, understanding bird (6)
24 Fine female donkey? (6)
26 '— anything, only don't cry' *(Lewis Carroll)* (8)
27 It's a bit sticky – he's gone into a dive! (8)
28 At a resting place, took nourishment natural to the mind (6)

DOWN

1 Self-confessed measurer of eight (7)
2 One who scratches a blemish on several pieces of china (3,7)
3 A Mr Sabre could be made to serve as a soldier (4,4)
4 Strip of cloth given Cologne Water for an eye bandage (7)
5 Astute about the bar (6)
6 Knocks up for the fight (4)
7 'In states unborn, and — yet unknown' *(Julius Caesar)* (7)
14 Magnificent, soft piece of furniture (5,5)
17 A means of communication? Perish the stuff! (8)
18 Take the chair into cheap residential area (7)
19 Official seats Cardinal with Companion of Honour among the busy ones (7)
20 Divides half a second into fractions! (7)
22 Scots girl! (6)
25 In a Swedenborgian Garden (4)

256

ACROSS

1 'Prize for Harmony'—revised version of film now in another language (6,6)

9 Some, we hear, wildly impugn the judge's duty (7,2)

10 'And make a—of the devil himself' *(King Henry V)* (5)

11 Make precious object to be placed in front of organ (6)

12 Coal broken down into proper state (8)

13 Discourses to leaders of party in cautious stages (6)

15 Counter with three articles—all fine stuff! (8)

18 Armed body of men in remote d— country enclosure (8)

19 After the manner of a spirit warning (6)

21 '— in the mystery of words' *(Wordsworth)* (8)

23 Shaw's God-searching girl has lost her head and is way out (6)

26 Sly fellow has included fifty-two points (5)

27 Insist upon it coming back to me in a matter of seconds (5,4)

28 Taking very little from ruined crypt at Ely, about half an em (5,7)

DOWN

1 Two certain keys lock up the fruit (7)

2 Christened little Edward in the morning? Just the reverse! (5)

3 The rule of a few holy characters given out about crag climbing after one (9)

4 They are smoked and bullied (4)

5 I am a fairy boy and completely magnificent! (8)

6 'His — wit degenerating into clenches' (Dryden on Shakespeare) (5)

7 What an awkward position! Cover up the girl! (7)

8 He gives a pi-jaw before the account is delivered to the girl (8)

14 Circle in a fable making a metaphor (8)

16 It's all one—revolver or reptile (9)

17 It costs you nothing and could give you free eats too (4,4)

18 As sheep and sucker may be (7)

20 'You would pluck out the heart of my—' *(Hamlet)* (7)

22 Recipient of a bit of beef, underdone (5)

24 Banished person captured by Felix *(Eliot's Radical)* in the rising (5)

25 Secure liberation of the Italian undergraduate (4)

ACROSS

8 Handy light (8,5)
9 Insect food (4)
10 Note in the chime provided by lower part of organ (5)
11 Noble listener left at the end (4)
12 I may set about outside work that causes short-sightedness (6)
14 Take away some of the badly made tachographs (6)
16 Angry, and may fool about for ages (3,4,1,4,3)
17 After North America, ship gets to the French island capital (6)
20 Stock of provisions to fatten the Queen (6)
22 'And gentlemen in England, now —, Shall think themselves accurs'd' *(King Henry V)* (4)
24 Doctrine in palindrome form (5)
25 Slightly tainted noble (4)
26 No coward takes such advice (5,3,5)

DOWN

1 Almost two points scored by Lear's uncle (6)
2 'I'll set a bank of rue, sour — of grace' *(King Richard II)* (4)
3 Imaginary state formed in the mind without opiates (6)
4 The plotting of some flat dwellers (6,9)
5 Impassive Head of Television is in a strong position (6)
6 Loud bird set at liberty (4)
7 Performed by a choir, which is a bit upset by its leader (6)
13 Puss, minus tail goes round half the Manx cats (5)
15 Ferocious creature making a row about a certain key (5)
18 Sailor girl attains high office in a convent (6)
19 In duty free arrangement, which is not in order (6)
20 Excused and discharged (3,3)
21 Crews that take large shoes (6)
23 Harrow gives a gay party (4)
24 Big embrace given by sweetheart (4)

258

ACROSS

1 Enigmatic composer (3,6,5)
9 Art is half the test for a performer (7)
10 Shakespearean merchant (7)
11 In short, do in like manner (5)
12 River or cobra in trouble (3,6)
13 Marsh grass around southern water provided the answer (9)
15 Two generations present member of secret society (5)
16 One of the hunters of the Snark (5)
18 All the more reason it should be in Latin (1,8)
21 Have canal re-diverted for a fall (9)
23 Common in the Athenaeum (5)
24 Editor provided that sweet building (7)
25 He wrote songs for a barber (7)
26 Present for one's first ceremony (11,3)

DOWN

1 Model servant writes an outstanding leader (8,6)
2 Goes round or up with Scottish portions (7)
3 'Since Cleopatra died, I have liv'd in such —' (Antony & Cleopatra) (9)
4 Proved a very red letter is missing (7)
5 Small type gem (7)
6 More towards the end of the canal at Erith (5)
7 They shelter from the sun (7)
8 'No Surrender' act (2,4,8)
14 Fancy was called a deceiving one by Keats (3)
15 Naomi the novelist (9)
17 Like Jack! (7)
18 Old name for one down (7)
19 Went too far (7)
20 Book for the devout (7)
22 One book, one plea (5)

ACROSS

9 Had communication with Italian boy about the performance (9)
10 'The other, — crust, A regular patrician' *(HMS Pinafore)* (5)
11 What a cigar has to give up (7)
12 Burden of paper work comes first (7)
13 Doll's expression (5)
14 Irreplaceable? Very amusing! (9)
16 A play of irritable retrospection (4,4,2,5)
19 Just change this military command! (5,4)
21 His rod is golden (5)
22 It's a pity about the walrus (7)
23 'Pray in penitential robe'—see Church Service (7)
24 The elder may box, for example (5)
25 Construction of Abelard IV (9)

DOWN

1 Having one more side than a 50p (10)
2 The effect here is decidedly incisive (8)
3 He wrote about the Left, with difficulty (6)
4 Stupefy with crazy turn (4)
5 At mid-noon, I upset counsel (10)
6 Order some bean soup, well cooked (8)
7 It's round here, below the second pedal (6)
8 Goddess embracing river god (4)
14 Worn by a Gainsborough lady, it gets a Film Salute (7,3)
15 Wrestler's aim is fastness (10)
17 Only 'Hair' gets support (8)
18 Member of the madder family (8)
20 A piercing bore! (6)
21 'I may — eternal Providence' *(Paradise Lost)* (6)
22 Cycle going up a hill (4)
23 A lot of larks (4)

260

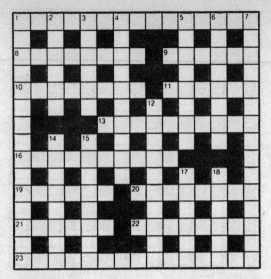

ACROSS

1 Father had potato mashed on the smallest provocation (2,3,4,2,1,3)
8 GI learnt complicated musical instrument (8)
9 'Just for a handful of — he left us' *(Browning)* (6)
10 City's Senior Citizen is a help at cleaning (4,4)
11 City shop or town market? Look within (6)
13 Poor crop had bravest arrangement (3,7)
16 Netted a tit-bit into the bag (10)
19 One spoon bent by a malignant influence (6)
20 Regarding as equal, two notes with quaint, quaint contents (8)
21 Design a location for the camper (6)
22 Blue bloomers for this girl! (8)
23 What one does to stimulate the brainpan (7,4,4)

DOWN

1 Lives written by DIY men (15)
2 The days of April (6)
3 Sterne, maybe, but another name than Laurence (6)
4 By altering the reel, one animal can be freed (10)
5 Heartless Fanny embraces Notorious Jack for useless trifles (8)
6 Town bred characters provide support for the patient (5-3)
7 Military command to UN draught? True, in an odd way (4,3,3,5)
12 Royalty on board (5,5)
14 The more austere Saint Richter has no aspiration (8)
15 A long-handled dipper, or possibly spoon, etc (5-3)
17, 18 Swift, for example (6,6)

ACROSS

8 Cover spread round worker returning for a little sleep (6)
9 'The voice of many thunderings, saying —' *(Revelation)* (8)
10 Fish without a tail is needed for this game (4)
11 Ethereal Celsius in a dream – as a delicious extra! (5,5)
12 Refuse in wine-making, one girl gets the stuff (8)
14 Deuterium carries inflammation risk (6)
15 Our future King? (7,3,5)
18 Perhaps the plan includes the Youth Hostels Association (6)
21 Is it embraced by the unsatisfactory Mohammedan? (8)
22 Seize the officer who has seized the English (10)
23 Some of the crop at harvest time which is trodden down (4)
24 Pass on from North to South in a mine vehicle to get it (8)
25 'We, in some unknown Power's — Move on a rigorous line' *(Arnold)* (6)

DOWN

1 A reaction the Head of Harrow saw! (8)
2 Spike put up by a bloodsucker (4)
3 One pound, and another, captured by playing card – it's an ace! (8)
4 Ariette, No. 1, meant for a Queen (5,10)
5 Following the song, the Editor is savagely criticised (6)
6 A Lieutenant takes monkey round the Scottish Island town (10)
7 He takes the top of the Papal Cross (6)
13 Take hat to pieces and dip it in red dye (10)
16 Regal arrangement, in the end, is more extensive (8)
17 Allowance, including occupational therapy, results in a recurrent order (8)
19 Prophet goes round the old city, putting down discreditable love affairs (6)
20 Leafy hat (6)
23 Bishop and Poet (4)

262

ACROSS

1 Two kinds of pastry and temper (5,3,5)
10 Self-conscious being meets mature VIP (9)
11 Adjective for certain galleries and grinders (5)
12 'Allow not nature more than nature —' (King Lear) (5)
13 The blamelessness of a pub—once it gets round the church! (9)
14 What is the idle baker doing? (7)
16 Sees about three notes and withdraws (7)
18 'A—man, proud in heart and mind' (King Lear) (7)
20 Much disputed territory (7)
21 Taking matters to the extreme—to me, that's foolish (2,3,4)
23 Spiked part of the rear edgebone (5)
24 A theory of certain consequence (5)
25 Clown has been, we hear, to get food (5,4)
26 Be quiet! (4,4,5)

DOWN

2 Stuffing of jade fibre? (9)
3 'The singing masons building—of gold' (Henry V) (5)
4 Deducting from the money in a pouch (7)
5 Governess's charges include a backward girl (7)
6 'Ay springes to catch —' (Hamlet) (9)
7 Lord of the Marbles (5)
8 Disconcertingly pink, Handel's on board and he's tall and thin (13)
9 Wit is below and in pain (13)
15 This travelling—is it in time to cover the Northern Territory? (9)
17 This ought to put one off! (9)
19 Comedian has the sulks over nothing (7)
20 Possibly an RAC outmotor (7)
22 Adjective for certain lights and lilies (5)
23 Time to a Muse (5)

ACROSS

1 Old fogy of 99 has affinity with them in a horsey establishment (5-2-3-3)
9 ' "Is there — there?" said the traveller' *(de la Mare)* (7)
10 Heed this ghastly spectre! (7)
11 High ground surrounds the river in flood (5)
12 Bribe, to reduce friction (9)
13 Large spoon left in Scottish mill-stream (5)
15 The clarity of Uncle Sid's letters (9)
17 Want support to be given to UN weapon (6-3)
18 A long time back in space (5)
19 He saves swimmers career – and watch! (9)
22 Eddy putting his head inside, the surly fellow! (5)
23 Very small stones taken to Heath ground (7)
24 Arena for a sport in which one looks nicer in knickers (3-4)
25 As a rule, it's permanent (8,5)

DOWN

2 This little pet could be made to yodel about the river (3,6)
3 Sing softly with the sly fellow? That's about right (5)
4 Heartless ditty inserted into hurtful story of rusticity (5)
5 Mixed Asian diet from one part of A-ia (4,5)
6 Town girl discovers tropical plant (5)
7 Fielder in Father's fly (5-4-4)
8 Being diplomatic, he first announces one of the same kind (13)
10 Polish one, to study the Italian stream (7)
14 Free from prejudice (9)
15 The convict is to drag up the one who's behind (7)
16 Two letters snub four oriental persons who administer government (9)
20 Fellow isn't vulgar – just a bit dim (5)
21 Performing animal – about one inch! (5)
22 Plain free from obstruction (5)

264

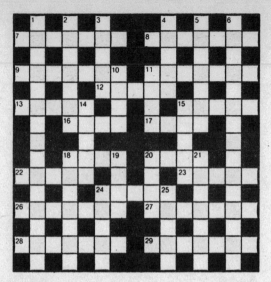

ACROSS

7 Throw away – Mark did without (7)
8 Trundled the boy round the brook (7)
9 The Yard, having captured many in retreat, is moving force (7)
11 I am meeting the journalists to produce a profound effect (7)
12 Row north to the river in France (5)
13 Frequent the circle on foot to some extent (5)
15 Discovered nothing in the store (5)
16 Boy embraces love willingly (4)
17 To bring to one listener the overture to 'Norma' (4)
18 A pound's nothing – and it's just as well! (4)
20 A circular figure is placed in the middle of the direct current (4)
22 All taken separately, and always to the letter (5)
23 There's nothing in the beach store (5)
24 Bore to meet the Duke, getting dressed (5)
26 Dealer in bloomers (7)
27 Remembering India in China (7)
28 The final course is to leave around the end of Christmas (7)
29 'Hateful to the nose, — to the brain' (James I on Tobacco) (7)

DOWN

1 Disentangle ivy leaf – let holly bloom (4,2,3,6)
2 Trusty comrade bought provisions (7)
3 Doctor has his own Scots filter (5)
4 Two notes about Border Act gravely wrong (5)
5 Family gathers around the river, making the sound of the trumpet (7)
6 She provides an example (8,7)
10 Old-fashioned food (4)
11 'The — is full of noises' (The Tempest) (4)
14 Could be only about a Baron in a lordly manner (5)
15 Cheeky note might be hers! (5)
18 Part of a chair or sling (7)
19 Leave out nothing – time nearly up! (4)
20 Judge puts up the reward (4)
21 Study to mend misspelt sentence (7)
24 Despots putting out the stars (5)
25 Primadonna to name a collection of poems (5)

ACROSS

1 Popular non-U tree (6)
4 Bind together three strings (8)
10 He puts his foot down and leaves the reader (7)
11 Scrap suits rum chaps to a T (7)
12 Woman and Nationalist leader in the same plane (5)
13 3D representation (7,3)
16 Provides from broken crates (6)
17 A voter, drunk before beginning of election, obviously had too much (7)
20 Girl has instrument which records volume of particular verse (7)
21 Dressed hippy style and engaged (2,4)
24 'He only can behold With unaffrighted eyes — — of the deep' *(Campion)* (3,7)
25 Film featuring motorway and street (4)
27 Falls backward again in front of sun-god (7)
29 Page precedes nobleman in Scottish lace (7)
30 'The — School of Criticism' *(Rossetti title)* (8)
31 Chestnut and bay achieve hilltop by opposite directions (6)

DOWN

1 Game operatic heroine (8)
2 The gift to send up now (8)
3 Helps maids who have lost a lot (4)
5 I have underwear that is rather humorous (8)
6 Revolutionary surly fellow gets ham and fruit (3,7)
7 Familiar name of old cabinet minister in any English government (3)
8 Legal bars in the judge's top story (6)
9 Convincing evidence provided by piano lid (5)
14 Fairy Queen legally presents Iolanthe's relation to Phyllis (6-2-3)
15 Open contest in which strip of sail comes in for overall (4,3,3)
18 Stuff the fish and get a ticking off! (8)
19 Old shilling subscription obtains the MSS (8)
22 'You are not — but men' *(Julius Caesar)* (6)
23 Doctor overworks and falls exhausted (5)
26 Two giving a quiet tune (4)
28 Period in which the viola germinates (3)

266

ACROSS

8 Irresistible light may break! (8)
9 Industrial leader in the factory is easily influenced (6)
10 Wader presenting a lengthy bill (6)
11 Paris Ace somehow gets room to breathe (8)
12 Gets ready by wrapping cloth in skins (8)
13 Father is to hire one who has a child (6)
14 Extend term of imprisonment (7)
16 A form of rude tin, not yet put to the test (7)
19 Food one left after a fast (6)
21 Coming upon the stage, is put under a spell (8)
23 In a particular tone of voice, I would chance the answer (8)
25 A performer, in this part, is tortured (6)
26 'The — tree shall flourish, and the grasshopper shall be a burden' (Ecclesiastes) (6)
27 Sweet made hard in the fridge (3-5)

DOWN

1 Ingenious introduction of case at the bar (6)
2 Portion of Christmas fare, a minute piece, perhaps (5-3)
3 Rich lot are absurdly over-decorated (10)
4 Go round some of the shabby passages (6)
5 'I have no — to prick the sides of my intent' (Macbeth) (4)
6 Ripped out bird (6)
7 Settle three quarters on little Connie and the Civil Engineer (8)
13 Sees through talks about string lace (10)
15 Used for binding a young animal under the gallows (4-4)
17 I care not to make a response (8)
18 One not to be doubted (7)
20 Delphic stool (6)
22 Coins spread about around a gaming-house (6)
24 Two Scandinavian books (4)

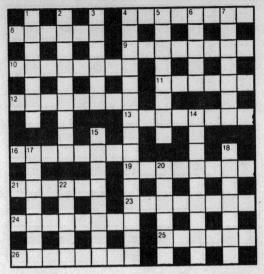

ACROSS

4 This friar is a monkey! (8)
8 Prim old style, a sensitive plant (6)
9 Fool breaks into an unusual choir of birds (8)
10 Now, perhaps, the Doctor gets round us, all very admirable (8)
11 Points made by Protestant Episcopal among the wood cutters (6)
12 Ridiculous rug meant as evidence (8)
13 Bullied son of King Edward (8)
16 Listen twice for this sound of approval (4,4)
19 Upper-class boy in lacy dress could be the end! (8)
21 The French bachelor at our political party (6)
23 Zigzag through Northern Territory? Indeed! (8)
24 Important in the past, and this, to Richard III, contains it (8)
25 It is idle to look at the back hair of the head (6)
26 Field of operations includes parking – for a tortoise! (8)

DOWN

1 The excessive zeal of a great Tory, perhaps (7)
2 Pentose found in many plants (4-5)
3 Girl gathering seaweed in abundance (6)
4 Scotch Robin sure somehow to take a decisive step (5,3,7)
5 Tourist centre gets a letter written in an act of mortification (8)
6 Run away – that's a smart girl! (5)
7 Iris's family show keen resentment about the plan (7)
14 Excel in dress with a ring, do, and a cloak (9)
15 A sweet pendant (4-4)
17 Question from a letter, one belonging to me (7)
18 River bird seen under alternating current (7)
20 'I'd — safely home and die – in bed' *(Siegfried Sassoon)* (6)
22 The animal inside this is not terribly fierce (5)

268

ACROSS

1 Slay her, the spoil-sport! (7)
5 He might have called one Jill coy (7)
9 Ineffectual, a Texan vegetable juice (5)
10 Odd 'Athene' bud in flower (3,6)
11 Arnold's fishy character (6)
12 You might get a windfall from these steely-hearted monsters (8)
14 Block of our last letter incorporated with the Greek omicron (5)
15 Head Archer in a broken voice proclaims act of annulment (9)
18 Half-witted offer about hydrant spot (3,3,3)
20 'Embryos and idiots, eremites and —s' *(Paradise Lost)* (5)
22 He fell in love with two girls and into lake river! (8)
24 Dull court room (6)
26 Neither stern nor forward, just somewhere in between (9)
27 Patriarch is one in a hundred (5)
28 Audience may think I deposit money for Medical Surgery Fund (3,4)
29 Sailor, mark the refrain! (7)

DOWN

1 River where hartebeest goes round fifty animals kept in captivity (9)
2 'Pillar Queen,' on presently (5,2)
3 Jo, put axes in proper order, put one beside the other (9)
4 Himalayas' answer to Loch Ness? (4)
5 Drive out the seducer (10)
6 Plant put in for a child (5)
7 This could be true in a non-particle (7)
8 Inspector, he asks the birds (5)
13 It may shed light on Hamlet material (10)
16 Flowers packed in a box which slid off a donkey cart when backing (9)
17 Ireland, in back study holding a peace conference (9)
19 Easily split one if less jumble outside (7)
21 Goddess follows in state (7)
22 'Occasion smiles upon a second—' *(Hamlet)* (5)
23 One star hotel harbours her (5)
25 Gigantic step on the way to heaven (4)

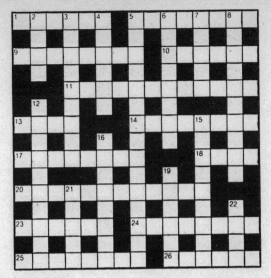

ACROSS

1 Company's waste wool (6)
5 In the middle of golf, a death – one way to die! (4,4)
9 Lie with a lover – a flaming affair! (8)
10 Disposition to harm Master of Arts, the nasty little things (6)
11 Sister Susie's sewing shirts as an example (12)
13 Man disturbing an artist portraying a bird (4)
14 Boldly phone leader of the Liberals within 24 hours (8)
17 Whereon the ghost in *Hamlet* walks (8)
18 It's a job to ask love to go away (4)
20 Diana's assets possibly destroyed (12)
23 Found in backward African mulatto girl student (6)
24 Meant getting betrothed (8)
25 It's good in France to go round the correct fashionable resort (8)
26 Hear about the French restorer (6)

DOWN

2 National emblem (4)
3 Red at worker being disposed to fight (9)
4 Explosives making an inferno on board (6)
5 Some say it's time for us to end him – in error! (6,9)
6 Brown sugar could be – dear me! – radium! (8)
7 'See how the Fates their gifts —' *(The Mikado)* (5)
8 Charles & Son disaster, and no sign of hope (10)
12 Sounds as if Jack is all in one piece, he deals in bulk (10)
15 Make no fuss over the woollen tapestry centre – it's moths! (9)
16 Faithful Vanbrugh character (8)
19 A sharp pain in the chest – it chokes one too! (6)
21 Wood left inside a vessel (5)
22 A pool and nothing more (4)

270

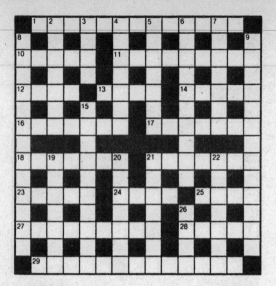

ACROSS

1 A clean one, dead drunk, might keep one unnecessarily involved (4,3,1,5)
10 A learner driver and one unaccompanied (5)
11 Professional writer put on the death list (9)
12 Note the fruit juice bubble (4)
13 Evil characters converted by priestly tribe (4)
14 New Zealander and I wander back (5)
16 Old city trees chopped up to make inner ducts (7)
17 Friend comes in, though briefly, about the call (5-2)
18 'When forty winters shall — thy brow' *(Shakespeare Sonnet)* (7)
21 Belonging to an island in the south latitude in the United Arab Republic (7)
23 Lands in the sea (5)
24 Somewhat grim morning for a top Moslem (4)
25 Porgy and Bess finally caught up (4)
27 Revolutionary leader takes the biscuit (9)
28 Old kitchen feature fitted with appliances set in a row (5)
29 How handy! Since this provides something for tea (5,8)

DOWN

2 Talk of oneself – and note it goes all wrong (7)
3 Cooks Peter Rabbit's aunts and sisters (4)
4 Some beneficiaries of nepotism (7)
5 Gallant character – a Sir Tom Foolery! (7)
6 To complete account, pacifist politician left his letters about (10)
7 One of the Marx brothers on railway coffee mix (7)
8 A connection of Sydney is to entertain with a game of cards (7,6)
9 Dr Johnson, for example (13)
15 Can be turned into poetry again? (10)
19 Lear is wrong to love one in *The Merchant of Venice* (7)
20 Food in bed? I bless the idea! (7)
21 A kind of iron nail put up under a palm tree (7)
22 Short Spartan (7)
26 'Wears upon his baby — the round And top of sovereignty' *(Macbeth)* (4)

ACROSS

1 Industrial employee, his charge is no light one (13)
10 Where are the actors filming in 'Assault'? (5)
11 Money for the Queen (9)
12 Meal left for a duck (4)
13 He tells a story backing the bird (4)
14 Retired Head of Eton with Head of Blundell's in bed (5)
16 Seek to improve the soak, give him a brooch (7)
17 ' 'Tis not so sweet now as it was before' *(Twelfth Night)* (6)
19 Set aside one rig, it must be altered (6)
22 Girl detectives are not at all sharp (3-4)
25 Miss Doone? Not really! (5)
26 God returned vexed (4)
27 Eg box made for a boot (4)
29 Number One S in S Row (9)
30 They travel in one sense, but from right to left (5)
31 Apparel of romantic knight of old (7,6)

DOWN

2 Pre-prepared this month (7)
3 Bête noire (4)
4 Impatient exclamation was at first spiteful (7)
5 Inns servant possibly (7)
6 Pantomime characters . . . (10)
7 . . . of sweet disposition (7)
8 Turn with Italian to the right (7)
9 Dishonest team takes in the point (5)
15 Gold tomato in more or less a high degree of mechanisation (10)
18 Unfavourable short notice on poetry (7)
20 Decorate the fish with sliced-up leg of beef (7)
21 'And not by — windows only, When daylight comes, comes in the light' *(Clough)* (7)
22 Maid in waiting at Belmont (7)
23 Animal Race—where? In Paris (7)
24 27 to help the carpenter (5)
28 Check part of a written note (4)

272

ACROSS

1 The applause of Jupiter? (12)
8 At least three boys are needed for the drums (3-4)
9 Taxi backs into another vehicle before a game (7)
11 Queen is back in America to meet North Eastern European (7)
12 Faces with plaster (7)
13 A figure of one who prays or one who works (5)
14 Limp characters possibly spelling danger for a Kentish feature (3-6)
16 Assembly to study the race (9)
19 Book-like container of records, one left by a dissolute fellow (5)
21 Father, with Christian Endeavour, for example, has a note for the Easter offering (4,3)
23 Infatuated offspring going round one American city (7)
24 Relatives surrounded by pets and lots of small flowers (7)
25 'I had a little —, nothing would it bear' *(Nursery rhyme)* (3,4)
26 Accentor protects himself with a quiet weapon (5-7)

DOWN

1 Cover over a tree under which there's a show (7)
2 Circus tent in a Scottish island, fit for an idealist (7)
3 Make a-weigh! (9)
4 Possibly sober garb (5)
5 Actual arrangement around the top of the cactus plant (7)
6 Funny case inside another, yet it's all one (7)
7 Adjective for a situation seen from two slightly different angles (12)
10 Being inattentive to surroundings, sailor is sent to heed the Editor (6-6)
15 An illness I name upon dissection (9)
17 Part of a shirt to fasten with a scarf (7)
18 A number in the GPO coming up for the vacancy (7)
19 He hears them applaud it – or part of it (7)
20 Scatter heads of endive, sage and thyme into the brew (7)
22 Narrow passages containing sulphur blasts (5)

ACROSS

1 Eg Othello gets the bird twice (7)
5 Charlie's the fellow who gets nothing back (7)
9 The musician who has already got the bird (3)
10 Son keeping a very thin slice (7)
11 'The — English drunkard made the — English road' *(Chesterton)* (7)
12 Rise – a bad sign! (5)
13 'Trouble in Crete' Editor returns to act as peacemaker (9)
14 Oriental escort, he used to carry a shield (7)
16 Cupbearers cheek the Royal Society (7)
18 Begged the little pedestrian to show the way in (7)
20 Doctor has to look round the circle for the old gun (7)
22 Silent informer of the distance walked (9)
24 Central character of 'The Virginians' splits the tree trunk to make a scarecrow (5)
25 Swimmer's letters are enough to make one blush if read this way (5)
26 Violin used in Shetland by Ezra, silly monkey! (7)
27 Self evident in 'The Go-Between' (3)
28 Broadcast song interrupting musical instrument (7)
29 No motorway to the north is followed by a learner driver, so-called (7)

DOWN

1 The service takes a long time – there's the rub! (7)
2 Ode about quails being prepared for a member of the harem (9)
3 Men who succeed one in what really belongs to a woman (5)
4 Silly niggle made about oriental loose gown (7)
5 Coward interrupts the hints given by clergymen (7)
6 'The ice was here, the ice was there, The ice was — ' *(Coleridge)* (3,6)
7 Learning about one flower (5)
8 Dark lady has a name that's way-out (7)
15 Secure in my end, if it is so organised (9)
17 Eg box (9)
18 It is pleasing to find a letter hidden in a tree (7)
19 Irritated by old coin being abandoned (7)
20 Father overlooks scrap on model (7)
21 All-round protection (7)
23 To conquer in war could make one bleed (5)
24 Fish caught right inside part of ship (5)

274

ACROSS

1 Windows (ten) in a S.E. fort, by arrangement (12)
8 Where the German sheep-dog comes from? (7)
9 Causes a change of teams, taking in Utah (7)
11 Coiling organ (7)
12 Friendly, asking if I have the strength (7)
13 One has left the cities' summons (5)
14 Could be saved with rope from waterfall (9)
16 One who counts (9)
19 Artist is given a note that's higher (5)
21 Conservative, once outside, is cut short (7)
23 Mixed gin I've put beside top of hand-rail (7)
24 Autumnal activity some singers claim they do in May (7)
25 Sad state of Irish nun with no aspiration (2,5)
26 In the chair that's quietly suitable for occupation (12)

DOWN

1 Quick! A number's coming up to see the lighthouse (7)
2 'The inhuman dearth Of noble —' *(Keats)* (7)
3 Features of Chinese Empresses (5,4)
4 Strange ball! Only half a dance! (5)
5 Mac's potatoes (7)
6 The month for 24 (7)
7 Prince, with one manipulation on the van . . . (12)
10 . . . altering the places—see—wins the race (12)
15 Colour of weasels, perhaps, when they've swallowed up the fruit juice (9)
17 Senior pupil has egg in the back room (7)
18 Fruit comes down, about half size (7)
19 Reverend sire upset the game (7)
20 First one to egg one to get a pound (7)
22 'For secrets are — tools' *(Dryden)* (5)

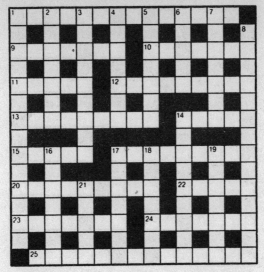

ACROSS

1 Re-edited, I'd call it a green editorial (7,7)
9 Wild flower the Queen comes to see, all in vain (7)
10 Venetian making a demand on the river (7)
11 Tooth of one girl is filled with gold (5)
12 More than one prodigal's death is among the chips (9)
13 Interpreter and Artist take two Poles to it in the process of being transported (2,7)
14 'Love virtue, she alone is free, She can teach ye how to —' *(Milton)* (5)
15 Love me being vulgar! (5)
17 Vehicle from Southport bears some mark of injury (6,3)
20 Contracting or warning letters? (9)
22 Latin written into a religious Christmas decoration (5)
23 Deteriorated fruit juice hurried outside (7)
24 Tropical American region (7)
25 Easy money made out of steel tie-pins, Mr! (6,8)

DOWN

1 Love potion producer (4-2-8)
2 Where one literally takes off (7)
3 I get Nancy disguised as Shakespeare's Bottom, at all events! (2,3,4)
4 GIs seen making an old book (7)
5 Show honour to what is enshrined in the padre's pectoral cross (7)
6 Is shown the way to become isolated (5)
7 Siren learning to garland (7)
8 Bird by mistake put in open pastry dish (10,4)
14 The constable to apprehend a foreigner (9)
16 Famous Italian Mother and Roman Catholic appearing at one (7)
17 Five hundred and fifty creatures about to defraud (7)
18 A means of communicating information on a method of investigation (7)
19 Picture made from bits of gold lace mostly (7)
21 Animal given a kiss and a flower (5)

276

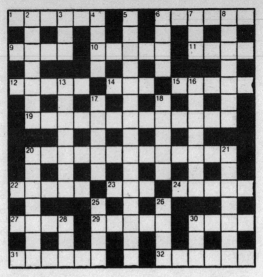

ACROSS

1 Help the dull fellow with a stone (6)
6 Funeral day for Mr Grundy (6)
9 Latin toy bird (4)
10 Piano top provides convincing evidence (5)
11 Low Northern satellite (4)
12 Adjective for certain fish and flowers (5)
14 Leather this child! (3)
15 'The End of Cedric' – reckless disaster! (5)
19 They can't go by themselves, but they help some pedestrians (7-6)
20 A sixth of Scotland (5,3,5)
22 Short second tilt (5)
23 Sash always kept in the robing-room (3)
24 Show us the woman! (5)
27 The first man to make an embankment (4)
29 One left another one solitary (5)
30 What some producers do, getting the seventh row of the stalls (4)
31 The rod that catches a sun-fish (6)
32 '— when young did eagerly frequent Doctor and Saint' *(Omar Khayyam)* (6)

DOWN

2 Shakespeare's Justice (7)
3 Adjective for certain bags and bottles (3)
4 Record the sound of a knock on an egghead (4)
5 Reducing print to pulp, or doctoring the digits? (7,3,5)
6 A second of time? Not so loud! (4)
7 Shakespeare's Corporal (3)
8 Nothing in this stratagem, as put out, alarms (7)
13 Captain of a Carrollian crew (7)
16 Discs of Ruddigore overture, unfortunately scored (7)
17 The solution found at the hairdressers (5)
18 Corpse causing a fit, written up in science fiction (5)
20 The fellow to bundle up a bird (7)
21 Umpire has to work outside, putting down the plant (7)
25 Westwood Bay on the East Coast (4)
26 The part of the ship that is made of hardwood (4)
28 Little Matthew raising his cap (3)
30 Empty talk of helping cook? (3)

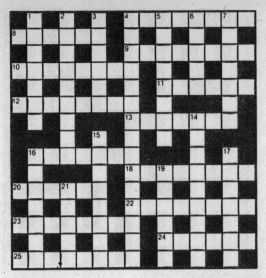

277

ACROSS

4 Curiosity (8)
8 Stitching us up with true knot (6)
9 'So truly —, though infinite can never meet' *(Marvell)* (8)
10 Playful quartet in presto movement (8)
11 Wolf putting Mac's grandchild in a place meant for animals (6)
12 Vegetable gives brother bad colic (8)
13 Southlander writes out a false report (7)
16 Difficulty presented by girl with infectious disease (7)
18 Where one gets clean thro' a mob riot (8)
20 Tempestuous character (6)
22 Postponed scrap (4,4)
23 Twice in a hole, backing the fiddler (8)
24 He leaves no issue (6)
25 Saint, wrongly beheaded, powerfully portrayed (8)

DOWN

1 Strengthen with drink after drink (7)
2 Its teeth operate on chestnuts, etc (5-4)
3 One doctor gets another to swallow diced dice (6)
4 Ie British imply a peculiar permanency (15)
5 Reverse covering for rat (8)
6 Generally the last part of a tennis match (5)
7 She left the soak, putting him up in the asylum (7)
14 Hunter catches two animals (4-5)
15 By means of which Ivy climbs up with a hundred and fifty-two mixed gins (8)
16 20 resorted letters and the twentieth letter is glowing (7)
17 The power of a revolving ladder in a dovecote (7)
19 To a Fellow, recompense is sweet (6)
21 Version of Ivanhoe heard in the past in America (5)

278

ACROSS

9 A cause contended for by King and Queen in equal arrangement (7)
10 Plan a sad drama about love, with piano accompaniment (4,3)
11 'God be praised, the Georges —!' *(W.S. Landor)* (5)
12 Risk a set of false teeth being broken by violent leader (9)
13 Tip for a cool drink (9)
15 Brother and distinguished airman make a couple (5)
16 One verse among four shows partiality (6)
18 Invent ailments to bring on as an inevitable consequence (6)
21 The habitual drink for normal health (5)
22 An old soldier and his weapon (4-5)
24 Barley, perhaps, for the bird (9)
26 Steered over badly at the end of the road (5)
28 Swiss lake plant (7)
29 Laura, mad about old gambling game, wins the crown (7)

DOWN

1 Extraordinary query re official (7)
2 Desert tract in 'Troilus and Cressida' (4)
3 Game with a cake, something suitable for afternoon tea (6,4)
4 Intertwine the branches of the fruit tree about the end of April (6)
5 Gallery displaying surrealist art and poetry (8)
6 One half of an underhand pledge (4)
7 I am placed at one, on a censure (10)
8 'Make thy two eyes, like stars, start from their —' *(Hamlet)* (7)
14 Mad uncle comes in late, after following the wind (10)
15 Rose up into the fight for a bat (10)
17 Obviously embarrassed by the American Indian book (3-5)
19 County people understand us climbing to top of fell (7)
20 Old soldier and French Queen in the wagon (7)
23 Girl in the embrace of insane woman, beside herself with frenzy (6)
25 River making a sudden forward movement (4)
27 It's nothing to toss up a coin (4)

ACROSS

8 Warm drink (7)
10 Plant conceals account for the immunising preparation (7)
11 Forth Bridge stopping-place (7)
12 Something entrusted to another's care is put back in the storehouse (7)
13 A rod for a twist of hair (3)
14 Before the end, served another Order of Merit (7)
15 Ran back at speed for the recount (7)
16 Organ getting attention (3)
18 Venomous mathematician (5)
20 Left them briefly outside the wood (3)
24 Tokens in glass, perhaps (7)
25 Dull sound accompanied by some percussion (7)
27 Tea *from* China? No, *in*! (3)
28 Flow out from Lac Leman at eventide (8)
29 Baron and famous Lord burn with scathing words (7)
30 'Down, thou climbing sorrow! Thy —'s below' *(King Lear)* (7)
31 Lattice work made from broken tillers (7)

DOWN

1 Squeeze a lot of people into the stage? No ta! (8)
2 'Caesar's angel' (6)
3 Divert the disjointed tripods (7)
4 English half dozen to study Council of Europe testimony (8)
5 Odd respect is shown here for the staff (7)
6 Gallery man's daughter is to affirm falsely (8)
7 Pretty awkward fish vessel! (6)
9 Horribly clean boy! (5)
17 Good quality material for two newspapers (3,5)
19 Raid on southern slopes (8)
21 Note:- 'Get up cause to be remembered' (8)
22 There's one in the cattle trough for the organiser (7)
23 Politician seen in a Republic's dominions (7)
24 Vegetables for certain Europeans (6)
25 'Costly thy — as thy purse can buy' *(Hamlet)* (5)
26 Tart cooked by the French vivacious talker (6)

280

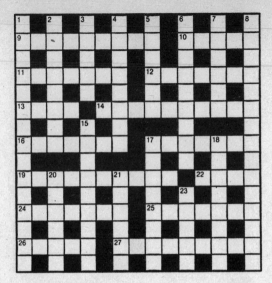

ACROSS

9 German and stoat dig beneath (9)
10 She might be nice to embrace, initially (5)
11 One comes to measure a flower (7)
12 Like a sloth, eg, in the dental surgery (7)
13 It assembles almost every day (4)
14 Once a mark of conviction (5,5)
16 It covers . . . (7)
17 . . . a postal district with consumer protection (7)
19 The Spanish make a mistake in china fruit (10)
22 Pole, possibly (4)
24 Sounds like a dog-cart (7)
25 Duchess departed right, and another character left (7)
26 I do one in with a masculine expression peculiar to the country (5)
27 With which Mr Mantalini threatened to fill his pockets (4-5)

DOWN

1 Invitation to revisit after a snub (3,3,4,5)
2 Dave—is he making a steady attachment? (8)
3 Newly wed stable-man (5)
4 Being two-faced, possibly lied hard (8)
5 Dream girl (6)
6 Anticipates worker, strangely sedate (9)
7 The first one on the right is put into lively action (6)
8 He goes the same way (6,9)
15 Theme of *The Third Man* (5,4)
17 'Say not the — naught availeth' *(Clough)* (8)
18 Permissive? Later on, perhaps, after tea (8)
20 Doctor goes over operation, in making a call (4,2)
21 'Rolled round in — diurnal course' *(Wordsworth)* (6)
23 Breaks up bridges (5)

ACROSS

7 Drink, with rather watery content? Not at all! (7)
8 Plain, but unwrinkled (7)
10 Part of the answer verges on a deviation (6)
11 Allowance from the French bird might be due (8)
12 Keen as a hero (4)
13 'Pedal in Enamelled Design' is entered on the list (10)
14 Given an inch, Nina returns to stoneworker immediately (2,2,7)
19 Eight pints in fewer bottles (4,6)
22 Adjective for certain ferns and frogs (4)
23 Circle to murmur about one of mixed descent (8)
24 Only seen in summer Elysian fields (6)
25 'I've a neater, sweeter maiden in a cleaner — land!' *(Kipling)* (7)
26 Contemptuous of opposition, and fainted in a dreadful fit (7)

DOWN

1 No Welsh in this rich City (7)
2 'Boy embraces Girl' article written by a dramatist (8)
3 Stick – and where to put it (6)
4 'I'll never Be such a gosling to obey —' *(Coriolanus)* (8)
5 Let nothing be put up as a stone over the window (6)
6 More prepared to meet death in the rear (7)
9 How the manacled show appreciation? (4,2,5)
15 It's a pity turned-up noses outside should cause mental disturbances (8)
16 Not the avifauna of a region – they are birds (8)
17 Agreement obtained from Italian with a measure of wood (7)
18 Man with a Flower Cure (7)
20 Revelled with river boy (6)
21 The time of the adder (6)

282

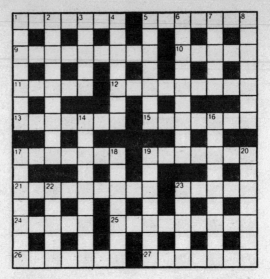

ACROSS

1 Low hoop – it serves to confine a ship (7)
5 Began by getting radiotelephone instead? Wrong! (7)
9 He wrote some of the best evensong hymns (9)
10 Farquhar's man-of-all-work – and what he had to do? (5)
11 One letter hidden in another tree (5)
12 Adjective for certain pilots and pistols (9)
13 I give a hint to listeners with this (3-4)
15 The right to slip away and slide (7)
17 Begins active operations with a strategical move in a back street (7)
19 Theologian in slippers potters about (7)
21 Weather-glass is nothing to me in the midst of traffic (9)
23 Society Academician to draw a French composer (5)
24 The animal doctor to employ (5)
25 His stupidity is of short duration (5,4)
26 The No No girl (7)
27 Animal outside came face to face with goddess (7)

DOWN

1 'Ah, pray make no —, We are not shy' *(The Mikado)* (7)
2 Rex and Head of Eton, in the open, do too much (9)
3 Girl caught in the wire netting (5)
4 Wartime wear (3-4)
5 This ancient Roman could be one star (7)
6 Fool, Oriental and Doctor, under control, all met together (9)
7 It's up to the sailor first to put down a card (5)
8 A sudden flood of water left cab overturned in the river (7)
14 Income is misspelt and criminal is lying (9)
16 Comparatively small vessel has a prize snake in its hollow (5-4)
17 Mixed bun meal for food (7)
18 Gratify fully with this tea – it's a spread! (7)
19 King Arthur's nephew has a colourful end (7)
20 Stupidly rest all of the stars! (7)
22 Debauchee making a point in France (5)
23 Melchizedek's kingdom (5)

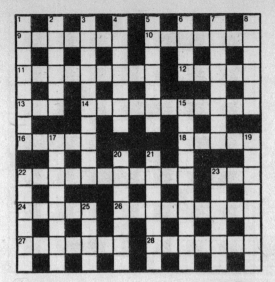

ACROSS

9 The fifteenth letter comes in, it's mainly about the allowance (7)

10 Six love? Let's gather flowers! (7)

11 A capitalist in France? I could be (9)

12 Entertainment provided by Doctor and h-dropping nurse (5)

13 Wicked Willy's heart (3)

14 This is taken without permission (6,5)

16 Run in the next race (5)

18 Five note instrument (5)

22 Room left by Scotland's own VIP (11)

23 Heads of Royal Opera talk nonsense (3)

24 '. . . Eros: the long day's task is done' (*Antony and Cleopatra*) (5)

26 Member of class presenting letters from Master B in order (9)

27 Possibly without a bowler (7)

28 Artist returns with opponent reaching destination (7)

DOWN

1 A certain length of a peculiar film in drag (4-4)

2 Name four numbers (6)

3 Number in balloon, if displaced, get something to eat (4,2,4)

4 They give the author's name, besides the poet's work (7)

5 Eager desire for wealth, and drink goes against the grain (7)

6 Possibly frozen fish, about a pound (4)

7 It might be a trap—look around and disconnect (8)

8 'And wish the . . . o' the world were now undone' (*Macbeth*) (6)

15 Stone fruit and stoneless fruit (10)

17 Badly recorded tape at self-conscientiously artistic social gathering (3-5)

19 Funny lot, dying in this foolishly affectionate manner (8)

20 One who favours pot is to make dissent (7)

21 Home built by Tabitha (7)

22 Dismissed for anything after scoring a hundred (6)

23 Intermediate class transfer (6)

25 Inheritors of the earth (4)

284

ACROSS

1 Intelligent animal could be a lion (8)
4 Spring revolutionary treated mercifully (6)
9 Runs together with a girl going to the dogs (7)
11 Passing from place to place, I'm returning with the General (7)
12 Jumble sale held in a room for provisions – for jocularity (10)
13 Golden-coloured sow (4)
15 Swimmer observed within eastern coastline (3-4)
17 Plant used for signalling (5)
19 Verse in a Christmas Book (5)
21 'What say you to a piece of beef and —?' *(The Taming of the Shrew)* (7)
24 An object of admiration in the aforesaid old play (4)
25 Unattractive ace in vingt-un in a misdeal (10)
28 Heraldic eagle, lacking three features (7)
29 Old paving stone made by worker gathering a fortune round him (7)
30 Rank taking its place among the best at Easter (6)
31 'What God hath —, that call not thou common' *(The Acts)* (8)

DOWN

1 Directions for making something mature, two notes included (6)
2 Old coins for the leather workers (7)
3 Beheading a priest is a crime (5)
5 One side of a leaf that has got soft with time (4)
6 What are you doing? (7)
7 Palm treated badly at the beginning of Easter (4-4)
8 Brightens up Society with animals (8)
10 Infirm of purpose and incapable? Get a good man in! (8)
14 A garment is put back on for wearing away (8)
16 I am with my people and not heartlessly threatening (8)
18 Personal hint (8)
20 'Fierce End of Agamemnon' in colour (7)
22 In taking dead aim, I ostentatiously impress the Oriental Nobles (7)
23 One, overcoming deadly sin, gave assent (6)
26 'Where the intrepid go to climb, scene of a plane crash (5)
27 Formal order for a foreign car (4)

ACROSS

1 Leather unobserved by one –
  what a game! (5,4,4)
8 Bottle shaped block of wood for
  Asiatic Association? (6,4)
9 Water colour (4)
11 Made off with rural instrument on
  the ebbing tide (6,2)
12 Before the leaders of the opposition
  got right inside the cave (6)
14 Girl returns an item of property (5)
15 Scoundrels' point, causing a great
  evil (5)
16 Black pier (5)
17 Village of turncoats (5)
20 Builder is married and has one
  child (5)
22 The Land of More (6)
23 'Of the earth, earthy' *(Corinthians)*
  (8)
25 Row Mark on the river (4)
26 Divide in violent fashion (5,2,3)
27 He does wonders with strings and
  bows (6,7)

DOWN

1 Clever as a cask in a coastal resort
  (6,2,1,6)
2 Sheltered in the Doctor's pocket, a
  pair of spectacles (7)
3 'To throw away the — thing he
  owed, As 'twere a careless trifle'
  (Macbeth) (7)
4 He hammers in decisive fashion (10)
5 Cut up the cakes (4)
6 Smoother way to coax (7)
7 Inn sign makes a particular bloomer
  and has the bird in half (3,4,3,5)
10 Boy putting up glossy material (4)
13 Where there are a good many cows,
  a river surrounds six or seven
  characters (6,4)
18 A domestic art – or a crafty
  practice? (7)
19 Tale heard by a queue (4)
20 Number 1049 put on a wild beast (7)
21 Casual devil! (7)
24 Up river, jazz style (4)

286

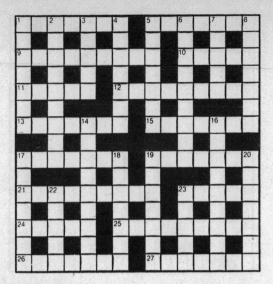

ACROSS

1 Possibly a Brontë Peer (7)
5 Shakespearean conspirator (7)
9 Tropic Isle of Grain? (9)
10 The peculiar charm of a romantic introduction (5)
11 Revolutionary King (5)
12 Harbour light, not quite all in the picture (7)
13 Lace rig makes slow mover (7)
15 His Hero was a girl (7)
17 Played (but were his notes true?) (7)
19 Favoured the younger in bed (7)
21 'Children of the future age Reading this — page' *(Blake)* (9)
23 Rewards me with abbreviated editions (5)
24 A strong beat in evidence all thro' Beethoven work (5)
25 The chosen ones travelled with the conductor (9)
26 The end of four beasts and cads (7)
27 Take away the dust cart Edward backed inside (7)

DOWN

1 Reversing the support (7)
2 Reproof concerning formal article to a degree (9)
3 Rain storm over northern county (5)
4 He swears he's a soldier! (7)
5 Regulation check (7)
6 Flight which may include more than one landing (9)
7 Substance found in walrus or in plant (5)
8 'I am thine husband, not a — soul' *(Tennyson)* (7)
14 Letters from Liege Bill rendered unreadable (9)
16 She was smothered with affection (9)
17 Waste food (7)
18 Sid made absurd crowns (7)
19 It's a bit thick, nevertheless, take care (3-4)
20 Pluto, roused to ecstacy by a difference of opinion (7)
22 Was bold enough right inside the grave (5)
23 Composition that suits Old May to a T (5)

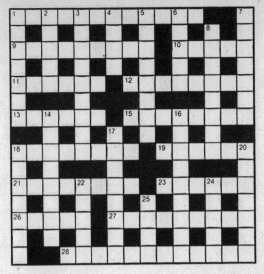

ACROSS

1 He perpetrated brief error with unnatural stuff (3-4,5)
9 Nurse with a portable shelter (5,4)
10 'I'll make a — of him that lets me' *(Hamlet)* (5)
11 Perfect types, as the ungrammatical trader might say (6)
12 Woman driver in bust bodice: the AA is involved (8)
13 Heads of Food Association, rather indignant, now ask for a meal (6)
15 Make sure in Civil Service sentences (8)
18 Harrow leaders take the guard's compartment (5-3)
19 Metal provides two thirds of her income (6)
21 Opening the covers, they have been rather trampled upon (8)
23 'There are few sorrows . . . in which a good — is of no avail' *(Logan Pearsall Smith)* (6)
26 Man has a whip round – he's dishonest! (5)
27 The party we support claims the fish (5,4)
28 Skipped school drama, and utter disaster as well! (6,6)

DOWN

1 Dog the hopeless person following mother (7)
2 Such impudence is never put out (5)
3 'Under The Greenwood Tree' possibly fair maiden is even fairer (3,6)
4 Made up food in a spherical shape (4)
5 '— Hot Muffin and Crumpet Baking and Punctual Delivery Company' *(Nicholas Nickleby)* (8)
6 Punctilious soldier going in free (5)
7 Naval weapon made of copper – old sailor turns up with a second (7)
8 Once inside, creditor takes to a certain musical composition (8)
14 Peruse what is written about a port (4,4)
16 Muscle in – the rotten pinchers have hidden half of it! (9)
17 Undergraduate's late illegitimacy (8)
18 They make topless dresses more respectable (7)
20 'Down, thou climbing sorrow! Thy —'s below' *(King Lear)* (7)
22 Britannia describes certain conductor (5)
24 Author in tears for you? I dare say! (5)
25 The old take part in a village drama (4)

288

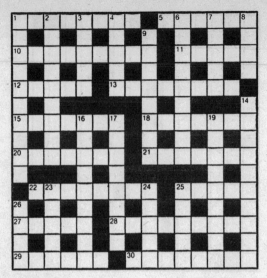

ACROSS

1 Echo some of the fanfares on at Edinburgh (8)
5 Traces of kisses (6)
10 '— certainly gives one werry gentlemanly ideas' *(Mr Jorrocks)* (9)
11 He's in the drink, catching the old cold in the head (5)
12 It is forbidden also to embrace a sailor (5)
13 Withdraws as far as pamphlets are concerned (8)
15 Poet going from right to left around the remains of the burnt cafe (3-4)
18 Tea to stir dear, this poses a riddle! (7)
20 Holy book about a worker produces its own philosophy (7)
21 This voter is an Oriental reader (7)
22 Strikes about first class Liberal agents (8)
25 Fifty four around for food! (5)
27 Shakespearian lady is about on horseback (5)
28 Disreputable person, that is, isn't bad as a supplementary instrumentalist (9)
29 Congregation coming from the capitals of France and Holland (6)
30 Gems on the road, giving a night show (4-4)

DOWN

1 An unmelodious part of the opera (10)
2 Nautical right-hand (9)
3 Poona in ruins and good-for-nothing (5)
4 Adjective for certain wolves and woods (5)
6 Preserve the odd alarm made outside (9)
7 Taking a whip round, he is a fraud (5)
8 Prophet raised by a heathen god (4)
9 Appearing under canvas, Alec put out a feeler (8)
14 The title Barrie borrowed from the Bard (4,6)
16 They catch fish in which the palmist is interested (4-5)
17 Basis of French dish for Monsieur (8)
19 Permission written by one who writes it at the end of May (9)
23 A boring affair to the French backward boy (5)
24 Pink half is in water colour (5)
25 Lets out the sound of a band (5)
26 Character played by an actor put up a ladder (4)

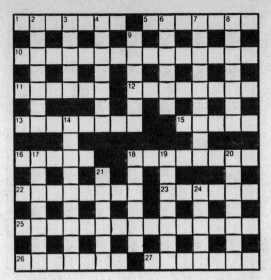

ACROSS

1 Marks grave, possibly (7)
5 The third party to a secret (7)
10 Funny author. Nelly read for twelve months (3,3,4,5)
11 Turning aside the women in service (6)
12 'Laugh, heart, again in the grey —' (8)
13 Deal with the short answer in the leaflet (8)
15 The author of the 12 across clue (5)
16 Holiday in a castle, a very old one (5)
18 Moor space (4,4)
22 PL is to join in the fight, a hand-to-hand fight (4-4)
23 Organ for intake of water might be on ship (6)
25 'No. Ten use it' as published here in the press, leads to over-assumption (15)
26 In surrealist style, we enter in a charming manner (7)
27 Glad greeting (7)

DOWN

2 Hostility, during which the gloves are on? (4,3)
3 '. . . Caesar, in his nightgown' (Shakespeare) (5)
4 Girl sat here rather awkwardly (7)
6 Attention given to covering insect (6)
7 He takes a mean advantage, possibly, making it for peer (9)
8 Musical success (4-3)
9 Verse, not necessarily erotic (6)
14 New palindrome, something to read (9)
17 Cockney intellectual, we hear, might cause it to be raised (7)
18 Wisconsin town is below it, out West (6)
19 Some cut out a dress (7)
20 Creature declares 'O I can' in Latin (7)
21 'It's been shelled'—sounds like a military man (6)
24 A number caught under the vessel take fright (5)

290

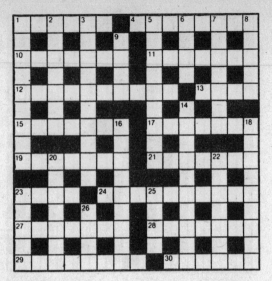

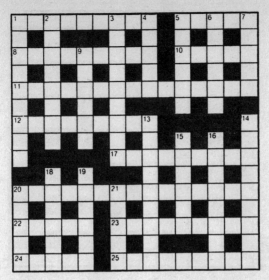

ACROSS

1 Bird caught by Father on the right has a crest (9)
5 I believe this is set to music in church (5)
8 Second year student, with false hopes about room being rebuilt (9)
10 We cut Ted some cloth (5)
11 Self sewn plant? (9,6)
12 In France where this starts off a racing-boat (9)
17 Polite excuse for not receiving a visitor (3,2,4)
20 The twelve-monthly circle, in and out of season (3,3,4,5)
22 Within his shell, a terrapin is slower (5)
23 Unhindered, I dumped mess about north and east (9)
24 Exhausted page sent out (5)
25 Collects fuel rising around the river (7,2)

DOWN

1 Go by formal accounts and records of financial business (4-5)
2 The greed of a business centre after a strike (8)
3 Small drink for doping lunatic (4,2,3)
4 Balances girl on two poles (5)
5 Trades Union Congress returns to eat the evening meal which is chops (4,2)
6 Items provided by fair chance about the end of August (6)
7 'Evening on the —, the golden sea of Wales' *(James Elroy Flecker)* (5)
9 Singular drink for operatic Eugene (6)
13 Lover of ceremony observed in the spiritualist meeting (9)
14 Out of the deep, I duly surrendered (7,2)
15 After a race, reprove the array (6)
16 Nearly spherical, in the manner of circular buildings (8)
18 He's a fool, and he's under cover (6)
19 Eager desire, this is about right at beginning of term (6)
20 Giant book (5)
21 Crazy guy – no junior (5)

292

ACROSS

1 Annual gift (8,7)
8 Overstrain puts artist in a spin (6)
9 A lot of people issue from right to left and note weapon (4-4)
11 Father, a fantastic figure, gets furious (7)
12 Get intensely interested therefore, even about . . . (7)
14 . . . the number of Spanish ships in *The Revenge (5-5)*
17 'For she had a tongue with a —' *(The Tempest)* (4)
18 Might be described as coffee or kidney (4)
19 Indication of omission and mess-up too, perhaps (10)
21 He says he puts money into circulation (7)
23 He used to perform in 'The Extortioner' (7)
25 It might be Ancient *and* Modern (4-4)
27 Time for deciding about a river (6)
28 I am to consider 'skill' and this causes the mind to boggle! (15)

DOWN

2 I am followed by a stupid reply about letters of intent, irrelevantly (13)
3 Eg, Mark Two (5)
4 He may give you the drill (7)
5 Invaluable diamond left in the closet (9)
6 It occurs in the ventriloquist's act (5)
7 I travel under quarter of a mile (3)
10 This postman is upset about two letters and he hates everybody (13)
13 Salute given to heartless Bishop (5)
15 Might be past being strained (5)
16 Hope and Beryl combine to form a rhetorical figure (9)
20 The motor with a meter (4-3)
22 Dressin' the bird (5)
24 'St Agnes' Eve—Ah, bitter—it was' *(Keats)* (5)
26 Make a face and a head of hair (3)

ACROSS

1 IRA redeployed gunners – I would attack! (3-4)
5 Market backs on to course track (7)
9 Give soldier a rude violin, it's common in old suites (5)
10 Money needed to take the railway to the Antarctic (9)
11 Books returned by one Köchel, an Eastern European (6)
12 Hoarse cries, so they say (8)
14 Tip out contents from cups, etc. (5)
15 Duke, being confused with wrong total, filibustered (9)
18 Period following palindrome (9)
20 Cock is hanging (5)
22 Let in lively small horse (8)
24 Circle reformed by clergyman (6)
26 Proportion engaged in honest work (9)
27 Quiet Gaelic Johnny in the river (5)
28 Mark embraces me and you bear up (7)
29 Most employed us and one more in the highest position (7)

DOWN

1 Bitter old place in Venezuela (9)
2 Areas where religions lose some life (7)
3 Possibly late flower sampler (3-6)
4 Town grass (4)
5 Clown from the Criterion (10)
6 Girl in an outfit of pale grey (5)
7 Hamlet follows the conflict with a character from King Henry V (7)
8 Old quizzes (5)
13 Tribe, after scoring a century (or a duck!) describes a certain rite (10)
16 Worker bolts with the jumpers (9)
17 Nurse's word for Romeo (8)
19 Counters display less than two yards, the rest perhaps is outside (7)
21 Carriage is a long time going under the gateway (7)
22 Fair outside comment (5)
23 State in which two Maharajahs rule (5)
25 Thackeray character (4)

294

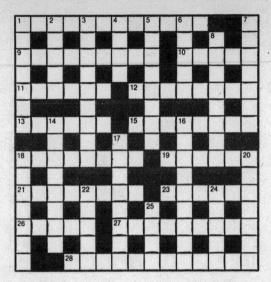

ACROSS

1 Biographer's same job? Well, could be! (5,7)
9 Penultimate state of Shakespeare's Richard III (9)
10 Found in the wash, a kolinsky fur cap! (5)
11 Kind and true, an anagram (6)
12 Investigation of river reaches has come to grief (8)
13 Was jealous of five, that is, in the end (6)
15 Actor jeers – 'They ought to be hung!' (8)
18 Heroic fighter discovered cold in ebbing sea (8)
19 Scribble nineteenth letter at a stroke! (6)
21 Measuring instrument confuses me with Mother (8)
23 Awkward arias, calling initially for lung extension (3-3)
26 Interior of pub "The Queen" (5)
27 Cat I love is in the river – what a business! (9)
28 Affectionate way to address Don (2,4,6)

DOWN

1 Jack Point:- that is, a fool (7)
2 Rebel and coward undergraduate (5)
3 Lady from a dramatic school (9)
4 Free love letter writer (4)
5 Child holds a weaver's reed for a Methodist (8)
6 Lake island material (5)
7 Adjective for certain horse and moth (7)
8 Possible part taken by a chemical firm over a girl (8)
14 Very strong man meets me in the opening (8)
16 Plot with partner about Eastern country (9)
17 Revere, or perhaps enervate (8)
18 Worshipping act in a circle (7)
20 Liberal Unionist about to recognise scene of mutiny (7)
22 We hear why nobleman leads in good time (5)
24 Accomplishment of a runner over two lengths (5)
25 Opening Act – or the Finale? (4)

ACROSS

1 Capital punishment, to compel study of a world's wonder, it's a feature (7,6)

9 One objective case fools the lower classes (3,6)

10 'In a wood of — they bay'd the bear' ('AMND') (5)

11 Interjection used to startle still Shakespearian character (5)

12 General in some degree altered the usual adjective for one monster (5-4)

13 Incomplete design in heaven (7)

15 A single jade is not so big (7)

17 Solve: 'The King in Jamshyd's seven-ringed Vessel' (5,2)

19 Conveyor bird (7)

21 Sea god, having one instead of his tail, swum half the unstable element (9)

23 Norris and Jobiska? (5)

24 A cut of the unlawful riches for the fictional murderer (5)

25 In a nice argument it meant glory to Humpty Dumpty (5-4)

26 Adjusted elbow rest, it's left for a writer (6,7)

DOWN

2 It can be lit, yet put out by a boy in 'The Card' (9)

3 Soldier on, little one and big one! (5)

4 It is also very easy on the eye (7)

5 They may turn some into these (7)

6 'Study in Scarlet' has an unfinished item which is obscure (9)

7 Lamentation from square leg? Yes! (5)

8 The Red Queen pockets a note—one needed by the White Queen (6)

9 Some of the brass in the Bantu base (5)

14 Ornament and disfigurement (9)

16 She complains of molesters from a famous seven (6,3)

17,22 Two of them, could be, ride over to the audience (6,5)

18 Buck up with note under target (7)

19 Fiddler supplies army with crude oil (7)

20 'We are — and stand upright' (Psalms) (5)

22 See 17

23 Oblique request—we rise to follow (5)

296

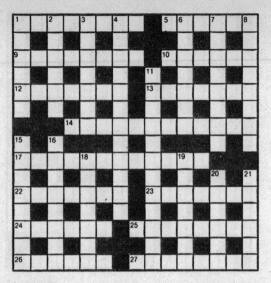

ACROSS

1 Member of the underground, caught in the act, is shown here (8)
5 The rascals pitch tent into the Sunday School (6)
9 Making a request to have a meal in the opening (8)
10 Girl gunners go against the grain (6)
12 Get along, do, into the boat (7)
13 Unproved red unit needs reforming (7)
14 Take the fruit and bring up a string of pack animals (7,5)
17 'To — — away they go' *(Trial by Jury)* (6,6)
22 Prince and priest have the power to present one with a large bill (7)
23 Living in the ocean, I'm a Teredo (7)
24 The resident surgeon inches towards the bird (6)
25 Punishments in plenty (8)
26 Half-baked Senator, not even in! (6)
27 Murders parent on board (8)

DOWN

1 Medical man on the brink captures the oyster-catcher (6)
2 Boy in a film (6)
3 Up in the piano merchant's place for fiddles (7)
4 Alienation of European Trade leaders, including Oddfellows (12)
6 Bird left in garment, it appears (4-3)
7 'What woeful stuff this — would be' *(Pope)* (8)
8 Remaining rigid and in pain (8)
11 Arouse undertaker with warning device (7,5)
15 Caught in September by the Indian Civil Service, they have no conviction (8)
16 Marooned one, dead and buried in turf (8)
18 Fodder from the lake (7)
19 'Fair is too foul an — for thee' *(Marlowe)* (7)
20 Red Indian uncle (6)
21 Time indicators (6)

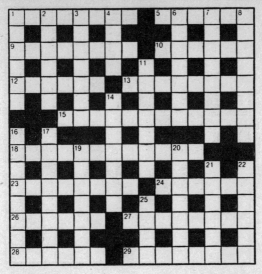

ACROSS

1 Carriage carrying the French politician's spectacles (3-5)
5 This may hold up his breakfast, eg, before George Cross gets up (6)
9 Priest to tempt the novice (8)
10 Quiet sweetheart given the bird (6)
12 Thou art not so — as man's ingratitude' *(As You Like It)* (6)
13 Republic might give it a spank! (8)
15 Forbidding notice that's no notice to German with brown Civil Engineer (2,10)
18 One of the office staff, in good condition for speaking? (7,5)
23 Cricketers' sabbath? (5,3)
24 Double row of trees provides a meeting place (6)
26 Riotous revels when gore is spilt (6)
27 Drag garment (8)
28 Pervert might be said to gain weight (6)
29 Emphasised backtracking the final courses (8)

DOWN

1 Mineral obtained by college servant with money (6)
2 When they joined, then was the tug of war (6)
3 Venetian merchant (7)
4 Stepfather once finished . . . (4)
6 . . . got about entirely on one old boat (7)
7 Eagerly desiring the customer to ring (8)
8 Funereal arrangement seen going up the mountains (8)
11 Flavour making one sick in the V and A (7)
14 Beside the kidneys, girl must separate the quarters of lard (7)
16 A great many coins divided by a courageous man (8)
17 Got the mean old people round the girl (8)
19 Human arches (7)
20 Get another price quoted for Little Albert in the Revue (7)
21 Cards dealt out by Jack Point (6)
22 A King comes in to dine, as dreaded! (6)
25 Climber get a hard nut cracked (4)

298

ACROSS

1 Translated fish indeed! (7)
5 Good man and social worker first in this time (7)
9 One girl is wrong (5)
10 Resting place which might be dubbed 'Leo' (6,3)
11 Calvin and Luther, eg (9)
13 Shocked initially at inside material (5)
14 Secret power of soldier in protective garb (5)
16 Knows leaf as a flower! (9)
17 Lines of irregular length, all very irregular (4,5)
18 Disinclined to act in the liner Titanic (5)
20 Has to make solemn appeals (5)
21 Left it to one to divide a gift in the end (9)
24 Cart comes back with a slab, it's all easily drawn (9)
26 Cosy little home given to a girl (5)
27 Bent down to take root (7)
28 After an effort, Bob and Edward agreed to meet (7)

DOWN

1 Girl with a metric measure for the figure (7)
2 'O sweet and far from—and scar' *(Tennyson)* (5)
3 Church worker has austere neckline — is it in the Fashion House? (8,7)
4 Italian VIP pockets the old coin, a mean trick (5)
5 Acknowledgement of debt given in a pious manner (3)
6 'First of the First' nicely suffices, oddly enough, for egoism (15)
7 Judge a recipe by bite to a certain extent (9)
8 'Those move easiest who have learned—' *(Pope)* (2,5)
12 Bone-black china (5)
15 Large number at 'Man in Grey' (5,4)
16 A bit of 'Up the airy skyways, Down the country too' (5)
17 Altar hanging made out of a saffron tallith (7)
19 Vessel built by the boat population of Canton Road (7)
22 It's obvious the head is understanding too much (5)
23 Inserted leaves in a badger's burrow (5)
25 Adjective for certain lands and language (3)

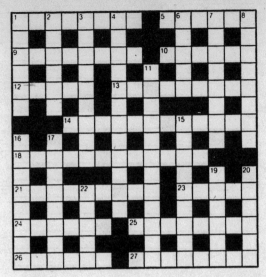

ACROSS

1 Material for moulding perch for Dickens' Noah? (8)
5 Queer cove goes within at getting the bird (6)
9 They are used 'pour encourager les autres' (4-4)
10 There's a place for old Francis here (6)
12 '— of all loiterers and malcontents' *(Love's Labour's Lost)* (5)
13 Will privates in the army enter the match? (9)
14 What is he to his Siamese twin? (4,8)
18 They war about semi-religious initiators of light (12)
21 Old soldiers make even teams (9)
23 Woolly-headed inhabitants of Florentine grotto (5)
24 Two women make a complaint (6)
25 Creatures with long hair occupying public transport (8)
26 Pistol, money in pocket, fixing an engagement (6)
27 Smell the jerry – it's an offensive object (8)

DOWN

1 Wicked little thing (6)
2 'Winds of the World, give —' *(Kipling)* (6)
3 Little by little, we hear it is hardly a bun fight (9)
4 Their charge is said to have been a mistake (5,7)
6 She has only one undergarment (5)
7 Extraordinarily beastly about him who deteriorated little by little (8)
8 'Years he number'd scarce —' *(Jonson)* (8)
11 Like the first Ordinary Seaman, gets clubs, eg, as protection (8,4)
15 . . . Beside the kidneys in a hormone (9)
16 Strong hearted deaf characters took the alternative to swearing (8)
17 Current issue of volume contains King on 'Obstruction' (8)
19 Its contents are almost sure to be cracked! (3-3)
20 County cod at Teesside (6)
22 Battle for chair (5)

300

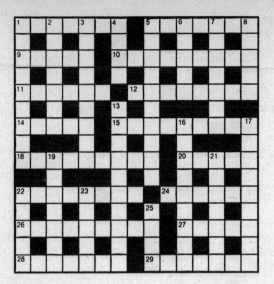

ACROSS

1 Sauerkraut on fried bread (7)
5 Venus or Vesta, perhaps (7)
9 French one the German is beneath (5)
10 One has left the port for the Princess (9)
11 Small bird, small man or small weight (6)
12 Different hats in the City show refinement of style (8)
14 Broadest part of a bottom? What nonsense! (5)
15 '— — and glittering in the smokeless air' *(Wordsworth)* (3,6)
18 Pardonable sex clue rewritten about sailor (9)
20 He added notes to Macbeth and Falstaff (5)
22 Braced framework with a long lock caging in a backward sow (8)
24 Being impelled, I have to interrupt Doctor Newton (6)
26 Bird, right inside the skeleton, carried by train (9)
27 Ancient Britons featured in a historic enigma (5)
28 He graphically described the progress of the immoral (7)
29 Altogether six balls? Quite! (7)

DOWN

1 Sociable number bursting a bubble (9)
2 A service-book, dead in fashion, and spoken about (7)
3 They achieve a piercing line-up (8)
4 The first conservationist? (4)
5 Note the sliced loaves she shares equally between two (4,6)
6 Pulls up the turf (5)
7 Circling round and round, boy takes a mixed gin (7)
8 Half-hose may twist, showing the joins (5)
13 Walk around watery London feature (6,4)
16 Another watery location in town *and* country (9)
17 Nine characters in a law suit lasting three years (9)
19 '— the food of sweet and bitter fancy' *(As You Like It)* (7)
21 Water colour artist to contend with another artist in depicting warm coastal resort (7)
22 Adjective for certains songs and dances (5)
23 Steal up to The Academy leaders' drum (5)
25 Nothing ends in nothing (4)

SOLUTIONS

No. 1

ACROSS: 1 Host 3 Assemble 9 Limbo 10 Rapture 11 Balance 13 Reef 14 Undo 17 Corner 19 Arabia 21 Leaf 23 Isle 25 Strange 28 Apostle 29 Crane 30 Hilarity 31 Peel

DOWN: 1 Half-back 2 Sampler 4 Screen 5 Emperor 6 Brute 7 Even 8 Moon 12 Cure 15 Daft 16 Farewell 18 Elector 20 Bondage 22 Aspect 24 Spoil 26 Rock 27 Bath

No. 2

ACROSS: 1 Madras 4 Abacus 9 Scuttle 10 Spree 11 Optic 12 Gosling 13 Meter 15 Drift 20 Replace 22 Dirty 24 Forgo 25 Decimal 26 Trowel 27 Almond

DOWN: 1 Mascot 2 Doubt 3 Article 5 Basis 6 Cardiff 7 Sleigh 8 Neigh 14 Esparto 16 Radical 17 Profit 18 Ready 19 Eyelid 21 Abode 23 Romeo

No. 3

ACROSS: 1 Soap 6 Ramp 9 Container 10 Ever 12 Mass 14 Postcard 15 Ibis 16 Duff 18 Incident 20 Stranger 21 Rite 22 Sent 24 Painters 28 Tree 29 Idea 30 Arrogance 31 Wary 32 Knot

DOWN: 1 Step 2 Aces 3 Port 4 Stealing 5 Wind 6 Reminder 7 Arab 8 Pass 11 Volunteer 13 Signature 17 Flattery 19 Carnival 22 Stew 23 Near 24 Pool 25 Tick 26 Eden 27 Salt

No. 4

ACROSS: 1 Leicester 8 Evian 9 Trainee 10 Dollop 11 Welfare 13 Logic 15 Bored 16 Elude 18 Sleeper 21 Orbits 22 Quality 23 Susan 24 Gateshead

DOWN: 2 Eerie 3 Chiefs 4 Steer 5 Remould 6 Village 7 Inspector 11 Warehouse 12 Earns 14 Rubbish 15 Belting 17 Health 19 Louse 20 Extra

No. 5

ACROSS: 1 Fail Safe 5 Show 9 Arise 10 Trailed 11 Middle 12 Radio 14 Lilian 16 Sleeve 19 Visit 21 Weight 24 Trainer 25 Skull 26 Reel 27 Detector

DOWN: 1 Flap 2 Initial 3 Speed 4 Fitter 6 Holed 7 Wide-open 8 Patrol 13 Elevator 15 Acting 17 Exhaust 18 Swerve 20 Stage 22 Issue 23 Blur

No. 6

ACROSS: 1 Punjab 4 Scales 8 Strand 10 Handle 11 Tides 12 Plea 14 Attic 15 Speed 17 Rock 19 Eggs 20 Score 21 Corgi 23 Lull 26 Roars 28 Hidden 29 Desist 30 Riding 31 Penned

DOWN: 1 Passport 2 Nurse 3 Aunt 5 Coast 6 Lodging 7 Shed 9 Diversion 10 Headboard 13 Ask 16 Isolated 18 Clouded 19 Eel 22 Green 24 Union 25 Char 27 Sere

No. 7

ACROSS: 1 Greens 4 Walton 7 Component 9 Boon 10 Dope 11 Hoses 13 Lesson 14 Rupert 15 Pumped 17 Tenant 19 Lever 20 Cant 22 Scar 23 Guarantee 24 Twinge 25 Silent

DOWN: 1 Gambol 2 Eton 3 Siphon 4 Winner 5 Land 6 Newest 7 Consuming 8 Tolerance 11 Hotel 12 Super 15 Packet 16 Degree 17 Tennis 18 Threat 21 Turn 22 Seal

No. 8

ACROSS: 1 Strike 4 Order 7 Dip 8 Collide 9 Point 10 Near 11 Miss 12 Tar 14 Wellingtons 18 Rip 20 City 21 Dial 23 Malta 24 Oration 25 Din 26 Singe 27 Astray

DOWN: 1 Second 2 Release 3 Knit 4 Opposite 5 Drift 6 Return 7 Designation 13 Blockade 15 Noisier 16 Trumps 17 Plenty 19 Pylon 22 Pass

No. 9

ACROSS: 1 Ogress 4 Checks 8 Emblem 10 Island 11 Point 12 Solo 14 Ferry 15 Wheel 17 Aden 19 Adze 20 Notes 21 Naomi 23 Prod 26 Ascot 28 Repose 29 Normal 30 Greens 31 Reform

DOWN: 1 Overseas 2 Rebel 3 Step 5 Haste 6 Chaired 7 Side 9 Modernise 10 Inflation 13 Own 16 Pendulum 18 Example 19 Asp 22 Mason 24 Romeo 25 Drag 27 Tome

No. 10

ACROSS: 1 Dragoon 5 Rails 8 Eight 9 Canasta 10 Limit 12 Arena 14 Tasty 16 Vigo 17 Tree 19 Skids 21 Asset 23 Enemy 26 Improve 27 Elude 28 Nurse 29 Slender

DOWN: 1 Diet 2 Angling 3 Outfit 4 Nick 5 Runway 6 Issue 7 Seafarer 11 Tank 13 Aviation 15 Tide 18 Remould 19 Stroke 20 Sneeze 22 Super 24 Pets 25 Gear

No. 11

ACROSS: 1 Identity 5 Ache 9 Coast 10 Meaning 11 Signal 13 Along 15 Best 17 Genial 19 Newton 21 Nero 23 Onset 25 Object 28 Ailment 29 Delta 30 Tool 31 Friendly

DOWN: 1 Itch 2 Elation 3 Titan 4 Tumble 6 Cairo 7 Engaging 8 Palate 12 Able 14 Ignorant 16 Snob 18 Anthem 20 Tickled 22 Rotter 24 Salvo 26 Judge 27 Mary

No. 12

ACROSS: 1 John Bull 5 Amps 9 Ideal 10 Miracle 11 Embrace 14 Venal 15 Urge 17 Adder 19 Arrow 21 Sect 24 Paint 25 Leather 27 Rotates 28 Nesta 30 Song 31 Adhesive

DOWN: 1 Joiner 2 Hoe 3 Balsa 4 Lumber 6 Macintosh 7 Stella 8 Driver 12 Badminton 13 Cure 16 Gate 18 Estate 20 Sports 22 Closed 23 Crease 26 Annie 29 Ski

No. 13

ACROSS: 1 Scholar 5 Angus 8 Relic 9 Matting 10 Paint 12 Cheap 14 Gross 16 Roll 17 Isis 19 Heard 21 Cargo 23 Kerry 26 Cricket 27 Antic 28 Essay 29 Panther

DOWN: 1 Surf 2 Holdall 3 Lacing 4 Rims 5 Attics 6 Glide 7 Signpost 11 Tree 13 Tricycle 15 Sark 18 Stretch 19 Hockey 20 Detain 22 Rails 24 Stop 25 Scar

No. 14

ACROSS: 1 Acceleration 8 Channel 9 Ideas 10 Leg 11 Fine 12 Stall 15 Enough 16 Report 19 Voice 21 Hugh 22 Air 25 Cling 26 Evasive 27 Inverted loop

DOWN: 1 Arch 2 Cram 3 Landing 4 Rolled 5 Twigs 6 Operator 7 Isolate 13 Service 14 Position 17 England 18 Threat 20 Eagle 23 Fido 24 Peep

No. 15

ACROSS: 1 Trailers 5 User 9 Smart 10 Nervous 11 Expense 14 Voter 15 Urge 17 Power 19 Aroma 21 Seas 24 About 25 Springs 27 Painter 28 Llama 30 Tank 31 Playmate

DOWN: 1 Tested 2 Aga 3 Luton 4 Runner 6 Sportsman 7 Resort 8 Driver 12 Promotion 13 Sure 16 Gasp 18 Estate 20 Carpet 22 Astral 23 Escape 26 Rally 29 Ada

No. 16

ACROSS: 1 Mudguard 5 Opts 9 Dread 10 Channel 11 Stirrup 14 Usher 15 Neat 17 Unwed 19 Nepal 21 Soft 24 Burst 25 Leaflet 27 Counter 28 Rally 30 Step 31 Inflator

DOWN: 1 Modest 2 Due 3 Under 4 Recipe 6 Punchball 7 Salary 8 Salute 12 Inner Tube 13 Undo 16 Ante 18 Estate 20 Abacus 22 Florin 23 Stayer 26 April 29 Lot

No. 17

ACROSS: 1 Fortress 5 Boss 7 Soar 9 Hannay 10 Pounce 12 Dig 13 Disarm 15 Null 16 All 17 Beef 19 Excess 21 Lit 22 Repaid 26 Single 27 Pull 28 Knot 29 Scramble

DOWN: 1 Fist 2 Reap 3 Earn 4 Schedule 5 Benign 6 Stabilise 8 Rota 11 Direction 14 Mattress 18 Flight 20 Clip 23 Poor 24 Dumb 25 Blue

No. 18

ACROSS: 1 Canvas 4 Jampot 8 Anthem 10 Pillow 11 Cable 12 Host 14 Inlay 15 Odium 17 Loop 19 Bean 20 Those 21 Lasso 23 True 26 Psalm 28 Loofah 29 Sandal 30 Basket 31 Melody

DOWN: 1 Coal-hole 2 Notes 3 Alec 5 Alien 6 Pillage 7 Town 9 Macintosh 10 Plimsolls 13 Top 16 Underlay 18 Orators 19 Bet 22 Space 24 Radio 25 Club 27 Make

No. 19

ACROSS: 1 Controls 5 Spit 7 Lots 9 Divide 10 Octane 12 Sun 13 Hectic 15 Gear 16 Ali 17 Tiff 19 Patrol 21 Ops 22 Hummed 26 Stella 27 Nene 28 Crew 29 Titanium

DOWN: 1 Call 2 NATO 3 Olga 4 Sideslip 5 Saving 6 Indicator 8 Scot 11 Perimeter 14 Camshaft 18 Follow 20 Then 23 Mist 24 Demi 25 Beam

No. 20

ACROSS: 1 Operations 7 Avid 8 Telegram 10 Needled 12 Angus 14 Tangled 17 Ill 18 Arc 19 Plaster 22 Extra 23 Tracing 26 Training 28 Sore 29 Diet Sheets

DOWN: 1 Out-patient 2 Eel 3 August 4 Ivan 5 Saddle 6 Life 9 Meagre 11 Discharges 13 Gulp 15 Absent 16 Dart 20 Locked 21 Relish 24 Room 25 Grit 27 Ice

No. 21

ACROSS: 1 Propulsion 8 Night 9 Adverse 10 Ted 11 Valve 12 Scene 13 Right 15 Gyro 16 Ache 18 Genoa 20 Tessa 22 Sonic 23 Arc 24 Overlap 25 Evens 26 Map Reading

DOWN: 2 Regular 3 Putter 4 Lead 5 Invest 6 Nurse 7 References 8 Navigation 14 Gun 17 Canteen 18 Gallop 19 Ascend 21 Steam 23 Apse

No. 22

ACROSS: 1 Crosswind 8 Solo 9 Passenger 11 Dimple 13 Terse 15 From 16 Tenth 17 Cites 18 Cocoa 19 Anne 20 Agent 22 Undoes 25 Reference 26 Sewn 27 Standards

DOWN: 2 Read 3 System 4 Wings 5 Need 6 Component 7 Nosewheel 10 Rifts 12 Off Course 13 Touch-down 14 Extra 17 Cater 19 Angela 21 Green 23 Seat 24 Iced

No. 23

ACROSS: 1 Aviation 8 Outfit 9 Forecast 10 Alight 12 Party 14 Silver 16 Paid 18 Sign 19 Nimbus 20 Scare 23 Studio 26 Nuisance 27 Bikini 28 Category

DOWN: 2 Viola 3 Agent 4 Iran 5 Notables 6 Stripes 7 Dish 11 Trance 12 Pupils 13 Rain 14 Subsonic 15 Rita 17 Disdain 21 Clang 22 Racer 24 Trim 25 Tilt

No. 24

ACROSS: 1 Instruments 7 Disc 8 Crow 9 Torrent 11 HMSO 13 Asks 16 Transport 17 Via 18 One 19 Generator 22 Noel 24 Bend 26 Essence 29 Kiev 30 Revs 31 Link Trainer

DOWN: 1 Idiom 2 Sector 3 Rear 4 Mile 5 Nectar 6 Shock 10 Reserve 11 Haven 12 Stage 14 Store 15 Speed 20 Eleven 21 Oberon 23 Oriel 25 Never 27 Slot 28 Nora

No. 25

ACROSS: 1 Grotesque 6 Kip 8 Austria 9 Blade 10 Suit 11 Tropics 13 Eye 14 Rural 15 Car 16 Formula 18 Cape 20 Raged 21 Tornado 22 Err 23 Personnel

DOWN: 1 Graf 2 Obscure 3 Egret 4 Quartermaster 5 Embroil 6 Khaki 7 Pleasure 12 Perforce 14 Round Up 15 Captain 17 Roger 18 Cargo 19 Foul

No. 26

ACROSS: 1 Strike 4 Level 7 Ice 8 Mission 9 Arson 10 Iris 11 Spin 12 Ton 14 Unwarranted 18 Art 20 Rite 21 Spot 23 Tunic 24 Operate 25 Kin 26 Rings 27 Ironed

DOWN: 1 Summit 2 Russian 3 Knit 4 Learning 5 Visit 6 Lining 7 Inspiration 13 Barracks 15 Explain 16 Master 17 Attend 19 Tenon 22 Veer

No. 27

ACROSS: 5 Avon 7 Air-pockets 8 Keen 9 Kite 12 Emits 13 Neighs 14 Nicety 16 Stream 18 Tripod 19 Enter 20 Else 23 Disc 24 Horsepower 25 Oslo

DOWN: 1 Bank 2 Fret 3 Screws 4 Resign 5 Asks 6 Operations 10 Identities 11 Eagle 15 Crime 17 Motors 18 Turret 19 Echo 21 Lawn 22 Earl

No. 28

ACROSS: 1 Defuse 4 Eight 7 Ann 8 Promote 9 Goner 10 Risk 11 Down 12 Sea 14 Employments 18 One 20 Trap 21 Calm 23 Strip 24 Inertia 25 Inc 26 Latin 27 Secret

DOWN: 1 Depart 2 Flotsam 3 Snow 4 Engineer 5 Gents 6 Tarmac 7 Aerodynamic 13 Flat Spin 15 Tractor 16 Dorsal 17 Impact 19 Egret 22 Here

No. 29

ACROSS: 1 Classic 5 March 8 Mocha 9 Monsoon 10 Sum 11 Cairo 12 Asses 13 Nanny 14 Rank 15 Play 17 Locks 19 Force 21 Tight 23 Tea 24 Swahili 25 Tacit 26 Lemon 27 Nacelle

DOWN: 1 Comic 2 Auction 3 Season 4 Communication 5 Monday 6 Roots 7 Honesty 14 Refusal 16 Logical 17 Legion 18 Static 20 Realm 22 Title

No. 30

ACROSS: 1 Carburettor 7 Bomb 8 Rave 9 Blotter 11 Seal 13 Eire 16 Sergeants 17 Ali 18 Lei 19 Directive 22 Then 24 Etch 26 Fireman 29 Mimi 30 Emma 31 Atmospheric

DOWN: 1 Close 2 Rubble 3 Undo 4 East 5 Turret 6 River 10 Treacle 11 Shaft 12 Aside 14 Islet 15 Edith 20 Infirm 21 Veneer 23 Haifa 25 Comic 27 Ribs 28 Myth

No. 31

ACROSS: 1 Logistics 6 Era 7 Ems 9 Relic 10 Tread 11 Inter 12 Exact 13 Baton 15 Elect 17 Inset 21 Swung 23 Eject 24 Heron 25 Ogres 26 Drill 27 Dim 28 Ass 29 Personnel

DOWN: 1 Lament 2 Garden 3 Sultan 4 Incite 5 Settle 6 Established 8 Strategists 14 One 16 Low 18 Shrimp 19 Tender 20 Merino 21 Stolen 22 Unreal

No. 32

ACROSS: 1 Bertha 4 French 8 Oxford 10 United 11 Pains 12 Lisp 14 Depot 15 Lathe 17 Copy 19 Asti 20 Orbit 21 Manna 23 East 26 Erode 28 Netted 29 Yankee 30 Thrust 31 Recess

DOWN: 1 Bootlace 2 Rafts 3 Harp 5 Rinse 6 Nations 7 Hide 9 Dartboard 10 Underbody 13 Ply 16 Distress 18 Planter 19 Ate 22 Needs 24 Ankle 25 Knot 27 Ease

No. 33

ACROSS: 1 Mountain 5 Dope 7 Clip 9 Common 10 Tumble 12 Tin 13 Bullet 15 Dole 16 Eve 17 Eric 19 Summer 21 Ham 22 Intake 26 Prison 27 Earl 28 Edge 29 Listless

DOWN: 1 Mock 2 Unit 3 Arab 4 Niceties 5 Demand 6 Propeller 8 Pull 11 Quartered 14 Terminal 18 Chaste 20 Make 23 Toss 24 Ease 25 Plus

No. 34

ACROSS: 1 Forward 5 Heart 8 Right 9 Skipper 10 Eve 11 Tudor 12 Hinge 13 Night 14 Boys 15 Undo 17 Might 19 Ivory 21 Amigo 23 Man 24 Theatre 25 Known 26 Leave 27 Turbine

DOWN: 1 First 2 Rigidly 3 Astern 4 Disengagement 5 Height 6 Aspen 7 Torpedo 14 Bristol 16 Nairobi 17 Myrtle 18 Tanker 20 Opera 22 Ounce

No. 35

ACROSS: 1 Maintenance 7 Bacon 8 Discord 10 Emus 11 Pair 13 Tea 15 Kit Inspection 17 Oar 19 Item 20 Asti 22 Numbers 24 Crate 25 Instruments

DOWN: 2 Account 3 Nine 4 End 5 Abstract 6 Clout 7 Breakdown 9 Drainpipe 12 Ample 14 Incident 16 Instant 18 Roman 21 Ache 23 Sou

No. 36

ACROSS: 5 Late 7 Turbulence 8 Face 9 Plan 12 Shoot 13 Abroad 14 Merlin 16 Divert 18 Static 19 North 20 Hand 23 Otto 24 Silhouette 25 Edge

DOWN: 1 Stop 2 Area 3 Closed 4 Inform 5 Left 6 Technician 10 Lubricated 11 Noose 15 Reach 17 Thrill 18 School 19 Nose 21 Ante 22 Deed

No. 37

ACROSS: 5 Give 7 Inspection 8 Also 9 Thug 12 Inert 13 Rating 14 Tiffin 16 Ampere 18 Bandit 19 Bigot 20 Lays 23 Etna 24 Regulation 25 Free

DOWN: 1 List 2 Esau 3 Acting 4 Direct 5 Gnat 6 Visibility 10 Headmaster 11 Guide 15 Final 17 Engage 18 Battle 19 Bare 21 Axis 22 Sand

No. 38

ACROSS: 1 Longitude 6 Coo 7 Mar 9 Cling 10 Rogue 11 Evans 12 Talon 13 Italy 15 Tokyo 17 Idiot 21 Heaps 23 Alive 24 Alter 25 Climb 26 Moist 27 Etc 28 Age 29 Technical

DOWN: 1 Loggia 2 Nicety 3 Icicle 4 Urgent 5 Embark 6 Certificate 8 Responsible 14 Leo 16 One 18 Intact 19 Tarmac 20 Vision 21 Hectic 22 Animal

No. 39

ACROSS: 1 Communication 8 Panel 9 Reign 10 Alarm 11 Omen 12 Aught 14 Stern 17 Home 18 True 20 Gamma 23 Naval 25 Soup 26 Inlet 28 Yield 29 Ukase 30 Unserviceable

DOWN: 1 Cope 2 Minimum 3 Uhlans 4 Intake 5 Airman 6 Icing 7 Nineties 13 Thank You 15 Tea 16 Rum 19 Rhubarb 20 Glider 21 Malawi 22 Astute 24 Views 27 Here

No. 40

ACROSS: 1 Clearance 8 Mist 9 Indicator 11 Dinner 13 Dated 15 Keel 16 Hello 17 Chest 18 Reach 19 Rear 20 Steer 22 Cutter 25 Fire-power 26 Eire 27 Celestial

DOWN: 2 Link 3 Animal 4 Aware 5 Clod 6 Signaller 7 Starboard 10 Right 12 Sky-rocket 13 Departure 14 Dress 17 Chief 19 Report 21 There 23 Rise 24 Vera

No. 41

ACROSS: 1 Golf Jacket 8 Integer 9 Error 10 Sprat 11 Wedlock 13 Else 15 Lustre 17 Ladles 19 Ness 21 Teapots 23 Truro 25 Ought 26 Alights 27 Racketeers

DOWN: 2 Outer 3 Fighter 4 Arrows 5 Knead 6 Turmoil 7 Brake-shoes 8 Insulation 12 Eels 14 Lent 16 Stagger 18 Astride 20 Estate 22 Optic 24 Usher

No. 42

ACROSS: 1 Instrumental 8 Leaflet 9 Motor 10 Era 11 Fido 12 Ditch 15 Things 16 Gander 19 Tenon 21 Earl 22 Oil 25 Occur 26 Isobars 27 Metal Fatigue

DOWN: 1 Idle 2 Stay 3 Rolling 4 Meteor 5 Nomad 6 Altitude 7 Archery 13 Station 14 Pinnacle 17 Airport 18 Relief 20 Norma 23 Bang 24 Isle

No. 43

ACROSS: 1 Streamer 5 Save 7 Draw 9 Throbs 10 Dakota 12 Tin 13 Outfit 15 Gate 16 Ran 17 Arts 19 Gallon 21 Ian 22 System 26 Bantam 27 Race 28 Beer 29 Together

DOWN: 1 Side 2 Road 3 Mayo 4 Rotating 5 Spring 6 Vibration 8 Waif 11 Lubricate 14 Transmit 18 Sitter 20 Leer 23 Song 24 Mash 25 Gear

No. 44

ACROSS: 1 Athens 4 Stick 7 Cut 8 Barrage 9 Alert 10 Raze 11 Stud 12 Lee 14 Indifferent 18 Sew 20 Neck 21 Late 23 Owing 24 Tornado 25 Hue 26 Trent 27 Intact

DOWN: 1 Albert 2 Horizon 3 Near 4 Standard 5 Ideal 6 Kitten 7 Certificate 13 Midnight 15 Niagara 16 Escort 17 Report 19 Whine 22 Iron

No. 45

ACROSS: 1 Longitude 6 Roe 7 Fit 9 Least 10 Venal 11 Obese 12 Ideal 13 Large 15 Deter 17 Twang 21 Debut 23 Range 24 Ounce 25 Stoic 26 Alive 27 Six 28 Ill 29 Energetic

DOWN: 1 Leaner 2 Nellie 3 Images 4 Untold 5 Effect 6 Revolutions 8 Theoretical 14 Gun 16 Eve 18 Annexe 19 Grease 20 Ending 21 Desert 22 Bionic

No. 46

ACROSS: 1 Wavelength 8 Attic 9 Gentian 10 Ice 11 Joint 12 Layer 13 Eagle 15 Shed 16 Port 18 Homer 20 Morse 22 Optic 23 Bat 24 Neutral 25 Troll 26 Discharged

DOWN: 2 Astride 3 Excite 4 Edge 5 Gentle 6 Hairy 7 Uncritical 8 Adjustment 14 Gum 17 Outcome 18 Hearts 19 Rotter 21 Round 23 Blah

No. 47

ACROSS: 1 Transit 5 Scrap 8 River 9 Exhaust 10 Err 11 Wince 12 Midge 13 Those 14 Crew 15 Chin 17 Pound 19 Lover 21 Owlet 23 Lad 24 Whistle 25 Gates 26 Reedy 27 Reserve

DOWN: 1 Throw 2 Advance 3 Street 4 Thermonuclear 5 Scheme 6 Round 7 Pattern 14 Cold War 16 Holster 17 Pretty 18 Dodges 20 Voice 22 Taste

No. 48

ACROSS: 1 Operationally 8 Await 9 Crank 10 Heart 11 Line 12 Awash 14 Motor 17 Item 18 Calm 20 Repel 23 Ounce 25 Open 26 Canon 28 Aught 29 Drape 30 Entertainment

DOWN: 1 Oral 2 Examine 3 Anthem 4 Intact 5 Nectar 6 Llama 7 Yokohama 13 Pilotage 15 Owe 16 One 19 Average 20 Rector 21 Panama 22 London 24 Night 27 West

No. 49

ACROSS: 1 Homing 4 Super 7 Imp 8 Martian 9 Eject 10 Etch 11 Grit 12 Sun 14 Serviceable 18 Wag 20 Raid 21 Star 23 Tango 24 Neutral 25 Ass 26 Hoard 27 Outlay

DOWN: 1 Hamper 2 Miracle 3 Nail 4 Spectral 5 Press 6 Rating 7 Infractions 13 Overload 15 Lateral 16 Switch 17 Brolly 19 Genoa 22 Lulu

No. 50

ACROSS: 1 Monte Carlo 8 Fishing 9 Glide 10 Oiled 11 Rhenish 13 Lose 15 Runner 17 Astern 19 Asti 21 Instant 23 Tales 25 Error 26 Treated 27 Manchester

DOWN: 2 Ousel 3 Twiddle 4 Cigars 5 Rogue 6 Orifice 7 Mechanised 8 Floor Tiles 12 Heat 14 Oran 16 Nostrum 18 Sitters 20 Stitch 22 Apron 24 Lathe

No. 51

ACROSS: 1 Facsimile 6 Mar 7 All 9 Ropes 10 Aimer 11 Eaten 12 Occur 13 Upset 15 Torso 17 Evoke 21 Bland 23 Rouse 24 Elder 25 Tiger 26 Ambit 27 Tea 28 Lay 29 Ladybirds

DOWN: 1 Frames 2 Carrot 3 Impact 4 Insert 5 Easter 6 Measurement 8 Londonderry 14 Erk 16 Oil 18 Ordeal 19 Errand 20 Hubbub 21 Better 22 Angels

No. 52

ACROSS: 1 Straight Ahead 8 Medal 9 Tagus 10 Angle 11 Scan 12 Rotor 14 Derby 17 Ally 18 Dope 20 Dress 23 Assay 25 Apex 26 Natal 28 Opera 29 Again 30 Airworthiness

DOWN: 1 Sump 2 Radical 3 Inland 4 Hangar 5 Artery 6 Eight 7 Deserter 13 Parabola 15 Ear 16 Bus 19 Operate 20 Dynamo 21 Extent 22 Salami 24 Spear 27 Onus

No. 53

ACROSS: 1 Passport 8 Afraid 9 Flapjack 10 Exempt 12 Sweat 14 Spoils 16 Grey 18 Yell 19 Relief 20 Screw 23 Ladles 26 Heliport 27 Pronto 28 Dog-fight

DOWN: 2 Allow 3 Sepia 4 Oral 5 Takes Off 6 Briefly 7 Limp 11 Tallow 12 Signal 13 Ewer 14 Slipshod 15 Seer 17 Yelling 21 Capri 22 Earth 24 Airy 25 Flog

No. 54

ACROSS: 1 Approval 8 Airman 9 American 10 Divert 12 Psalm 14 Seesaw 16 Stew 18 Lawn 19 Shield 20 Bench 23 Doctor 26 Invasion 27 Violin 28 Gangster

DOWN: 2 Pumps 3 Rural 4 Vice 5 Land's End 6 Trivial 7 Pair 11 Trench 12 Passed 13 Aces 14 Steering 15 Warn 17 Whittle 21 Eases 22 Close 24 Omit 25 Avon

No. 55

ACROSS: 5 Tree 7 Uniformity 8 Reel 9 Thin 12 Dance 13 Pretty 14 Report 16 Nether 18 Menace 19 Oiled 20 Lily 23 Swan 24 Controller 25 Free

DOWN: 1 Suit 2 Kiwi 3 Friday 4 Winner 5 Tyre 6 Electrical 10 Horsepower 11 Notch 15 Panel 17 Relent 18 Modern 19 Once 21 Idle 22 Yard

No. 56

ACROSS: 1 Damp 3 Bald 6 Bid 9 Trace 10 Cleaner 11 Shunted 12 Moor 14 Grease 16 Grocer 19 Tail 21 Heating 24 Advance 25 Crane 27 Pal 28 East 29 Vent

DOWN: 1 Dot 2 Measure 4 Arcade 5 Dreamer 6 Bingo 7 Dirt 8 Beat 11 Sign 13 Brag 15 Silence 17 Climate 18 Wheels 20 Anvil 22 Arch 23 Ramp 26 Eat

No. 57

ACROSS: 1 Compressed 8 Valve 9 Gallant 10 Toe 11 Sight 12 Crest 13 Yeast 15 Body 16 Fido 18 Speed 20 Limit 22 Erica 23 Kit 24 Tension 25 Amity 26 Right Angle

DOWN: 2 Obliged 3 Pretty 4 Edge 5 Select 6 Drake 7 Stationary 8 Visibility 14 Awe 17 Initial 18 String 19 Detain 21 Minor 23 Knot

No. 58

ACROSS: 1 Promoted 8 Outfit 9 Hong Kong 10 Summit 12 Testy 14 Propel 16 Ayot 18 Root 19 Worthy 20 Scope 23 Steppe 26 Newcomer 27 Tactic 28 Engineer

DOWN: 2 Rhone 3 Might 4 Tool 5 Dog's-body 6 Stammer 7 Mimi 11 Turtle 12 Thames 13 Show 14 Patience 15 Loco 17 Towpath 21 Crown 22 Piece 24 Team 25 Twig

No. 59

ACROSS: 1 Boring 4 Staple 8 Lascar 10 Engine 11 Terms 12 Wind 14 Pedal 15 Equal 17 Yarn 19 Peep 20 Buyer 21 State 23 Over 26 Anger 28 Unrest 29 Secret 30 Ladder 31 Veneer

DOWN: 1 Bulawayo 2 Resin 3 Neat 5 Tense 6 Private 7 Even 9 Recumbent 10 Employees 13 Den 16 Operator 18 Retired 19 Pro 22 Taste 24 Verse 25 Pull 27 Rene

No. 60

ACROSS: 1 Streamer 5 Bear 7 Opus 9 Vanity 10 Tattoo 12 Lie 13 Squall 15 Read 16 Use 17 Miss 19 Repaid 21 Ebb 22 Esteem 26 Censor 27 Race 28 Stun 29 Diplomat

DOWN: 1 Stop 2 Rout 3 Mist 4 Revolver 5 Banner 6 Automatic 8 Saga 11 Equipment 14 Lumbered 18 Season 20 Pier 23 Trip 24 Maim 25 West

No. 61

ACROSS: 1 Midnight 5 Leaf 9 Waste 10 Nothing 11 Grotto 12 Treat 14 Asylum 16 Astern 19 Steep 21 Plunge 24 Overrun 25 Crate 26 Tote 27 Defender

DOWN: 1 Mown 2 Destroy 3 Inert 4 Hendon 6 Exile 7 Fighting 8 Status 13 Passport 15 Umpire 17 England 18 Sponge 20 Erect 22 Uncle 23 Heir

No. 62

ACROSS: 1 Design 4 Close 7 Rio 8 Chinese 9 Rifle 10 Mope 11 Solo 12 Rig 14 Present Arms 18 Lob 20 Avid 21 Edge 23 Guard 24 Retreat 25 Eye 26 Tudor 27 Trusty

DOWN: 1 Decamp 2 Skipper 3 Glen 4 Corporal 5 Offer 6 Emerge 7 Reconnoitre 13 Islander 15 Madness 16 Flight 17 Sentry 19 Brand 22 Star

No. 63

ACROSS: 1 Obliterate 8 Pylon 9 Compete 10 Och 11 Odour 12 Radio 13 Ensue 15 Aunt 16 Nora 18 Scrap 20 About 22 Alibi 23 Fat 24 Decline 25 Rooks 26 Regardless

DOWN: 2 Balloon 3 Ignore 4 Etch 5 Admire 6 Emend 7 Aerobatics 8 Propaganda 14 Sir 17 Ominous 18 String 19 Patrol 21 Occur 23 Fear

No. 64

ACROSS: 1 Method 4 Hover 7 Hoe 8 Surface 9 Arson 10 Exit 11 Dial 12 Tie 14 Development 18 Air 20 Tote 21 Acre 23 Attic 24 Regular 25 Ass 26 Atoll 27 Defeat

DOWN: 1 Master 2 Turbine 3 Oral 4 Headlamp 5 Visit 6 Ranked 7 Helicopters 13 Vertical 15 Nacelle 16 Canada 17 Secret 19 Ratio 22 Ogre

No. 65

ACROSS: 1 Accident-prone 8 Cross 9 Eager 10 Elder 11 Spar 12 Catch 14 Theme 17 Card 18 Plan 20 Prong 23 Berth 25 Lute 26 Idaho 28 Angel 29 Wrong 30 Disappearance

DOWN: 1 Arch 2 Chopper 3 Desert 4 Needle 5 Pierce 6 Ought 7 Earphone 13 Scabbard 15 Her 16 Man 19 Let Down 20 Philip 21 Oracle 22 Glower 24 Rages 27 Ogle

No. 66

ACROSS: 1 Servicing 8 Life 9 Concourse 11 Streak 13 Quits 15 Drum 16 Eaten 17 Anger 18 Ellen 19 Moon 20 Train 22 Toffee 25 Latitudes 26 Reel 27 Interests

DOWN: 2 Eton 3 Vacuum 4 Count 5 Ness 6 Direction 7 Reckoning 10 Ether 12 Adventure 13 Qualified 14 Sight 17 Angel 19 Minute 21 Rhine 23 Earn 24 Beat

No. 67

ACROSS: 1 Dropping 5 Flap 9 Tutor 10 Germane 11 Morsel 12 Arena 14 Hither 16 Degree 19 Moral 21 Attack 24 Imposed 25 Brave 26 Nile 27 Streamer

DOWN: 1 Duty 2 Outpost 3 Parts 4 Niggle 6 Leave 7 Prepared 8 Grease 13 Champion 15 Enlist 17 Reclaim 18 Bandit 20 Repel 22 Table 23 Beer

No. 68

ACROSS: 1 Password 8 Icarus 9 Fearless 10 Patrol 12 Steep 14 Matter 16 Curb 18 Noah 19 Launch 20 Radar 23 Tattoo 26 War-horse 27 Course 28 Ramparts

DOWN: 2 Alert 3 Serge 4 Open 5 Dispatch 6 Canteen 7 Judo 11 Lather 12 Secret 13 Earl 14 Manpower 15 Road 17 Battery 21 Aroma 22 Asset 24 Atom 25 Drum

No. 69

ACROSS: 1 Forward 5 Comic 8 Aisle 9 Station 10 Rot 11 Skids 12 Clear 13 Ernie 14 Sand 15 Bull 17 Stunt 19 Aware 21 Ahead 23 Sub 24 Through 25 Large 26 Range 27 Ditched

DOWN: 1 Flaps 2 Russian 3 Averse 4 Distinguished 5 Chance 6 Maine 7 Central 14 Shatter 16 Unearth 17 Secure 18 Tablet 20 Apron 22 Dread

No. 70

ACROSS: 1 Corporal 5 Seek 7 Slab 9 Number 10 Defend 12 Foe 13 Demand 15 Rate 16 Eel 17 Door 19 London 21 Ali 22 Ginger 26 Fasten 27 Dark 28 Tyre 29 Rationed

DOWN: 1 Cast 2 Read 3 Rome 4 Landfall 5 Summer 6 Execution 8 Beta 11 Secondary 14 Designer 18 Rattle 20 Need 23 Newt 24 Rain 25 Skid

No. 71

ACROSS: 1 Rocket 4 Guard 7 Roe 8 Pancake 9 Nears 10 Iron 11 Area 12 Mar 14 Emplacement 18 Nap 20 Ivan 21 Emma 23 Apron 24 Liaison 25 Cue 26 Ensue 27 Censor

DOWN: 1 Repair 2 Conform 3 Exam 4 Gendarme 5 Alarm 6 Desert 7 Retractable 13 Alliance 15 Nemesis 16 Intake 17 Banner 19 Paris 22 Lane

No. 72

ACROSS: 1 Speculate 8 Adam 9 Passenger 11 Meteor 13 Sound 15 Room 16 Untie 17 Strut 18 Queen 19 Eric 20 Slave 22 Exempt 25 Satellite 26 Cage 27 Plastered

DOWN: 2 Peak 3 Custom 4 Linen 5 Them 6 Adventure 7 Emergency 10 Rebut 12 Frequency 13 Sovereign 14 Darts 17 Snaps 19 Evolve 21 Leeds 23 Tail 24 Stye

No. 73

ACROSS: 1 Critical 8 Output 9 Embarked 10 Errand 12 Count 14 Totter 16 Epic 18 Ring 19 Tanker 20 Radar 23 Crates 26 Outburst 27 Relief 28 Fighting

DOWN: 2 Romeo 3 Train 4 Cake 5 Lodestar 6 Starter 7 Burn 11 Danger 12 Cleric 13 Unit 14 Takes Off 15 Rind 17 Captain 21 Adult 22 Anson 24 Reel 25 Stag

No. 74

ACROSS: 1 Marching 5 Dope 7 Sent 9 Upshot 10 Garden 12 Tar 13 Bunker 15 Tote 16 Eye 17 Flap 19 Tattoo 21 Ali 22 Muster 26 Savage 27 Keen 28 Blue 29 Transmit

DOWN: 1 Mess 2 Ring 3 Iced 4 Gauntlet 5 Desert 6 Promotion 8 Tank 11 Bugle Call 14 Regiment 18 Parade 20 Trek 23 Saga 24 Ream 25 Knit

No. 75

ACROSS: 1 Engineering 7 Stun 8 Trim 9 Nut-case 11 Base 13 Nags 16 Prospects 17 Air 18 Ice 19 Appointed 22 Kite 24 Year 26 Release 29 Miss 30 Lute 31 Transmitter

DOWN: 1 Extra 2 Gunner 3 Newt 4 Ella 5 Intent 6 Going 10 Captive 11 Blank 12 Sprat 14 Aside 15 Swear 20 Persia 21 Eyelet 23 Idiot 25 Alter 27 Loss 28 Anti

No. 76

ACROSS: 1 Oscillate 8 Pair 9 Contacted 11 Divine 13 Angle 15 Nile 16 Trail 17 Seedy 18 Edict 19 Town 20 Tower 22 Credit 25 Parachute 26 Pier 27 Deterrent

DOWN: 2 Show 3 Intone 4 Local 5 Tied 6 Navigator 7 Greenland 10 Dirty 12 Intercept 13 Altimeter 14 Event 17 Strip 19 Tether 21 Orate 23 Tape 24 Stun

No. 77

ACROSS: 1 Circular 8 Elated 9 Terminal 10 Idling 12 State 14 Debtor 16 Reel 18 Noon 19 Coffee 20 Space 23 Nation 26 Cylinder 27 Crease 28 Stalling

DOWN: 2 Inert 3 Comet 4 Land 5 Reliable 6 Balloon 7 Mean 11 Glance 12 Screen 13 Alec 14 Defences 15 Rota 17 Logical 21 Panel 22 Clean 24 Acre 25 Flea

No. 78

ACROSS: 1 Receiver 5 Show 7 Item 9 Porter 10 Winter 12 Ink 13 Snails 15 Eats 16 Tea 17 Bird 19 London 21 Rig 22 Geared 26 Attire 27 Door 28 Frog 29 Shortage

DOWN: 1 Rain 2 Crew 3 Vest 4 Reprisal 5 Strike 6 Operation 8 Mimi 11 Indicator 14 Staggers 18 Drying 20 Need 23 Alto 24 Dora 25 Free

No. 79

ACROSS: 1 Carburettor 7 Grid 8 Vamp 9 Derange 11 Pose 13 Rank 16 Crosswind 17 USA 18 Dot 19 Long-range 22 Beer 24 Army 26 Dredger 29 Ogre 30 Note 31 Self-starter

DOWN: 1 Cargo 2 Rudder 3 User 4 Even 5 Tavern 6 Roman 10 Assured 11 Plumb 12 Scale 14 Adder 15 Kitty 20 Ordeal 21 Garnet 23 Edges 25 Motor 27 Eros 28 Gaga

No. 80

ACROSS: 1 Vibration 6 Sea 7 Use 9 Gorge 10 Lying 11 Amble 12 Ariel 13 Other 15 Sprig 17 Edges 21 Satan 23 Panic 24 Tenor 25 Haiti 26 Igloo 27 Spa 28 Gas 29 Naturally

DOWN: 1 Vanish 2 Beggar 3 Afraid 4 Ideals 5 Number 6 Silhouettes 8 Emergencies 14 Eve 16 Pea 18 Gunman 19 Sprint 20 Angler 21 School 22 Twiggy

No. 81

ACROSS: 1 Decode 4 Cable 7 Sea 8 Capture 9 Lying 10 Near 11 Ivan 12 Sag 14 Interchange 18 Mar 20 Iran 21 Papa 23 Light 24 Log-book 25 Eye 26 Ahead 27 Terror

DOWN: 1 Decent 2 Captain 3 Drum 4 Calendar 5 Blips 6 Engage 7 Serviceable 13 Deviated 15 Glamour 16 Amelia 17 Tanker 19 Rogue 22 Ague

No. 82

ACROSS: 1 Revolution 6 Iced 10 Steward 11 Implies 12 Sidelong 13 Range 15 Organ 17 Socialist 19 Life-style 21 Super 23 Crawl 24 Shipmate 27 Intense 28 Terrain 29 Earl 30 Playfellow

DOWN: 1 Rust 2 Viewing 3 Leave 4 Tediously 5 Owing 7 Chianti 8 Dissenters 9 Spartans 14 Collective 16 Nestling 18 Chemistry 20 Flatter 22 Pitfall 24 Steel 25 Morse 26 Snow

No. 83

ACROSS: 1 Ascend 9 Economical 10 Tent 11 Agree 12 Accent 14 Threat 15 Thespian 17 Harvest Festival 20 Stigmata 22 Assume 24 Appeal 26 Naked 27 Doom 28 Comparison 29 Strike

DOWN: 2 Sweetheart 3 Estate 4 Detritus 5 Moment Of Madness 6 Forage 7 Acre 8 Platen 13 Capri 16 Alarm-clock 18 Vague 19 Slackens 20 Starch 21 Allure 23 Sadder 25 Pump

No. 84

ACROSS: 1 House Of Lords 9 Nostalgia 10 Gecko 11 Test 12 Fiend 13 Warm 16 Opening 18 Russian 19 Actress 21 Madonna 22 Iraq 23 Moira 24 Rank 28 Excel 29 Price List 30 Suffragettes

DOWN: 2 Oasis 3 Shaw 4 Ongoing 5 Learner 6 Rage 7 Sectarian 8 Common Market 9 Nationalised 14 Linen 15 Aside 17 Entrances 20 Stopper 21 Morning 25 Alive 26 Clef 27 Beat

No. 85

ACROSS: 1 Train Of Thought 10 Ashen 11 Awe-struck 12 Traits 13 Decadent 15 Nose 16 Confidence 20 Fellowship 21 Asti 23 Relative 26 Sedate 28 Octagonal 29 Aught 30 Surprise Attack

DOWN: 2 Rehearsal 3 Innate 4 Opal 5 Theme 6 Outwards 7 Gauge 8 Take The Liberty 9 Fast And Furious 14 Boss 17 Fair 18 Nostalgic 19 Cottager 22 Repast 24 Later 25 Venus 27 Plea

No. 86

ACROSS: 1 Security Council 9 Italian 10 Bargain 11 Listen 14 Elapse 15 Rivalry 16 Duty 18 Ages 19 Chalice 20 Noon 21 Herb 23 Blossom 25 Misery 26 Recall 30 Die-hard 31 Opulent 32 Caught Red-handed

DOWN: 1 Skilled 2 Class 3 Raider 4 Tank 5 Cuba 6 Unruly 7 Champagne 8 Lingers 12 Nightly 13 Hapless 14 Erector 17 Trousseau 20 Nomadic 22 Belated 23 Breath 24 Medusa 27 Ahead 28 Oder 29 Wood

No. 87

ACROSS: 1 Campaigner 6 Club 10 Ethical 11 Know-all 12 Tart 13 Ready Money 16 Renew 17 Strut 18 Ago 19 Due 20 Slang 21 Visit 22 Collateral 24 Scum 27 Lambent 29 Surpass 30 Dent 31 Passengers

DOWN: 1 Chest 2 Maharanee 3 Arch 4 Galley-slave 5 Elk 7 Learn 8 Billy-goat 9 Formative 14 Dark Glasses 15 Two-seater 16 Ridiculed 18 Associate 23 Lemon 25 Moses 26 Iron 28 Tea

No. 88

ACROSS: 1 Chatham 5 Objects 9 Ell 10 Manufacture 11 Inspection 13 Heap 15 Transport 18 Oiler 20 Shred 21 Terminals 23 Roll 25 Breakwater 29 Consultants 31 Aga 32 Storage 33 Seepage

DOWN: 1 Chemist 2 Atlas 3 Humberside 4 Manet 5 Off 6 Jack 7 Crude 8 Sleeper 12 Outer 14 Solid Waste 16 Air 17 Otter 19 Lea 20 Spruces 22 Surface 24 Lingo 26 Agnes 27 Tiara 28 Cuba 30 Tie

No. 89

ACROSS: 1 Java 3 Soup 6 Carol 10 College 11 Truffle 12 Braise 13 Helping 16 Breadcrumb 17 Idle 19 Each 21 Engagingly 24 Gelatin 25 Mature 29 Vanilla 30 Boilers 31 Larks 32 Even 33 Peel

DOWN: 1 Jacob 2 Village 4 Oven 5 Potted Meat 6 Chumps 7 Refined 8 Leek 9 Bedside 14 Frangipane 15 Bevy 16 Beef 18 Vitamin 20 Cleaner 22 Gruyere 23 Tables 26 Easel 27 Oval 28 Able

No. 90

ACROSS: 1 Bristol Fashion 9 Refloat 10 Madeira 11 Earl 12 Insulation 15 Product 17 Enlarge 18 Our 19 Rainbow 21 Seconds 23 Hovercraft 25 Pits 28 Sailors 30 Flavour 31 Central Heating

DOWN: 1 Barge 2 Inferno 3 Tool 4 Latin 5 Arm 6 Hydraulics 7 Olivier 8 Painters 13 Users 14 Rubber Boat 15 Purchase 16 Tower 20 Invoice 22 Nairobi 24 Fifth 26 Shrug 27 Saga 29 Sea

No. 91

ACROSS: 1 Statesman 6 Malta 9 Plotter 10 Tartars 11 Starvation Wage 14 Volga 15 Brim 16 Emma 18 Real 19 Eton 20 Equal 22 Rhode Island Red 25 Infidel 27 Spencer 28 Elgar 29 Sheltered

DOWN: 1 Saps 2 Amontillado 3 External 4 Maria 5 Nutrition 6 Marine 7 Lea 8 Answerable 12 Armoured Car 13 Overpraise 15 Bath Salts 17 Head-rest 21 Leader 23 Aisle 24 Fred 26 Fig

No. 92

ACROSS: 1 Construction 8 Atom 9 Operations 11 Devised 12 Colander 14 Abstains 16 Eton 17 Gongs 19 Messy 21 Etna 22 Designer 25 Shipment 27 Steamer 29 Solid Waste 30 Mule 31 Deteriorated

DOWN: 1 Choice 2 Needle 3 Trainees 4 Unite 5 Tend 6 Navigate 7 Modernise 10 Sense 13 Rangers 15 Momentous 18 Grimaced 19 Manpower 20 Knees 23 Teaset 24 Attend 26 Haiti 28 Rose

No. 93

ACROSS: 1 Secretary-bird 8 Terrible 9 Piping 10 Callow 11 Tributes 14 Idea 16 Registered 18 Contractor 19 Toss 21 Regiment 24 Castor 26 Addict 28 Priority 29 Window-cleaner

DOWN: 1 Steward 2 Carol 3 Elbow-grease 4 Agent 5 Yap 6 Imprudent 7 Dance 12 Instructive 13 Sides 14 Incur 15 Attrition 17 Gut 20 Spotter 22 Endow 23 Topic 25 Siren 27 Two

No. 94

ACROSS: 1 Air-conditioned 10 Paced 11 Viciously 12 Capitulate 13 Half 15 Treacly 17 Scuttle 19 Attired 21 Ransack 22 Even 24 Escutcheon 27 Look Ahead 28 Plain 29 Royal Enclosure

DOWN: 2 Incipient 3 Cadet 4 Novelty 5 Incites 6 Iron 7 Nesta 8 Day Of Reckoning 9 Space Traveller 14 Turn 16 Card 18 Trade Fair 20 Discern 21 Roundel 23 Ebony 25 Copes 26 Tall

No. 95

ACROSS: 1 Raft 3 Scot 6 Packs 10 Console 11 Equally 12 Please Turn Over 14 Ahead 16 Hamburger 18 Labyrinth 21 Bless 22 Hot-water Bottle 26 Auditor 27 Freight 28 March 29 Lily 30 Stir

DOWN: 1 Receptacle 2 Fence 4 Cheetah 5 Theorem 6 Pluto 7 Colleague 8 Styx 9 Consider 13 Prospector 15 Embroider 17 Unbroken 19 Natural 20 Harmful 23 Witch 24 Tight 25 Calm

No. 96

ACROSS: 1 Christmas Spirit 9 Deflated 10 Outing 12 School 14 Moderate 16 Norseman 18 Iceman 19 Arctic 20 Retainer 21 Gardenia 23 Mosaic 25 Eskimo 27 Informer 29 Dick Whittington

DOWN: 2 Hoe 3 Igloo 4 Total 5 Abdomen 6 Snow-drift 7 Inter 8 Inn 9 Disentangle 11 Greengrocer 13 Hire-car 15 Ammonia 17 Macintosh 20 Realist 22 Drink 23 Mufti 24 Sprig 26 Ski 28 Ego

No. 97

ACROSS: 1 Water-cooling 8 Rout 9 Natural Gas 10 Upward 11 Walk 12 Natal 14 Tirade 18 Maker 20 Drama 21 Plumb 23 Rebel 24 Drifts 28 Tarry 29 Able 31 Timber 33 Exasperate 34 Semi 35 Common Market

DOWN: 1 Windward 2 Total 3 Rare 4 Oil Tanker 5 Insult 6 Grower 7 Purred 13 Smart 15 Imply 16 Arum 17 Taxi 19 Robertson 22 Basement 25 Raider 26 Fabric 27 Stream 30 Black 32 Vera

No. 98

ACROSS: 1 Accept 4 Thatcher 9 Tom-tom 11 Romantic 12 Rabid 13 Nook 15 Keen 16 Liberator 17 Mind 19 Diver 20 Cigar 24 Nero 26 Fraternal 27 Ally 28 Wall 30 Psalm 32 Theories 33 Yellow 34 Eventful 35 Terror

DOWN: 1 Autonomy 2 Compound 3 Poor 5 Hood 6 Trap 7 Hitler 8 Recant 10 Manifesto 11 River 14 Capitally 15 Koran 18 Diary 21 Retailer 22 Follower 23 Brass 25 Castle 26 Fleece 29 Grit 30 Peru 31 Mere

No. 99

ACROSS: 1 Proletarian 9 Professor 10 South 11 Creeps 13 Sanction 15 Agronomist 16 Shoe 18 Bard 20 Attainment 23 Aquarium 24 Deepen 26 Chain 27 Importune 29 Brotherhood

DOWN: 1 Pioneer 2 Ode 3 East 4 Air Marshal 5 Insect 6 Nourish 7 Special Branch 8 Channel Tunnel 12 Punt 14 Amateurish 17 Knee 19 Rhubarb 21 Expound 22 Franco 25 Spur 28 Rio

No. 100

ACROSS: 1 Busman's Holiday 9 Exploited 10 Crawl 11 Deal 12 Remainders 14 Natural 16 Deirdre 18 Barrack 20 Torpedo 21 Typewriter 23 Limp 26 Exact 27 Traveller 28 Comrades-in-arms

DOWN: 1 Bread And Butter 2 Sepia 3 Atom 4 Sitwell 5 Old Hand 6 Incendiary 7 Aware 8 Plaster Of Paris 13 Breakwater 15 Tar 17 Due 19 Knitted 20 Toecaps 22 Plato 24 Idler 25 Peon

No. 101

ACROSS: 1 Bury The Hatchet 9 Satirical 10 Motto 11 Afraid 14 Motion 15 Pelican 16 Sack 18 Farm 19 Limpets 20 Oval 21 Dean 22 Chatham 24 Insert 25 Pilaff 29 Accra 30 Emulation 31 Sleeping Beauty

DOWN: 1 Busman's Holiday 2 Rotor 3 Turnip 4 Each 5 Able 6 Common 7 Extricate 8 Young Man's Fancy 12 Delight 13 Dispute 14 Mantrap 17 Classical 22 Crease 23 Mirage 26 Adieu 27 Peri 28 Rung

No. 102

ACROSS: 1 Cottage Loaf 7 Coo 9 Pork-pie 10 Seafood 11 Niece 12 Aces 13 Burn 15 Potage 17 Shorter 19 Quinces 21 Tender 23 Anne 24 Pour 25 Ladle 28 Hooting 29 Inkling 30 Dip 31 Caster Sugar

DOWN: 1 Capons 2 Torte 3 Apple Sauce 4 Elevate 5 Oysters 6 Flan 7 Croquette 8 Ordinary 14 Cornflakes 16 Onion Soup 18 Squashed 20 Sponges 21 Terrine 22 Beggar 26 Doing 27 Zinc

No. 103

ACROSS: 1 Radical 4 Emerald 8 Discouraged 11 Dais 12 Drum 13 Poser 14 Weight 16 Edison 18 Grammatical 21 Shorts 23 Slings 24 Table 25 Lard 27 Stir 28 Double Dutch 29 Entries 30 Intrude

DOWN: 1 Run-down 2 Iris 3 Accept 5 Meagre 6 Reed 7 Diamond 8 Diving-board 9 Unspeakable 10 Dress-length 15 Heart 17 Ducal 19 Isolate 20 Astride 22 Stable 23 Sequin 26 Door 27 Scar

No. 104

ACROSS: 1 Civil Engineer 8 Opencast 9 Extent 10 Germs 12 Violinist 17 Bubbling 18 Design 19 Idiocy 21 Maintain 22 Scholarly 26 Stews 30 Gazebo 31 Dockside 32 Manufacturers

DOWN: 1 Copse 2 Venom 3 Lead 4 Nothing 5 Ideal 6 Eaten 7 Rungs 10 Gubbins 11 Rubbish 13 Ice 14 Imitate 15 Tenants 16 Tidy 18 Drip 20 Col 21 Melodic 23 Charm 24 Ocean 25 Aloof 27 Taste 28 Wades 29 Ecru

No. 105

ACROSS: 1 Milestone 6 Basin 9 Ragtime 10 Shallow 11 Sites 13 Agent 14 Sea 15 Barrage 16 Topmast 18 Express 21 Miracle 23 Kit 24 Solve 25 Snaps 27 Opinion 28 Example 30 Noted 31 Estimator

DOWN: 1 Marks 2 Lighter 3 Ski 4 Operate 5 Easiest 6 Boast 7 Silesia 8 Newcastle 12 Slate 15 Breakdown 17 Parts 19 Patriot 20 Silence 21 Meekest 22 Coal-pit 24 Spied 26 Steer 29 Aim

No. 106

ACROSS: 1 Swimmers 6 Axle 10 Tired 11 Plant Hire 12 Resolve 13 Skimp 14 See 15 Seasons 17 Amnesia 20 Andante 23 Storage 24 Mat 25 Cream 27 Eastern 30 Pipe-dream 31 Learn 32 Alec 33 Serenity

DOWN: 2 Works Band 3 Model 4 Express 5 Swansea 6 Artisan 7 Luigi 8 Stir 9 Template 15 Seascape 16 Nut 18 Met 19 Spare Part 21 Nomadic 22 Empress 23 Steamer 26 Expel 28 Solon 29 Nine

No. 107

ACROSS: 1 After A Fashion 8 Fair 9 Stump 10 Love 11 On Top Of The World 15 Enraged 17 Seminal 19 Tractor 21 Embroil 24 Ploughman's Lunch 29 Aged 30 Leave 31 Ivan 32 Curiosity Shop

DOWN: 1 Again 2 Torso 3 Restore 4 Faulty 5 Supreme 6 Igloo 7 Novel 11 Onestep 12 Tornado 13 Run Down 14 Delilah 16 Gut 18 Mob 20 Othello 22 Mastery 23 Salami 25 Logic 26 Under 27 Uriah 28 Champ

No. 108

ACROSS: 1 Cash On Delivery 9 Abundance 10 Capri 11 Kidnap 14 Donors 15 Lounger 16 Nick 18 Burn 19 Station 20 Char 21 Mean 22 Rancour 24 Employ 25 Muddle 29 Sigma 30 Plentiful 31 Telescopic Lens

DOWN: 1 Chalk And Cheese 2 Sound 3 Ordeal 4 Dent 5 Lien 6 Victor 7 Reproduce 8 Pins and Needles 12 Portray 13 Unstuck 14 Decorum 17 Champagne 22 Rotate 23 Rustic 26 Defoe 27 Epic 28 Peep

No. 109

ACROSS: 1 Baron Of Beef 9 Unpin 10 Agitators 12 Shinwell 13 Peridot 14 Lectern 15 General 17 Igor 18 Mast 20 Raw Deal 22 Enslave 23 Rubicon 25 Testator 27 Sectioned 28 Theme 29 Labour Party

DOWN: 2 Angle 3 Outsider 4 Outcome 5 Bars 6 Furnace 7 Ephemeral 8 Inclination 11 Shallow 13 Police State 15 Goose-step 16 Reredos 18 Manitoba 19 Caramel 21 Doubter 24 Overt 26 Reno

No. 110

ACROSS: 1 Demonstration 8 Sweden 9 Examiner 12 Tropic 15 Nicety 18 Cactus 19 Parliamentarian 20 Choker 22 Person 24 Dearth 27 Ridicule 29 Leader 30 Pioneer Spirit

DOWN: 1 Dawn 2 Middle 3 Ninety 4 The Worse For Wear 5 Arabic 6 Iris 7 Nye 10 Reasoning 11 Inspector 13 Carafe 14 Stairs 16 Carrot 17 Toiled 21 Refuse 22 Philip 23 Repair 25 Tito 26 Left 28 Imp

No. 111

ACROSS: 1 Production 6 Rota 9 Subtitling 10 Stir 12 Issue 14 Predicted 15 Guest-room 18 Dance 19 Apple 20 Extremism 22 Overtrain 24 Organ 25 Stay 26 Make-weight 28 Duke 29 Trespasser

DOWN: 1 Passing 2 Orb 3 Unite 4 Telephone 5 Ounce 7 Outstanding 8 Abridge 11 Fiddle 13 Steeplejack 16 Twenty 17 Mutineers 19 Aroused 21 Monster 23 Adair 24 Opera 27 Gas

No. 112

ACROSS: 1 Decline And Fall 9 Annie 10 Plainsman 11 Oran 12 Break 13 Solo 16 Despair 17 Against 18 Exploit 21 Grumble 23 Diet 24 Troll 25 Knee 28 North-west 29 Omaha 30 State Of Affairs

DOWN: 1 Diamond Wedding 2 Canvass 3 Ilex 4 Emperor 5 Niagara 6 Font 7 Lampoon 8 One Of These Days 14 Wagon 15 Vague 19 Pierrot 20 Torpedo 21 Galatea 22 Bengali 26 What 27 Loaf

No. 113

ACROSS: 1 Cakewalk 5 Barrel 9 Ripeness 11 Parson 12 Throb 13 Oven 16 Fool 17 Roquefort 18 Beer 20 Party 21 Angus 22 Head 24 Croquette 27 Puma 28 Yarn 29 Magic 32 Unseat 33 Decanter 34 Yankee 35 Peppered

DOWN: 1 Carrot 2 Kipper 3 Wine 4 List 6 Arab 7 Rissoles 8 Landlord 10 Shift 11 Porringer 14 Nomad 15 Butter-pat 18 Butty 19 Chop-suey 20 Parmesan 23 Squid 25 Easter 26 Snored 29 Mace 30 Cede 31 Wasp

No. 114

ACROSS: 1 Highland Fling 8 True 9 Saver 10 Loud 11 Rector 14 Literate 19 Donated 21 Fragile 22 Woe 23 Cremate 24 Replace 25 Latterly 30 Decent 33 Wool 34 Slang 35 Part 36 Flying Trapeze

DOWN: 1 Horse 2 Guest 3 Laser 4 Novel 5 First 6 Idler 7 Gaunt 11 Radical 12 Concert 13 Outrage 15 Infer 16 Example 17 Animate 18 Element 20 Dwell 26 Aloof 27 Tally 28 Risen 29 Yeast 30 Dogma 31 Copse 32 Nurse

No. 115

ACROSS: 1 Construction 8 Oven 9 Natural Gas 10 Vain 11 Ewer 12 Little 13 Ruby 14 Shifts 16 Earns 17 Items 19 Debar 21 Nicks 24 Nassau 26 Star 27 Carbon 28 Itch 29 Plus 30 Ineligible 31 Rope 32 Fire Fighting

DOWN: 1 Conversion 2 Scan 3 Routine 4 Charter 5 Ingress 6 Nose-dive 7 Defect 9 Nimble 15 Surprising 18 Mischief 20 Bottle 21 Nuclear 22 Cardiff 23 Storing 25 Action 29 Plot

No. 116

ACROSS: 1 Dress Rehearsal 10 Rocky 11 Pinnacled 12 Convention 13 Chic 15 Aligned 17 Tapioca 19 Reeling 21 Bennett 22 Roll 24 Past Master 27 Tangerine 28 Ankle 29 Conquering Hero

DOWN: 2 Recondite 3 Style 4 Reputed 5 Hand-out 6 Agag 7 Sylph 8 Lady Chatterley 9 Armchair Critic 14 Span 16 Nail 18 Overtaker 20 Glazier 21 Bittern 23 Linen 25 Awash 26 Beau

No. 117

ACROSS: 1 Cairngorm 6 Oasis 9 Arrival 10 Overall 11 Shaggy 12 Imported 15 Bus 16 Typing 17 Menu 19 Nile 21 Cemini 22 Awl 24 Engineer 25 Severn 28 Initial 30 Heating 31 Green 32 Assistant

DOWN: 1 Claws 2 Inroads 3 Navigate 4 Oils 5 Mao 6 Oberon 7 Seattle 8 Solid Fuel 13 Mendip 14 Sphere 15 Bunkering 18 Minerals 20 Lignite 22 America 23 Indian 26 Night 27 This 29 Lea

No. 118

ACROSS: 1 Researcher 6 Scum 10 Donegal 11 Refrain 12 Carriage 13 Edith 15 Risks 17 Hard Times 19 Sustained 21 Dodge 23 Ditto 24 Prentice 27 Nearest 28 Terrier 29 Yoke 30 Short Sight

DOWN: 1 Rude 2 Sandals 3 Anger 4 Callaghan 5 Eerie 7 Cranium 8 Manchester 9 Affected 14 Presidency 16 Seasoned 18 Red Letter 20 Setback 22 Ducking 24 Pitch 25 Tires 26 Fret

No. 119

ACROSS: 1 Intrepid 5 Bright 10 Neighbour 11 Byron 12 Regency 13 Stubble 14 Streaker 17 Delve 19 Opens 21 Rhetoric 24 Fascism 25 Million 27 Syrup 28 Red Square 29 Deride 30 Sleepers

DOWN: 1 Ignore 2 Thing 3 Enhance 4 Ivory 6 Rebound 7 Garibaldi 8 Tendered 9 Preserve 15 Treasurer 16 Karl Marx 18 Confused 20 Snipped 22 Oblique 23 Kneels 25 Model 26 Irate

No. 120

ACROSS: 1 Face The Music 9 Jasmine 10 Alberta 11 Collop 14 Please 15 Restore 16 Even 17 Jean 18 Distant 19 Pawn 21 Jaws 23 Colonel 25 Threat 26 Rattle 29 Trotter 30 Perfect 31 Keep-fit Class

DOWN: 2 Absolve 3 Editor 4 Heel 5 Moan 6 Subtle 7 Corsage 8 Make Ends Meet 9 Jacket Potato 12 Peridot 13 Station 14 Printer 20 Warlock 22 Actress 23 Castle 24 Laurel 27 Graf 28 Spot

No. 121

ACROSS: 1 Know The Score 9 Dig 10 Rogue 11 Fence 12 Enlist 13 Discover 16 Seasonable 18 Diet 20 Nook 21 False Teeth 23 Diagonal 24 Geneva 27 Worst 29 Droop 30 Tut 31 Demoralising

DOWN: 2 Nigel 3 Workshop 4 High 5 Specialist 6 Office 7 Eon 8 Heart To Heart 9 Dressing Down 14 Voice 15 Salamander 17 Aroma 19 Attempts 22 Bottom 25 Eaten 26 Cool 28 Red

No. 122

ACROSS: 1 Distributor 9 Emits 10 Debauched 12 Roulette 13 Jetties 14 Left Half 15 Dots 16 Roan 17 Eaves 19 Star 21 Tots 22 Londoner 24 Carrion 26 Balanced 28 Sing Small 29 Nosed 30 Opportunity

DOWN: 2 Irene 3 Traction 4 Increase 5 User 6 Reflate 7 Distracts 8 Isle of Grain 11 Done 13 Jodrell Bank 14 Lover 15 Dauntless 18 Straight 19 Storeman 20 Tornado 23 Eyes 25 Owlet 27 Dido

No. 123

ACROSS: 1 Election Agent 8 Feminist 9 Iceman 10 Advent 13 Fastest 14 Oscar 16 Anent 18 Idiot 19 Engaged 20 Stars 22 Abate 24 Notch 26 Protest 28 Locate 32 Collie 33 Roulette 34 Strike-breaker

DOWN: 1 Emend 2 Elite 3 Twists 4 Oath 5 Anita 6 Ejected 7 Transport 11 Vie 12 Notes 13 Fright 15 Cogent 17 Notorious 18 Idaho 21 Rattler 23 Ada 25 Clause 27 Steak 29 Check 30 Tutor 31 Grub

No. 124

ACROSS: 1 Appointment 9 Inlet 10 Quoted 11 Defraud 12 Exist 13 Rats 15 Natter 16 Cure 17 Rovers 18 Tear 20 Semi 21 Smoker 22 Ride 23 Offing 25 Ants 27 Local 28 Interim 29 Attend 30 Alter 31 Merchandise

DOWN: 2 Pamela 3 Operator 4 Thud 5 Extra 6 Tides 7 Altitude 8 Stuttering 10 Quarryman 13 Revokes 14 Turnround 15 Natural Gas 19 Abdicate 20 Suffered 24 Noises 25 Alarm 26 Tutor 28 Inch

No. 125

ACROSS: 1 Final Touch 6 Cold 10 Laggard 11 Raiment 12 Hate 13 Darlington 16 Delhi 17 Doubt 18 Dot 19 Tub 20 Pinch 21 Rover 22 Heaven-sent 24 Wrap 27 Viscous 29 Glazier 30 Noel 31 Presidency

DOWN: 1 Filth 2 Night-club 3 Lead 4 Odds And Ends 5 Cur 7 Overt 8 Detonator 9 Signature 14 Laughing Gas 15 Simpleton 16 Dutch Oven 18 Diversion 23 Aisle 25 Party 26 Wand 28 Sir

No. 126

ACROSS: 1 Runner Beans 7 Des 9 Chowder 10 Utensil 11 Clear 12 Cave 13 Swap 15 Accept 17 Trotter 19 Central 21 Sugary 23 Acid 24 Abba 25 Noble 28 Elegant 29 Ivories 30 Dot 31 Marshmallow

DOWN: 1 Rococo 2 Noose 3 Elderberry 4 Borscht 5 Aquavit 6 Seed 7 Dishwater 8 Salt Pork 14 Gorgonzola 16 Condiment 18 Scrag-end 20 Lobster 21 Spanish 22 Seesaw 26 Brill 27 Farm

No. 127

ACROSS: 1 Reprobate 6 Idled 9 Shorter 10 Express 11 Manifesto Group 14 Alive 15 Cool 16 Echo 18 Done 19 Wage 20 Ocean 22 Narrow Majority 25 Station 27 Mandate 28 Adele 29 Resisters

DOWN: 1 Rash 2 Probationer 3 Outsider 4 Agree 5 Electrode 6 Impugn 7 Lie 8 Disappoint 12 Orchestrate 13 Sandinista 15 Coal-miner 17 Torrents 21 Polite 23 James 24 Less 26 Age

No. 128

ACROSS: 1 Labour Relations 9 Brother 10 Marvell 11 Riddle 14 Gamble 15 Dreamer 16 Lump 18 Cant 19 Escaper 20 Club 21 Idol 23 Topical 25 Retain 26 Latins 30 Incense 31 Ennoble 32 Freedom Fighters

DOWN: 1 Liberal 2 Broad 3 Uphold 4 Rare 5 Lame 6 Tartar 7 Overboard 8 Solvent 12 Erosion 13 Fanatic 14 General 17 Moustache 20 Cardiff 22 Listens 23 Tinned 24 Launch 27 Imbue 28 Term 29 Kepi

No. 129

ACROSS: 1 Stainless Steel 9 Chaotic 10 Lucerne 11 Shed 12 Apprentice 14 Cargo 15 Stoic 17 Gut 18 End 20 Gasps 23 Annoy 25 Supervisor 26 Pier 29 Treadle 30 Roll Off 31 Representative

DOWN: 1 Socks 2 Amateur 3 Note 4 Escapes 5 Salerno 6 Technician 7 Earning 8 Recently 13 Rough-rider 14 Creosote 16 Tip 19 Deplete 21 Spiders 22 Sporran 24 Nairobi 27 Rifle 28 Flea

No. 130

ACROSS: 1 Crocodile Tears 10 Truro 11 Porterage 12 Redden 13 Doorstep 15 Idea 16 Tablespoon 20 Abdication 21 Stub 23 Entrance 26 Ottawa 28 Candidate 29 Paint 30 Partner In Crime

DOWN: 2 Roundhead 3 Clover 4 Dope 5 Largo 6 Theorise 7 Adapt 8 Sleeping Beauty 9 Storm In A Teacup 14 Salt 17 Look 18 Ostracism 19 Occasion 22 Stupor 24 Tuner 25 Chair 27 Mean

No. 131

ACROSS: 1 Arch 3 Iced 6 Sated 10 Protein 11 Souffle 12 Chilli 13 Sweeter 16 Sugar Mouse 17 Asti 19 Oats 21 Water-melon 24 Cake-mix 25 Morsel 29 Spinach 30 Pink Gin 31 Event 32 Nosh 33 Mesh

DOWN: 1 Aspic 2 Cooking 4 Cans 5 Dishwasher 6 Saucer 7 Toffees 8 Diet 9 Cellars 14 Soda Siphon 15 Sign 16 Shop 18 Impound 20 Tea-time 22 Lasagne 23 Repast 26 Lunch 27 Isle 28 Opus

No. 132

ACROSS: 1 Captain 4 Obliged 8 Composition 11 Play 12 Nail 13 Cocoa 14 Select 16 Nought 18 Out And About 21 Exhort 23 Drawer 24 Angle 25 Gold 27 Drag 28 Pocket-sized 29 Amended 30 Inspire

DOWN: 1 Compass 2 Troy 3 Impact 5 Batman 6 Iron 7 Deflate 8 Call For Help 9 Second Sight 10 Naughty Word 15 Cater 17 Odour 19 Pergola 20 Brigade 22 Tackle 23 Design 26 Down 27 Deep

No. 133

ACROSS: 1 Powerline 6 Tours 9 Seasons 10 Adder 11 Ocean 12 Ethos 13 Stern 14 Beat 15 Sorts 17 Morsel 18 Tub 20 Packet 22 Trier 24 Snap 25 Range 26 Offer 28 Drink 29 Igloo 30 Steered 31 Elsie 32 Roadstone

DOWN: 1 Paste 2 Weather 3 Riots 4 Insolent 5 Expert 6 Transport 7 Undress 8 Sprinkler 15 Supervise 16 Stevedore 19 Black Sea 21 Candles 23 Inferno 24 Sailor 26 Opens 27 Ridge

No. 134

ACROSS: 1 Stage-door Johnny 9 Meat Loaf 10 Remote 12 Chaste 14 Casanova 16 Observer 18 Loving 19 Caller 20 Armorial 21 Predator 23 Bionic 25 Cherub 27 Carnival 29 Needle And Thread

DOWN: 2 Tie 3 Gates 4 Drone 5 Officer 6 Jerusalem 7 Human 8 Net 9 Microscopic 11 Evangelical 13 Absolve 15 Opinion 17 Veritable 20 African 22 Dared 23 Beret 24 Osier 26 Hue 28 Ada

No. 135

ACROSS: 1 Commonwealth 9 Startling 10 Laura 1' Pair 12 Mover 13 Veto 16 Remorse 18 Dallied 19 Titanic 21 Zambesi 22 Then 23 Divan 24 Boss 28 Olive 29 Evocation 30 Garden Suburb

DOWN: 2 Okapi 3 Mate 4 Noisome 5 Egghead 6 Lily 7 Housewife 8 Harold Wilson 9 Superstition 14 Front 15 Plump 17 Muttering 20 Chinese 21 Zealots 25 Osier 26 Bear 27 Lamb

No. 136

ACROSS: 1 Polling Station 9 Rebellion 10 Ranch 11 Yell 12 Salamander 14 Restore 16 Epistle 18 Grammar 20 Command 21 Aristocrat 23 Epic 26 Mitre 27 Usherette 28 Brothers In Arms

DOWN: 1 Party Programme 2 Label 3 Idle 4 Grimace 5 Tonnage 6 Terra Firma 7 Owned 8 Charles Dickens 13 Commitment 15 Spa 17 Tea 19 Recluse 20 Clashes 22 Inter 24 Peter 25 Iron

No. 137

ACROSS: 1 Despot 4 Spartans 9 Cherub 11 Frighten 12 Sadat 13 Avid 15 Prow 16 Prisoners 17 OPEC 19 Nancy 20 Axiom 24 Fire 26 Condition 27 Amin 28 Miss 30 Helen 32 Prepared 33 Doctor 34 Transfer 35 Hatred

DOWN: 1 Dictator 2 Specimen 3 Onus 5 Port 6 Rags 7 Actors 8 Sinews 10 Barricade 11 False 14 Unexposed 15 Proof 18 Canon 21 Minister 22 Censured 23 Steed 25 Carpet 26 Cinema 29 Mass 30 Here 31 Nora

No. 138

ACROSS: 1 Cucumber 5 Hot-pot 9 Enticing 11 Carrot 12 Aloof 13 Stew 16 Ache 17 Tipsy Cake 18 Sole 20 Vegan 21 Scrap 22 Lois 24 Cafeteria 27 Pate 28 Brie 29 Curry 32 Abacus 33 Tomatoes 34 Kisses 35 Tia Maria

DOWN: 1 Cheese 2 Cutlet 3 Mace 4 Etna 6 Olaf 7 Pork Chop 8 Tethered 10 Glace 11 Corkscrew 14 Wines 15 Asparagus 18 Sahib 19 Flapjack 20 Victuals 23 Heart 25 Armour 26 Persia 29 Cure 30 Yogi 31 Warm

No. 139

ACROSS: 1 Redress 5 Ballast 9 Upset 10 Rio 11 Clara 12 Borrowed Plumes 14 Heel 15 Cheapskate 19 Royal Birth 20 Miss 22 Social Standing 26 Inept 27 Oil 28 Bathe 29 Tantrum 30 Slender

DOWN: 1 Rout 2 Discovery 3 Extort 4 Straw 5 Broadcast 6 Luckless 7 Alarm 8 Transverse 13 Short Skirt 16 Hailstorm 17 Alienated 18 Oleaster 21 Edible 23 Clean 24 Atlas 25 Near

No. 140

ACROSS: 1 Breakthrough 9 Trailing 10 Egret 12 Roll 13 Kilt 14 Wear 15 May 17 Limbo 19 Owing 20 Ink-well 22 Inter 23 Tight 24 SOS 25 Garb 26 Bolt 27 Open 31 Image 32 Educated 33 Site Engineer

DOWN: 2 Rural 3 Acid 4 Tricky 5 Regulate 6 Used 7 Hardening 8 Storage Tank 11 Drilling Rig 15 Moira 16 Volts 18 Motorways 21 Kerosene 24 Strung 28 Piece 29 Deft 30 Main

No. 141

ACROSS: 1 Cold Tap 5 Limited 9 Night 10 Earmarked 11 Expense Account 15 Sheet 17 Epitomise 19 Overrates 20 Riser 21 Asset-strippers 25 Promotion 27 Naomi 29 Display 30 Enlarge

DOWN: 1 Conversion 2 Log 3 Titan 4 Precedent 5 Lyric 6 Moa 7 Taking Issue 8 Dado 12 Pretensions 13 Odour 14 Regressive 16 Three 18 Insurance 22 Shiny 23 Panel 24 Spud 26 Oil 28 Oar

No. 142

ACROSS: 1 Articulated 9 Ewell 10 Harvester 12 Dislodge 13 Whistle 14 Gantries 15 Cede 16 Good 17 Dress 19 Char 21 Toot 22 Bulkhead 24 Deposit 26 Importer 28 Catamaran 29 Green 30 Grangemouth

DOWN: 2 Reach 3 Invested 4 Unsolved 5 Aged 6 Deflate 7 Headlight 8 Fleet Street 11 Rita 13 Weighbridge 14 Greed 15 Collapsed 18 Steerage 19 Colorado 20 Shoring 23 Alec 25 Inapt 27 Rain

No. 143

ACROSS: 1 Light Fantastic 9 Ready-made 10 Deter 11 Statue 14 Stroke 15 Trouble 16 Nude 18 Juno 19 Asinine 20 Lath 21 Left 22 Printer 24 Dundee 25 Rescue 29 Extol 30 Crescendo 31 Promising Start

DOWN: 1 Lords And Ladies 2 Ghana 3 Try-out 4 Away 5 Twee 6 Sedate 7 Introduce 8 Order Of The Boot 12 Erasure 13 Running 14 Slender 17 Detonator 22 Peplum 23 Reacts 26 Conga 27 Acts 28 Mean

No. 144

ACROSS: 1 Pleasure Cruise 9 Apple 10 Challenge 11 Loom 12 Cause 13 Opal 16 Optimum 17 Stretch 18 Warrant 21 Monster 23 Silk 24 Grasp 25 Alps 28 Operative 29 Unite 30 Feel The Draught

DOWN: 1 Pearls Of Wisdom 2 Exploit 3 Stew 4 Reclaim 5 Chassis 6 Ugly 7 Sand-pit 8 Healthy Respect 14 Smear 15 Frank 19 Relieve 20 Turkish 21 Mislead 22 Telling 26 Wall 27 Cuba

No. 145

ACROSS: 1 Precipitate 9 Noose 10 Ideologue 12 Gavottes 13 Comrade 14 Niggler 15 Courage 17 Ahoy 18 Item 20 Extreme 22 Lampoon 23 Inflict 25 Bandages 27 Dialectic 28 Untie 29 Restitution

DOWN: 2 Radio 3 Choirboy 4 Plodder 5 Trug 6 Engorge 7 Postulate 8 Measurement 11 Earnest 13 Cheap Labour 15 Community 16 Amended 18 Implicit 19 Dowager 21 Ringlet 24 Cairo 26 Sift

No. 146

ACROSS: 1 Black And White 8 Resign 9 Workmate 12 Lifted 15 Replay 18 Rental 19 Bolt From The Blue 20 System 22 Stones 24 Darwin 27 Sapphire 29 Trojan 30 Detached House

DOWN: 1 Beer 2 Animal 3 Kindly 4 News From Nowhere 5 Warder 6 Irma 7 Eat 10 Edelweiss 11 Proboscis 13 Defect 14 Stalin 16 Polish 17 Alfred 21 Maniac 22 Snatch 23 Ormolu 25 Spot 26 Wave 28 Aid

No. 147

ACROSS: 1 Proletarian 9 Polemical 10 Plaza 11 Norman 13 Eggshell 15 Immaterial 16 Etna 18 Gape 20 Mercantile 23 Eyesight 24 Tea-set 26 Nylon 27 Underwear 29 State Secret

DOWN: 1 Pilgrim 2 Ohm 3 Each 4 Allegiance 5 Impose 6 Neatest 7 Spinning Jenny 8 Parliamentary 12 Acts 14 Greenhouse 17 Knee 19 Peebles 21 Inspect 22 Vienna 25 Edge 28 RUR

No. 148

ACROSS: 1 Edible 9 Meadow-lark 10 Tsar 11 Tuned 12 Gallon 14 Matron 15 Overstay 17 Chequered Career 20 Free Trip 22 Repeat 24 Adonis 26 Lower 27 Turn 28 Coat-hanger 29 Normal

DOWN: 2 Dishwasher 3 Barter 4 Eminence 5 Handsome Apology 6 Boggle 7 Paul 8 Skinny 13 Loser 16 Alexandria 18 Queen 19 Careworn 20 France 21 Rascal 23 Porter 25 Oval

No. 149

ACROSS: 1 Detachment 8 Hermit 9 Spare Rib 11 Lorgnette 13 Oust 15 Flip Side 18 Sister 19 Sawn 20 Ingle 21 Loot 23 Rotten 24 Retailer 25 Enid 26 Evocative 31 Enshrine 32 Scream 33 Pessimists

DOWN: 1 Disconsolate 2 Transistor 3 Chef 4 Mail 5 Thug 6 Friends 7 List 10 Boxing-glove 12 Evening Dress 14 Africa 16 Sherry 17 East Indies 22 Teacher 27 Vice 28 Temp 29 Ends 30 Them

No. 150

ACROSS: 1 Watches 5 Radical 9 Realm 10 Gold-miner 11 Inverted Commas 15 Socks 17 Academies 19 Extrovert 20 Space 21 Monkey Business 25 Wristband 27 Dodge 29 Pattern 30 Dialect

DOWN: 1 Warminster 2 Tea 3 Homer 4 Segregate 5 Relic 6 Dam 7 Contaminate 8 Lark 12 Vacationist 13 Meets 14 Assessment 16 Shock 18 Astounded 22 Yearn 23 India 24 Swap 26 Tie 28 Due

No. 151

ACROSS: 1 Combustion 8 Inrush 9 Abstains 11 Donkey-man 12 Border 14 Oath 15 Vents 17 Noon 20 Manufacture 22 Dump 23 Ratio 25 Spar 27 Stroke 29 Escalator 31 Nominees 32 Income 33 Table Linen

DOWN: 1 Coal-bunker 2 Mushroom 3 Usage 4 Tend 5 Nicks 6 Greybeard 7 Ushant 10 Southampton 13 Rogue 16 Stephenson 18 Navigator 19 Stars 21 European 24 Assent 26 Cadet 28 Twill 30 Roll

No. 152

ACROSS: 1 Fire Fighting 8 Eton 9 Retirement 11 Sweeper 12 Ailments 13 Managed 14 Disc 16 Creek 18 Sob 19 Doc 23 Ingot 24 Race 25 Marking 27 Accident 29 Beaches 31 Rear-lights 32 Free 33 Warehouseman

DOWN: Forwards 2 Ruthless 3 Farmer 4 Gamut 5 Tons 6 Generator 7 Foremen 10 Tweak 13 Memo 15 Corkscrew 17 Rung 20 Caterham 21 Jettison 22 Madeira 23 Infer 26 Cities 28 Cargo 30 Sete

No. 153

ACROSS: 1 Redistribution 10 Outward 11 Vessels 12 Exactions 13 Tote 15 Tatters 17 Salvage 19 Toilers 22 Segment 24 Flat 26 Appraisal 29 Arc-lamp 30 Evident 31 Data Processing

DOWN: 2 Extract 3 Inapt 4 Tedious 5 Invests 6 Upset 7 Inertia 8 Nose 9 Potentate 14 Ventilate 16 Eye 18 Log 20 Illicit 21 Shampoo 22 Supreme 23 Eastern 25 Tramp 27 Amiss 28 Wand

No. 154

ACROSS: 1 Portsmouth 6 Acts 10 Massing 11 Initial 12 Distance 13 Tepid 15 Agnes 17 Sightseer 19 Lohengrin 21 React 23 Agree 24 Squatter 27 Earache 28 Niagara 29 Tank 30 Retrospect

DOWN: 1 Pomp 2 Russian 3 Shift 4 Organiser 5 Twice 7 Cripple 8 Solidarity 9 Dictator 14 Parliament 16 Sentence 18 Gun-runner 20 Hard-run 22 Average 24 Scene 25 Teams 26 Pact

No. 155

ACROSS: 1 Austria 5 Primate 9 Lemon 10 Tar 11 Thumb 12 Unwelcome Guest 14 Plum 15 Accusative 19 Electorate 20 Acre 22 Hot And Bothered 26 Extra 27 Err 28 Opera 29 Saladin 30 Wrestle

DOWN: 1 Ally 2 Simon Pure 3 Runner 4 Antic 5 Paramount 6 Integral 7 Abuse 8 Embittered 13 Speechless 16 Caribbean 17 Inclement 18 Standard 21 Repose 23 Total 24 Throw 25 Wage

No. 156

ACROSS: 1 Snap Decision 9 Pad 10 Aloof 11 Dylan 12 Unrest 13 Panorama 16 Second-rate 18 Stud 20 Alma 21 Man Of Parts 23 Beach Hut 24 Couple 27 Urges 29 Corgi 30 Wit 31 Donkeys' Years

DOWN: 2 Nadir 3 Praising 4 Eros 5 Infraction 6 Indoor 7 Nil 8 Incandescent 9 Prussian Blue 14 Alter 15 Great-uncle 17 Comma 19 Apposite 22 Chosen 25 Power 26 Arms 28 God

No. 157

ACROSS: 1 Oust 3 Smug 6 Pupil 10 Pension 11 Minaret 12 Sheep's Clothing 14 Tudor 16 Extirpate 18 Oppressed 21 Treat 22 Vanishing Cream 26 Initial 27 Enliven 28 Tryst 29 Rind 30 Arts

DOWN: 1 Opposition 2 Sense 4 Monocle 5 Gumboot 6 Punch 7 Parentage 8 Late 9 Disperse 13 Sentiments 15 Depravity 17 Reticule 19 Scholar 20 Dungeon 23 Idiot 24 Elver 25 Lift

No. 158

ACROSS: 1 Backward 5 Access 10 Salisbury 11 Enter 12 Candied 13 Genteel 14 Bulgaria 17 Rhine 19 Rates 21 Absolute 24 Samurai 25 Compact 27 Eaten 28 Tractable 29 Temper 30 Tendered

DOWN: 1 Bisect 2 Colon 3 Washing 4 Round 6 Cleaner 7 Extremist 8 Stroller 9 Eyeglass 15 Ultimatum 16 Realists 18 Prospect 20 Strange 22 Limited 23 Attend 25 Crate 26 Amber

No. 159

ACROSS: 1 Fratricide 6 Tsar 9 Lock-keeper 10 Loss 12 Ramps 14 Inspector 15 Motor-ship 18 Irene 19 Scrub 20 Shopfloor 22 Elaborate 24 Rated 25 Tail 26 Port Of Call 28 Rite 29 Starveling

DOWN: 1 Fulcrum 2 Arc 3 Rakes 4 Cherishes 5 Dress 7 Smoothed Out 8 Reserve 11 Relief 13 Materialist 16 Ribbon 17 Protester 19 Shelter 21 Red Flag 23 Aloft 24 Rifle 27 Ali

No. 160

ACROSS: 1 Installation 8 Omega 9 Own 10 Roads 12 Listing 13 Operate 14 Newcastle 17 Okapi 19 Shrub 21 Essential 23 Outpost 25 Coal-gas 27 Keats 28 Eve 29 Again 30 Raw Materials

DOWN: 1 Ideas 2 Stamina 3 Along 4 Londoners 5 Torpedo 6 Omaha 7 Rolling-stock 11 Specialising 15 War 16 Treatment 18 Ali 20 Blossom 22 Niagara 24 Tiara 25 Clear 26 Grabs

No. 161

ACROSS: 1 Sack 3 Gong 6 Piper 10 Rissole 11 Sirloin 12 Teapot 13 Broiler 16 Red Currant 17 Inns 19 Duck 21 Vermicelli 24 Glucose 25 Potted 29 Caramel 30 Bouquet 31 Dress 32 Date 33 Beer

DOWN: 1 Sprat 2 Custard 4 Oven 5 Gastronome 6 Parkin 7 Protein 8 Rind 9 Coconut 14 Green Salad 15 Asti 16 Rude 18 Octopus 20 Calorie 22 Lettuce 23 Scamps 26 Deter 27 Iced 28 Abet

No. 162

ACROSS: 1 Conservation 8 Ache 9 Unattached 11 Millers 12 Sinkable 14 Isobar 15 Forces 17 Gash 20 Epee 23 Carton 24 Censor 25 Disposal 28 Ravenna 30 Experience 31 Mere 32 Resettlement

DOWN: 1 Cruising 2 Neatness 3 Extra 4 Vocal 5 Them 6 Nail-hole 7 Wharfage 10 Divisions 13 Boom Crane 16 Cur 18 Averages 19 Hastener 21 Presence 22 Effluent 26 Inept 27 Poise 29 Axle

No. 163

ACROSS: 1 Merganser 6 Harem 9 Musical 10 Comment 11 Lord Chancellor 14 Omaha 15 Slip 16 Agra 18 Laid 19 Here 20 Easel 22 Constitutional 25 Imprint 27 Aniline 28 Elect 29 Repellent

DOWN: 1 Mimi 2 Restoration 3 Arcadian 4 Sylph 5 Recondite 6 Hammer 7 Rue 8 Materially 12 Legislative 13 Collective 15 Spectator 17 Memorial 21 Strict 23 Tramp 24 Beat 26 Poe

No. 164

ACROSS: 1 Refuse 4 Passable 10 Amsterdam 11 Inner 12 Sash 13 Ferry 14 Lean 17 Deposit 19 Limpid 21 French 23 Polygon 25 Host 26 Canal 27 Solo 31 Loose 32 Immingham 33 Prestige 34 Shored

DOWN: 1 Roadside 2 Fists 3 Shed 5 Admiral 6 Sail 7 Bunkering 8 Errand 9 Advent 15 Using 16 Smelt 18 Periscope 20 Informed 22 Heating 23 Psalms 24 Philip 28 Other 29 West 30 Inch

No. 165

ACROSS: 1 Account 5 Meddler 9 Hands 10 Awl 11 Sniff 12 Nine Days' Wonder 14 Unit 15 Opposition 19 Non-starter 20 Acre 22 Spring-cleaning 26 Inter 27 Use 28 Olive 29 Groupie 30 Tempest

DOWN: 1 Ache 2 Condition 3 Ulster 4 Tiara 5 Milestone 6 Despotic 7 Laird 8 References 13 Furnishing 16 Parachute 17 Incentive 18 Eton Crop 21 Inform 23 Ratio 24 Erect 25 Belt

No. 166

ACROSS: 1 Airship 5 Miracle 9 Double Bed 10 Smash 11 Even 12 Diplomatic 14 Scratch 16 Lateral 17 Oppress 18 Scolded 20 Solidarity 22 Opal 25 Reign 26 Mendacity 27 Element 28 Adopted

DOWN: 1 Address 2 Route 3 Hulk 4 Publishes 5 Model 6 Resumption 7 Chartered 8 Ethical 13 Attendance 15 Repulsive 16 Lusitania 17 Observe 19 Delayed 21 Remit 23 Paint 24 Dado

No. 167

ACROSS: 1 Scarlet Woman 9 Measure 10 Stretch 11 Number 14 Petrol 15 Deliver 16 Fork 17 Glad 18 Declare 19 Each 21 Wool 23 Discuss 25 Tiptoe 26 Speech 29 Reissue 30 Arizona 31 Entomologist

DOWN: 2 Charmer 3 Routed 4 Ewer 5 Wish 6 Murder 7 Natural 8 Philadelphia 9 Man Of Letters 12 Reverie 13 Dialect 14 Peeress 20 Capsize 22 Onerous 23 Dorset 24 Spring 27 Term 28 Rail

No. 168

ACROSS: 1 Property Owner 8 Engaging 9 Arrive 10 Schism 13 Manacle 14 Taste 16 Where 18 Tepid 19 Portico 20 Class 22 Tough 24 Probe 26 Frigate 28 Emboss 32 Moment 33 Thatcher 34 Sit On The Fence

DOWN: 1 Panic 2 Okapi 3 Enigma 4 Toga 5 Omaha 6 Narrate 7 Revolving 11 Hoe 12 Steps 13 Mexico 15 Stripe 17 Hilarious 18 Totem 21 Segment 23 UFO 25 Behalf 27 Titan 29 Bacon 30 Scene 31 Itch

No. 169

ACROSS: 1 Precious 6 Pipe 10 Channel 11 Initial 12 Moira 13 Projector 14 Dimension 16 Heron 17 Rover 19 Partridge 21 Carthorse 24 Ellen 26 Opaline 27 Gateman 28 Stay 29 Saturday

DOWN: 2 Realism 3 Container 4 Orlop 5 Shipowner 6 Pride 7 Painter 8 Scum 9 Clarence 14 Director 15 Importers 16 Harvester 18 Variant 20 Dilemma 22 Hairy 23 Eight 25 Nine

No. 170

ACROSS: 1 Attorney-General 9 Angular 10 Minicab 11 Cutest 14 Linear 15 Horatio 16 Yard 18 Seal 19 Slavery 20 Mean 21 Grab 23 Erasure 25 Herons 26 Yum Yum 30 Manager 31 Noodles 32 The Fat Of The Land

DOWN: 1 Anarchy 2 Tight 3 Relish 4 Earn 5 Game 6 Nuncio 7 Racketeer 8 Liberal 12 Toilers 13 Canvass 14 Library 17 Rearrange 20 Mahomet 22 Bemused 23 Enigma 24 Europe 27 Yalta 28 Trio 29 Knit

No. 171

ACROSS: 1 Stripling 6 Cupid 9 Pensive 10 Onerous 11 Rhone 12 Twenty-one 13 Sentiment 15 Opera 16 Night 18 Esplanade 20 Hydrangea 23 Grasp 25 Tremble 26 Imagine 27 Canoe 28 Noiseless

DOWN: 1 Super 2 Runcorn 3 Price-list 4 Inept 5 Goose-step 6 Chest 7 Propose 8 Desperate 13 Synthetic 14 Evergreen 15 Orangeade 17 Gudgeon 19 Avarice 21 Amble 22 Alibi 24 Press

No. 172

ACROSS: 1 Scrutineer 6 Ours 9 Ingratiate 10 Edge 12 Price 14 Hard Times 15 Rapturous 18 Owner 19 Cloth 20 Rivalries 22 Overladen 24 Dogma 25 Beer 26 Laceration 28 Ruth 29 Chancellor

DOWN: 1 Slipper 2 Reg 3 Trade 4 Neighbour 5 Enter 7 Undemanding 8 Spenser 11 Stroll 13 Improvement 16 Uphold 17 Seventeen 19 Clobber 21 Spanner 23 Death 24 Drake 27 Ill

No. 173

ACROSS: 1 Cash 3 Epic 6 Bogus 10 Praline 11 Oysters 12 Edible 13 Hot Cake 16 Vegetarian 17 Inch 19 Also 21 Sweet Tooth 24 Garnish 25 Plaice 29 Helping 30 Tea-time 31 Title 32 Rare 33 Tray

DOWN: 1 Copse 2 Sealing 4 Peel 5 Chocolates 6 Bisect 7 Gherkin 8 Sash 9 Giblets 14 Brown Sugar 15 Shah 16 Veal 18 Italian 20 Shallot 22 Olivier 23 Endive 26 Enemy 27 What 28 Stir

No. 174

ACROSS: 1 Statesmanlike 8 Scargill 9 Reside 10 Isolde 13 Cheddar 14 Adder 16 Stern 18 Groom 19 Collier 20 Usage 22 Alert 24 Great 26 Peerage 28 Fetish 32 Remiss 33 Whitelaw 34 Schoolteacher

DOWN: 1 Socks 2 April 3 Exiled 4 Milk 5 North 6 Insider 7 Endeavour 11 One 12 Dance 13 Cruise 15 Deluge 17 Tasteless 18 Grate 21 Garnish 23 Eli 25 Africa 27 Gusto 29 Teeth 30 Stair 31 Twit

No. 175

ACROSS: 1 Armhole 5 Purport 9 Mousehole 10 Fence 11 Notes 12 Preferred 13 Close-fisted 16 Hoe 17 Nag 18 Photography 20 Monstrous 22 Crass 24 Dusty 25 Harmonium 27 Curator 28 Day-book

DOWN: 1 Almanac 2 Mount 3 Oversleep 4 Ego 5 Pretentious 6 Rifle 7 Ownership 8 Treadle 12 Philosopher 14 Organiser 15 Directory 17 Nomadic 19 Yashmak 21 Tryst 23 Amigo 26 Red

No. 176

ACROSS: 1 Distributor 8 Alibi 10 Invented 12 Directed 13 Charity 14 Deplores 17 Polar 18 Puffin 19 Impair 20 Diana 21 Enlarged 23 Mistral 25 Speeding 28 Slanting 29 Rates 30 Contracting

DOWN: 2 Irish 3 Tavern 4 Ignition 5 Used 6 Race 7 Victorian 9 Industrial 11 Diver 13 Compressor 14 David 15 Lima 16 Effluents 17 Pier 19 Insignia 20 Deans 22 Strict 24 Argon 26 Disc 27 Glut

No. 177

ACROSS: 1 Poverty Line 9 Frail 10 Carpenter 12 Romantic 13 Meander 14 Dresser 15 Restore 17 Lied 18 Disc 20 Fanatic 22 Overall 23 Moisten 25 Amersham 27 Designate 28 Ruche 29 Draughtsman

DOWN: 2 Orate 3 Expanded 4 Tangent 5 Leer 6 Effaced 7 Fantastic 8 Electrician 11 Roedean 13 Millionaire 15 Reference 16 Offload 18 Dissents 19 Waisted 21 Abolish 24 Extra 26 Menu

No. 178

ACROSS: 1 Staggered Hours 9 Character 10 Ebony 11 Anew 12 Perishable 14 Shut Out 16 Gondola 18 Chimera 20 Obelisk 21 Racialists 23 Scar 26 Tract 27 Transport 28 Clerical Worker

DOWN: 1 Social Security 2 Awake 3 Gear 4 Retreat 5 Darling 6 Open-handed 7 Rhomb 8 Hyde Park Orator 13 Forecaster 15 UDI 17 Obi 19 Asiatic 20 Outfall 22 Crawl 24 Crook 25 Oslo

No. 179

ACROSS: 1 Strike-breaker 8 Rabbit 9 Resisted 12 Leader 15 Allege 18 Remote 19 Dubious Blessing 20 Louder 22 Intern 24 Demean 27 Paradise 29 Arises 30 Demonstration

DOWN: 1 Sham 2 Rebate 3 Kettle 4 Bargain Basement 5 Easter 6 Kiss 7 Roe 10 Divergent 11 Hand-clasp 13 Reason 14 Police 16 Labour 17 Gloved 21 Region 22 Indaba 23 Tahiti 25 Warm 26 Bean 28 Aid

No. 180

ACROSS: 1 Stephenson 8 Limit 9 Liverpool 10 Egotism 13 Salt 14 Glide 15 Norman 16 Alps 18 Ascot 20 Sold 21 Load 23 Verse 25 Lena 26 Gemini 27 Cilla 29 List 30 Ruffled 33 Land-owner 34 Diver 35 Adventurer

DOWN: 1 Sales Mnager 2 Envelops 3 Hard 4 Noodles 5 Oiled 6 Pictorial 7 Kiss 11 Gentle 12 Manufacturer 17 Solid Fuel 18 Advice 19 Cur 22 Designer 24 Silence 28 Idled 31 Unit 32 Port

No. 181

ACROSS: 1 Power Politics 8 Foremost 9 Lather 10 Little 11 Reformer 14 Dora 16 Sir or Madam 18 Complacent 19 East 21 Stranded 24 Ousted 26 Person 28 Carriage 29 Holiday Resort

DOWN: 1 Proviso 2 Wrest 3 Rhode Island 4 Otter 5 Ill 6 Interlace 7 Scene 12 First Course 13 Remit 14 Ducks 15 Appraisal 17 Rye 20 Sleight 22 Teeth 23 Decay 25 Sligo 27 Nod

No. 182

ACROSS: 1 Scrapped 5 Tahiti 10 Laden 11 Container 12 Newcastle 13 Fret 16 Owing 18 Desperado 21 Engineers 24 Extra 25 Nick 27 Wearisome 31 Strongest 32 Ratio 33 Drowsy 34 Chemical

DOWN: 1 Sale 2 Reddening 3 Panic 4 Excised 6 Away 7 Inner 8 Irrational 9 Angles 14 Modernised 15 Mere 17 Gang 19 Err 20 Automatic 22 Eyelet 23 Stretch 26 Cargo 28 Strum 29 Onus 30 Toll

No. 183

ACROSS: 1 Going Straight 8 Cope 9 Digit 10 Sham 11 Settle Old Scores 15 Endorse 17 Engaged 19 Lioness 21 Idyllic 24 Castles In The Air 29 Menu 30 Token 31 Gaff 32 Debt Collector

DOWN: 1 Globe 2 Inept 3 Goddess 4 Toggle 5 Artisan 6 Gusto 7 Trade 11 Shellac 12 Tedious 13 Regalia 14 Seducer 16 Rue 18 Guy 20 Sceptic 22 Detente 23 Nickel 25 Ahead 26 Thumb 27 Eight 28 Infer

No. 184

ACROSS: 1 Castro 4 Scrapper 9 Oil-rig 11 Redstart 12 David 13 Song 15 Once 16 Mine-shaft 17 Ahem 19 Repay 20 Liver 24 Ream 26 Handshake 27 Peel 28 Real 30 Beans 32 Improver 33 Glassy 34 Gendarme 35 Dealer

DOWN: 1 Crossbar 2 Silencer 3 Raid 5 Cued 6 Also 7 Plaint 8 Rotten 10 Garibaldi 11 River 14 Shrinking 15 Offer 18 Metal 21 Reversal 22 Employer 23 Cheer 25 Spring 26 Hempen 29 Soda 30 Beam 31 Sloe

No. 185

ACROSS: 1 Guillotine 6 Eric 9 Prosperity 10 Wage 12 Impel 14 Overrated 15 Sectarian 18 Floor 19 Draft 20 Title-page 22 Pretender 24 Royal 25 Shed 26 Bill Poster 28 Tell 29 Stay-at-home

DOWN: 1 Gypsies 2 ILO 3 Lapel 4 Terrorist 5 Nitre 7 Reactionary 8 Cheddar 11 Trifle 13 Package Deal 16 Anthem 17 Naturally 19 Deposit 21 Enlarge 23 Drift 24 Roost 27 Two

No. 186

ACROSS: 1 House Of Lords 9 Jerusalem 10 Mourn 11 Cask 12 Party 13 Shoe 16 Imitate 18 Diabolo 19 Oppress 21 Planter 22 Fool 23 After 24 Abet 28 Copse 29 Realistic 30 Union Meeting

DOWN: 2 Ogres 3 Sash 4 Oil-cake 5 Limited 6 Ramp 7 Southport 8 Undemocratic 9 Jack-in-office 14 Haven 15 Salad 17 Impromptu 20 Saffron 21 Prepare 25 Baton 26 Semi 27 List

No. 187

ACROSS: 1 Cross-purposes 9 Replica 11 Voice 12 Grist 13 Aped 15 Realm 17 Divergent 21 Item 22 Oscar 23 Seal 24 Economist 28 Roach 30 Shoe 31 Alibi 33 Claim 34 Granite 35 Branch Meeting

DOWN: 2 Regina 3 Stream 4 Pipped 5 Rail 6 Onager 7 Excise 8 Overtime Pay 10 Stately Home 14 Discuss 16 Lemon 18 Earl 19 Gusto 20 Form 25 Oliver 26 Origin 27 Thrive 28 Recent 29 Amazon 32 Bath

No. 188

ACROSS: 1 Arch 3 Dish 6 Token 10 Pancake 11 Meat Pie 12 Emends 13 Endives 16 Tonic Water 17 User 19 Ripe 21 Ginger-snap 24 Delight 25 Starch 29 Utensil 30 Avenues 31 Fudge 32 Edam 33 Levy

DOWN: 1 Apple 2 Canteen 4 Idea 5 Ham And Eggs 6 Tragic 7 Kippers 8 Need 9 Haddock 14 Danish Blue 15 Drop 16 Tart 18 Fritter 20 Pretend 22 Nurture 23 Tissue 26 Hasty 27 Duff 28 Java

No. 189

ACROSS: 1 Wilmington 6 Loaf 10 Niggled 11 Service 12 Harm 13 Massive 17 Lightship 20 Loose 21 Ellen 22 Represent 23 Pantile 25 Tree 30 Founder 31 Nominee 32 Rake 33 Persistent

DOWN: 1 Winchelsea 2 Lager 3 Isle 4 Godfather 5 Oasis 7 Omit 8 Feel 9 Traveller 14 Standards 15 Mole 16 Settlement 18 Gulf 19 Pipelines 24 Three 26 Range 27 Afar 28 Bulk 29 Amps

No. 190

ACROSS: 1 Works Outing 9 Performed 10 Strut 11 Raider 13 Prolific 15 Assimilate 16 Mere 18 Rock 20 Uneconomic 23 Guardian 24 Odessa 26 Might 27 Intending 29 Strongholds

DOWN: 1 Worries 2 Rio 3 Sump 4 Understock 5 Insult 6 Giraffe 7 Spartan Regime 8 Stock Exchange 12 Emma 14 Elongation 17 Enid 19 Charges 21 Mystics 22 Editor 25 Itch 28 Nil

No. 191

ACROSS: 1 Shadow Minister 9 Elaborate 10 Edict 11 Kilt 12 Duplicator 14 Resolve 16 Silence 18 Carlyle 20 Sisters 21 Repression 23 Stir 26 Enrol 27 Abominate 28 Between Friends

DOWN: 1 Speakers' Corner 2 Avail 3 Oboe 4 Measure 5 Needles 6 Speechless 7 Evict 8 Starter's Orders 13 Playfellow 15 Sir 17 Nye 19 Eustace 20 Show Off 22 Purge 24 Train 25 Hi-fi

No. 192

ACROSS: 1 Imperial College 9 Spanner 10 Pothole 11 Ganges 14 Revoke 15 Regular 16 Temp 18 Fist 19 Saladin 20 Malt 21 Stub 23 Topical 25 Redcar 26 Lender 30 Apostle 31 Outrage 32 Test Of Endurance

DOWN: 1 Insight 2 Plain 3 Runner 4 Aura 5 Copy 6 Litter 7 Economist 8 Element 12 Senator 13 Lunatic 14 Radical 17 Melodious 20 Mordant 22 Burmese 23 Tattoo 24 Letter 27 Drain 28 Here 29 Gold

No. 193

ACROSS: 1 Opening Night 9 Caravan 10 Isolate 11 Lapel 12 Tempting 14 Ivor 15 Notes 16 Heir 17 Tunisia 20 Lair 22 Ditto 24 Edam 25 Lavender 28 Ounce 30 Moisten 31 Chimera 32 Eleventh Hour

DOWN: 2 Parapet 3 Novelist 4 Nine 5 Noise 6 Group 7 Tea-time 8 Beggar's Opera 9 Colonel Blimp 12 Trainer 13 Mimi 18 Used 19 Admonish 21 Invoice 23 Tonneau 26 Nitre 27 Ernie 29 Scut

No. 194

ACROSS: 1 Tolerable 6 Champ 9 Organic 10 Panache 11 Estrange 12 Retina 14 Diet 15 Importance 17 White House 19 Bolt 22 Raisin 23 Elephant 26 Glazier 27 America 28 Trent 29 Title-page

DOWN: 1 Those 2 Legatee 3 Runway 4 Backgammon 5 Espy 6 Confetti 7 Auction 8 Prevalent 13 Consultant 14 Downright 16 Feminist 18 Imitate 20 Ocarina 21 Sphere 24 Trace 25 Fret

No. 195

ACROSS: 1 Welsh Rabbit 7 Boa 9 Flatter 10 Skillet 11 Lunch 12 Open 13 Ogle 15 Ragout 17 Skewers 19 Apricot 21 Copper 23 Down 24 Anon 25 Racer 28 Iron Age 29 Epicure 30 Hot 31 Dining-table

DOWN: 1 Waffle 2 Learn 3 Hotchpotch 4 Airport 5 Baskets 6 Twin 7 Bolognese 8 Actressy 14 Peppermint 16 Arrowroot 18 Sandwich 20 Tintern 21 Canteen 22 Freeze 26 Crumb 27 Lard

No. 196

ACROSS: 1 Important 6 Aloof 9 Chopped 10 Ribston 11 John Brown's Body 14 Knife 15 Snap 16 Near 18 Tail 19 Amok 20 Roads 22 Banana Republic 25 Andorra 27 Channel 28 Dread 29 Dispelled

DOWN: 1 Inch 2 Proposition 3 Repented 4 Alder 5 Throwback 6 Ambush 7 Opt 8 Fancy Dress 12 Operational 13 Skateboard 15 Samarkand 17 Cribbage 21 Ingrid 23 Packs 24 Glad 26 Due

No. 197

ACROSS: 1 Run-down 5 Bandage 9 Bustard 10 Tripper 12 Spar 14 Apron 15 Tent 18 Insect 20 Blessing 22 Long Shot 24 Sprout 25 Them 28 Score 29 Dean 31 Partial 32 Parable 33 Wheezes 34 Adverse

DOWN: 2 Usurp 3 Deter 4 Warrant 6 Arrange 7 Depot 8 Green 11 Probation 12 Skillet 13 Absence 16 Episode 17 Tighten 19 Cos 21 Sip 23 Hostage 24 Steward 26 Heath 27 Metre 29 Drake 30 Atlas

No. 198

ACROSS: 1 Fruit-machine 9 Gibraltar 10 Cache 11 Anti 12 Sleep 13 Slur 16 Shallot 18 Thereat 19 Outcome 21 Pointer 22 Each 23 Sudan 24 Saga 28 Aroma 29 Animosity 30 Eleventh Hour

DOWN: 2 Robot 3 Ivan 4 Matelot 5 Current 6 Itch 7 Excellent 8 Secret Treaty 9 Gladstone Bag 14 Blood 15 Merit 17 Artichoke 20 Emulate 21 Pianist 25 Adieu 26 Wage 27 Both

No. 199

ACROSS: 1 Tea-chest 5 Grapes 9 Beetroot 11 Larder 12 Tried 13 Eddy 16 Asti 17 Soup Spoon 18 Lace 20 Steel 21 Flail 22 Bath 24 Mincemeat 27 Rice 28 Char 29 Berry 32 Expels 33 Novelist 34 Nutmeg 35 Skittles

DOWN: 1 Tables 2 Amends 3 Hard 4 Spot 6 Read 7 Pedestal 8 Sardines 10 Tripe 11 Leg Of Lamb 14 Youth 15 Appetites 18 Lilac 19 Aberdeen 20 Stockpot 23 Scorn 25 Thrill 26 Crates 29 Blue 30 Yolk 31 Lent

No. 200

ACROSS: 1 Charterhouse 8 Tool 9 Automation 10 South 12 Mine 13 Lorries 16 Sol 17 Reach 18 Nineveh 19 Collect 20 Capri 21 Aye 22 Reverse 25 Grub 26 Their 29 Wharfinger 30 Wave 31 Refrigerated

DOWN: 1 Coal Merchant 2 Attendance 3 Tame 4 Ratio 5 Odour 6 Ethos 7 Port 10 Service 11 Half-timbered 14 Rail-car 15 Shelter 16 Shipwright 22 River 23 Ether 24 Shrug 27 Heat 28 Pier

No. 201

ACROSS: 1 French Bread 7 Ash 9 Torpedo 10 Liberal 11 Ethos 12 Lard 13 Owed 15 Grocer 17 Economy 19 Cracker 21 Hearty 23 Ante 24 Spam 25 Diced 28 Breathe 29 Emotive 30 Elf 31 Dressed Crab

DOWN: 1 Fatter 2 Earth 3 Cheesecake 4 Broiler 5 Enlarge 6 Dabs 7 Arrowroot 8 Holidays 14 Hot And Cold 16 Roast Beef 18 Scramble 20 Replete 21 Hampers 22 Adverb 26 Crier 27 Stud

No. 202

ACROSS: 1 Splinter Group 8 Storage 9 Bramble 11 Open 12 Attic 13 Carp 16 Service 17 Harness 18 Eastern 21 Chateau 23 Away 24 Junta 25 Mama 28 Drinker 29 Promise 30 Miracle-worker

DOWN: 2 Pioneer 3 Ivan 4 Trestle 5 Rubbish 6 Road 7 Umbrage 8 Shop-steward 10 Expostulate 14 Liver 15 Broad 19 Swahili 20 Neutral 21 Cat's-paw 22 Examine 26 Skua 27 Hour

No. 203

ACROSS: 1 Subtle 4 Chessman 9 Baltic 11 Prorogue 12 Roman 13 Then 15 Seal 16 Amendment 17 Glen 19 Dotty 20 Super 24 Rein 26 Reformist 27 Pied 28 Pure 30 Steam 32 Oligarch 33 Naples 34 Tingling 35 Placid

DOWN: 1 Sabotage 2 Believed 3 Lair 5 Horn 6 Sort 7 Magnet 8 Needle 10 Commotion 11 Paint 14 Ombudsman 15 Sneer 18 Noted 21 Republic 22 Incensed 23 Smith 25 Sprout 26 Resign 29 Rail 30 Scan 31 Mail

No. 204

ACROSS: 1 Solidity 5 Decamp 10 Forestall 11 Susie 12 Elevate 13 Referee 14 Bandsman 17 Lilac 19 Attic 21 National 24 Heckler 25 Skipper 27 Trace 28 Terminate 29 Crying 30 Opencast

DOWN: 1 Soften 2 Large 3 Discard 4 Trade 6 Easeful 7 Australia 8 Pretence 9 Clarinet 15 Autocracy 16 Minority 18 Pathetic 20 Colleen 22 Opinion 23 Urgent 25 Scrap 26 Plaza

No. 205

ACROSS: 1 Substitute 6 Wait 10 Prior 11 Measuring 12 Affluent 13 Upset 15 Leaflet 17 Rebecca 19 Creator 21 Curates 22 Smart 24 Valuable 27 Impudence 28 Inner 29 Hock 30 Restaurant

DOWN: 1 Sept 2 Brief-case 3 Tyrol 4 Tempest 5 Tractor 7 Alias 8 Tight Waist 9 Cucumber 14 Blacksmith 16 Latitude 18 Catalonia 20 Revenue 21 Collect 23 Aspic 25 Adieu 26 Writ

No. 206

ACROSS: 1 Contract 6 Ducat 10 Unloads 11 Reclaim 12 Logs 13 Lima 14 Lathe 16 Tidings 17 Oil Drum 19 Absence 22 Harbour 24 Ariel 26 Snug 27 Itch 29 Esparto 30 Italian 31 Derby 32 Furnaces

DOWN: 2 Obliged 3 Teak 4 Assails 5 Tornado 6 Ducal 7 Charter 8 Timber Merchant 9 Full Steam Ahead 15 Anon 18 Lord 20 Skipper 21 Ease Off 22 Haulier 23 Outside 25 Lorry 28 Java

No. 207

ACROSS: 1 Parliament 6 Onus 10 Reflect 11 Station 12 Factious 13 Those 15 Range 17 Impartial 19 Freighter 21 Latin 23 Stain 24 Probable 27 Impress 28 Iron Age 29 Need 30 Weightless

DOWN: 1 Port 2 Refrain 3 Inept 4 Methodist 5 Nests 7 Nairobi 8 Sunderland 9 Pastoral 14 Profession 16 Engineer 18 Parroting 20 Example 22 Tillage 24 Paste 25 About 26 Bess

No. 208

ACROSS: 1 Cabbages 5 Rabbit 9 Canister 11 Parkin 12 Satin 13 Ling 16 Ewer 17 Aubergine 18 Plum 20 Gravy 21 Scull 22 Heed 24 Beanfeast 27 Neat 28 Hash 29 Stock 32 Trifle 33 Kindness 34 Agenda 35 Strainer

DOWN: 1 Cockle 2 Banana 3 Apse 4 Eyes 6 Alan 7 Bakewell 8 Tantrums 10 Range 11 Picnicker 14 Guard 15 Serviette 18 Plush 19 China Tea 20 Gelatine 23 Snack 25 Tavern 26 Chaser 29 Slid 30 Kilt 31 Edna

No. 209

ACROSS: 1 Hundred Days 9 Obnoxious 10 Clara 11 Sample 13 Propound 15 Monday Club 16 Heel 18 Rapt 20 Washington 23 Overlaid 24 Barrel 26 Doing 27 Nattering 29 Metalworker

DOWN: 1 Hangman 2 Nix 3 Roof 4 Distraught 5 Accept 6 Stature 7 Consumer Goods 8 Daddy-long-legs 12 Lead 14 Occasional 17 Inca 19 Premium 21 Terrier 22 Alight 25 Otto 28 Elk

No. 210

ACROSS: 1 Spotted Dick 7 Lam 9 Coconut 10 Doleful 11 Agree 12 Atom 13 Corn 15 Cutlet 17 Showers 19 Codfish 21 Splash 23 Aura 24 Aria 25 Notch 28 Bromide 29 Improve 30 Ewe 31 Kitchenette

DOWN: 1 Social 2 Oscar 3 Tenderloin 4 Detract 5 Indoors 6 Kale 7 Left-overs 8 Mildness 14 Rolling-pin 16 Underdone 18 Scramble 20 Harvest 21 Spanish 22 Cheese 26 Trout 27 Sink

No. 211

ACROSS: 1 Womankind 6 Codas 9 Canonical 10 Anger 11 Span 12 Smock-frock 14 Teledu 15 Overdid 16 Pachisi 18 Enrols 20 Osteopathy 21 Harm 24 Trout 25 Ill-omened 26 Demur 27 Eccentric

DOWN: 1 Wicks 2 Mintage 3 Nine 4 Incommunicative 5 Dolichocephalic 6 Chauffeurs 7 Dogwood 8 Stroked 13 Helicopter 16 Plotted 17 Cutworm 19 Learner 22 Medoc 23 Amen

No. 212

ACROSS: 1 Misdealt 4 Silent 8 Tiverton 11 Pastry 12 Pill 13 Eat 14 Attach 15 Shanghai 18 Atop 20 Magic 21 Stare 22 Coot 24 Footwear 28 Busoni 29 Ill 30 List 32 Avenue 34 Easiness 35 Turkey 36 Skylight

DOWN: 1 Mother 2 Errata 3 Loop 5 Ida 6 Entracte 7 Toyshops 9 Vets 10 Night 11 Plaistow 16 Heat 17 Nail-file 18 Area 19 Icy Blast 20 Mouse-ear 23 Goose 25 Espial 26 Rime 27 Closet 31 Talk 33 Use

No. 213

ACROSS: 1 Santiago 5 Warsaw 9 Linkboys 10 Unfair 12 Algebra 13 Rebecca 14 Prince Albert 17 Globe Trotter 22 Gudgeon 23 Average 24 Orants 25 Learning 26 Pandas 27 Eye-water

DOWN: 1 Sultan 2 Nonage 3 Imbiber 4 Guy Mannering 6 Annabel 7 Starched 8 Warranty 11 Greek Tragedy 15 Age Group 16 Cordwain 18 Electra 19 Eyebrow 20 Papist 21 Beggar

No. 214

ACROSS: 1 Icy 5 Molasses 10 Revolt 11 Lot 12 Staccato 13 Wilton 14 Ass 15 Sent Up 18 By Hook Or By Crook 21 Under The Weather 25 Fitter 26 Cut 28 Gibbon 29 Recitals 31 Rig 32 Combat 33 Descried 34 Led

DOWN: 2 Crows 3 Yetis 4 Portico 6 Out 7 Ascetic 8 Shampoo 9 Shoemaker 16 Elbows 17 Bothie 18 Blundered 19 Ode 20 Rat 22 Defects 23 Rotator 24 Alabama 26 Coral 27 Unite 30 Lie

No. 215

ACROSS: 1 Predestination 9 Oration 10 Paucity 11 Entertain 12 Phial 13 Thrips 14 Shagreen 17 Thousand 19 Tragic 22 Enter 24 Establish 26 Orlando 27 All Star 28 Undermentioned

DOWN: 1 Prone 2 Exactor 3 Epigraphs 4 Tankas 5 Nepenthe 6 Trump 7 Orifice 8 Cyclonic 13 To The Top 15 Garibaldi 16 Anteroom 18 Ortolan 20 Glisten 21 Attain 23 Range 25 Hared

No. 216

ACROSS: 1 Hecate 4 Addendum 10 Roadway 11 Sledges 12 Unschooled 13 Lira 15 Because 17 Bagshot 19 Sockeye 21 Elegant 23 Carl 24 Dressmaker 27 Raising 28 Singeth 29 Eye-tooth 30 Uses Up

DOWN: 1 Harquebus 2 Classic 3 Town Houses 5 Dissemble 6 Ewer 7 Dogfish 8 Massa 9 Tyro 14 Agreements 16 Eyebright 18 Tutorship 20 Cursive 22 Anklets 23 Curse 25 Sash 26 Tito

No. 217

ACROSS: 1 Racist 4 Scuttle 9 Operas 10 Ambrosia 11 Botanic 13 Raiment 14 Phantasmagoria 16 Man In The Street 20 Impasse 22 Ditches 23 Eardrums 24 Alpine 25 Prelate 26 Adages

DOWN: 1 Rhombs 2 Cleft Chin 3 Shannon 5 Compromised 6 Turning 7 Lisle 8 Mantra 12 Crash Helmet 15 Re-echoing 16 Maiden 17 Nostril 18 Rattled 19 Asters 21 Parer

No. 218

ACROSS: 1 Spender 5 Pea-soup 9 Storm-cone 10 Easel 11 Afeard 12 Derelict 14 Naturalist 16 Lake 18 Dour 19 Hollow Eyes 22 Faceache 23 Served 26 Alter 27 Unbridles 28 Tussled 29 Negress

DOWN: 1 Sustain 2 Evoke 3 Demerara 4 Room 5 Prehensile 6 Abeles 7 Obstinacy 8 Palette 13 Bloodhound 15 Truncates 17 Sweeting 18 Defiant 20 Sadists 21 Laurel 24 Value 25 Oban

No. 219

ACROSS: 1 Primrose 5 Gander 9 Operator 10 Maniac 12 Pre-empt 13 Rotator 14 Spring Greens 17 Lyric Theatre 22 Massage 23 Giddier 24 Needle 25 Aigrette 26 Odours 27 Adscript

DOWN: 1 Prompt 2 Icemen 3 Road Map 4 Short-sighted 6 Alastor 7 Drift-net 8 Rock-rose 11 Mrs Gradgrind 15 Flamenco 16 Prospero 18 Crawler 19 Roderic 20 Viotti 21 Urgent

No. 220

ACROSS: 1 Calypso 5 Loose 9 Bagatelle 10 Occur 11 Noel 12 Beeswing 15 Good Samaritan 16 Beyond The Pale 17 Friction 18 Heir 22 Arkle 23 Rigmarole 24 Kites 25 Enhance

DOWN: 1 Cabins 2 Leg Before Wicket 3 Path 4 Oslo 5 Look Slippy 6 Once In A Blue Moon 7 Enrage 8 Telepathy 13 Adroitness 14 Cardboard 17 Flank 19 Reeve 20 Ogee 21 Cash

No. 221

ACROSS: 8 Inconsequential 9 Selvage 10 Limp 11 Retain 12 Istle 13 Chic 14 Dabchick 16 Renounce 19 Roux 21 Nabob 22 Irises 24 Esse 25 Honoria 26 Phosphorescence

DOWN: 1 Anguish 2 Conspicuousness 3 Isolation 4 Squared 5 Reger 6 Stretcher-bearer 7 Cardiac 15 Barbarism 17 Earache 18 Ensnare 20 Unstuck 23 Shahs

No. 222

ACROSS: 1 Adipose Tissue 9 Expedient 10 Taboo 11 Annal 12 Sea-breach 13 Sea-lion 15 Twitter 17 Antwerp 19 Evening 21 Half-truth 23 Bruno 24 Runic 25 Monoplane 26 Red Letter Days

DOWN: 2 Dependant 3 Pedal 4 Stepson 5 Tetract 6 Saturnine 7 Umbra 8 Mother 9 Exams 14 Identical 16 Tributary 17 Adhere 18 Plummet 19 Enhance 20 Goose 22 Lance 23 Biped

No. 223

ACROSS: 1 Abbreviation 9 Four 10 Bondslave 12 Little 13 Judicial 15 Compromise 16 Sees 18 Case 20 Delegation 23 Rhetoric 24 Irises 26 Apprehend 27 Aces 28 The Gentle Sex

DOWN: 2 Burglary 3 Ruby 4 Vanquished 5 Aussie 6 Imagine 7 Needlessness 8 Tom-tom 11 Black Currant 14 Impediment 17 Marriage 19 Steeple 21 Instep 22 Cohere 25 Idle

No. 224

ACROSS: 1 Chocolate 5 Chaff 8 Moguls 9 Scorpion 11 Conspire 12 Camera 14 Pests 16 Abandon 18 Realist 19 Relic 20 Rotter 22 Presaged 26 Mastodon 27 Prayer 28 Steer 29 Halfpenny

DOWN: 1 Comic 2 Organiser 3 Orlop 4 Etch 5 Coriander 6 Arise 7 Fantastic 10 Arcadia 13 Battery 14 Panoramas 15 Stage Door 17 Nell Gwynn 21 Taste 23 Strap 24 Derby 25 Nosh

No. 225

ACROSS: 1 Stretchers 6 Koko 10 Evade 11 Neuralgia 12 Pitcairn 13 Picnic 15 Ivan 16 Isle 17 Elihu 20 Cabal 21 Etty 22 Went 24 Police 26 Arrogate 29 Bathsheba 30 Adder 31 Erne 32 Staff Nurse

DOWN: 1 Steep 2 Roast Lamb 3 Theban 4 Huntresses 5 Roup 7 Organ 8 On Account 9 Canines 14 Better Half 15 Incapable 18 Icelander 19 Glucose 23 Domain 25 Latin 27 Eyrie 28 Welt

No. 226

ACROSS: 1 Perpendicular 9 Elegant 10 Chinese 11 Orris 12 Hottentot 13 Rigid 15 Translate 17 Metronome 18 Lasso 19 Tormentor 22 Throw 23 Soldier 24 Popular 25 Hypochondriac

DOWN: 2 Eyebright 3 Plans 4 Notch 5 Universal 6 Alert 7 Melodramatist 8 Centre Forward 10 Cottage 14 Duodecimo 15 Trotter 16 Australia 20 Rally 21 Ripon 22 Tapir

No. 227

ACROSS: 1 Companion Ladder 9 Tearful 10 Biscuit 11 Obtrude 13 Dreamer 14 Seven Dials 16 Ajar 19 Body 20 Kettledrum 22 Comment 23 Dolores 25 Lacking 27 Proudie 28 Commonplace Book

DOWN: 1 Cottons 2 Meant 3 Affluent 4 Ill 5 Nub 6 Auster 7 Drum-major 8 Rotor 12 Evident 13 Diluted 15 Vade-mecum 17 Rump-steak 18 Bell-rope 19 Bucolic 21 Merino 24 Radio 26 Gyp 27 Pea

No. 228

ACROSS: 1 Behest 4 Brown Owl 10 Baronet 11 Walking 12 Hoof 13 Bell The Cat 16 Odious 17 Terrain 20 Thomas a 21 Becket 24 Hundred Per 25 Otic 27 Stomata 29 Present 30 Softness 31 Stamen

DOWN: 1 Babyhood 2 Harmoniphon 3 Sink 5 Rowelled 6 Wild Horses 7 Obi 8 Legate 9 Steed 14 Cricket Team 15 Summer Rain 18 Used Cars 19 Stockton 22 Theses 23 Tempo 26 Cent 28 Off

No. 229

ACROSS: 1 Pie 3 Amalgamator 9 Evergreen 10 Unarm 11 Stalls 12 Kerosene 14 Robin-redbreast 17 Brighthelmston 21 Nineteen 22 Salome 25 Idola 26 Imitation 27 Monseigneur 28 Sol

DOWN: 1 Pressure 2 Ewe Lamb 3 Angel 4 Ales 5 Ginger Beer 6 Mausoleum 7 Teasers 8 Romper 13 Feathering 15 Nightmare 16 Infernal 18 Runcorn 19 Tropics 20 Infirm 23 Adair 24 Mite

No. 230

ACROSS: 1 Pack-ice 5 Nudists 9 Narcotics 10 Moped 11 Arena 12 Star-shell 13 Entailing 16 Debar 17 Onion 18 Dead March 20 Crustacea 23 Sober 25 Abana 26 Indweller 27 Doe-skin 28 Emerson

DOWN: 1 Pancake 2 Carve 3 Isolation 4 Emits 5 Nostalgia 6 Dimes 7 September 8 Saddler 14 Triturate 15 Induction 16 Damascene 17 Orchard 19 Hard-run 21 Thank 22 Addle 24 Bills

No. 231

ACROSS: 1 Alderman Cute 8 Hair Shirt 9 Ulcer 11 Niello 12 Triolets 14 Wellington 16 Dido 18 Omri 19 Inner Light 21 Echoless 22 Troika 25 Tithe 26 Intensive 27 Cornish Cream

DOWN: 1 Alice 2 Disclaim 3 Rail 4 Arterioles 5 Coupon 6 Ticketing 7 The New Forest 10 Rose Of Tralee 13 Agonistics 15 Larghetto 17 Clarence 20 Aldern 23 Ilium 24 Otic

No. 232

ACROSS: 8 Pool 9 Astronomer 10 Staccato 11 Knotty 12 Psyche 13 Nuthatch 15 Symphony Concert 18 Brunette 20 Canton 21 Finish 23 Ethereal 24 Maidenhair 25 Stub

DOWN: 1 Soothsayer 2 Blackcap 3 Savage 4 Attorney-general 5 Cockatoo 6 Corona 7 Neat 14 Coriolanus 16 Outshine 17 Contrast 19 Naiads 20 Cohort 22 Iras

No. 233

ACROSS: 1 Misplaced 8 Lalo 9 Trilateral 10 Unwept 12 Sound 13 Amen 15 Easter 18 Double-barrelled 19 Hussar 22 Hymn 23 Anger 24 Rarest 26 Intolerant 27 Eyas 28 Nerve-cell

DOWN: 1 Mark 2 Sullen 3 Lutist 4 Circumnavigator 5 Delude 6 Parentally 7 North Riding 11 Card-sharper 14 Equestrian 16 Axes 17 Flea 20 Ration 21 Grilse 22 Hearse 25 Anil

No. 234

ACROSS: 1 Pandas 4 Emphasis 10 Totally 11 Thistle 12 Northanger 13 Onan 15 Asepsis 17 Inertia 19 Exhumes 21 Greener 23 Alps 24 Apple Carts 27 Betitle 28 Yenisei 29 Yearning 30 Became

DOWN: 1 Potentate 2 Nut Tree 3 All The Same 5 Mothering 6 Heir 7 Satinet 8 Stern 9 Lyon 14 Senescence 16 Sisyphean 18 Arrestive 20 Hypatia 22 Nerissa 23 Abbey 25 Lays 26 Stun

No. 235

ACROSS: 8 Wet Paint 9 One Way 10 Tropic 11 Tincture 12 Schedule 13 Cereal 14 Lady Day 16 Imbibes 19 Otiose 21 Palisade 23 Amethyst 25 Curate 26 Enlist 27 Manacled

DOWN: 1 Cedric 2 Apoplexy 3 Discourage 4 Statue 5 Moon 6 Mentor 7 Carriage 13 Complacent 15 Antimony 17 Instruct 18 Epitome 20 Oxtail 22 Dotted 24 Yeti

No. 236

ACROSS: 8 Elgin 9 Placeman 10 Shortbread 11 Side 12 Inhere 14 Modified 15 Scab 16 Yacht 18 Ajax 20 Chloride 23 Breath 24 Bled 25 Absolutist 28 Near Side 29 Tosti

DOWN: 1 Mechanic 2 Eger 3 Snobbery 4 Apse 5 Candid 6 Persiflage 7 Saddle 13 Embroidery 14 Macle 17 Tabulate 19 Artistic 21 Halved 22 Italic 26 Seed 27 Test

No. 237

ACROSS: 1 Freeling 5 Ash-can 9 Whipcord 10 In Turn 12 Skill 13 Obstacles 14 Face The Music 18 Complication 21 Note-paper 23 Shore 24 Animal 25 Estimate 26 Signet 27 Assyrian

DOWN: 1 Fewest 2 Elicit 3 Local Call 4 Narrow Escape 6 Senna 7 Clueless 8 Nonesuch 11 Aspheterises 15 Moonshiny 16 Scandals 17 Omitting 19 Somali 20 Severn 22 Plate

No. 238

ACROSS: 9 Outredden 10 Neath 11 Demesne 12 Tallboy 13 Whoa 14 Speedwell 17 Robin Goodfellow 19 Hesitated 21 Aunt 23 Silence 24 Between 25 Penal 26 Spaghetti

DOWN: 1 Wordsworth 2 Atom Bomb 3 Sense 4 Adze 5 Unattended 6 Unfledged 7 Ramble 8 Shay 14 Short Lease 15 Lawn Tennis 16 Instantly 18 Laureate 20 Selina 22 Itchy 23 Saps 24 Brag

No. 239

ACROSS: 1 Characteristic 8 Amateur 9 Bondage 11 Side 12 Settlement 14 Ridden 16 Fledge 17 Nigeria 18 Posted 20 Entrap 24 Overriding 25 Oslo 27 Inertia 28 Rhenish 29 Hundred Per Cent

DOWN: 1 Claustrophobia 2 Awarded 3 Amen 4 Target 5 Robots 6 Sunderland 7 Weather Prophet 10 Amend 13 Penetrated 15 Nid 16 Fie 19 Siege 21 Respite 22 Ideate 23 Enwrap 26 Lear

No. 240

ACROSS: 1 Crumpets 5 Coffer 9 Accoutre 10 Cedric 12 Brocade 13 Wastage 14 Remainderman 17 Saint Swithin 22 Treacle 23 Eustace 24 Rookie 25 Bears Out 26 Cobweb 27 Odyssean

DOWN: 1 Crambo 2 Unclog 3 Plumage 4 Three Day Week 6 Oversee 7 Fire-arms 8 Recreant 11 Swing The Lead 15 Esoteric 16 Dive-bomb 18 Tactile 19 Insures 20 Galore 21 Teuton

No. 241

ACROSS: 7 Potage 8 Dogberry 10 Span 11 Springtime 12 Mutton 14 Nosiness 15 Adverse 17 Essence 20 Bend Down 22 Posset 23 Colleagues 24 Peep 25 Thatcher 26 Launch

DOWN: 1 Compound 2 Lawn 3 Person 4 Adoring 5 Centeniers 6 Cramps 9 Genesis 13 Theodolite 16 Stomach 18 Credence 19 Inquire 21 Epochs 22 Pestle 24 Paul

No. 242

ACROSS: 1 Rapprochement 10 Outrush 11 Crumbly 12 Gaulish 13 Cellar 15 Undo 16 Ill-starred 18 Fallacious 20 Amin 23 Remedy 24 Chrisom 26 Neglige 27 Empiric 28 Archimandrite

DOWN: 2 Astound 3 Plug In 4 Ophthalmic 5 Hack 6 Mouse-ear 7 Nibbler 8 Long-suffering 9 Hydrodynamics 14 Escutcheon 17 Band-fish 19 Lamiger 21 Musk-rat 22 Draper 25 Herm

No. 243

ACROSS: 1 Raffia 4 Paraffin 9 Parody 10 Sinecure 12 Isabella 13 Ordeal 15 Ache 16 Yardsticks 19 Targeteers 20 Deal 23 Untied 25 Asperate 27 Pub Crawl 28 Strich 29 Toyshops 30 Orange

DOWN: 1 Replica 2 Forgather 3 Indeed 5 Acis 6 Aberrate 7 Flute 8 Needles 11 Pleases 14 Address 17 Cremation 18 Research 19 Trumpet 21 Leechee 22 Letter 24 Tabby 26 Swap

No. 244

ACROSS: 8 Continuo 9 Rhesus 10 Tapeti 11 Toilsome 12 Star 15 Gradient 16 Procrastination 18 Maryland 20 Nose 22 Bradshaw 23 Cancan 25 Disown 26 Radiance

DOWN: 1 Monastery 2 Stye 3 Ending 4 Portmanteau Word 5 Fruition 6 Kensington 7 Rummy 13 Richardson 15 Constance 17 Anything 19 Decade 21 Braid 24 Neat

No. 245

ACROSS: 1 Permit 5 Relate 10 Tread 11 Nightmare 12 Level Best 13 Adela 14 Duty 15 Penicillin 19 Indicative 20 Aces 22 Dealt 24 Stricture 26 Angel-cake 27 Brigg 28 Needle 29 Sprags

DOWN: 2 Enervated 3 Medal 4 Tenderest 5 Right 6 Lothario 7 Trade 8 Stolid 9 Remain 16 Inverness 17 Lecturing 18 Scuttled 19 Indian 21 Sledge 23 Argue 24 Stake 25 Caber

No. 246

ACROSS: 1 Amiable 5 Reached 9 Ordinee 10 Yardarm 11 Piccadilly 12 Idol 13 Tot 14 Aminobutene 17 Christendom 19 Pat 20 Buss 22 Petrol Tank 26 Arizona 27 Village 28 Delight 29 Letters

DOWN: 1 Apoop 2 Indicator 3 Bandana 4 Elemi 5 Royal Road 6 Aire 7 Hoard 8 Demulcent 13 Tack-board 15 Inelegant 16 Esplanade 18 Melilot 21 Still 23 Revel 24 Keels 25 Dong

No. 247

ACROSS: 1 Clamps 5 Pediment 9 Dark Hair 10 Shouts 11 Territorials 13 Bear 14 Minsters 17 Question 18 Rasp 20 Flower Garden 23 Accent 24 Ice Cubes 25 Anderson 26 Shawms

DOWN: 2 Liar 3 Make Terms 4 Starry 5 Parliamentarian 6 Dismount 7 Maori 8 Nettlerash 12 Republican 15 Tarantula 16 Nitrates 19 Adders 21 Where 22 Seam

No. 248

ACROSS: 8 Parliament House 9 Beginner 10 Copper 11 Chin 12 Arras 14 Rank 15 Agreed 16 Sadist 18 Smug 20 Storm 21 Lout 22 Manner 23 Draughts 24 Make A Fresh Start

DOWN: 1 Gave The Game Away 2 Alliance 3 Barnyard 4 Heir 5 Stocks 6 Romper 7 As Keen As Mustard 13 Rondo 16 Sympathy 17 Delights 19 Gannet 20 Strife 23 Does

No. 249

ACROSS: 1 Breton 4 Roebucks 8 Manciple 10 Tranio 12 Alibi 13 Woundwort 14 Order 16 Midinette 17 Swept Away 19 Cadet 21 Discourse 22 Adair 24 Loudly 25 Stop-cock 26 Antidote 27 Trilby

DOWN: 1 Bummalo 2 Ennui 3 Olivier 5 Borodin 6 Contorted 7 Smoothe 9 Lawnmowers 11 Sunday Best 15 Dress Suit 17 Sedilia 18 Tootled 19 Clapper 20 Turnkey 23 Atoll

No. 250

ACROSS: 9 Oatmeal 10 Epitome 11 Chart 12 Diagnosis 13 Piecemeal 15 Gasps 16 Stream 18 Clover 21 Enact 22 Numerator 24 Good Taste 26 Pilot 28 Ice-floe 29 Epicure

DOWN: 1 Forceps 2 Etna 3 Settlement 4 Pledge 5 Metallic 6 Sign 7 Consistent 8 Persist 14 Extra Cover 15 Geographic 17 Menasseh 19 Penguin 20 Written 23 My Eyes 25 Tale 27 Laud

No. 251

ACROSS: 7 Peeler 8 Tramping 9 Mercator 10 Llamas 11 Black 12 Fortunate 14 Interest Rates 16 Interpose 18 Busby 21 Stroll 22 Exertion 23 Maternal 24 Venice

DOWN: 1 Reveal 2 Black-cat 3 Broth 4 Tall Story 5 Sprain 6 Unearths 8 Tortoise-shell 13 Drop A Line 14 Ignatian 15 Trusting 17 Eroded 19 Broach 20 Heave

No. 252

ACROSS: 1 Sinbad 4 Anchoret 9 Secret 10 Trinculo 12 Nautical 13 Asleep 15 Arne 16 Bottom Gear 19 Saltigrade 20 Peke 23 Amours 25 Bullfrog 27 Ice Cream 28 Maybug 29 Graphite 30 Ostend

DOWN: 1 Susanna 2 Nocturnal 3 Amelia 5 Norm 6 Handsome 7 Rouse 8 Trooper 11 Favours 14 Stadium 17 Execrable 18 Hierarch 19 Shaving 21 Engaged 22 Clears 24 Opera 26 Cast

No. 253

ACROSS: 1 Lucknow 5 Blanche 9 Nonet 10 Morse Code 11 Furrow 12 Cemetery 14 Rules 15 How Goes It 18 Eldest Son 20 Tudor 22 Canister 24 Busoni 26 Mezzanine 27 Bilbo 28 Long Leg 29 Faraday

DOWN: 1 Land Force 2 Central 3 Net Losses 4 Womb 5 Barley Wine 6 Abele 7 Coopers 8 Enemy 13 Whispering 16 Outnumber 17 Territory 19 Denizen 21 Drooled 22 Camel 23 Stall 25 Leaf

No. 254

ACROSS: 1 Destruction 9 Have Dinner 10 Eire 11 Beetles 12 Caterer 14 Again 16 Insoluble 19 Crayoning 20 Umbel 22 Wintery 24 Measure 27 Hoar 28 Aristocrat 29 Momentarily

DOWN: 2 Electrify 3 Trivet 4 Urns 5 Toreador 6 Obese 7 Face 8 True Blue 13 Anent 15 Garrison 17 Unmusical 18 Increase 21 Better 23 Torso 25 Roan 26 List

No. 255

ACROSS: 8 Ampere 9 Allspice 10 Measured 11 Vortex 12 Terror 13 Arrogate 15 Inst 16 Cora 21 True Blue 23 Godwit 24 Assess 26 Consider 27 Adhesive 28 Innate

DOWN: 1 Ammeter 2 Tea Service 3 Bear Arms 4 Bandeau 5 Clever 6 Spar 7 Accents 14 Grand Piano 17 Organdie 18 Preside 19 Benches 20 Bisects 22 Lassie 25 Eden

No. 256

ACROSS: 1 Dunmow Flitch 9 Summing Up 10 Moral 11 Endear 12 Proclaim 13 Topics 15 Barathea 18 Farmyard 19 Alarum 21 Embodied 23 Egress 26 Colon 27 Exact Time 28 Petty Larceny

DOWN: 1 Dessert 2 Named 3 Oligarchy 4 Fags 5 Imperial 6 Comic 7 Dilemma 8 Preacher 14 Parabola 16 Alligator 17 Free Seat 18 Fleeced 20 Mystery 22 Donee 24 Exile 25 Bail

No. 257

ACROSS: 8 Electric Torch 9 Grub 10 Pedal 11 Earl 12 Myopia 14 Detach 16 For Many A Long Day 17 Nassau 20 Larder 22 Abed 24 Tenet 25 High 26 Stand And Fight

DOWN: 1 Nearly 2 Herb 3 Utopia 4 Window Gardening 5 Stolid 6 Free 7 Choric 13 Pumas 15 Tiger 18 Abbess 19 Untidy 20 Let Off 21 Eights 23 Drag 24 Huge

No. 258

ACROSS: 1 Sir Edward Elgar 9 Artiste 10 Antonio 11 Ditto 12 Rio Branco 13 Responded 15 Mason 16 Baker 18 A Fortiori 21 Avalanche 23 Heath 24 Edifice 25 Rossini 26 Christening Mug

DOWN: 1 Standard Bearer 2 Rotates 3 Dishonour 4 Averred 5 Diamond 6 Later 7 Awnings 8 Go Down Fighting 14 Elf 15 Mitchison 17 Knavish 18 Ancient 19 Overran 20 Orarium 22 Alibi

No. 259

ACROSS: 9 Contacted 10 Upper 11 Abandon 12 Oppress 13 Golly 14 Priceless 16 Look Back In Anger 19 Right Turn 21 Aaron 22 Remorse 23 Beseech 24 Trees 25 Adverbial

DOWN: 1 Octangular 2 Intaglio 3 Hardly 4 Stun 5 Admonition 6 Subpoena 7 Sphere 8 Eros 14 Picture Hat 15 Stronghold 17 Buttress 18 Gardenia 20 Gimlet 21 Assert 22 Rota 23 Bevy

No. 260

ACROSS: 1 At The Drop Of A Hat 8 Triangle 9 Silver 10 Bath Soap 11 Oporto 13 Bad Harvest 16 Reticulate 19 Poison 20 Equating 21 Intent 22 Veronica 23 Scratch One's Head

DOWN: 1 Autobiographies 2 Thirty 3 Ernest 4 Releasable 5 Frippery 6 Hover-bed 7 Turn Out The Guard 12 White Queen 14 Stricter 15 Scoop-net 17, 18 Famous Divine

No. 261

ACROSS: 8 Catnap 9 Alleluia 10 Skat 11 Dairy Cream 12 Marcella 14 Danger 15 Charles The Third 18 Mayhap 21 Islamite 22 Commandeer 23 Path 24 Transmit 25 Employ

DOWN: 1 Backwash 2 Gnat 3 Spadille 4 Marie Antoinette 5 Flayed 6 Altrincham 7 Pirate 13 Carthamine 16 Enlarged 17 Rotation 19 Amours 20 Panama 23 Pope

No. 262

ACROSS: 1 Short And Sweet 10 Personage 11 Organ 12 Needs 13 Innocence 14 Loafing 16 Secedes 18 Serving 20 Alsatia 21 At The Most 23 Eared 24 Karma 25 Cocoa Bean 26 Shut Your Mouth

DOWN: 2 Horsehair 3 Roofs 4 Abating 5 Duennas 6 Woodcocks 7 Elgin 8 Spindleshanks 9 Understanding 15 Itinerant 17 Deterrent 19 Groucho 20 Autocar 22 Torch 23 Erato

No. 263

ACROSS: 1 Stick-in-the-mud 9 Anybody 10 Respect 11 Drown 12 Lubricant 13 Ladle 15 Lucidness 17 Needlegun 18 Arena 19 Lifeguard 22 Churl 23 Gritted 24 Ice-rink 25 Standing Order

DOWN: 2 Toy Poodle 3 Croon 4 Idyll 5 East India 6 Urena 7 Daddy-long-legs 8 Statesmanlike 10 Rubicon 14 Enlighten 15 Laggard 16 Executive 20 Faint 21 Doing 22 Clear

No. 264

ACROSS: 7 Discard 8 Trilled 9 Dynamic 11 Impress 12 Noise 13 Often 15 Found 16 Soon 17 Earn 18 Also 20 Disc 22 Every 23 Hoard 24 Tired 26 Florist 27 Minding 28 Dessert 29 Harmful

DOWN: 1 Lily Of The Valley 2 Achates 3 Drain 4 Crime 5 Clarion 6 Personal Pronoun 10 Corn 11 Isle 14 Nobly 15 Fresh 18 Armrest 19 Omit 20 Deem 21 Condemn 24 Tsars 25 Divan

No. 265

ACROSS: 1 Poplar 4 Astringe 10 Treader 11 Oddment 12 Even 13 Contour Map 16 Caters 17 Overate 20 Dimeter 21 In Gear 24 The Horrors 25 Mist 27 Niagara 29 Pearlin 30 Stealthy 31 Browns

DOWN: 1 Patience 2 Present Time 3 Aids 5 Sportive 6 Red Currant 7 Nye 8 Estops 9 Proof 14 Mother-in-law 15 Free For All 18 Reproach 19 Writings 22 Stones 23 Drops 26 Pair 28 Age

No. 266

ACROSS: 8 Almighty 9 Pliant 10 Avocet 11 Airspace 12 Prepares 13 Parent 14 Stretch 16 Untried 19 Ientil 21 Entrance 23 Accident 25 Artist 26 Almond 27 Ice-bound

DOWN: 1 Clever 2 Mince-pie 3 Rhetorical 4 Bypass 5 Spur 6 Dipper 7 Ensconce 13 Penetrates 15 Tree-calf 17 Reaction 18 Certain 20 Tripod 22 Casino 24 Edda

No. 267

ACROSS: 4 Capuchin 8 Mimosa 9 Ornithic 10 Wondrous 11 Apexes 12 Argument 13 Hectored 16 Hear Hear 19 Ultimacy 21 Labour 23 Indented 24 Historic 25 Lollop 26 Terrapin

DOWN: 1 Bigotry 2 Wood-sugar 3 Galore 4 Cross The Rubicon 5 Penzance 6 Cutie 7 Irideae 14 Outmantle 15 Pear-drop 17 Examine 18 Acheron 20 Toddle 22 Otter

No. 268

ACROSS: 1 Killjoy 5 Spooner 9 Latex 10 The Danube 11 Merman 12 Orchards 14 Zinco 15 Avoidance 18 Off Her Dot 20 Friar 22 Lysander 24 Wooden 26 Amidships 27 Isaac 28 Eye Bank 29 Abstain

DOWN: 1 Kalamazoo 2 Later On 3 Juxtapose 4 Yeti 5 Steerforth 6 Orach 7 Neutron 8 Rheas 13 Candlewick 16 Daffodils 17 Eirenicon 19 Fissile 21 Indiana 22 Leave 23 Nesta 25 Ossa

No. 269

ACROSS: 1 Flocks 5 Fade Away 9 Flambeau 10 Malice 11 Alliteration 13 Rhea 14 Daringly 17 Platform 18 Task 20 Assassinated 23 Alumna 24 Intended 25 Brighton 26 Healer

DOWN: 2 Lily 3 Combatant 4 Shells 5 Fourth Dimension 6 Demerara 7 Allot 8 Anchorless 12 Wholesaler 15 Notodonta 16 Constant 19 Stitch 21 Almug 22 Mere

No. 270

ACROSS: 1 Lead One A Dance 10 Alone 11 Proscribe 12 Boil 13 Levi 14 Maori 16 Ureters 17 Tally-ho 18 Besiege 21 Insular 23 Isles 24 Imam 25 Scup 27 Garibaldi 28 Range 29 Honey Sandwich

DOWN: 2 Egotise 3 Does 4 Nephews 5 Amorist 6 Accomplish 7 Chicory 8 Harbour Bridge 9 Lexicographer 15 Reversible 19 Salerio 20 Edibles 21 Italian 22 Laconic 26 Brow

No. 271

ACROSS: 1 Nightwatchman 10 Onset 11 Sovereign 12 Teal 13 Liar 14 Ebbed 16 Retouch 17 Sourer 19 Ignore 22 Non-acid 25 Lorna 26 Sore 27 Tree 29 Noisiness 30 Tubes 31 Shining Armour

DOWN: 2 Instant 3 Hate 4 Waspish 5 Taverns 6 Harlequins 7 Amiable 8 Contort 9 Snide 15 Automation 18 Adverse 20 Garnish 21 Eastern 22 Nerissa 23 Caribou 24 Plane 28 Stem

No. 272

ACROSS: 1 Thunderclaps 8 Tom-toms 9 Baccara 11 Russian 12 Stuccos 13 Orant 14 Hop-garden 16 Concourse 19 Album 21 Pace Egg 23 Madison 24 Catkins 25 Nut Tree 26 Hedge-sparrow

DOWN: 1 Tamasha 2 Utopist 3 Disanchor 4 Robes 5 Lactuca 6 Peascod 7 Stereoscopic 10 Absent-minded 15 Pneumonia 17 Necktie 18 Opening 19 Auditor 20 Bestrew 22 Gusts

No. 273

ACROSS: 1 Moorhen 5 Chaplin 9 Emu 10 Shaving 11 Rolling 12 Aries 13 Intercede 14 Esquire 16 Saucers 18 Pleaded 20 Pedrero 22 Pedometer 24 Bogle 25 Lubfish 26 Guereza 27 Ego 28 Relayed 29 Nominal

DOWN: 1 Massage 2 Odalisque 3 Heirs 4 Negligé 5 Curates 6 All Around 7 Loire 8 Negress 15 Indemnify 17 Evergreen 18 Popular 19 Ditched 20 Paragon 21 Overall 23 Debel 24 Bream

No. 274

ACROSS: 1 Fenestration 8 Alsatia 9 Mutates 11 Tendril 12 Amiable 13 Cites 14 Eavesdrop 16 Numerator 19 Raise 21 Concise 23 Inveigh 24 Nutting 25 In Ruins 26 Presidential

DOWN: 1 Fastnet 2 Natures 3 Small Feet 4 Rumba 5 Tatties 6 October 7 Pantechnicon 10 Steeplechase 15 Vermilion 17 Monitor 18 Raisins 19 Reversi 20 Initial 22 Edged

No. 275

ACROSS: 1 Leading Article 9 Vervain 10 Salerio 11 Ivory 12 Spendalls 13 In Transit 14 Climb 15 Lumme 17 Sports Car 20 Narrowing 22 Holly 23 Spoiled 24 Neogaea 25 Simple Interest

DOWN: 1 Love-in-idleness 2 Airport 3 In Any Case 4 Genesis 5 Respect 6 Isled 7 Lorelei 8 Gooseberry Tart 14 Catchpole 16 Marconi 17 Swindle 18 Organon 19 Collage 21 Oxlip

No. 276

ACROSS: 1 Assist 6 Sunday 9 Lark 10 Proof 11 Moon 12 Globe 14 Kid 15 Crash 19 Walking-sticks 20 James The First 22 Scant 23 Obi 24 Usher 27 Adam 29 Alone 30 Grow 31 Switch 32 Myself

DOWN: 2 Shallow 3 Ink 4 Tape 5 Cooking The Books 6 Soft 7 Nym 8 Arouses 13 Bellman 16 Records 17 Rinse 18 Stiff 20 Jackdaw 21 Trefoil 25 Wash 26 Helm 28 Mat 30 Gas

No. 277

ACROSS: 4 Interest 8 Suture 9 Parallel 10 Sportive 11 Coyote 12 Broccoli 13 Slander 16 Rubella 18 Bathroom 20 Adrian 22 Left Over 23 Paganini 24 Eunuch 25 Strongly

DOWN: 1 Support 2 Curry-comb 3 Medico 4 Imperishability 5 Turncoat 6 Rally 7 Shelter 14 Deer-hound 15 Clinging 16 Radiant 17 Potence 19 Toffee 21 Idaho

No. 278

ACROSS: 9 Quarrel 10 Road Map 11 Ended 12 Adventure 13 Refresher 15 Brace 16 Favour 18 Entail 21 Usual 22 Demi-lance 24 Fieldfare 26 Drove 28 Lucerne 29 Aureola

DOWN: 1 Equerry 2 Sand 3 Bridge Roll 4 Pleach 5 Traverse 6 Pawn 7 Imputation 8 Spheres 14 Flatulence 15 Battledore 17 Red-faced 19 Suffolk 20 Veteran 23 Maenad 25 Dart 27 Obol

No. 279

ACROSS: 8 Cordial 10 Vaccine 11 Outspan 12 Deposit 13 Cue 14 Deserve 15 Narrate 16 Ear 18 Adder 20 Elm 24 Signals 25 Humdrum 27 Cha 28 Emanate 29 Blister 30 Element 31 Trellis

DOWN: 1 Scrowdge 2 Brutus 3 Disport 4 Evidence 5 Sceptre 6 Misstate 7 Kettle 9 Lance 17 Rag Paper 19 Descents 21 Memorise 22 Manager 23 Empires 24 Swedes 25 Habit 26 Rattle

No. 280

ACROSS: 9 Undermine 10 Niece 11 Anemone 12 Edental 13 Dail 14 Broad Arrow 16 Overall 17 Sweater 19 Elderberry 22 Slav 24 Growler 25 Goneril 26 Idiom 27 Halfpence

DOWN: 1 Cut And Come Again 2 Adhesive 3 Groom 4 Dihedral 5 Helena 6 Antedates 7 Bestir 8 Fellow Traveller 15 Harry Lime 17 Struggle 18 Tolerant 20 Drop In 21 Earths 23 Snaps

No. 281

ACROSS: 7 Nothing 8 Unlined 10 Swerve 11 Latitude 12 Acid 13 Empanelled 14 In An Instant 19 Four Quarts 22 Tree 23 Octoroon 24 Merely 25 Greener 26 Defiant

DOWN: 1 Norwich 2 Sheridan 3 Inhere 4 Instinct 5 Lintel 6 Readier 9 Clap In Irons 15 Neuroses 16 Notornis 17 Concord 18 Healing 20 Rioted 21 Summer

No. 282

ACROSS: 1 Mooring 5 Started 9 Stevenson 10 Scrub 11 Abele 12 Automatic 13 Eye-wink 15 Relapse 17 Attacks 19 Muddles 21 Barometer 23 Satie 24 Mouse 25 April Fool 26 Nanette 27 Demeter

DOWN: 1 Mistake 2 Overexert 3 Irene 4 Gas-mask 5 Senator 6 Assembled 7 Tarot 8 Debacle 14 Incumbent 16 Pilot-boat 17 Albumen 18 Satiate 19 Mordred 20 Stellar 22 Rouen 23 Salem

No. 283

ACROSS: 9 Alimony 10 Violets 11 Financier 12 Drama 13 Ill 14 French Leave 16 Extra 18 Greed 22 Chamberlain 23 Rot 24 Unarm 26 Tribesman 27 Hatless 28 Arrival

DOWN: 1 Half-mile 2 Lionel 3 Loin Of Lamb 4 Bylines 5 Avarice 6 Cold 7 Separate 8 Estate 15 Loganberry 17 Tea-party 19 Dotingly 20 Protest 21 Habitat 22 Caught 23 Remove 25 Meek

No. 284

ACROSS: 1 Rational 4 Spared 9 Concurs 11 Migrant 12 Pleasantry 13 Gilt 15 Sea-line 17 Bugle 19 Novel 21 Mustard 24 Idol 25 Uninviting 28 Alerion 29 Pantile 30 Estate 31 Cleansed

DOWN: 1 Recipe 2 Tanners 3 Arson 5 Page 6 Reading 7 Date-tree 8 Smartens 10 Unstable 14 Abrasion 16 Imminent 18 Intimate 20 Violent 22 Daimios 23 Agreed 26 Nepal 17 Fiat

No. 285

ACROSS: 1 Blind Man's Buff 8 Indian Club 9 Lake 11 Hooked It 12 Grotto 14 Asset 15 Curse 16 Jetty 17 Ascot 20 Mason 22 Utopia 23 Telluric 25 Tier 26 Break In Two 27 Yehudi Menuhin

DOWN: 1 Bright As A Button 2 Indoors 3 Dearest 4 Auctioneer 5 Snub 6 Flatter 7 The Rose And Crown 10 Eric 13 Cattle Farm 18 Cookery 19 Tail 20 Million 21 Scratch 24 Trad

No. 286

ACROSS: 1 Baronet 5 Cassius 9 Capricorn 10 Aroma 11 Ixion 12 Portrayal 13 Glacier 15 Leander 17 Fiddled 19 Blessed 21 Indignant 23 Meeds 24 Throb 25 Electrode 26 Rotters 27 Detract

DOWN: 1 Backing 2 Reprimand 3 Nairn 4 Trooper 5 Control 6 Staircase 7 Ivory 8 Smaller 14 Illegible 16 Desdemona 17 Fritter 18 Diadems 19 Butt-end 20 Dissent 22 Durst 23 Motet

No. 287

ACROSS: 1 Man-made Fibre 9 Sarah Gamp 10 Ghost 11 Ideals 12 Boadicea 13 Farina 15 Censures 18 Brake-van 19 Chrome 21 Doormats 23 Income 26 Cheat 27 Right Side 28 Played Truant

DOWN: 1 Mastiff 2 Nerve 3 Ash Blonde 4 Edam 5 Improved 6 Rigid 7 Cutlass 8 Concerto 14 Read Over 16 Sphincter 17 Bastardy 18 Bodices 20 Element 22 Metal 24 Ouida 25 Aged

No. 288

ACROSS: 1 Resonate 5 Smacks 10 Champagne 11 Rheum 12 Taboo 13 Retracts 15 Tea-shop 18 Charade 20 Vedanta 21 Elector 22 Bailiffs 25 Flour 27 Regan 28 Ripienist 29 Parish 30 Cats-eyes

DOWN: 1 Recitative 2 Starboard 3 Napoo 4 Tiger 6 Marmalade 7 Cheat 8 Soma 9 Tentacle 14 Dear Brutus 16 Hand-lines 17 Platform 19 Authority 23 Auger 24 Sepia 25 Frees 26 Trap

No. 289

ACROSS: 1 Accents 5 Bedpost 10 All The Year Round 11 Swerve 12 Twilight 13 Transact 15 Yeats 16 Leave 18 Back Room 22 Pell-mell 23 Siphon 25 Pretentiousness 26 Sweetly 27 Welcome

DOWN: 2 Cold War 3 Enter 4 Theresa 6 Earwig 7 Profiteer 8 Song-hit 9 Sextet 14 Novelette 17 Eyebrow 18 Beloit 19 Costume 20 Opossum 21 Kernel 24 Panic

No. 290

ACROSS: 1 Te Deum 4 Addendum 10 Aquaria 11 Windows 12 All Hallows 13 Spry 15 Gas-fire 17 Reredos 19 Rescues 21 Sugared 23 Knar 24 Esplanades 27 Agitate 28 Antonio 29 Epiphany 30 Frosts

DOWN: 1 Trafalgar 2 Doubles 3 Uproarious 5 Downwards 6 Etna 7 Dropped 8 Misty 9 Fall 14 Originator 16 East Sheen 18 Side Shows 20 Swahili 22 Rodents 23 Knave 25 Lear 26 Gash

No. 291

ACROSS: 1 Partridge 5 Credo 8 Sophomore 10 Tweed 11 Bachelor's Button 12 Outrigger 17 Not At Home 20 All The Year Round 22 Later 23 Unimpeded 24 Spent 25 Gathers Up

DOWN: 1 Pass-books 2 Rapacity 3 Drop Of Gin 4 Evens 5 Cuts Up 6 Events 7 Olden 9 Onegin 13 Ritualist 14 Yielded Up 15 Attrap 16 Rotundas 18 Clothe 19 Thirst 20 Atlas 21 Young

No. 292

ACROSS: 1 Birthday Present 8 Sprain 9 Time-bomb 11 Frantic 12 Enthuse 14 Fifty-three 17 Tang 18 Bean 19 Apostrophe 21 Utterer 23 Exactor 25 Hymn-book 27 Crisis 28 Imponderability

DOWN: 2 Impertinently 3 Twain 4 Dentist 5 Priceless 6 Event 7 Ego 10 Misanthropist 13 Hatto 15 Tense 16 Hyperbole 20 Taxi-cab 22 Robin 24 Chill 26 Mop

No. 293

ACROSS: 1 Air-raid 5 Tramway 9 Gigue 10 Southerly 11 Slovak 12 Whinnies 14 Upset 15 Out-talked 18 Afternoon 20 Tapis 22 Galloway 24 Cleric 26 Operation 27 Piano 28 Sustain 29 Busiest

DOWN: 1 Angostura 2 Regions 3 Ale-taster 4 Diss 5 Touchstone 6 Ashen 7 Warwick 8 Yoyos 13 Coronation 16 Antelopes 17 Dishclout 19 Tellers 21 Portage 22 Gloss 23 Omaha 25 Snob

No. 294

ACROSS: 1 James Boswell 9 Horseless 10 Shako 11 Nature 12 Research 13 Envied 15 Hammocks 18 Achilles 19 Scrawl 21 Ohmmeter 23 Air-sac 26 Inner 27 Avocation 28 My Dear Fellow

DOWN: 1 Johnnie 2 Marat 3 Sneerwell 4 Open 5 Wesleyan 6 Lisle 7 Clothes 8 Patricia 14 Vehement 16 Machinate 17 Venerate 18 Adoring 20 Lucknow 22 Early 24 Skill 25 Door

No. 295

ACROSS: 1 Hanging Garden 9 The Masses 10 Crete 11 Boyet 12 Green-eyed 13 Sketchy 15 Slimmer 17 Clear Up 19 Creeper 21 Neptunium 23 Aunts 24 Ulric 25 Knock-down 26 Osbert Sitwell

DOWN: 2 Acetylene 3 Giant 4 Nosegay 5 Gaspers 6 Recondite 7 Elegy 8 Redder 9 Tubas 14 Carbuncle 16 Moping Owl 17 Cinque 18 Pricket 19 Campoli 20 Risen 22 Ports 23 Askew

No. 296

ACROSS: 1 Depicted 5 Scamps 9 Entreaty 10 Sandra 12 Gondola 13 Untried 14 Baggage Train 17 Castle Moated 22 Pelican 23 Animate 24 Intern 25 Lashings 26 Sodden 27 Smothers

DOWN: 1 Dredge 2 Patina 3 Cremona 4 Estrangement 6 Coal-tit 7 Madrigal 8 Standing 11 Burglar Alarm 15 Sceptics 16 Isolated 18 Lucerne 19 Epithet 20 Pawnee 21 Tenses

No. 297

ACROSS: 1 Gig-lamps 5 Eggcup 9 Prentice 10 Plover 12 Unkind 13 Pakistan 15 No Admittance 18 Invoice Clerk 23 Lord's Day 24 Avenue 26 Orgies 27 Pullover 28 Sadist 29 Stressed

DOWN: 1 Gypsum 2 Greeks 3 Antonio 4 Pace 6 Galliot 7 Coveting 8 Pyrenees 11 Vanilla 14 Adrenal 16 Millions 17 Averaged 19 Insteps 20 Revalue 21 Knaves 22 Feared 25 Hunt

No. 298

ACROSS: 1 Decoded 5 Instant 9 Amiss 10 Double Bed 11 Reformers 13 Satin 14 Magic 16 Snowflake 17 Free Verse 18 Inert 20 Oaths 21 Abolition 24 Tractable 26 Nesta 27 Layered 28 Trysted .

DOWN: 1 Diagram 2 Cliff 3 District Visitor 4 Dodge 5 IOU 6 Self-sufficiency 7 Arbitrate 8 To Dance 12 Spode 15 Great Many 16 Syria 17 Frontal 19 Tankard 22 Overt 23 Inset 25 Bad

No. 299

ACROSS: 1 Claypole 5 Avocet 9 Nest-eggs 10 Assisi 12 Liege 13 Testament 14 Near Relative 18 Firelighters 21 Ironsides 23 Negro 24 Malady 25 Bullocks 26 Dating 27 Stinkpot

DOWN: 1 Candle 2 Answer 3 Piecemeal 4 Light Brigade 6 Vesta 7 Chimeric 8 Thirteen 11 Asbestos Suit 15 Adrenalin 16 Affirmed 17 Brooklet 19 Egg-cup 20 Dorset 22 Sedan

No. 300

ACROSS: 1 Crouton 5 Goddess 9 Under 10 Alexandra 11 Bantam 12 Chastity 14 Bilge 15 All Bright 18 Excusable 20 Verdi 22 Trestles 24 Driven 26 Railborne 27 Iceni 28 Hogarth 29 Overall

DOWN: 1 Clubbable 2 Ordinal 3 Threaders 4 Noah 5 Goes Halves 6 Draws 7 Eddying 8 Seamy 13 Marble Arch 16 Riverside 17 Triennial 19 Chewing 21 Riviera 22 Torch 23 Tabor 25 Zero